Praise for *The Underground Is Massive*

"Finally: the epic tale of how a b[...] gearheads and crooks turned a p[...] into a worldwide movement tha[...] *Underground Is Massive* follows [...] and turns of dance music and [...] beats from Detroit to Berlin to Brooklyn—from a master story-teller and a hardcore fan."

—Rob Sheffield, *New York Times* bestselling author of
Love Is a Mix Tape and *Turn Around Bright Eyes*

"*The Underground Is Massive* is the richly researched, vividly detailed chronicle that America's electronic dance culture has long deserved. Essential reading for scene believers and curious onlookers alike."

—Simon Reynolds, author of *Energy Flash* and *Generation Ecstasy*

"Hip-hop and dance music have ever been kin, like musical first cousins, sometimes estranged but often in sync. Michelangelo Matos's massive history of electronic dance music, told in an unprecedented epic sweep, is like seeing a familiar face in your family as if for the first time—to finally appreciate the depth of their genius and the scope of their struggle, and to revel in their triumph."

—Dan Charnas, author of
The Big Payback: The History of the Business of Hip-Hop

"*The Underground Is Massive* is a staggering work of research, organization, and synthesis, and yet Michaelangelo Matos never loses his wit or his deft way with a sentence. He is the Barbara Tuchman of EDM!"

—Luc Sante, author of
Low Life and *The Other Paris*

THE UNDERGROUND
IS MASSIVE

THE UNDERGROUND
IS MASSIVE

DEY ST.
AN IMPRINT OF
WILLIAM MORROW *PUBLISHERS*

How Electronic Dance Music
Conquered America

Michaelangelo Matos

DEY ST.

THE UNDERGROUND IS MASSIVE. Copyright © 2015 by Michaelangelo
Matos. All rights reserved. Printed in the United States of America.
No part of this book may be used or reproduced in any manner
whatsoever without written permission except in the case of brief
quotations embodied in critical articles and reviews. For information address HarperCollins Publishers, 195 Broadway, New York,
NY 10007.

HarperCollins books may be purchased for educational, business,
or sales promotional use. For information, please e-mail the Special
Markets Department at SPsales@harpercollins.com.

A hardcover edition of this book was published in 2015 by Dey
Street Books, an imprint of William Morrow Publishers.

FIRST DEY STREET BOOKS PAPERBACK EDITION PUBLISHED 2016.

Designed by Paula Russell Szafranski

Library of Congress Cataloging-in-Publication Data has been applied for.

ISBN 978-0-06-227179-2

HB 08.07.2023

CONT

ENTS

Ain't nothin' goin' on but history.

—BASEMENT JAXX, "RED ALERT" (XL, 1999)

INTRODUCTION

LATE SUNDAY NIGHT on Memorial Day weekend 2013, outside of 1515 Broadway in Detroit, I was introduced to a DJ I'd spoken with some weeks earlier over the phone about the city's electronic-dance-music history, its party scenes—including specific parties—and its peccadilloes and controversies. He'd indulged me for two hours, but I'd smelled an undercurrent, and in person it didn't take long to emerge. "Why aren't you going to focus on the hidden gems?" he asked. "Why are you talking all the obvious shit?"

If only I'd had the presence of mind to ask when he was going to play a two-hour set that included his entire record collection. "The obvious shit" to him is almost completely unknown to nearly everybody else in the country. When electronic dance music wasn't popular in the United States, we consumed it very differently than the rest of the world. Now that it dominates our concert business—which essentially *is* the music business now—we still consume it differently than other countries. *The Underground Is Massive* is an attempt to understand how, and why, those things happened.

The book is not an expanded listicle of Greatest Parties Ever; a number of the events covered, not just the ones in the chapter titles, bombed. The loudest, in retrospect, may have been the World Party, at Joe Louis Arena on June 18, 1994—the precursor to the utter triumph of the first Detroit Electronic Music Festival six years later. Glasgow's

Keith McIvor (Twitch; today, JD Twitch, half of Optimo), a huge fan of Detroit techno, was thrilled when he saw the lineup: "We really believed we were going to be playing the best party in the history of the world." Instead, the arena reached less than five percent capacity. McIvor was dumbfounded when kids approached him after he'd played some Detroit classics and asked: "Where is that from?" McIvor responded: "Er . . . *here.*"

Yet *here* has never been adequately documented in full. *Here* operates on a very different apparatus than the rest of the world. The book's subtitle—*How Electronic Dance Music Conquered America*—is deliberately chosen: This is a story about a culture forming, taking over every part of the world except its creators' own—only to rear up and take center stage after mutating into something its inventors barely recognized. It's also about people who took it to audiences it hadn't reached. To recount them all would take an encyclopedia; this book could have been many times larger with little effort.

Two things I knew going in: I wasn't writing a history of either Chicago house or Detroit techno. Each is a story for other books than this one. Nevertheless, there will be people who fault it for that before anything—for overlooking "the hidden gems" in favor of a through line that has existed for decades, sometimes purely local, sometimes intersecting with the larger listening world. Hence, many major electronic dance careers are shortchanged in these pages, including those of people I spoke to at great length. So are entire movements, genres, scenes, and events that, with a shift of emphasis, could have been swapped out with many others here.

Then there were the many stories I couldn't crowbar in without necessitating entire new passages, or chapters. Just a few examples: Low End Theory, Daddy Kev's path-breaking L.A. club night, starting in 2006. Most of the history of Miami's Winter Music Conference— loads of Florida history generally. The Boston scene, up to and including DJ/rupture, whose two-part mix *Gold Teeth Thief* (2001) is the most resonant post-9/11 recording I know by anyone. The infamous Raymond Frances, the East Coast mixtape king, and the RIAA-engineered raids on NYC and D.C. mixtape vendors in 1994. Huge swaths of New York house history. San Francisco's feminist party collective Your Sister's House, 1993–1994. The forty-five-hundred-word feature I wrote after following Minneapolis crew Family Werks around as they threw their Valentine's Day 1999 party Love, which I'd originally planned to drop into the narrative as is, just to give the flavor and specifics of the time and place. MTV's "reality" hit *Jersey Shore* (2009–2012), which brought house music into millions of homes via series lead DJ Pauly D. Metro Area and the reclaiming of "disco." DFA Records generally—and Ninja Tune, Dust Traxx, Submerge/430 West, Asphodel, and Spinnin', just for starters. MUTEK 2002. Decibel Festival 2012. The 2013 Brooklyn Electronic Music Festival. A spring 2013 visit to an actual rave at Bedford-Stuyvesant's Electric Warehouse in the midst of EDM-festival madness—two months before the venue was shut down by local authorities. Chicago's mid-nineties jungle scene. Illbient. And the 2014 Electric Zoo, manned by heavy security and police dogs, yet another harbinger—in a season frighteningly full of them—of the U.S. turning into a police state.

If you'd told me at Winter Music Conference in 2000 that I'd someday write a history of the music I loved, I'd have raver-hugged you. If you'd added that I'd have to cut both Danny Tenaglia and Josh Wink's "Higher State of Consciousness" out of it, I'd have shanked you. Yet that's what it came down to here. Tenaglia is one of the dozen greatest DJs I've ever heard; he's done as much to spread house music as anyone alive. He just did it away from the center of the events I've focused on. Ditto the many names above—and so many others—as well.

For what it's worth, I attended precisely zero of the events for which the chapters are named—though I'll also mention that the chapter configurations changed constantly through the book's gestation; at one point or another about forty parties were mooted as chapters before I whittled it down to the eighteen in the book.

One defining dichotomy of dance music is that it is, by definition, populist—and that many of its most ardent fans are anything but. That's one reason we still deal with people who, every time a new genre emerges, insist that somebody just made up a name to hoodwink everybody, and never mind that if you can't tell jungle from house, you probably can't tell the Byrds from Slayer, either. The dance side sometimes gets anxious: "Quit calling it something else, because people think it's a fad anyway."

But America knows now what many of us have for decades: Electronic dance music is not a fad but a staple. Country stars use detonating dubstep bass. Pop and R&B and hip-hop radio are awash in synths that sound like they could have been on a Ministry of Sound compilation anytime in the late nineties or early 2000s—and sometimes feature music that was. There are DJ-themed reality competition shows.

Maybe someday we'll get a book about EDM Babylon, a from-the-trenches report that treats the whole thing like a glitter parade and is full of salacious shenanigans from the lighting technicians. Hey, I'll read it. But while I didn't shy from dirt, that isn't the viewpoint of the story that follows. It's written from a fan's perspective, as well as that of a journalist and critic who's been on a couple of junkets (both of which, in different ways, made their way into the text: the Red Bull Music Academy confab in Palm Springs, California, February 2011; and Tomorrowland, in Boom, Belgium, July 2013). But it's not quite an insider's view. I've never had the money to jet off to Berlin and stay up for three days while glimpsing the universe with my new best friends; nor have I done PR, started a label, attempted to spin (beyond just playing records like a college-radio DJ), produced or remixed a track, or written DJ bios. Within the ultra-DIY world of electronic dance music, this makes me an oddity; many of the people with the most to say in these pages wear many of those hats.

But what they and everyone else says is filtered through my natural skepticism, as well as my instinctive love for the music and the overlapping sets of cultural possibility it represents—meaning that any and all mistakes in this book are mine alone. Nothing's "objective." Not even machines.

AUTHOR'S NOTE

THIS BOOK UTILIZES a score of secondary data in addition to first-hand interviews, a great deal of it from uncopyedited sources, and in the interest of readability I imposed uniformity—cleaning up typos and misspellings and punctuation and wEirD cApitAliZatioN, without imposing brackets unless absolutely necessary. (The exceptions are chosen on purpose.) For cohesion's sake, I've simplified and made uniform the punctuation and capitalization of the names of Hyperreal's mailing lists: MW-Raves, NE-Raves (originally NE_Raves), NYC-Raves (nyc-raves), PB-CLE-Raves (Pb-Cle-Raves), and SF-Raves (SFRaves). It might otherwise have been a visual-noise riot.

In the long notes available online or in the e-book edition, I cite specific mailing list posts by e-mailer name, if given. When not, the first half of the e-mail address, before the @, is used without the rest. Chances are that 99 percent of those addresses are defunct, but there's a limit to exploiting others' privacy—which I tried not to do, overall, particularly regarding the mailing lists. The few personal details gleaned from them, and a number of rave zines and Web sites, are intended to stand in for attributes shared by many in the community, and that's how I hope they read. I tried not to misrepresent anybody's intentions, though there is no such thing as a perfect interpretation. My apologies to anyone whose meanings I may have trampled in pursuit of my own.

Quotes taken from author interviews conducted between 2011 and

2014 are in present tense ("says Derrick May"), unless the subject was discussing an upcoming event now past. Quotes taken from secondary sources are in past tense ("Richie Hawtin said"). When expedient, the first introduction into the book's narrative of a character who operates under an alias (such as a DJ) gives their birth names in parentheses—ex. Tommie Sunshine (Thomas Lorello)—or vice versa—ex. Joel Bevacqua (Deadly Buda). If the first name is the same for both, only the birth surname is in parentheses—ex. Robbie Hardkiss (Cameron). Most of the story's actors zip in and out of the narrative, and are ID'd by where they were living at the time. Dance music is a migratory business.

America is very shy when it comes to electronics. It's still a highly schizophrenic situation. People have all the latest state-of-the-art technology, and yet they put wood panels on the front to make them feel comfortable. Or they develop new plastics and try to imitate the appearance of wood. They use modern technology to try to re-create the Middle Ages. This is stupid.

—RALF HUTTER OF KRAFTWERK, 1982

>1

THE POWER PLANT

"DON'T DO IT!"

Juan Atkins was beside himself. Twenty-one years old in 1983 and already a recording artist, as half of an electro-funk duo called Cybotron, Atkins was still struggling to make it beyond his hometown of Detroit. He'd had a great idea—take what Kraftwerk, the German synth-pop group, was doing, but make it funky. Not just funky the way he knew them to be—a group whose 1977 album *Trans-Europe Express* could keep a dance floor going—but funky in a way that the rest of the world could hear.

Atkins was a DJ, and so was his best friend Derrick May—two years younger, brash and forthright where Juan was bookish and reserved. Together, they'd founded a mobile DJ company called Deep Space Soundworks. Juan named it and set its course. Deep Space, as its name implied, wasn't content to play the big R&B hits of the day. Atkins was a seeker, enamored of new technology. His Kraftwerk fandom attested to that.

So did his secret weapon—a Roland TR-909 drum machine Atkins played underneath the records he was spinning, to keep the groove going and goose it. That way you stood out in a crowded field—and the DJ teams of suburban Detroit's high school party scene were fiercely competitive. There was a bustling trade in invitational events for several hundred, mostly posh African American kids who took style cues from Paul Schrader's 1980 film *American Gigolo*. "It was so organized, so professional, you wouldn't believe it," says May.

But May was still unready for what he'd hear while visiting his mom in Chicago. Shopping for records in the Loop at Importes Etc., one rack there caught his attention. It was filled with older hits from the Philadelphia International and Salsoul labels, synth-heavy Italian imports, and British twelve-inches like Bo Kool's "Money (No Love)" backed with T. W. Funkmasters' "Love Money." The section bore an unusual header: "House Music."

May was impressed by the selection and puzzled by the jargon—not to mention the names. "They were saying: 'This one is Frankie's big record of the moment; Ronnie is really playing this lots; Farley is playing this one.' I didn't have any idea who these people were. But I would soon learn that Frankie was Frankie Knuckles and Ronnie was Ronnie Hardy and Farley was Farley Keith. I wanted to find out more: 'Where does Frankie play this music?' 'At the Power Plant, of course.'"

Located at 2210 South Michigan Avenue, the Power Plant—so named for the transmitters standing visible from the club's entrance—was Frankie Knuckles's second DJ home; the first had been the Warehouse, also in the Loop, and the source of the name "house music." Ron Hardy, of the Muzic Box on the north side, and "Funkin'" Farley Keith, of WBMX-FM, were the other key disseminators of the sound Importes was pushing, but Knuckles had created the blueprint.

That night, May went to the Power Plant for the first time—"I didn't go with a group of people; I was always alone, man"—and promptly had his skull peeled back. The Detroit teen parties were professional, but this was *church*. The crowd—largely underage, mostly gay and black—moved harder than the kids May was spinning for, and Knuckles played louder, freer, more powerfully. He was sweet and easygoing, but he had a corporal's command over the crowd. After a couple of visits, May saw an angle. He had a second TR-909, he needed cash, and he'd heard from Importes manager Craig Loftis that Knuckles wanted a drum machine: Game, set, match. When May told him his plan, Atkins panicked. "Juan begged me not to. Nobody had a 909 yet."

The previous summer, Atkins had taken boxes of the first two Cybotron singles, 1981's "Alleys of Your Mind" and 1982's "Cosmic Cars," to New York. In Detroit, he could just hand the singles to local DJs and they'd play them. Out east, the game was a lot tougher. On his final day in the city, he turned on the radio and heard Afrika Bambaataa and the Soul Sonic Force's "Planet Rock"—a rap song set to replayed chunks of Kraftwerk's "Numbers" and "Trans-Europe Express." "The station was like, 'We got it first, nyah, nyah!'" Atkins told journalist Dan Sicko. Juan returned home, deflated. He may have told May, "Don't do it," but he could have been saying: *Not again.*

Worse, his carless friend had arranged a driver for the five-hour journey to Chicago: Juan's baby brother, Marcellus. That night, a furious Atkins went to see May's roommate, Eddie Fowlkes, another member of the Deep Space crew. "You know what this motherfucker did?" Atkins fumed. "Derrick went and gave away the fucking sound!"

BORN FRANK NICHOLLS on January 18, 1955, and raised in the South Bronx, Frankie Knuckles went to an arts high school in Manhattan, where he also went clubbing with his best friend, Larry Philpot. Together, they attended the clubs—the Loft on lower Broadway, Better Days on West Forty-ninth Street—where disco was born.

In 1973, Knuckles and Philpot began working at the Gallery in SoHo, blowing up balloons and lacing the punchbowl with LSD for DJ and proprietor Nicky Siano, who pioneered the smooth beat-mixing that eventually became the standard for dance DJs. That July they went to the Continental Baths. Situated in an opulent hotel basement on West Seventy-fourth Street, it featured several rooms of entertainment (the cabaret was where Bette Midler, accompanied by pianist Barry Manilow, became a star) as well as a swimming pool, saunas, and private nooks for homosexual men to live out long-held fantasies. Larry changed his surname to Levan. Knuckles handled lights there. He could DJ but dismissed it as a career: "I'm not going to wake up one day and be thirty-two years old and still doing this."

But he'd take an opportunity. In March 1977, Knuckles spent two weeks in Chicago at the invitation of Robert Williams, whom he'd first met in the early seventies—they went to the same clubs, but more important, when Frankie and Larry were nabbed by the cops for swiping doughnuts from a midtown delivery truck while walking home from a club at dawn, Williams had been their juvenile officer. It was one of a handful of careers Williams had tried on after being ejected from Columbia Law School.

In Chicago, Williams opened U.S. ("us") Studios, inspired by the all-night, nonalcoholic "juice bars" exemplified by the Loft. At the end of 1976, Williams was preparing a new, six-hundred-capacity venue at 206 South Jefferson Street—a slender brick building with oblong windows in the Loop, between Chicago's North and South Sides. Williams's first pick to DJ his new members-only club was Levan. Larry demurred—impresario Michael Brody was building a disco for him in a SoHo parking garage.

But Knuckles was between jobs—the Baths had gone bankrupt that bicentennial year. By July Knuckles had moved into the building, both living and working there for two years. The place boasted a high-velocity sound system designed by New Yorker Richard Long, who was also outfitting Larry's new SoHo venture. There was no sign; eventually it officially took on its nickname: the Warehouse.

In 1979, Knuckles and his friend Erasmo Rivera, a sound-engineering student, began editing extended versions of his favorite tracks on reel-to-reel tape. The big one was "Let No Man Put Asunder," a spare, gospelly plea by Philly girl group First Choice, on Salsoul. It wasn't just the long DJ hours that necessitated these edits. The same year, on July 12, across town at Comiskey Park, shock-jock DJ Steve Dahl had presided over the public dynamiting of thousands of disco records, inciting a riot. The incident was a farce, but it reflected a record-biz shake-up that led to a substantial cutback on disco releases. The re-edits helped fill the gap on Frankie's floor.

By the early eighties, Knuckles's DJ sets—traveling through the city on cassettes traded by true believers—were becoming storied; so was the space, which Williams had begun to lease on off-nights. By the end of 1981, the Warehouse was no longer members only—and the door charge doubled, from four dollars to eight.

For the new crowd, the place was a revelation. "It was the holy grail of teen dances," says Vince Lawrence, then a South Side Chicago teenager. "There was a rumor that there was acid in the punch." (Was there? "I don't know, man. I had such a good time, I might have *thought* I was high.") Rachael Cain, a.k.a. Screamin' Rachael, a white punk singer who promoted shows at Space Place, an illegal venue around the corner from the Warehouse, saw Knuckles for the first time on the night the Chicago police shut her club down. "It was like nothing I'd ever heard, how it would build and peak," she recalls. Frankie wasn't terribly enamored of his new crowd, though—the Warehouse had become dangerous. He defected in November 1982, leaving to spin Friday nights at the Riverside Club. In December, it became the Power Plant. It wasn't long before Derrick May wandered in.

There were similarities between Knuckles's playlist and that of the Deep Space crew, but so many differences that made what May heard at the Power Plant—where Frankie played far more disco than Derrick heard in Detroit—seem more exotic. "I had not really been out that much," says May. "To see a high-performance DJ in a club environment like that, with gay people and straight people at four o'clock in the morning—and I'm still there, and people singing along to the songs and stomping on the floor, and the smell of the place—it was an indoctrination. It was the moment that changed my life."

The Warehouse's DJ booth had stood on a loading dock. By contrast, the Power Plant's booth was luxurious—an enclosed space one-and-a-half feet off the dance floor, with room enough for a small clutch of Knuckles's friends as well as a lighting board and his enormous record collection. When May knocked on the booth's door, Craig Loftis answered. "I have a 909 for sale," said May. Loftis whispered into Knuckles's ear. Frankie looked up and demanded: "Go get it." He bought the drum machine on the spot. Just as quickly he took Derrick under his wing.

"I found myself somehow making friends with this man," says May. "Yeah, he's gay—but I never felt like he was trying to get close to me because of his sexuality. He just admired me as a kid aspiring to do something. He really felt close to that. He sort of adopted me. It was an amazing feeling." Frankie also gave Derrick some DJ advice: "Find somebody who is motivating you, and only play for them."

BORN ON DECEMBER 9, 1962, in Detroit, Juan Atkins had started playing keyboards before kindergarten—his grandmother took him to a local piano store, where he toyed with the synthesizers in back. His father served hard time for most of Juan's formative years; after he was out, he gave Juan an electric guitar for his tenth birthday. By junior high, the kid was playing drums and bass in garage funk bands with his neighbors. "You could hear the music in a three- or four-block radius," Atkins said.

Atkins met May in high school, after he and his brother Aaron moved to the rural suburb of Belleville; they lived on a dirt road, and Juan was bused to school. Aaron and Derrick were on the football team together, and Juan began playing chess with Derrick. In

1979, Juan gave Derrick a tape with some Tangerine Dream and Giorgio Moroder; they began to DJ together within a couple of months, though they didn't play out much at first.

On the football team with Derrick and Aaron Atkins was six-foot-one Kevin Saunderson. At nine, he'd left trash-strewn Bushwick, Brooklyn, for the bucolic Midwest with his mother after she'd divorced his father. "I was a quiet leader," says Saunderson. "I wasn't the kind to get up in front of people and talk a lot. But I would *do*. I would step in any situation and deliver." This solidity contrasted sharply with May's flippancy. "At that age, he was very annoying," says Saunderson, adding: "He's probably sometimes *still* annoying." Not long after meeting, May and Saunderson made a five-dollar sports bet. Saunderson was ready to pay if he lost, which he didn't. May welshed. So Kevin socked him in the mouth. (May's lip still bears the scar.)

Both loved danceable R&B—the kind Atkins was already making. Older and more aloof, Juan conducted himself as a serious artist. He was a huge Parliament-Funkadelic fan—particularly the 1978 R&B number-one, "Flash Light," thanks to keyboardist Bernie Worrell's pitch-bent Moog-synth bass line. Along with Kraftwerk and futurist author Alvin Toffler's *The Third Wave* (1980)—with its hybridized words like "metrocomplex," referring to the idea that the world's cities would eventually balloon in size until they met at the edges and merged—"Flash Light" represented the sci-fi groove Atkins aspired to. At home, he recorded demos, crafting rhythm tracks by tweaking the filters of his Korg MS10 analogue synth to imitate various drum sounds.

Juan had first encountered Kraftwerk via *The Midnight Funk Association*, on WGPR (107.5 FM), an overnight program hosted by Arkansas-born Charles Johnson, known on-air as the Electrifying Mojo. "Mojo was one of the first FM DJ icons," says Atkins. "WGPR was the first black station that had an AOR format—they would play a whole side of an album." Mojo was as likely to play Kraftwerk, the

B-52's, or Peter Frampton as he was James Brown, Prince, or P-Funk. Every night, Mojo would "land the Mothership"—à la Parliament's 1975 album, *Mothership Connection*—using sound effects, John Williams's *Close Encounters of the Third Kind* score, and his own delectably theatrical voice instructing his listeners to turn on their flashlights.

Atkins formed Cybotron with Rik Davis—a reclusive Vietnam veteran and fellow sci-fi nerd with an impressive synth collection—at Washtenaw Community College. Their name was a Tofflerian word-splice, combining "cyborg" and "cyclotron." May took Mojo a cassette demo of "Alleys of Your Mind"—Atkins drolly intoning sci-fi paranoia over synths more Euro-new-wave than midwestern funk. "If you guys put this out, I will play it," Mojo said. Juan issued it on his own Deep Space Records. "We were like his disciples," says May. "We would do whatever he told us to do." Mojo encouraged another local group, A Number of Names, whose "Sharivari" featured a similarly serrated synth groove with lyrics about driving around in Porsches listening to cassettes—the good life, via GQ and *The Face*.

"Mojo made it okay for young black people to listen to 'white' music," says Neil Ollivierra, also a Detroit teenager at the time. "When they saw that was possible, they realized you could tear down similar boundaries in terms of fashion and music and literature and style and friendships and culture. They realized you could change all kinds of stuff about your life."

Soon Atkins and May involved themselves directly. "We started doing mixes for Mojo under the table," says Atkins. "He kept it under wraps, as if it was him mixing. But it was really us." It began with edits of the B-52's "Mesopotamia" and Prince's "Controversy" and "Private Joy"—similar to what Frankie Knuckles did in Chicago. "Once we did an edit on a record, he would play that version," says Atkins. "Every time he played 'Mesopotamia,' [ours] was the one he played." Eventually they moved up to crafting several ten-to-fifteen-minute megamixes a week, still anonymously. Instead of credit, the DJ would give them cryptic on-air shout-outs, drawling, "Uh, *deep space*," or, "Everything is on the *one*." Explains May: "He didn't call Juan *Juan*. He called Juan *One*." The two seethed at not receiving credit, but the anger also motivated them to work.

Atkins and May listened to music together analytically. "We talked about: 'What were they thinking about that made them want to do this? How did they process this information in their minds?'" says May, who admired his friend's unshakeable work ethic. "Juan read the book *This Business Called Music*—a four- or five-hundred-page book—as a fucking teenager. Juan had this vision when he was fourteen or fifteen years old. He knew that he was going to do it by himself. He knew that, being a young black artist making electronic music, nobody was going to sign him. We talked about these things as kids all the time."

One label did take a chance: San Francisco's Fantasy Records signed Cybotron in 1983. *Enter* did modestly; the group remained largely a local concern. Atkins had made its best track, "Clear," by himself at home: pure machine funk, smooth as his heroes Kraftwerk. In the can he had something even better: "Night Drive," which pulsed with new menace. "Time—space—*transmat*," chanted a scrunched warble; the latter word was another Tofflerism, for teleportation (*transfer* + *matter*). He wanted it to be a stand-alone Cybotron single. Davis overrode him in favor of his own, rock-leaning "Techno City" (1984).

BORN APRIL 6, 1963, and raised by a single mother, Derrick May ended up in Belleville after a peripatetic childhood in and around Detroit. "I went to four or five elementary schools, one junior high school—which was amazing—and two high schools," he says. (Of his dad, May once said, "Basically his occupation was never to be my father.") Constantly adjusting to new environments, May became outgoing, broadcasting a constant stream of ideas. "He's totally unafraid to stir the pot and speak his mind," says Ollivierra, who met May in the late eighties. "It makes him a lot of fun to hang around with and talk to."

May's gift of gab even worked on his mom. She married a man with a corporate job waiting for him in Chicago, but Derrick had a football scholarship riding on his staying at Belleville High. At sixteen, he got permission not to join them. "My mother didn't want me to stay in Detroit," says May. "She was heartbroken. It was hard, believe me, to convince my mother to let me do that. I made a lot of mistakes after she left, because I basically stopped going to school for a while." May fell off the scholarship track—the opposite of Saunderson, who got a football ride to Eastern Michigan University. When Derrick called Kevin at school following his Damascene experience at the Power Plant, Saunderson was dismissive—he'd already heard Frankie Knuckles's best friend in action.

While visiting New York in 1982, the eighteen-year-old Saunderson and some friends and family trekked to SoHo to dance at Larry Levan's club, the Paradise Garage, and experienced a DJ beloved for his dramatic flair. Kevin had reacted much the way Derrick did in Chicago. "Seeing Larry Levan playing for hours and hours, nonstop—I thought that was amazing," says Saunderson, who quietly scoffed as May yammered breathlessly about the Power Plant: "We're traveling the same world, but I'm thinking, 'You don't know what a real party is,' and he's probably thinking the same thing about me." Soon, Saunderson was also DJing—and using a drum machine in his sets.

Soon Derrick had gathered a Chicago road-trip posse—high school friends George Baker, Alton Miller, and Chez Damier (Anthony Pearson). Baker or Miller drove: "I didn't have a car until I was thirty-five years old," says May, who sometimes took the train: "Sometimes I would go to Chicago just to go to the party and I didn't even see my mother—just drive right back in the morning. And they had never seen anything like that before, either. Once they went to hear Ronnie play at the Muzic Box and Frankie at the Power Plant, that was it, man. That was the defining moment in their lives, as well."

The Muzic Box was Robert Williams's new club after Knuckles left the Warehouse, located at 326 North Michigan Avenue. Ron Hardy had played at Den One in the late seventies—one of Chicago's few white gay bars open to black clientele—and spent some time in L.A. The differences between Hardy and Knuckles were remarkable. Knuckles's beats-per-minute (BPM) would peak around 128—fast for disco, but not too fast—and he had a restrained touch, maintaining energy while still letting things breathe. Hardy, a notorious heroin addict, hammered away, more apt to play left-field rock records—the Clash, the Police, Talking Heads, even the Residents' "Diskomo." His crowd was younger, straighter, druggier. "It was a lot more raw at the Music Box," says Screamin' Rachael. "It was primal in there—very sexual." His cranked volume and tempos earned Ron the nickname "Heart Attack Hardy."

It didn't take nearly as much effort to hear Farley Keith Williams— or, as he was first known, "Funkin' " Farley Keith. He was part of the Hot Mix 5, a DJ team that broadcast for five hours every weekend on WBMX's *Saturday Night Live, Ain't No Jive—Chicago Dance Party.* He'd been hired in 1980, along with Scott "Smokin'" Silz, Kenny "Jammin' " Jason, Mickey "Mixin' " Oliver, and "Rockin' " Ralphi Rosario. The showbiz names are quaint now, but the Hot Mix 5 had a million listeners a week; they'd rotate time slots each Saturday to keep the fans, and themselves, on their toes.

"They were the Michael Jordans of DJs in Chicago," says Vince Lawrence. "Their appearances at parties were a big frickin' deal." Farley was the most flamboyant, skilled, and beloved of the group; he'd hoist an empty turntable and tap out a beat on it mid-performance. Eventually he changed his name to Farley "Jackmaster" Funk. "Honestly, when I started, I didn't go out buying new records," he said. "I went out and regurgitated what Frankie Knuckles would play."

One of the places he did so was Mendel High, a south-side private Catholic prep school. The academy's gym held about two thousand and hosted many of the city's top DJs for afternoon dances—daytime mirrors of the Power Plant and Muzic Box. (The DJs weren't that much older than their audience; Ralphi Rosario was sixteen when WBMX hired him in 1980.) "They used to get Frankie Knuckles, Ron Hardy, Farley, Steve Hurley, Andre Hatchett," says Mike Dearborn, a native Chicagoan who attended the Mendel parties. Hurley spun at the South Side's Candy Store; Hatchett was part of a DJ crew called the Chosen Few.

"It was an effort to give the teens in the neighborhood something to do so they wouldn't get in trouble," says Charles Little II, another Mendel regular. Little was briefly involved with the notorious Chicago gang the Black P Stones; at the Mendel parties, the P Stones would side-eye their ascendant rivals, the Gangster Disciples, across the dance floor: "Black gay kids, the Gangster Disciple thugs from the Low End—the North Side, close to downtown—and the pretty boys from out south would all come together in this room." Another division was between the kids who liked full-fledged songs—"house"—and ones who preferred the stripped-down beats—"trax." House was soulful and had lyrics; trax, says Little, meant "kick drum, snare, and 808s," and little else. Both Dearborn and Little gravitated toward trax.

ANOTHER MEMBER OF the Chosen Few was Jesse Saunders. Cute and popular with girls, he also made his own edits (with a cassette deck's pause button) and used a drum machine in his sets—the Roland TR-808, the 909's cousin. The 808's huge low-end kick could rattle a city block. (Afrika Bambaataa had featured it on "Planet Rock.") Saunders also had a few killer exclusives—records no one else had, in particular a black-market twelve-inch by Mach, on Remix Records. "It was pieces of a bunch of records, but way before sampling technology happened," says Lawrence, friends with Saunders from high school. The B-side, "On and On," combined the bass from Play-back's "Space Invaders," chants from Donna Summer's "Bad Girls," and synth-horns from Lipps Inc.'s "Funkytown." "That bass line drove people crazy at the parties," says Lawrence.

Vince knew something about the music biz. His father, Nemiah Mitchell Jr., ran Mitchbal Records, a tiny blues indie. Father and son were not close: "I didn't have the most organized family structure from the get-go," says Lawrence. Nonetheless, in 1981, Mitchbal issued a single, "Fast Cars," by his son's band, Z-Factor; Vince had to talk his dad into issuing it on twelve- rather than seven-inch vinyl. "I explained how you sold a forty-five [rpm seven-inch] for a dollar, but if you put the same song on a twelve-inch, you could sell it for $2.30," says Lawrence.

Jesse Saunders joined the band for 1984's "Fantasy"; they lifted the "Space Invaders" bass line from the Remix Records bootleg, the melody from the Flirts' "Calling All Boys," a favorite of radio DJ Herb Kent, who hosted a late-night show on WXFM called *Punk Out*. Like the Electrifying Mojo in Detroit, Kent's show gave black, teenage Chicago a gateway into new wave. Jesse and Vince got Screamin' Rachael to sing "Fantasy," partly because she didn't sing it quite how Saunders wrote it, helping disguise its origins.

Then Saunders lost his Mach twelve-inch and decided to bootleg the bootleg, using his 808. Lawrence walked him through the motions— recording it in a studio, pressing it up, hand-drawing a logo; they called the label Jes' Say Records. For nine untethered minutes, a spiraling bass line girded 808 presets, ping-ponging voices uttering the title (with jarring interjections of "Bitch!"), and chintzy synth played by their friend Duane Buford. The bass line was played on a Roland TB-303, a bass synthesizer with a one-octave keyboard and several pitch-adjustment knobs. The year Jesse Saunders's "On and On" was released, Roland pulled the 303 from the market. Like disco, it was dead.

When Saunders began playing his own "On and On," his dance

floors exploded. A while later, Lawrence, Saunders, and Buford took a copy to Importes Etc. There, the buyer, Frank Sells, demanded, "Where did you get this record? We've been looking for this for months." They had a thousand copies in the car, and Importes took them all. Returning to the vehicle, the trio "literally screamed," says Lawrence. "We said, 'We're going to be a record company now.'" Lawrence promptly quit his job and started hustling the record to radio, DJs, and shops. He also ordered matching satin baseball jackets with the Jes' Say logo, with each principal's title near the lapel. "Mine said 'Marketing,'" says Lawrence. "Because Duane had a car, his said 'Distribution.' And Jesse's said 'President.'"

IF LARRY SHERMAN had a satin baseball jacket in 1984, it too would have said "President," with an insignia for Musical Products, Chicago's only pressing plant, which he'd purchased the year before. When the newly formed Jes' Say came back to re-press "On and On," Sherman promptly started a label, Precision, to feed the demand for more records like it. After visiting the Muzic Box, he put Lawrence in charge of a second imprint, named for the stripped-down stuff the kids were really flipping for: Trax Records. "He wanted actual songs on Precision, not just beat tracks," says Lawrence. "We'd take our beat-track records and put them out on Trax."

No one could believe these records. They were completely amateur-hour by most standards—but the kids who made them didn't care. They'd put on the parties. They'd saved up for the equipment. (Vince Lawrence had bought his first synthesizer for eight hundred dollars in 1979, saving up with a high school job at Comiskey Park, where he was stationed to collect the disco records the crowd—racists from the north side, in Lawrence's pithy recollection—came to mass-burn at Disco Demolition Night.) They'd gone into the studios and hauled the records around and gotten the attention and upped their appearance fees and were hood superstars. This music was *theirs*.

If you were a serious musician, its appeal was baffling. "That's a record?" said an unimpressed West Side bassist named Adonis Smith. "Everybody's got this record," the friend who played it for him responded. "This guy is famous." Smith took the hint. So did his neighbor, postal worker Marshall Jefferson, a Led Zeppelin fan who'd hated disco until he followed a comely coworker to the Muzic Box in 1982 and Ron Hardy rearranged his insides there. Jefferson heard "On and On" and figured he could do at least as well. "Back then the post office paid a ton of money," says Jefferson. One day he spent nearly ten thousand dollars of it on a home studio's worth of electronic music equipment, drawing catcalls from his friends who knew that Marshall could barely play "Chopsticks." Too late: Saunders's record had suspended all bets.

On the floors of the Power Plant and Muzic Box, a new style of dancing had taken off: jacking. "If you were to get hit from behind in an auto accident," Juan Atkins said, "that would be similar to jacking." Screamin' Rachael calls it "like fucking standing up." In March 1985, a DJ and Importes clerk named Chip Eberhard cut a cheap electronic twelve-inch of his own, the *Jack Trax* EP, credited to Mirage feat. Chip E. It was telling that he billed a machine—the Ensoniq Mirage, an early sampling keyboard—ahead of himself. (Joe Smooth, the DJ at Chicago's Smart Bar, played the Mirage.) The EP's two big tracks were the hypnotic "Time to Jack" and the stuttering "It's House." Two other cuts featured the word "house" in their titles as well; House Records, established by Farley Keith, issued the EP. Importes' handwritten bin card was now an actual musical style. "Just like New York rap is about rap and Washington go-go is about go-go," *Spin*'s Barry Walters wrote in 1986, "Chicago house is about house."

JUST AS THE SUGAR HILL GANG'S "Rapper's Delight" had done in New York in 1979, the 1984 issue of "On and On" in Chicago sired an explosion—the first for black music in the city since the early-seventies heyday of Curtis Mayfield and the Chi-Lites. Labels and producers popped up like baseballs at a riot-free double-header.

In August 1985, Marshall Jefferson cut a demo called "Move Your Body." In defiance of Larry Sherman, who scoffed that house music didn't have piano lines, Marshall nicknamed the song "The House Music Anthem," putting the word right at the top of every piano-driven line: "Gotta have HOUSE! Music! All night long!" The record sounded like a pop song. "When I first took it to Ron Hardy, he played it six times in a row," says Jefferson. "He told me not to take it to anybody else—he wanted an exclusive on it. I said sure. I didn't care, because I didn't want it out because it wasn't released yet." It soon spread around the city, on tapes traded by the faithful.

Hardy got another tape, brought in by a third party, from a shut-in bedroom singer-songwriter named Byron Walford, whose demos were recorded under the alias Jamie Principle. "He pretty much fashioned everything he was doing at that time around Prince," Knuckles said. "He was a real big Prince fan, hence the name Jamie *Prince*-iple." Not to mention Prince's own early alias, as writer-producer for the Time, Vanity 6, and Sheila E.: Jamie Starr.

Principle's songs quickly became Muzic Box staples, but when he wanted a producer, he went to Knuckles. In 1983, Salsoul released Frankie's warhorse re-edit of First Choice's "Let No Man Put Asunder," but he had no real studio experience—or studio; they made their first recording, the smeared-ethereal "Your Love," in the Power Plant's DJ booth. Their first actual release was "Waiting on My Angel," on the tiny imprint Persona; Jesse Saunders promptly and unflatteringly covered it note-for-note on Larry Sherman's Precision.

The difference between Knuckles's and Hardy's spinning styles was also manifest in their production work: Frankie the disco perfectionist versus Ronnie the wild man. Hardy's remix of 1986's "Donnie," produced by Chip E. as The It, sounds like an accident, partly because it was—Robert Owens's strained, hypnotic wail came from him teaching Harri Dennis the hook, which Hardy mixed in.

Off-key vocals and one-take production gave early Chicago house a feverish feel. Few styles were as frankly sleazy, as with Adonis's maniacally repetitive "No Way Back" or Hercules's "7 Ways to Jack," with its reptilian porno vocals: "Number six: Physically touch the body in front of you—in *every way imaginable* / Number seven: Lose complete mental control and *begin . . . to . . . jack*." Knuckles and Principle's greatest record, 1987's "Baby Wants to Ride," is one of the all-time great Prince rip-offs: lyrics via *Dirty Mind* ("When I go to bed at night / I think of you with all my might"), synth skid via *Controversy*.

The studio of choice for much of this output was Chicago Trax on Halstead Street—no relation to Trax Records. (Wax Trax! Records is no relation to either—it can be confusing.) Chicago Trax's Studio B was in constant use by the city's fledgling producers; Studio A was block-booked for a year by Ministry, whose leader Al Jourgensen was then in the first throes of serious rock-star debauchery; Vince Lawrence and Screamin' Rachael were frequent guests. Chicago Trax became the place to go after Steve "Silk" Hurley and Keith Nunnally, who recorded as J.M. Silk, made "Music Is the Key" there. It was one of the most polished house records yet; even the goofy rap ("Music is the KEY! To set yourself FREE!") is fully integrated into the song.

The Chicago house recording made in 1985 with the biggest impact wasn't a song at all. One day, DJ Pierre, (Nathaniel Pierre Jones), his cousin Earl "Spanky" Smith, and their friend Herbert Jackson—the trio Phuture—created "Acid Tracks" by accident. Spanky had picked up a Roland TB-303, the single-octave bass synth Jesse Saunders made "On and On" with, for forty dollars. Knobs controlled cutoff frequency, resonance, envelope modulation, decay, and accent—to tune the sound till it sounded right. But nobody could program the damn thing.

Instead, Pierre began turning the knobs to undulate the pitch. It sounded *crazy*—pure machine music with an obviously human touch, constantly warping. "I approached everything like Ron Hardy playing in the Muzic Box, thinking about how that crowd would react to it," says Pierre. Hardy asked for a copy immediately after hearing it the first time, playing it over and over till the crowd got it, about 4 A.M.—literally jumping off the walls. The original title was "In Your Mind," but when people started trading microcassettes of bootleg recordings of the track, it became known as "Ron Hardy's Acid Track." Originally 127 beats per minute, it dropped to 120 when Marshall Jefferson, who produced the finished record, told them, "This is too fast for New York."

"Acid Tracks" remains one of the oddest "hit" singles ever made: Twelve minutes of a machine eating its own wires, the 303 gibbering away over drum machine, hand claps, and referee's whistle. The flipside was a heartfelt, and scary, antidrug monologue called "Your Only Friend," which began, "This is cocaine speaking." In 1987, Spanky watched as a clutch of Chicago drug dealers waved wads of dollar bills while the track played at a local club, hooting: "This is our song!" He was horrified. "It was never our intention for it to be linked to drugs," Spanky told *The Wire*. "We thought of acid rock because it had the same sort of changing frequencies."

JUAN ATKINS LEFT CYBOTRON in 1985, setting up his own label, Metroplex Records, and releasing solo material as Model 500—first the jittery electro-funk "No UFOs," immediately one-upped by "Night Drive (Time, Space, Transmat)," a track baldly indebted to Kraftwerk but also on its own plane entirely. Every squiggling synth line was locked onto the skeletal, stop-start rhythm, and every beat intensified the synths' cumulative effect. It made becoming a robot seem not so much romantic, as Kraftwerk had done, as *urgent*, a body-led imperative.

Derrick May was going in the same direction. In addition to talking about starting a juice bar of their own in Detroit—he even had a name picked out: The Music Institute—Derrick played his rough demos to the Chicago road-trip crew. "Eighty-five, '86, '87, we spent a lot of time traveling, listening to what Derrick was doing," remembers Alton Miller. "We knew it was going to lead to something big."

These tracks were very different from Atkins's—sweeping, orchestral, studded with sudden stops and turnarounds, the percussion intricately layered. While briefly leading a Hot Mix 5–style show for WJLB-FM called *Street Beat* and spinning Friday nights at the downtown new wave club the Liedernacht (where management reined him in—he was attracting too many blacks), May was also carving a unique niche as a DJ. "Derrick has a really intense, physical swing," says Gamall Awad, a British-born dance-music publicist in Brooklyn. "It's never behind the one, it's never on the one—his swing is *ahead* of the one. If you think about the idea of the future: The future is pulling you, it's got momentum. The idea of futurism is ahead of the one."

Saunderson had also begun to produce. His brother Ron had road-managed seventies funk hit makers Skyy and Brass Construction—"He was very into MIDI and technology," says Saunderson—and showed his brother what to buy and how to use it. Kevin frequently stopped over at May and Fowlkes's apartment: "I would play whatever they had, and vice versa." In 1986, Metroplex issued "Triangle of Love" by Kreem—Saunderson and endearingly pitchy vocalist Je'nine Barker, with Atkins adding a bass line reminiscent of New Order. Kevin was a disco guy trying to write an Evelyn "Champagne" King record; Juan was a new waver. "It was just parts that I had that worked," says Saunderson. "He mixed it and I watched. Once I seen it, I knew how."

These tracks were well received in Chicago. "For us, Model 500's 'No UFO's' was a house record," Tyree Cooper, an early Chicago producer and vocalist, said. "It sounded different but for us it was still house." Sure, "Triangle of Love" could have been issued on Chicago imprints like Trax or the rising D.J. International, but May's first record, "Nude Photo" (1986), credited to Rhythim Is Rhythim, sounded little like what was on those labels. It was too tonally slippery, too rhythmically intricate. Anyway, Atkins had another name for what they were doing in Detroit. He called it "techno."

KEVIN AND DERRICK also took after Juan by starting their own labels—KMS for Saunderson (his middle name is Maurice), Transmat for May. This was a crucial difference between the two cities. Detroit was DIY by necessity and historical tradition: Motown still loomed over everything. But though plenty of smaller, black-owned house imprints popped up in Chicago—notably, Chicago Connection, a subdivision of Mitchbal; Dance Mania, another Saunders imprint; and producer Mark Imperial's House Nation—the big guns belonged to Chi-*caaah*-go's music-biz old-boy network, ready to cash in on the craze.

Rocky Jones had been the head of a record pool before starting D.J. International in 1985, starting with Chip E.'s "Like This," a huge bite of "Moody" by New York post-punks ESG—a Frankie Knuckles staple. In 1986, Jones signed D.J. International's lawyer, Jay B. Ross, to the label as the Rapping Lawyer. "Only in America could an attorney sell himself via 'Sue the Bastards' T-shirts with his name and number on the back," Sheryl Garratt noted in *The Face*.

Larry Sherman was so cheap he pressed records on recycled vinyl—center label and all. "There was this huge boiler, about as big as a room," says Screamin' Rachael. "You know how people complain about Trax records having pieces of cardboard in them? That's why." In addition to repurposing unwanted LPs ("We ground up a bunch of *Thrillers*," she says), they also reused the cardboard jackets, with old label insignias, of bigger indies like Tuff City and King Street. Trax Records—nothing but class.

Lewis Pitzele was a Chicago concert promoter who owned a local clothing chain called House of Lewis. "He was like P. T. Barnum," says Screamin' Rachael. "He was larger than life. Once he stopped an ambulance because Jerry Lee Lewis would not go on stage without towels. So Lewis pulled a stack from an ambulance." Pitzele knew there was money to be made overseas. He'd begun hearing rumors that people liked house music in England.

So had Marshall Jefferson, who received a call in 1985 from London record-shop clerk Michael Schiniou, a.k.a. pirate radio DJ Jazzy M. Jefferson, and sent the Englishman some cassettes. He didn't include "Move Your Body." He didn't have to. Schiniou had gotten a copy from Alfredo Fiorito, a.k.a. DJ Alfredo, an Argentinian DJ living on the Mediterranean island of Ibiza, who'd gotten *his* copy from Larry Levan in New York. On cassette mixtapes going hand to hand, house music was becoming international. But no one in her right mind could have predicted what would happen in 1987.

BBC reporter: Where do you think you're going?

Girl: We don't know.

Boy: That's the mystery about it. This is acid, man.

—"WE CALLED IT ACID," REPORT ON BBC-TV'S *WORLD IN ACTION*, 1988

>2

THE MUSIC INSTITUTE

DETROIT, MICHIGAN
November 24, 1989

ON JANUARY 21, 1987, England had a new number-one hit. J.M. Silk's "Jack Your Body" utilized a familiar First Choice bass line. "We stole 'Let No Man Put Asunder' a million times," Farley admitted on behalf of the city of Chicago. "We went down a note. We went up a note. We transposed it." J.M. Silk—Steve "Silk" Hurley and vocalist Keith Nunnally—didn't necessarily steal it *best*, but that didn't matter: The record sounded like nothing the English had heard. They knew little about the group, either: When the song hit the top, *The Chart Show* on Channel 4 was forced to show the duo's black-and-white photo for two and a half minutes.

"Jack Your Body" had been on a compilation called *The House Sound of Chicago*, put together in 1986 by London Records A&R man Pete Tong, from selections in the D.J. International catalog. The collection excited the music press's attention. "Lewis Pitzele was the one who got seven journalists to fly into Chicago and write about us—on Rocky's dime," says Screamin' Rachael. "They were interviewing me and my big stuff hadn't come out yet," recalls Marshall Jefferson. "That is when I got a clue that it was getting popular out there."

A number-one hit was one thing; a full-fledged scene was another. Up north, English cities like Birmingham, Manchester, and Sheffield had long nurtured rabid fan bases for imported African American records. Those were the audiences that greeted the visiting Chicagoans in early 1987, on the Chicago House Party package tour. "All the shows were packed," says Jefferson. "Rock City in Nottingham was complete pandemonium; same thing at the Haçienda in Manchester." But while DJs such as the Haçienda's Mike Pickering made house music a staple of their sets, it was slower to pick up in London, where club culture meant endless fashionista posing at haughty venues like the Wag or Samantha's, whose tight door policies contradicted the black-and-proud early-seventies funk being played inside. One night, the Wag refused entry to rapper KRS-One—whose group, Boogie Down Productions, was scheduled to play there the following evening.

THAT SUMMER, A QUARTET of English funk and soul DJs—Nicky Holloway, Paul Oakenfold, Danny Rampling, and Johnny Walker—vacationed on the Mediterranean island of Ibiza, which had been drawing draft dodgers and tourists since the sixties. The summer weather was balmy, the drug policy lax; they were there to celebrate Oakenfold's twenty-fourth birthday. The four of them visited their friends Trevor Fung and Ian St. Paul, who ran a night at Project Bar, near San Antonio, with a growing clientele of northern English tourists.

Eventually the group ended up in Amnesia, an enormous open-air venue in Ibiza Town run by DJ Alfredo, a journalist from Argentina who'd found asylum on the island following a right-wing military coup in 1976. Now he drew thousands of people, seven nights a week, to dance to his selections. Alfredo mixed a span of styles unusual in tightly regimented London—he had global tourists to please, after all. But the music wasn't all that pleased them.

MDMA—street name ecstasy—was first synthesized in 1912 by German chemist Anton Köllisch, a developer for the pharmaceutical giant Merck. It had been part of club life in the early eighties, particularly in New York, where it was popular with Paradise Garage regulars and visiting musicians. (The title of Soft Cell's NYC-recorded 1982 album, *Non Stop Ecstatic Dancing*, nodded to MDMA.) Typically presented in a pressed pill, with "purer" strains occasionally appearing in capsule form, ecstasy releases to the brain a jet stream of serotonin—a mood-enhancing chemical naturally produced by the body in smaller amounts than an MDMA dose opens up—and dopamine, a likewise naturally occurring stimulant.

On ecstasy, one's perception sharpens, but so does one's level of empathy; on it, nearly everything seems wonderful, almost indiscriminately so. If you were a self-consciously stylish English DJ in 1987, that meant everything from U2's "I Still Haven't Found What I'm Looking For" to the freakish tweaks of Phuture's "Acid Tracks." Oakenfold's crew imbibed for five consecutive nights.

In December, Rampling rented the mirrored basement of a fitness center in Bermondsey, South London, the other side of the world from West End pseudo-sophistication. He put smiley faces—a nod to the dystopian comic book *Watchmen*, by Brits Alan Moore and Dave Gibbons, not to mention Ibiza's blissful style—on the flyer: "Sensation seekers, let the music take you to the top." Shamelessly druggy hedonism taking place in the *echt*-eighties altar of self-improvement—a gym—made its own statement.

Rampling's night, Shoom, was, in his words, "a runaway train." At British pop culture's stodgiest period, the hug-your-neighbor vibe began a sea change in popular music and popular culture. House music was no longer a novelty; it was the future. At first, according to DJ and future A.R.E. Weapons member Thomas Bullock, "People would say, 'Are you going to go raving on the weekend?'" The term "rave," he says, "crept in in '88. We were doing something on a much more intimate level."

Not for long. In April 1988, Oakenfold kicked off Spectrum at the Charing Cross club Heaven, drawing fifteen hundred on Monday nights—three times Shoom's capacity. Two months later Holloway started the Trip at the Astoria on Tottenham Court Road, bringing in three thousand people wearing smiley T-shirts and smiley shoelaces and blowing smiley whistles while coming up on smiley pills. They'd still be buzzing when the club shut down, partying outside, defying police trying to shoo them home, boogying to the squad-car sirens while chanting: *Aciiieeed! Aciiieeed!* In seven months acid house had blown wide open. It wasn't for club insiders anymore. It was for *everybody*.

The first time DJ Pierre went to London, he says, "I didn't know what to play. I don't have previous experience playing for white people." On the night, his worry turned to amusement. "People in Chicago, they were *dancing*—spinning, jumping in the air. They just had the moves—you know the stereotype. In London it was more just jumping up and down, hands in the air." Jefferson is less diplomatic: "When I first went to Europe, they couldn't dance, man," he says with a laugh. "They were horrible and they didn't care. But they were having a good time, and that was what was most important."

EVEN THOUGH THEIR records were blowing up overseas, most of the Chicago producers were still living hand to mouth. Larry Sherman made sure of it. He calculated royalties on a sliding scale. "If I give an artist three thousand dollars to do a tune and it costs him, say, fifteen hundred to use a studio, that leaves him fifteen hundred to live on till he can produce another tune, because the reality is that we have to sell at least fifteen thousand records to pay back his advance and all his records will do is ten to fifteen thousand units," Sherman boasted to UK fanzine *Soul Underground* in late 1988. "When they get to the UK and they get on a compilation, the compilation may do up to fifteen thousand units. Even so, because it is one of the fifteen tracks on the record, the revenue will be so low that the advance is not recouped." Little wonder, as Sherman put it in the same interview, "Everybody with me still works together, so no one excels."

Sherman's didn't merely penny-pinch his artists, either. He insulted them: "People like Farley and Marshall and Hurley can't really play a note—they don't have the tools to be successful commercially," he said—two years after Hurley's UK number-one and Farley's top-ten "Love Can't Turn Around" (with large, screaming vocalist Darryl Pandy resplendent on *Top of the Pops* in a blue lamé top), and Jefferson a year away from his own British top-ten with the band Ten City. "I have artists who are musically capable and I've kept them out of the marketplace so that they don't get poisoned," the mogul continued, adding, heartwarmingly: "I try and help these kids out, and hell, they make me a lot of money, so seriously I have no bitch with them and I wish them all the luck in the world."

They needed it. Allegations of Sherman's business tactics run rampant where and whenever he is discussed—with artists persistently raising questions about copyright grants and royalty payments. DJ Pierre would go to the Trax office for his cut of publishing every quarter and be told by Sherman, "You didn't really earn any royalties. You know, it's just a Chicago thing. This house music isn't big all over."

"The part that I never understood was where the money was going on those deals," says Vince Lawrence, barely out of high school and doing Trax's A&R, plus producing on the side. "I never got paid." He laughs. "I was making good money but the real economics were oblivious to me." Figuring he had it made with Sherman, Lawrence turned down an offer from the Warner Bros.–distributed Tommy Boy Records, which had issued "Planet Rock," to run a house-music subsidiary. "What are you talking about? I've *got* my own label," he told them. "I didn't understand that they had established national and international distribution," says Lawrence. "Nobody understood the concept."

NEIL RUSHTON KNEW he'd missed the big train. An ex-journalist and soul fan, he'd cofounded Kool Kat Records in Birmingham in 1987 to issue black American club tracks (and local variants) in the UK. "Other UK labels had sewn up Chicago," he says. "From my fascination with Detroit sixties soul music, I was drawn to music from the place. And once I heard it I loved it."

He licensed Rhythim Is Rhythim's "Nude Photo," from Transmat, and "The Sound" by Reese & Santonio (Saunderson and Santonio Echols), from KMS, and grew friendly with the Belleville guys. Over Christmas 1987, May went to England to work on some remixes, staying with Rushton; they clicked immediately. "I think Derrick realized I was as mad as he was," says Rushton. On a handshake, he became May's manager.

Rushton quickly realized that he'd found a story. He approached Mick Clark from the Virgin subsidiary 10 Records, and signed on to produce a compilation of Detroit dance tracks. In spring 1988 he flew to Detroit to oversee it; soon Rushton was managing Atkins and Saunderson as well. May did much of the comp's legwork, encouraging other producers—Blake Baxter, Eddie Fowlkes, Anthony "Shake" Shakir—to get in on the windfall.

Atkins didn't like the name Rushton was planning to issue his collection under: *The House Sound of Detroit*. Juan's track was called "Techno Music," and that's the title he wanted for the album as well. "Techno" was a muscular word, and it fit music that sounded, proudly and deliberately, as if machines had made it. "Even though all my records weren't necessarily techno records," says Saunderson, "because I was from Detroit, the group I was around, that's what it was."

Saunderson's contribution to *Techno! The New Dance Sound of De-*

troit, "Big Fun," credited to Inner City, was the last track Rushton heard for consideration. Kevin had written it with help from musicians James Pennington and Art Forest, and got Chicagoan Paris Grey to sing it. "Not only did I say on the spot it was a single, I told Kevin it would be a worldwide smash and would change his life and he should consider quitting college," says Rushton. "He thought I was mad." It hit number eight in England, where the follow-up, "Good Life," reached number five—an even better record, and an absolutely convincing statement of unfettered positivity. Suddenly, the last of the Belleville three to become a DJ was its first bona fide pop star.

But Derrick became, in short order, a star of a different kind, beginning with his memorable definition of techno as sounding "like George Clinton and Kraftwerk are stuck in an elevator with only a sequencer to keep them company," as he told *The Face*'s Stuart Cosgrove in his feature on the sound, "Seventh City Techno." (It was, May says, entirely top-of-the-head.) Another feature by John McCready in *NME* confirmed it; May was the sharpest, most charismatic, most forthright of a group that wasn't exactly shy about its opinions.

Juan, Derrick, and Kevin eventually rented a building together in Detroit proper; 1486–1492 Gratiot Avenue, in Detroit's arty Eastern Market area, became headquarters for May's label, Transmat, as well as Atkins's Metroplex and Saunderson's KMS. "They just took over that whole area when they got money," says Alan Oldham, a DJ (as T-1000) and radio host who's known May since elementary school. "Juan lived right downstairs and Kevin was down the street." The block quickly became dubbed "Techno Boulevard."

Most of the area's buildings became live-work spaces on the sly. "The landlords would turn down money: 'You want a *refrigerator*? No—let's go,'" says Ollivierra, who also lived near Techno Boulevard. One of his other neighbors was a former Detroit Symphony bassoonist, then in her seventies. "One day she came over with a Froot Loops casserole," he says. "Or a stuffed crow. She was really into taxidermy.

There were a host of characters. Derrick and Kevin and Juan were part of that."

Metroplex sat on the Gratiot complex's ground-floor loft, a thirty-six-channel mixing board and scads of MIDI equipment occupying the center. May founded his label after the other two had founded theirs, and got ribbed for it. "We were the babies: 'Derrick May's trying to have a real record label,'" says Ollivierra. The first time Ollivierra brought his electric typewriter to work, Eddie Fowlkes looked up from a game of parking-lot basketball with Saunderson and exclaimed, "Oh, shit! Look! Transmat's got a typewriter, y'all! Shit's gettin' real!"

Techno Boulevard's denizens were like siblings, supportive and squabbling in equal measure. "There was a fierce competitiveness between the three that exists to this day," says Ollivierra. "Not as in, 'I want to be more famous, make more money, and sell more records than you.' Their goal was to compose music that would be new and different. They wanted to hear Juan say, *[low, hollow-throated]* 'That's some *new shit* right there.' They wanted Kevin to have to bow and say, *[laid-back growl]* 'Shit's hot, y'all! Is *hot.*' They wanted Derrick to say, *[slightly pinched, excitable]* 'Yo, that's the motherfucka!' It wasn't enough to have a good song. If you did something similar to the others, you'd get called out for it. Originality was even better than having a hot track."

One track in particular, though, was hotter than the rest. It began with piano chords, played by Derrick's friend Michael James, that May chopped up. It becomes apparent quickly that the piano is background for the song's real star—the Detroit Symphony's strings, recorded live and reconfigured by May, hitting from oblique angles. Played in real time, they add a subtle charge to meticulously programmed 909 snares and hi-hats. After Frankie Knuckles played it—more than once—for his Power Plant crowd, he told Derrick what to call it: "Strings of Life."

EARLY IN 1988, Kevin Saunderson visited London for some DJ gigs. "The clubs were very pop, very unaware," he recalls. "House music like 'Jack Your Body' was in the charts. It was what people had experienced. But by the time I came back in July, the shit had hit the fan." Saunderson went to Paul Oakenfold's Spectrum one Monday night and watched "Big Fun" decimate the crowd. Across the country, house and techno music were doing the same thing. "It was like a virus," says Saunderson. "It spread to everybody. Not just the young or old—everybody. You'd see them all at parties. You'd never seen nothing like it. I realized, 'This is some real shit. This is unbelievable.'"

The hinterlands were ready, decided Tony Colston-Hayter, a rich, twenty-one-year-old ex–blackjack player who'd gone to Shoom and the Trip. First, in August 1988, he threw an event, Apocalypse Wow, at Wembley Film Studios in Shepherd's Bush, selling five thousand advance tickets in the two weeks before the event. That fall, Colston-Hayter caravanned partiers to the country for the Sunrise Mystery Trip, where E'd-up punters could jump around inside a bouncy inflatable castle while they sucked on pacifiers ("dummies," the English called them) to ease the facial-muscle jitters brought on by MDMA, or rubbed Vick's VapoRub on the inside of gas masks to further stimulate the rush. The innocence-regained feel of Rampling's weekly was quickly hardening into a series of social tics.

Police shut down Sunrise, though the model was set: There would be more parties like it, many more. English news media—initially warm to the smiley craze—reverted to moral panic. *The Sun* went from giving away its own acid house T-shirt to the thundering headline, "Evil of Ecstasy," in a week, running a two-panel editorial cartoon in which the Devil wears a smiley mask and lures an innocent girl and boy to fall through a doormat reading "Welcome to Acid House" and into hell.

Jonah Sharp, a jazz drummer from Edinburgh who'd come to London via Newcastle in the mid-eighties, attended one of Colston-

Hayter's Sunrise events. "It was absolutely extraordinary—one of those huge outdoor raves," he says. "Completely blew my mind: twenty thousand people in a field. The music was really developing then." Sharp heard 808 State's "Pacific State" and Members of the KLF's "What Time Is Love?"; along with A Guy Called Gerald's "Voodoo Ray," a number-twelve UK chart hit, these led a wave of new tracks by English DJs and producers that emulated Chicago house while imbuing it with their own perspective.

As with the rise of gangsta rap in the U.S. around the same time, rave's illegal aura only enhanced its draw. But by mid-1989, what was sold as ecstasy was at least as likely to contain any number of other substances—aspirin, LSD, ketamine, caffeine, amphetamine—as it was MDMA. As a result, people began taking more pills to achieve the rush they'd come for. Increasingly, these parties took place alongside the Orbital, a motorway that circles London's suburbs, with thousands guided by pirate radio stations like Centre Force. "You'd hear about a party and directions being given out on radio and you're literally driving around to find it," says Sharp.

By 1989, the renegade party squads in England were beginning to go legit. They brought in larger DJ lineups, secured ever-more-outlandish spaces, piled on drug-enhancing extras. On May 27, 1989, an event called Energy took place at the Westway film studio, with five kitted-out rooms: one resembling imperial Rome, another à la *Blade Runner*, a third featuring a pyramid. Jazzy M, spinning on a twenty-foot scaffold in the Roman Empire room, cut back and forth between two copies "Strings of Life," teasing out the beatless intro until the crowd was ready to snap. Then he brought in the hook, and the place went berserk. The acid house generation had found its anthem.

"It was definitely a culture shock to me," says Atkins, who played some of the early film-studio parties in London. "In the USA, the races are polarized because [the country is] so big. There's no place you can go in England and not see people of different races, from everywhere. They're more used to that cultural mix-up, to where they don't think nothing of it. I'm thinking to myself, 'This would never happen in the USA.'"

BACK IN DETROIT, May, George Baker, Alton Miller, and Chez Damier decided to open a Muzic Box or Power Plant of their own. In 1987, they made an abortive attempt to renovate a former Firestone spark plug factory near Wayne State University. To fix it properly, says Miller, "would have taken an exorbitant amount of money"; instead, the group threw the occasional party in downtown's Harmonie Park neighborhood. "Those did very well," says Miller. "That was a barometer as to what was going on."

The group found an opening at 1315 Broadway, a black box that held five hundred; by early 1988 they'd begun turning it into the Music Institute. There was a main dance area, a second-floor balcony for the club's juice bar (selling warm Faygo for a dollar), and offices on the third floor. A lot of work was necessary: "We had to build a bar," says Miller. "We had to build the bathrooms. We had to sand an entire dance floor, and the one above it. I think we ended up doing the third floor, as well. Between building the bathrooms and sanding all those wooden floors"—he laughs—"I vowed that I would never touch another sander in my life."

The second-floor staircase had a heavy theater drape to dampen the sound. "You heard it just enough to make you want to come back downstairs and dance," says Miller. The Music Institute's DJ booth was an enclosed box fifteen feet above the floor, with a rectangular hole: "You could see Derrick's forehead—not the top of his head—down to his shoulders," says Ollivierra, who checked coats and designed flyers for the Music Institute. The booth's height and isolation allowed the club's DJs unparalleled control of the environment. "It became my tower," says May. "I was above the lights. I could see everything happening on that dance floor. It was an amazing feeling." Adds Miller: "The place was a box, so it was easy to get the sound right."

For two weeks before the club opened, its principals embarked on a membership drive, allowing people into the space to sign up. "The membership was derived from the fact that clubs in New York and Chicago did it," says May. "It wasn't really legitimate. But we had paper IDs. We made T-shirts." While the Music Institute was clearly tied to the early-eighties Detroit high school party scene, its membership wasn't, necessarily. "There were a lot of people I didn't know," says Miller. Eventually, some 250 people became members.

Initially, the Music Institute was supposed to be open only on Saturday nights; opening night shut down early due to a fire-code violation. But attendance built rapidly. "It took about a month, and then it exploded," says Miller. "We had lines literally down the street. That was unheard of for an after-hours in Detroit." It also spoke to the need for more nights. "We thought two nights would be a bit much, especially based on the hours of operation," says Miller. "Saturday held its own. But we felt that Derrick needed to be able to do his own thing over the course of a night." Kevin Saunderson was involved early on, but bowed out once Inner City took off.

May took the decks Friday nights after his regular opener, D-Wynn (born Darryl), spun from midnight to 3. "Darryl would tear them up," says May. "We were a great team." Once May was on the decks, everyone in the club knew it, even if no one could see him, thanks to his signature tracks. Two by Chicago house producer Lil Louis, in particular, became May's calling cards: "Blackout" and especially "French Kiss," a UK number-two record with a trick middle—it slowed nearly to a stop before resuming its normal tempo. May once played it, whole, five times in a night.

"He would play 'French Kiss' and slow it down incrementally over the period of a minute," says Ollivierra. May then ran the slurring track into a speeding locomotive from a sound effects record—an old Nicky Siano trick (he'd used an LP of a jet landing). "On a major sound system, a proper recording of a locomotive train was amazing," says May. "You could feel the ball of heat just rise through the floor." Then May would throw on a new track. "That was 100 percent Derrick May," says Ollivierra. "It would drive people crazy." May sent everyone home to the softer strains of Manuel Göttsching's *E2:E4*. "Just imagine," says Ollivierra, "Manuel Göttsching being played for a crowd of young black people in Detroit in 1988."

"I had no say in running it," says May of the Institute. "I was a resident, but we all lived there. We were all twenty-five years old. There was no real manager. I didn't even get paid to play the Music Institute." *Never?* "In the end, a couple of times: four hundred dollars. I did it because I loved it. It was our home. It was a labor of love."

THE MUSIC INSITUTE'S walls were black. There was no alcohol. "It was no frills," says Atkins, and so was the crowd. The first night Ollivierra went, in late 1988, he was struck by how busy it was: "You could lay down and take a nap in the middle of Gratiot Avenue at two in the morning and wake up not having been run over by a car," he says. "I'd never seen that many black people standing outside a bar or club anywhere in Michigan, ever. They all looked excited. They were all talking with one another. Those weren't the faces I'd seen of people queuing up to get into a club—anxious and a bit annoyed to be put out. It was more like a party at somebody's house."

Once inside, Ollivierra was equally amazed. "There was nobody, really, standing up against the wall," he says. "There were no chairs. There was no alcohol. There was some people coagulating at a bar—taking a breather—and they'd jump right back out there, because the music was so loud you couldn't really have a conversation, unless you were shouting point-blank in their ear." The crowd largely eschewed substances; dress was, by necessity, casual. "The humidity and the heat—it was like a jungle in there," says Ollivierra. "Nobody was there to get laid. Nobody was there to get drunk. Nobody was there to make a presentation of style with respect to their hair, their makeup, their clothing."

Carl Craig, an aspiring musician who'd been giving May his demo tapes, began going to the Music Institute after a friend from high school took him. "It was like walking into Nirvana," says Craig. "It was exactly what I wanted to experience. I loved everything that I heard." Craig attended the night May premiered Inner City's "Big Fun." "I've never seen a room, before that, explode—really, almost spontaneous combustion," says Craig. "These people just lost their freaking minds. I think he might have played it three times within an hour." Craig was also impressed by the fluid, expressive dancing—particularly compared to Detroit's other hot downtown spot of the time, the Shelter, which catered to all-elbows Goths, the worst dancers on earth. At the Music Institute, "they weren't doing flips, but, God, you thought they were going to. They were dancing together—not like, 'Can I have this dance?' You just kind of joined in. It was really exciting."

Along with May's loft, the club became a gathering place for Detroit's African American musical intelligentsia. "The MI and Derrick's loft were like the black, bourgie Detroit version of Warhol's Factory," says Oldham. Carl Craig, who hung out at both places, likens May to Giancarlo Esposito's character in *School Daze*: "When I went to Derrick's house, the impression I got when I left was that I'd met the real-life Big Brother Almigh-*ty*: the head of the fraternity, talking shit the whole time, the coolest guy."

The club's makeup changed subtly over time, in part thanks to Ollivierra, who began distributing flyers in the Detroit suburbs. "I told everybody I knew about it, black, white, Asian, what have you," says Ollivierra. This was unusual: "White people kinda stood out in those days," says Oldham. "Detroit was still Murder City to most suburbanites, especially that area of downtown, away from the well-lit areas like Greektown."

Among the newcomers were Richie and Matthew Hawtin, siblings from nearby Windsor, Ontario, who'd immigrated to Canada from England as kids. Richie was a DJ at the Shelter; his friend Kenny Larkin inaugurated the Hawtins into the Institute's growing cult. "It was part of the club circuit," says Matthew. "The Music Institute would be the post-post-club thing—this black box, strobe, loud music; always great music." The Hawtins became MI members in March of 1989.

Soon, May's places became a destination for out-of-towners as well. "I never knew any actual English people before I started hanging out at Derrick's," says Oldham, who met British electronic musicians A Guy Called Gerald and Darren Mohammed, from Adrenalin M.O.D., at May's loft. "All I knew about England was what I saw on TV. Hearing that accent in person was a big deal."

Chicago's DJ Pierre, the man who'd twisted the knobs of Phuture's "Acid Tracks," made a handful of five-hour treks to party at the Institute, much the way the club's founders had driven to Chicago to dance at the Power Plant and Muzic Box. "We were hearing about something happening: Kevin Saunderson, Derrick May, and Juan Atkins all at one party," says Pierre, for whom the Institute struck a balance between the simmering tempos of New York's clubs and Ron Hardy–style frenzy. "It was more balanced musically—it was a different vibe, but had the same energy, as the Muzic Box."

JUST AS DERRICK and his crew would travel to see Knuckles and Hardy in action, says Ollivierra, "There'd be people who'd travel from foreign countries to Michigan just to see this scene. It wasn't uncommon for the door to knock, and there'd be six Ne'erlanders with backpacks: 'Can we come in?' 'Sure.'" May made tea, took them to lunch, and bantered about the virtues of his hometown. "It wasn't even surprising after a while," says Ollivierra.

If May's provocative interviews with European magazines fired the imaginations of overseas listeners, Friday nights at the Music Institute had a similar effect at home. "Derrick made me say, 'This is something I want to do,'" says Robert Hood, an MI regular who'd begun rapping under the name Rob Noise and was starting to make records with Jeff Mills—a popular scratch DJ better known by his radio name, "The Wizard"—and local musician Mike Banks, as Underground Resistance. Another Detroit native, Stacey Pullen, drove eight hours north from his classes at Tennessee State University to visit family and dance till dawn at the Music Institute. "Derrick May was my idol," says Pullen. "I was all about him. That's who inspired me to get more involved in doing the music. You left your judgments at the door. I realized, 'This is what I'm about.'"

The Music Institute had only two bouncers. "They were friendly; they didn't throw around their weight," says Ollivierra. "Honestly, they didn't have to. They would sniff people out. Outside the whole time, the filtration was occurring." Anyone who came to the door in a goat-fur coat—popular with Detroit drug dealers of the eighties—would only be let in once they'd given up their firearms. "I never saw a fight," says Ollivierra. "I never saw anybody yelling at anyone—not once."

During the day, the Music Institute space would be rented out for yoga lessons and private parties, dance classes and video shoots. "We really wanted to make sure we were accessible to the community," says Alton Miller. "It was nominal. It didn't make or break us. But it was a way to supplement the budget of the club." Eventually, Miller began spinning on Wednesday nights as well, for an older crowd—fortyish, gay, "the whole *Interview* magazine, *Details* magazine, Andy Warhol, Paradise Garage set," says Ollivierra.

But May's career, like Atkins's and Saunderson's, had picked up so much momentum overseas that he began missing weeks at the Music Institute. For one London trip, May took Carl Craig along as his bandmate for a pair of live Rhythim Is Rhythim shows, opening for Inner City. "He was nervous because he'd never played as a musician in front of anybody," says Craig. "He always did it in the privacy of his own home, or if there were people over, he'd act crazy and make jokes out of it."

Craig had played in bands and was used to crowds; May wasn't. He got stage fright on the second night, at London's Town and Country venue: "That was when the Cindy Brady red-light-on-the-camera thing [happened]," says Craig. "He was over that." Craig, meanwhile, stayed in England for three months, with his London-based girlfriend, an artist named Sarah Gregory; they'd met months earlier, when she painted a mural on the Music Institute's wall. (One figure had eyes, recalls Stacey Pullen, "that looked like they were coming at you every time the strobe light would go on.")

With May out of the picture so much, Atkins began filling in. "I didn't have an actual residency," says Atkins. "I was the backup." The MI's regulars benefited from those London trips. "We would go over to record stores like Fat Cat and Blackmarket, buy all of this music, and come back and play it," says Atkins.

THROUGHOUT THE SUMMER OF 1989—the Second Summer of Love, per the British press—England's acid house parties began ramping up in size. On July 1, Karma Productions threw Energy Part 2, a sequel to their first Energy event the year before. Along with a smattering of the rising circuit's bigger names—Oakenfold, Jazzy M, and Fabio, soon to cofound the London club Rage—the promoters invited New Yorker Frankie Bones (Frank Mitchell), billed as "Franky" on the flyer.

Bones had started making freestyle—Latin hip-hop—in the mid-eighties before issuing a flurry of house tracks, often driven by break-beats, under a variety of pseudonyms: Bonesbreaks, the Break Boys, Lake Errie. A 1989 twelve-inch, "Just as Long as I've Got You," recorded by Bones with his onetime rival roller-skating DJ Lenny Dee—born Leonardo Didesiderio in Sheepshead Bay—as Looney Tunes, fit right in with England's hopeful vibe.

"We were used to selling three to five thousand units on our own," says Bones. "Then licensing deals started happening. We were getting large advances coming from labels in Europe. Suddenly we were moving ten thousand units. London was very interested in us. When we got the call in June 1989, it was very appealing to go somewhere outside of America and see our music being played."

Bones anticipated a crowd of five thousand people—the size of a giant NYC club such as the Tunnel—at Energy Part 2. Driving to the locale in Membury, Berkshire, someone handed Bones a pill. "I didn't know what ecstasy was," Bones told the zine *Massive*. "[We were] stuck in a traffic jam on a little country road with just two lanes and cars for miles." As they approached the venue, Bones continued, "Out of one car was one of my songs from one record and out of another car was another song from another record—as I am coming up from ecstasy. I pretty much lost my mind." Bones hit the decks as the sun came up. "I was a baby in diapers up onstage in front of twenty-five thousand people all on E at the same time at seven A.M.," Bones said. "That was probably my enlightenment."

"You've got to remember, everyone in England was dropping ecstasy like it was frickin' water," says Lenny Dee, who played London shortly after Bones, headlining the club Helter Skelter. "If there were nine hundred people there, there would be nine hundred people on ecstasy. That was the environment. I was dropping pills like nothing back then, being out of the country without my mother and father. It was like having a credit card with no limit on it."

BY LATE 1989, the Music Institute was having trouble paying its bills. "There were bad decisions on our part," says Miller. "It became a bit difficult to keep that budget, because we had to solely rely on proceeds from the door." The winter of 1989 was particularly rough. "The crowd had dissipated quite a bit—typical Detroit shit, that it started off strong, and then people started not coming so much," says Craig. There was, adds Miller, "inner turmoil between the four of us—the rigmarole of trying to run a business and trying to get four people on the same page. It was time to regroup. We all were getting older."

The Music Institute closed on short notice: "Maybe two weeks," says May. "I was pissed off. We weren't making any money, but we definitely felt the loss, because this was our place." Ollivierra's flyer declared:

With the nigh closing of **THE MUSIC INSTITUTE**, we join
the world-wide ranks of parties-gone past.
THE PARADISE GARAGE in New York,
THE POWER PLANT in Chicago,
and the PHANTASY parties in the U.K. to name a few.
We've progressed through the spectrum of the music, the media and
the masses, and with our last Friday night party, November 24, 1989,
we bring you the bang-end to this after-hours,
strobe-lit, juice bar, stank-box.
With every death there is a rebirth; look for the new salvation this spring.
We thank you for your past support, and this announcement
breaks us all up, but hey: THERE ARE 10,000 FLYERS ALL OVER THE CITY;
JUST LIKE THE ONE IN YOUR HAND.
We're going to pack this fucking box.
BE THERE.

The announcement brought the club renewed attention. "The local news showed up," says Ollivierra. "I remember going up to the DJ booth and Derrick going, 'Can you fucking believe this?' We looked down—there were guys with big shoulder-cameras, spraying bright light on the crowd." There was a lot of crowd to spray. "It was absolutely packed," says Robert Hood. "It reminded me of a New Year's Eve party—sort of a beginning, but an ending as well. Everybody was letting themselves go completely crackers in that place. People screaming, shouting, dancing; I remember times that night when they'd turn the music down and they'd *stomp* to make the four-four beat."

Carl Craig arrived promptly at midnight, as usual. Alan Oldham finished his shift hosting the dance-music show *Fast-Forward* on WDET-FM at 3 A.M., put his records back in the library, got to the club a half hour later, and placed himself near the speakers. Ollivierra caught the feeling while checking coats: "When Derrick plugged the set with all the familiar cues, people were crying. You could see it in the strobe lights."

May was seeing red, too, but for different reasons. During his set, he discovered that his girlfriend, who worked at the Institute, had left the building. "At the height of the party I said, 'D-Wynn, take over. Where's your car? Let me see your keys.' I went out the back door to go find out where my girlfriend was." May was gone about fifteen minutes, and swears he saw another DJ's car parked outside her place. He returned to the club and got back on the decks, shaken. "I finished, but I wasn't myself, and I didn't end it right," he says. "I was off my game completely. To put D-Wynn in that position was really rude and insulting. He didn't deserve it."

Nevertheless, the room felt electric: "It was a really intense energy," says Matthew Hawtin, there with his brother Richie. May began pulling out the stops. Out came "Big Fun"; out came "Sharivari." As the night wore on, May mixed "Strings of Life" with the tolling of clock-tower bells from another sound-effects record, which caused a dance-floor surge.

But instead of ending it with one of the usual MI biggies—with Beats Working's "Sure Beats Working," or Mory Kante's "Ye Ke Ke," or Adrenalin M.O.D.'s "Track This," or D-Mob's "We Call It Acieed," or the elaborate twelve-minute "Fruitness Mix" of Frankie Goes to Hollywood's "Welcome to the Pleasuredome," or his own remix of A Guy Called Gerald's "Automanikk"—May went for something brand new: 808 State's

"Pacific State," which he'd picked up on his most recent overseas trip. According to Oldham, May played it multiple times that night.

After that, it was all over for Derrick. The Music Institute re-opened in early 1990—two blocks away, at 1515 Broadway, both the venue's name and address owned by Chris Jaszczak. "Chris was an older gentleman, and he knew me as a kid," says May. "He was al-ways in love with any music happening in the city." Respectfully, May declined the invitation: "I was heartbroken when the club closed. I couldn't do it." Ollivierra went along, but it was finished by spring: "It just wasn't the same."

May sometimes threw parties at his loft. "It was simply word of mouth," he says. "But we would get seven or eight hundred people inside the actual garage, maybe another thousand people in the street. I got citations—not from the neighbors, 'cause there are no neighbors where my building is situated, but from the police." As an officer wrote a ticket, May protested: "But nobody's complaining." The cop retorted: "*I'm* complaining."

Alton Miller took a radio DJ gig in Toronto for a year in 1990. Chez Damier would go to Chicago, where in 1993 he and Ron Trent founded Prescription Records together, specializing in deep house rather than Detroit techno—Damier and Miller's musical remit ever since. George Baker became a fireman. The building at 1315 Broadway became Club Inferno: "All the lowdown ghetto/Luke-style/booty/bass/strip club shit you could stand and the diametric opposite of what was there before," Oldham wrote in 1998.

House music and techno splintered, in rapid order, into a hundred subcategories. And the party template inherited and promulgated by four young men in Detroit would take ever-stranger turns over the next few decades, from the margins to the dead center of pop culture. "It all lasted less than sixteen months," says Derrick May of his crucial blueprint. "Isn't that amazing?"

It started in Detroit,
But I'm out to exploit
The way I hear it.

—FRANKIE BONES, "CALL IT TECHNO"
(BREAKING BONES RECORDS, 1989)

> 3

STRANGER THAN FICTION

THE HEAT ROSE ALL WEEK during the 1990 New Music Seminar (NMS), nudging to the mid-nineties. The city hardly needed the extra temperature; unrest, much of it racial, tinged the air. The previous summer, Spike Lee's *Do the Right Thing* had caught the mood. Violent crime in New York reached its zenith in 1990, with 2,245 people killed—an increase of nearly 18 percent over 1989. The ugliest incident involved the Happy Land Social Club, a Bronx after-hours spot without fire exits or sprinklers that was popular with Central American immigrants. Ordered shut in late 1988, it operated illegally—until early March 25, 1990, when a spurned ex-lover of Happy Land's doorwoman splashed a dollar's worth of gasoline around the perimeter and lit a match. Eighty-seven people died; only five escaped.

"Wake Up America, You're Dead!" was the title of the July 17, 1990, NMS panel hosted by Factory Records founder Anthony Wilson. Provocation was his gift; the panel—also featuring Screamin' Rachael Cain, Marshall Jefferson, Derrick May, and Robert Ford, one of the first hip-hop producers—was set up to hype his newest big things, Happy

Mondays—sardonic, hardscrabble, working-class lads playing rock inspired by acid house. Skepticism filled the room. The Haçienda, Wilson's Manchester nightclub, had played house music before anyone in London, the 303's winding whine hitting the youth of England the way Elvis Presley's hips or Jimi Hendrix's feedback had. Homemade dance twelve-inches, with blank white labels and handwritten credits, were hitting the charts: Orbital's "Chime" had gone from a one-thousand-copy pressing to number seventeen in March. The Mondays' adaptation of the groove—like other "Madchester" bands such as the Stone Roses and the Beloved—was the next step.

That resonance was near meaningless in America—a reverse dog whistle to a mass audience drowning in hair-metal power ballads, Wilson Phillips, and Vanilla Ice. In England, punk had altered pop music; in the States, it was a cult blip. Dance music fared even less well. The U.S. rock underground had grown progressively harder and heavier as the eighties progressed, from Black Flag to Seattle grunge. By comparison, the Roses' and Mondays' light funk bottom seemed flimsy—where was the *rock?*

"The rest of the shit going on in the rest of this building is the *Old* Music Seminar," Wilson grandly announced. "This is the *New* Music Seminar." The audience's sizable English contingent snickered: Wilson's nature, like Manchester's, was to simultaneously proselytize and take the piss. "You used to know how to dance here. God knows how you fucking forgot." It hadn't—America danced to hip-hop. But Wilson knew his audience. "New Music Seminar was supposed to be all about new music, but that largely translated in the real world to white music," says New York clubbing veteran Bruce Tantum. "Some weirdo passing out a thousand copies of some drum-machine track was not going to turn anybody's head around."

The criminal class that hip-hop glorified differed sharply from that of England's post-rave milieu. "The raison d'être of Thatcherism was to do it for yourself, get off your arse, make some money," said panelist Nathan McGough, Happy Mondays' manager. "What developed was a mass criminal youth culture. When ecstasy came along, you could sell it for twenty, thirty pounds a tablet." The Mondays, he explained, "became the E dealers in Manchester. First it was the drugs, and then through drugs they found music."

"So in other words," Ford asked McGough, "your boys are drug dealers, they're not musicians?"

"Correct."

There were clear parallels with American hip-hop—switch some nouns and McGough could have been describing Eazy-E. But there was already an enormous divide between the Brits' drooling MDMA proselytizing and the relative abstinence of house and techno music's creators. At one point, Cain offered that Chicago dancers tended to take their acid house straight. Keith Allen—an English comedian on the panel playacting as a doctor who specialized in MDMA's effects—sneered, "I don't believe in natural highs. I think you should pay for it."

Jefferson and May were becoming agitated. "We as black people have always had to deal with the fact that we've had to be better because, since the beginning of time, we've had to walk into a white person's house and clean a white motherfucker's ass," May said.

"Listen, Derrick," Allen responded, "I might have white skin, but I'm black, for fuck's sake! Look at me, Derrick. Look at me—I'm black."

It didn't take long for things to hit the dirt; both Jefferson and May got up and left. Despite Jefferson producing and cowriting four English hit singles from the first album by Chicago group Ten City, fronted by Byron Stingily, Atlantic Records in America still complained after every expenditure: "The running joke was that we paid for En Vogue and Levert's promotion, because they didn't promote us at all." He tried working with SBK Records, home of Wilson Phillips and Vanilla Ice, only for his project to be shelved—after SBK put itself on the map with "Pump Up the Jam," a global hit by Belgian dance act Technotronic that baldly rewrote Jefferson's "Move Your Body."

Technotronic had spent the spring of 1990 opening for Madonna's Blonde Ambition Tour—keynoted by "Vogue," her hat-tip to the house-fueled New York drag "ball" scene. It spent three weeks at number one. Everybody, it seemed, was making more bank with the music he'd helped invent than Jefferson himself.

NEW YORK LATCHED ONTO house music as fast as it latches onto anything—immediately. "Little" Louie Vega, then a freestyle producer, began playing Trax and D.J. International sides alongside Latin freestyle, hip-hop, and DOR (dance-oriented rock—groove bands like Talking Heads and the B-52's) at the Devil's Nest in the Bronx. Bruce Forest, who played four nights a week at Better Days on West Forty-ninth Street in Manhattan, cultivated a similar mix. In 1985, Forest gave David Morales, who handled Thursday nights, his extra J.M. Silk and Chip E. twelve-inches, and Morales began playing house, too. In 1986, Vega landed at Heartthrob, on West Twenty-sixth Street in Manhattan—formerly the Fun House, the mid-eighties home of John "Jellybean" Benitez, the New York DJ best known for producing Madonna's "Holiday." But New York didn't fully occupy house music until Todd Terry.

Born and raised in Coney Island and Brighton Beach, Terry was equally inspired by Larry Levan's DJ tapes from the Paradise Garage and the hip-hop of the era. He began making beats for his friends to rhyme over, but couldn't find a label that was interested. Then he decided to fool around with the house music sound that had been sneaking into the clubs: "It had a more traveling type of deepness to it. It had the 909 [drum machine], so that gave it a stride—a lot of riffing over deep bass lines." Terry decided to stitch some current, popular house records together for a laugh: "I was doing it just to show my friends, 'I can do this shit. What's the big deal? The rap stuff is a lot harder to do than this.'"

House music wasn't just easier to make, it was easier to sell: Terry shopped the demo, titled "Party People" and credited to Royal House, to the small Brooklyn label Idlers. "I got a deal for that the next day," he says. Terry responded in kind, turning out tracks in a hurry—he even named his Black Riot single from 1988 "A Day in the Life" because that's how long it took to make. "I woke up in the morning, made the beat, did the music, and I was finished later that night," he says. (In 1992, he made an entire album, *The Todd Terry Project* on Champion, in a single day.) Terry's biggest pop hit, his 1995 remix of Everything but the Girl's "Missing," was done in a day and a half. "It was a pretty easy record to do because the song was there," he says. "Go in there, do it; felt good about it, handed it in."

Unlike the Chicago producers, who used samplers mostly to stutter their own voices, Terry layered and reconfigured his samples like a hip-hop producer. (Vega, who was transitioning out of freestyle, mixed many of Terry's tracks.) The link wasn't lost on his fellow New Yorkers. "Only Todd's stuff was really making the kids go manic," says Larry Tee, a resident DJ at the Tunnel, who says of his playlist circa 1989, "If it sounded like Todd Terry, we played it."

Rap fans initially resisted house music. When Frank Owen, an English music writer who'd moved to New York the day the stock market crashed in October 1987, began throwing parties that mixed acid house in with hip-hop at the multistory Alphabet City spot the World, he had to do a quick rethink. "Some homeboy stuck a gun in the DJ's face and told him if he played that crap again he'd shoot him," recalls Owen.

The World kept aggressively pushing rap and house as kin to its crowd, a mix of artists, b-boys, and fashionistas. "It was like Obi-Wan Kenobi: 'You will like hip-hop . . . you will like house music,'" World cofounder Steve Lewis wrote. Terry's music helped seal the gap. When "Can You Party" started hitting in hip-hop clubs as well as house ones, Terry put Idlers-signed rappers the Jungle Brothers on top of it; their version was called "I'll House You" (1988), which, inevitably, helped sire hip-house as a genre. But Terry was also audible in subsequent producers' work whose dance tracks appealed to the hip-hop crowd, such as Soho's "Hot Music" (1990), produced by Joseph Longo, a.k.a. Pal Joey. "That was a time when hip-hoppers didn't want to dance," says Longo. "That song made you dance or fight—it was one or the other."

FRANKIE BONES DECIDED to hit his potential audience—music-loving outer-borough kids like him—where they lived. He ran off five hundred copies apiece of three mixtapes—*Groove Promo 1, 2,* and *3*—and headed to South Brooklyn's premier cruising spot, beneath the elevated train on Eighty-sixth Street, with his brother Adam; together they handed out cassettes to kids in passing cars. "He would make a speech at the beginning," says Adam: " 'Hello party people! I just came back from England! And I just experienced this thing: The rave!' " His brother's salesmanship paid off: "[We'd wait] thirty minutes and they'd be on the rebound. You'd start hearing LFO coming out of the car: 'Cool. Got one.' "

On the back of the cassettes was an address on Avenue U where Bones opened a vinyl store on April 21, 1990. Groove Records, explains Adam, was instrumental in his older brother's master plan: "He opened the shop to break techno music in New York. Other shops in New York were selling techno—Vinyl Mania, Downtown Records. But they didn't push it as a movement. My brother wanted to make a scene around it." The giveaways didn't stop at Eighty-sixth Street: "Anybody that came in my store, we gave them the tape," says Bones. "Once they heard it they would come back for the music."

Frankie's friends got different kinds of cassettes: VHS tapes of camcorder footage he'd shot of the parties in England on his thousand-dollar Sanyo. "The motorway was packed with cars," says Adam. "Miles and miles of traffic, people getting out of their cars like it was Woodstock. You'd see just such a mix of people—as many black people as white people in England. I thought that was incredible, especially growing up here, where there was so much racial shit going on here. You couldn't even go into the next neighborhood without people trying to beat you down with a baseball bat. Every neighborhood was territorial."

Born in Bensonhurst, Brooklyn, in 1966, Bones began spinning records for roller skaters at fifteen. A few years later he began re-editing tracks for the dance floor with another teenage DJ from Brooklyn, Omar Santana. "He was getting projects from labels, and I was like, 'Why don't we just start writing the songs ourselves?'" says Bones. By 1987 he worked at the pressing plant for Northcott Productions, a studio and label complex in SoHo. By night, he'd go into the studios, alone and with colleagues like Lenny Dee, to cut tracks under a plethora of pseudonyms.

The most popular alias was Looney Tunes, whose "Just as Long as I've Got You" (1989, on Northcott imprint Nu Groove) captured the cresting rave scene's hopeful vibe. "Our records not only were selling in America, but licensing for bigger amounts of money," says Bones. "You would get a ten-thousand-dollar advance; even more sometimes. It went from being a shoestring budget to a multimillion-dollar operation within two years." Looney Tunes' co-producer, Dee, was amazed: "I couldn't even play 'Mary Had a Little Lamb,' and all of a sudden my first record sold fifteen thousand copies." Soon, London came calling.

A couple weeks after the shop opened, Bones returned from another trip to England with some small, round souvenirs. "I had never done E before," says Adam, who'd begun working at Groove after his graffiti-writing career (tag: VEN) put him under surveillance. Bones had become zealous about the substance—"Like some Jim Jones–crazy shit," says Adam with a laugh. Adam thought, *Why not?* "I was already into the music, but I wanted to understand what the hell he was raving on about."

Down went the gate; up went the volume; out went the party favors. "Everybody did it at once," says Bones. "This was back when it was first new, so the stuff then was good—it wasn't anything like what these kids be doing these days." Bones gave the crew—including Adam and local producers Jimmy Crash and Ray Love—the full treatment. "We pulled the gates down and turned the system up," says Adam. "In an hour I was like, '*Whoooaaa*.' On E, everything was much more clear. You weren't really hallucinating, but the music was really accented."

It couldn't have come at a better time, according to Adam: "I used to hang out with kids that smoked angel dust. You could be twice as strong as them, and you're not knocking them out. They will get up and kill you. And here you have this drug that's totally peaceful. People wanted to let go: *finally*, something that could chill people out. The people in the group told their friends, I told my friends, and it spread like wildfire, the whole idea of it." He too changed his name, to Adam X—"like Malcolm X," he says. "It was never related to drugs." For one thing, New Yorkers, like the English, called the good stuff "E." "On the West Coast," he says, "they were calling ecstasy 'X.'"

MDMA HAD LONG BEEN prevalent in Southern California. Not outlawed in the United States until 1985, it wasn't a law-enforcement priority for years after. "We had a steady stream of ecstasy from Texas," says Aldo Bender, a San Diego native who spun new wave and industrial at clubs in late-eighties Laguna Beach before becoming a rave DJ. (Today he's a lawyer.) "They were producing it in the labs in Austin until 1987, and a couple of guys would go back and forth to Houston. They would bring back the pure stuff."

Los Angeles was the perfect place for rave to take root in the United States—its most anglophile city, and the home of KROQ (106.7 FM), which broke British college rock hits in the U.S. like eggs at Sunday brunch. Santa Monica, on the city's Westside, housed a particularly large cluster of English expats in their early twenties. "Most of them were hooligans who had escaped from England for one reason or another," says London expat Steve Levy with a laugh. Many had been hobbyist DJs at home. "When you came to L.A. from London at that particular time, you could embellish your credentials," says Bender. "They'd come over here and be superstars."

The largely British local promoters formed the basis of a large mid-eighties after-hours party scene in downtown L.A.—roving, word-of-mouth affairs, often in halls or lofts, and short-lived by design. (Los Angeles clubs closed at 2 A.M.) One promoter, Solomon Mansoor, organized a series of them, including Palooka Joe's at the Hollywood Athletic Club. "Solomon rented out the penthouse and funneled a bunch of people upstairs to party till the sun rose," recalls Levy. It attracted hipsters and fashionistas of mixed races and sexuality, an ethos that ran against the Sunset Strip's homogeneous hair-metal crowds—the MTV-approved face of L.A. nightlife. "When we started playing dance music in L.A., there was still long hair all over Melrose Avenue," says Bender. Adds Levy: "At the time it was all Young MC and Tone-Loc in the Hollywood clubs." Unlike in New York, upscale clubs in Los Angeles didn't play house music. There were exceptions—like Marques Wyatt, an early house and garage loyalist—but they were few.

La Casa, a cavernous Mexican rental hall just south of downtown, became another locus. It was there that promoter Randy Moore began his irregularly scheduled, invitation-only Alice's House events. "Like anybody else, they had dead nights, so the rave scene took over in those places," recalls Bender. "It was smack dab in the ghetto," adds Doc Martin (Martin Mendoza) with a laugh. "The neighborhood was sketchy; a lot of gang activity. There were always crowds there, sometimes too big." It was common for the dance parties to happen alongside other events: "One time I went down a hallway and came across a Mexican *quinceañera*,"* says Jason Bentley, a native L.A. DJ who'd

. . . .
* A traditional Latin American coming-of-age ceremony for fifteen-year-old girls.

traveled to London in 1988 and seen the acid house explosion first-hand. "At the same time, there was a massive rave going on."

BY 1990, THE PARTIES WERE spreading to Orange County, where teenage promoters like Gary Richards (Destructo), Stephen Haupt-fuhr (Mr. Kool-Aid), and Daven "the Mad Hatter" Michaels catered to an underage base. "We had our own Orange County mafia, do-ing warehouse break-ins," says Bender. Eventually, O.C. promoters moved into Los Angeles. "There was a big focus in finding these ware-houses, paying off the landlord, and getting your sound set up," says Bender. "It all coalesced at the same time."

L.A.'s scene was generally drinking age. That was the crowd British-born brothers Steve and Jon Levy, in Santa Monica, catered to. The Levys had first put on events during the mid-eighties while attend-ing Pepperdine. In 1988, Steve returned to London for a few months, hitting Paul Oakenfold's Spectrum and several warehouse events. He returned to California at the beginning of 1989 and attended Palooka Joe's with Jon. "We were lying there as the sun rose and looked around at each other like, 'We could do an after-hours,'" says Levy.

They dubbed their own parties Moonshine, advertising with brown paper bags on which jugs with X's were drawn. "We started doing some less-than-legal warehouse parties," says Levy. "I think we ran fifteen times without getting shut down. Another big inspiration was in the middle of the Crenshaw district—literally a concrete box. They played proper Chicago house all night. It was Madonna, Cindy Crawford, Richard Gere showing up, and everyone getting crazy."

"You'd see Drew Barrymore hanging out," says Doc Martin, who moved to L.A. from San Francisco in September 1990, after play-ing DJ-promoter Sean Perry's party Where the Wild Things Are, alongside UK headliners A Guy Called Gerald and Adamski. "A lot of people into house music and techno back then also worked in the movie industry and were models. It bled over quite a bit."

After a smelly foray into the basement of a fish factory, Moonshine moved into an abandoned TV studio in Culver City, where the music drowned out the smoke alarm. "It was going to be our biggest night ever," says Levy. "We're about an hour in, a thousand people—all of the sudden, the fire department shows up. We're like, 'What's going on?' We had a couple of LAPD Vice cops doing security for us; the trouble was, Culver City was a different jurisdiction."

L.A.'s sprawl also cemented the idea of raving as road-trip culture, further extending the British rave mythos. An excess of industrial spaces in desolate areas was ideal for break-ins. "It was about the extent to which you would have to find the party," says Bentley. "The early flyers would just have a phone number. That would get you to a map point. The map point would get you to the actual event." Bender compares it to a scavenger hunt: "You had to go to two or three different locations, get all the different flyers, and put the puzzle pieces together to figure out what this thing was. The whole weekend was like that."

An infrastructure was forming. On and near Melrose Avenue, a number of record shops began specializing in the new sound: Prime Cuts, Street Sounds, DMC, and later Beats Nonstop. "People would walk that block back and forth all day between record stores," says Doc Martin, who pulled shifts at Prime Cuts. "We'd get all the Italian house, the really off-the-wall stuff. Street Sounds was more Chicago–New York–England."

Not long after Martin got to L.A. he began spinning an after-hours called Flammable Liquid. "There was one speaker, no monitor," he says. "Within three weeks, it really caught on. We would get eight hundred, nine hundred people sometimes, in spaces that held three hundred. We had to keep changing the number." The early Flammable crowds reflected the early L.A. scene's diversity—hippie spiritualists, service workers coming off the late shift, Europeans and gays who'd made up the pre-acid-house downtown scene. "It was a melting pot—

my ideal situation. There wasn't a lot of regulation. We'd do things in restaurants. We did something at the Reebok shoe factory. Mansions, lofts, churches—it would always be an adventure."

PRIOR TO THE RISE of house music, beat matching was rare among DJs of any stripe, even in the disco era. "Until 1987, '88, you could DJ in a big New York club without knowing how to beat-match," says Tantum. "Nobody really cared." The same was true in Los Angeles, especially among expats like the Alice's House DJs, such as Michael Cook. "Terrible," recalls Kevin Moo—an early-nineties L.A. partier who later took the DJ name Daddy Kev—of Cook. "Just comedy to me."

When Doc Martin moved to L.A. in the fall of 1990, his technical proficiency—strengthened by years of playing hip-hop in San Francisco—stood out. "I learned to mix in the headphones without a monitor," he says. "When I'd show up to gigs in L.A. in the early days there was no monitors. The DJs would train-wreck* all the time because you can't hear what you're doing. I was the type of DJ that would practice three hours a day, and I still do." Martin had already played nationally before he moved to L.A.: In 1990, he opened for New York trio Deee-Lite on the tour for their debut album, *World Clique*.

Formed in 1986 by Ukrainian émigré Dmitry Brill and brassy, New Agey military brat Lady Miss Kier (Kirby)—who'd hung out at Area (where Kirby briefly worked) and the Pyramid, where drag stars like Hapi Phace and Lady Bunny held court—Deee-Lite soon added Towa Tei, a Japanese DJ who had befriended the couple; among their early gigs was Wigstock, Lady Bunny's drag and arts festival. "They were the ones that gave people hope that they could make a lot of money doing dance music," said Tantum. "Deee-Lite went

----

* A train wreck is a mistimed blend—two records playing simultaneously and out-of-sync.

from nothing to 'Groove Is in the Heart.' Nobody knew about them until then."

"Groove Is in the Heart" became a pop smash, reaching number four on *Billboard*'s Hot 100 and spawning a gloriously kitschy, Day-Glo video that became ubiquitous on MTV. "A lot of people didn't like 'Groove Is in the Heart' because they thought it was a poppy, watered-down version of house music," says Tantum. "But everybody liked Deee-Lite because they were part of the scene and they were all funny people." And no one had anything bad to say about the B-side: "'What Is Love?' was much more accepted among hardcore clubbers," said Tantum. "Everybody has heard 'Groove Is in the Heart' so many billions of times that no one wants to hear it anymore. [But] there are still songs coming out with the vocals from 'What Is Love?'"

Deee-Lite weren't the only New Yorkers making house-infused hits in 1990. Keyboardist David Cole had been an accompanist to David Morales during his residency at the World, enhancing Morales's live-in-the-club remixes; they'd worked together on the 1987 club hit "Do It Properly," credited to 2 Puerto Ricans, a Blackman, and a Dominican—in billed order, Morales, Robert Clivillés, David Cole, and Chep Nuñez. Morales's "Def Mix" of the song gave the name to the production company he began with Frankie Knuckles—who'd moved back to New York in 1988 to become another of the World's residents—and their manager, Judy Weinstein.

When Clivillés and Cole struck out on their own, as C+C Music Factory, they tapped steely-voiced studio engineer Freedom Williams to bust some basic rhymes over their grinding hooks. Their 1990 debut, *Gonna Make You Sweat*, sold five million copies, with the title track going to number one on the pop chart. It launched them as producers for established acts—they made Mariah Carey's "Make It Happen" and Whitney Houston's "I'm Every Woman," among others—before Cole's death from spinal meningitis in 1995, at age thirty-two.

To American radio listeners in 1990, "Groove Is in the Heart,"

"Gonna Make You Sweat," and "Pump Up the Jam" were bright novelty hits—extensions of Paula Abdul and Milli Vanilli, whatever their underground roots. But the underground—more concerned with through-line DJ sets than pop crossover, with immersive, audience-as-star experience than stagecraft—was beginning to surface into public view. Its most prominent outing to date came on September 7, with an L.A. party called Stranger Than Fiction.

THROWN BY RANDY MOORE and featuring an installation by Laserium, Stranger Than Fiction took place at the Shrine Auditorium, near the USC campus. "Certain venues were more desperate and downtrodden, so they would entertain these young rave promoters because they really didn't have anything else going on," says Bentley. "That was the case with the Shrine."

Along with a bunch of local DJs (Moore, Marques Wyatt, Ron D. Core, Mark Lewis, and Steve LeClair) and Brit-rave stars Baby Ford and Trevor Fung, Stranger Than Fiction was a Northcott Productions family gathering: The other headliners were Frankie Bones and Vandal—Peter and Vanessa Daou. A keyboardist and arranger with a jazz background, Peter worked extensively with the Northcott's Nu Groove imprint. "Peter and I had just gotten married," says Vanessa. "I was just out of school, hanging out. I started becoming involved by virtue of being there."

A dancer who'd studied art history at Vassar, Vanessa was also active in local poetry readings; Lenny Dee and Victor Simonelli prompted her to write and sing. Their "It Could Not Happen," credited to Critical Rhythm, became a Nu Groove bestseller. The live Vandal set involved Peter playing and programming while Vanessa and a friend from Vassar improvised dance moves for twenty or thirty minutes. "That was the show at the Shrine," she says with a laugh. Occasionally in New York, they hired a bass player—a short, intense local club DJ and ex-punk everybody called Moby.

Vandal began gigging in Europe, where, says Vanessa, "The rave thing was starting to permeate the conversation. We were aware the music we were making was part of that conversation." In early 1990, Vandal traveled to Ghent along with Joey Beltram, a young Brooklyn producer making tracks for Nu Groove as well as for Belgium's R&S Records. Initially specializing in homegrown new beat—a slower, viscous industrial variant—R&S dove into international techno in the nineties. Cofounder Renaat Vandepapeliere drove the New Yorkers to their party: "We weren't sure where it was, because it was the kind of thing you only found out word of mouth," says Vanessa. "We were headed down on the autobahn with some crazy speed looking for this rave. The energy was very palpable. But it was not something people knew about here."

That energy permeated Stranger Than Fiction as well. "You felt this rebellion in there, in the spirit of it. It was a very radical act, even though it was at the Shrine," says Vanessa. The size helped. "That was actually the first massive—over three thousand people," recalls Bones. The promoters added bouncy castles and bumper cars in front: "This was the first time they put rides in the parking lot," says Bones. "They definitely had the vision of what was yet to come with the bigger festivals." Vanessa adds with a laugh: "It turned the Shrine inside out."

Seattle transplant DJ Dan (Daniel Lee Wherrett) had long been a clubber, but Stranger Than Fiction was his first rave. "It was very raw—minimal lighting, minimal lasers," he says. Minimal staging, as well: "All the performers were on one stage," says Vanessa. "The stage was kind of small. It wasn't really raised; I remember being, not level, but in the crowd, maybe slightly above. It was in the way back—or front, or whatever you want to call it—of the Shrine." DJ Dan recalls approaching the decks as Frankie spun Bonesbreaks tracks and Deee-Lite's "What Is Love?": "You could actually walk close to him"—though the music echoed everywhere. "It was during a time where sound wasn't as dialed in." The lasers, on the other hand, were spot-on. "It was really synchronized well with the music, providing a lot of energy," says Vanessa.

So did the party's sense of breakthrough. "I remember feeling like part of something that wasn't obvious to the world," says Vanessa. "I remember looking at the crowd and feeling like somehow this event brought together a subculture, because it was like home to a lot of people. It became the language that we were all understanding and speaking. There was something profoundly understood that was way beyond the music. It wasn't even like 'It's us against them.' It was like, 'It's *us.*'"

There weren't enough of *us* yet to turn a profit. Stranger Than Fiction drew less than half of the venue's capacity, losing a reported thirty thousand dollars. "The Shrine Auditorium was way too early," says Bones. "It was still 1990. You really didn't start to get bigger crowds until 1992."

Stranger Than Fiction was nevertheless a catalyst for growth. In its wake came a number of new parties, notably the Levy brothers' Truth, held at the Park Plaza Hotel. Copromoter Tef Foo's Hollywood crowd began merging into something else. "I would see people come in—the guy in an Armani suit and the girl in her skintight black dress and high heels," says Levy. "Those same people showed up the following week wearing overalls, ready to party. I knew we were converting a lot of people through that."

Frankie Bones had different ideas. Following Stranger Than Fiction, he decided to go after those crowds himself, at home—and far from the swank likes of the Park Plaza.

Wow! 35 subscribers in 24 hours!
This may get gigantic.

—BRIAN BEHLENDORF, SF-RAVES POST,
MARCH 4, 1992

>4

THE FINALE OF THE GATHERING
+ UFOS ARE REAL

San Francisco, California
April 11, 1992

FOR SAN FRANCISCO RAVERS, Saturday, April 11, 1992, was a lucky date: Not just one party by the city's biggest promoters, but two. Better yet, they were five minutes apart. For a newcomer (in 1992 America, that meant most everyone, though not necessarily in San Francisco), the two parties—UFOs Are Real, presented by Toon Town, on the roof of the Fashion Center; and the Finale of the Gathering, around the corner at SOMA—seemed basically alike. But going head-to-head, they exposed a rift emerging in the rave scene.

UFOs Are Real featured several of the scene's biggest names. The headliner was New Yorker Moby, who'd hit the British top ten the previous October with his song "Go," which mimicked (not sampled) Angelo Badalamenti's theme song from *Twin Peaks*, and was part of a second wave of rave anthems regularly charting overseas. Kevin Saunderson and Joey Beltram were billed but reportedly no-showed; ditto S.F. native Doc Martin, who'd grown in prominence since relocating to L.A. in the fall of 1990. Toon Town regular Markie Mark was also there—an English expat, like most of the San Francisco rave vanguard, whose billing fooled the two guys trying to resell their tickets outside. They'd mistaken him for "Good Vibrations" rapper Marky Mark (Mark Wahlberg).

Toon Town also advertised the party in both of the local alternative papers, *SF Weekly* and *SF Bay Guardian*. The indoor rotunda, where the party ended up, was, as Moby's manager Marci Weber puts it, "like a spaced-out Guggenheim: this atrium in the center, the floors wrap around, in a spiral." A spaceship "flew" above the stage, propelled from above, says Weber, "like a marionette."

Founded by Martin O'Brien, a highly organized Irishman who'd helped kick-start the Bay Area's rave scene a couple years earlier, the Gathering advertised by flyers and word of mouth, period. Though they would eventually host bigger names—Saunderson, in particular, became a regular—the April 11 party utilized no big out-of-towners, relying on regulars who went by first names only: Josh, Jenö, Garth. They were *purists*. On paper it wasn't a contest, but not unusually for San Francisco, reality was something else: Both parties drew well, but by midnight, around 150 were in line for the Gathering. Nobody was waiting to get into Toon Town.

That was emblematic of the differences at work. It helped that the Gathering was cheaper ($17 to UFOs' $23), and they'd enticed passersby with the main-room DJ sets pumping out of the speakers placed outside SOMA's entrance. More important was the Gathering's re-entrance with a hand-stamp, like a party; "NO IN-OUT," read the sign on the Fashion Center's door, like a concert. The Gathering was aggressively community oriented—"A no-frills party where music is the essence and the main participant is you," ran a slogan. UFOs Are Real exuded a heavy music-biz vibe: "You're name's not down, you're not coming in," one passerby heard a door staffer bark. The Gathering's floor was packed with dancers, despite the main room being carpeted; UFOs' was thick with bystanders.

Above the Gathering dance floor hung a twenty-foot globe with images of the earth projected onto it from three angles, while UFOs was festooned with lasers. UFOs was consistently under-volume. The Gathering, too, had audio trouble—an amp in the side room blew out and had to be restarted several times through the night. But patrons there were more forgiving, and for the many who stayed till the end, the party closer, Garth, finished with Sister Sledge's disco classic "We Are Family."

Passing Toon Town after leaving the Gathering at 6:30 A.M., nineteen-year-old L.A. native Brian Behlendorf, then a freshman at UC Berkeley, found the other party eerily quiet: "Not a soul to be found," he wrote a few days later. At the Gathering, he'd handed out buttons to a handful of people he'd arranged to meet—a group that, in an informal poll, had shown its preference for the Gathering two-to-one over Toon Town. They'd all been hitting parties for a while, but most had first met virtually, through SF-Raves, the mailing list Behlendorf had founded a month earlier.

THE RISE OF THE U.S. rave scene and the rise of the Internet, besides being concurrent, mirrored each other in many ways. Both mixed rhetorical utopianism with insider snobbery. Both were future-forward "free spaces" with special appeal to geeks and wonks. (It's hardly a coincidence that dance music's instruments of choice are referred to by their model numbers: 303, 606, 808, 909.) Both took root in the eighties and emerged in fits and starts through the mid-nineties, at which point both became part of the social fabric.

As a style whose digital nature was encoded into its very name, techno is the music of early adopters. Rather than the smoothly homogeneous World Wide Web of today, cyberspace was fragmented, and whether you were on CompuServe or AOL, the codes differed. "When [I] first signed up for the Internet in the early nineties, [I was] assigned a username, by first and last name," says Richie Hawtin. "Mine was RH199." Whoever next signed on who shared his initials, then, would have been RH200. Presuming that numbering system kept its pace, Hawtin says that today, "a number assigned anyone would be in the millions and billions. Having a two- or three-digit number dates you as early."

How early? Netscape, the first commercially available Web browser, didn't debut until 1994 (it was purchased by AOL four years later). That January, *The Today Show*'s Katie Couric guessed on-air that the "@" symbol translated to "about or around," while her cohost, Bryant Gumbel, read his show's e-mail address as "NBC, GE, com"—rather than pronouncing the "dot" separating each word on the screen, as he'd automatically do today. These were common mistakes: Few people outside Silicon Valley yet spoke this strange new language.

Many early technology adopters became acquainted with bulletin board services (BBS) as well as Vrave. "I got involved with BBS back in 1992," says Ariel Meadow Stallings, editor of the late-nineties L.A. rave zine *Lotus*. "It wasn't even the Internet. You were calling someone's hard drive, essentially, and typing messages back and forth."

"There was no World Wide Web," says Cleveland-born techno DJ and producer Jeff Samuel, whose experience typifies a lot of the local-leaning early BBS culture. "I was hanging around on music boards with [early dialup service provider] Prodigy. There was this thing called Cleveland Freenet, by Case Western Reserve University, a private college. Cleveland, of all places, was one of the first places [where] you could do real-time chat. You couldn't have Joe Schmoe getting on the Internet at that point. It just didn't happen."

When it did happen, a raver made it so: Behlendorf wrote code for the Apache Web server—the driver of nearly the entire modern-day Internet. "The whole West Coast was deep in it," says Matt Corwine, a Seattle tech entrepreneur and producer-DJ. "This early, pre-dot-com wave felt deeply connected to rave culture. Everyone knew each other. Everybody went to the same parties. Somebody would be working at this small company doing Internet stuff. Somebody else would be working at Wieden & Kennedy in Portland, trying to plug electronic music into ads. This creative culture coalesced around the rave scene."

DESPITE ITS EXPLICITLY GAY roots, house music barely creased gay San Francisco nightlife in the eighties. AIDS had ravaged the city's gay population, and its DJs responded by holding on to the good times. "There was still a lot of 'It's Raining Men,'" recalls Matt Adell, a Chicago native who moved to S.F. for college in 1986 and managed Streetlight Records, on Market and Castro Streets in the center of Boys Town. "A disco version of 'Jack and Diane' by John Cougar Mellencamp was getting a lot of circulation."

Streetlight was next door to a fledgling charity, Gay Men's Health Crisis. "I remember when the AIDS Quilt fit in the storefront," says Adell. "Of course, now you can't even get it in one place anymore." Adell made regular visits to grieving parents of fallen DJs to buy the record collections. "You'd have customers that you'd see once or twice a week, constantly, and then they'd just be gone. It was a tough time in that neighborhood."

One of the city's reigning DJs in the mid-eighties was Doc Martin, who'd grown up in the S.F. suburbs. In 1986 he began sneaking Mr. Fingers tracks into his sets. By 1987, Martin was playing mostly house music at his regular spots, DV8 and the DNA Lounge. "Hip-house really bridged the gap in San Francisco—Fast Eddie, Tyree Cooper," says Martin. "There was a big melting pot of different types of people. That's what made things exciting—to have death-rockers next to people in gold chains next to people riding Harley-Davidsons next to businessmen, people you wouldn't see anywhere else together."

Martin especially liked the "speakeasy" parties usually held in lofts: "We did quite a few two-hundred-people events—go all night and day. People would keep coming and coming. Sometimes they'd go for sixteen, eighteen hours." True to their name, the speakeasies were mostly alcohol fueled, but ecstasy was starting to make its way in as well. Amusingly for a town as chemically libertine as San Francisco, says Martin, "a lot of people were afraid to try it when it came in."

It didn't take long for that to change; ditto the size of the crowds. By the time Martin left San Francisco for L.A. in the fall of 1990, "We had a club called Townsend, doing up to eight hundred people on a Thursday night. We'd already done a show with Deee-Lite before they had hit big. That show did eleven hundred people. By the time things like Toon Town and the Gathering came around, the numbers started getting to three to five thousand."

BEFORE TOON TOWN and the Gathering, there was Wicked. English DJ Garth Wynne-Jones had spent the summer of 1989 in San Francisco. "My mother had married an American, so I had a green card handed to me. I always wanted to leave England anyway." After returning home, he became involved with Tonka—a former hip-hop scratch crew turned acid house purists at a time when the rest of the scene concentrated on giant events. "I never went to any orbital events," says fellow Tonka DJ Thomas Bullock. "Tonka was a sound system, but on a family scale; we're not talking Sunrise."

Tonka attracted anarcho-punks and wandering hippies—the elements of the traveling festival scene entrenched in England since the late sixties, now gone raving. But as 1990 progressed, says Wynne-Jones, "The free-party spirit was coming to a close over there." He decided to return to San Francisco. "I was surprised how quickly the guys joined me." Jenö showed up first. "The day after he came, it was a full moon, so we rented a little sound system, went down to Baker Beach, and threw the first Full Moon party. The timing was just perfect."

Calling themselves Wicked, the group created a groundswell, especially in Doc Martin's absence. While England went cuckoo for homemade "hardcore" anthems—many featuring samples of kids' cartoons, such as the Prodigy's "Charly," a number-three UK hit in 1991—San Francisco's raves were still using smiley-face imagery and cultivating a return-to-Eden vibe. Their California crowds reflected Tonka's mix of New Age and circle-A; the flyers quoted Dr. Timothy Leary. In mid-1992, Bullock called Wynne-Jones while on the East Coast, visiting his brother. Garth told Thomas: "You got your records? Come *now*."

JONAH SHARP HAD ATTENDED the Sunrise events, but like the Wicked guys he'd grown weary of the music's increasingly antic direction. "Hardcore got faster, until it was 140-BPM breakbeat stuff," says Sharp. "I wanted to be in the chill-out room." He'd spun ambient records at London's Brain Club, alongside Mixmaster Morris (Gould), a proselytizer for nod-off grooves; after arriving in San Francisco in March 1992, Sharp got a gig with Toon Town, which had secured a large warehouse space south of Market Street, where promoter Craig Valentine promptly invited him to organize the Friday-night chill-out room. "It was, 'Hey, he's English.'" Sharp laughs. "The Brits were showing everyone what to do."

African Americans and gays had largely been responsible for house and techno music, but as the rave party paradigm was adopted from the UK, and as Europeans were pumping out more and more of the popular tracks, the rave scene in America was increasingly becoming majority white and middle class—especially in counterculture-central San Francisco. By mid-1992, DV8—where Doc Martin's old partner Pete Avila had given the Wicked DJs some of their first local turntable time—was seen as passé by the rave scene. Saying you'd passed out party flyers there was a self-contained punch line on SF-Raves.

As with other scenes, San Francisco had its share of break-in parties. "People got pretty creative," recalls Glenn Fajardo of Seattle, who traveled frequently to party in S.F. "A lot of the parties we went to were in warehouses, disused businesses where there was enough space, basements of businesses. The cat-and-mouse game with the cops was intense. There were a lot of busts." DJ Dan recalls playing one in the Mission, in 1992: "We didn't even know it was a break-in party until we saw the police coming up. I threw my records in the crate and ran."

Oregon promoter Manoj Mathew attended, and took cues from, a 1992 S.F. event called Groove Asylum, put together by Toon Town cofounder Preston Lytton. "The first phase started at the Warfield Theater and ran until two or three in the morning, then moved to another venue. People with bone necklaces and drums were in the club, drumming along with the music. At the end of the evening we did a closed circle, all holding hands. It brought the spirit of everything together. Then we went to Golden Gate Park in the morning for a five-hundred-to-eight-hundred-person dance event. We had this incredible picnic-dance party out in the day."

The Portland and Seattle scenes were essentially outposts of San Francisco's. Both were rock towns—Seattle especially, in the wake of Nirvana and Pearl Jam—far more than dance ones. Seattle native DJ Dan had learned his trade there, but was gone by 1991, eventually taking Donald Glaude, a regular at the Underground, in Seattle's Belltown neighborhood, with him to San Francisco, where they started a troupe called Funky Tekno Tribe. Like S.F., Seattle was a major tech hub, its IT workforce comprising some "ten to fifteen percent" of the early scene there, according to Fajardo (himself a tech worker).

Much of the early action in Seattle took place in clubs, not raves, though by 1992 that began to change. One notorious Seattle party that year was Follow the Yellow Brick Road. (Seattle's nickname is the "Emerald City.") "This event will trip your world," brayed the flyer, a promise its promoters made good on, according to Matt Tuttle, a.k.a. DJ Shoe, a Las Vegas native who played it: "They gave away five hundred hits of acid, free at the door. One of the people that threw it was an apprentice chemist. You could definitely feel a certain electricity in that room."

• • • •

EARLY-NINETIES SAN FRANCISCO was full of affordable warehouse space. "I remember paying a hundred dollars a month for a room, shared with four or five people, in a twenty-seven-hundred-square-foot loft in the Mission," says Sharp. "It's not the Market, so nobody really bothered with it, because it was so bleak back then. It was just businesses; it wasn't really residential." Later, when Sharp began his record label, Reflective, he set up shop in the same warehouse. Around the corner was the office of *Wired*, a magazine start-up, whose staff would show up at the parties; one helped Sharp set up his first e-mail account. "Freaky, geeky, psychedelic, raver, Grateful Deadheads—these nerdy dudes."

Early-nineties San Francisco was also full of affordable drugs. "Around 1991 to 1993, if you were under thirty-five in San Francisco and weren't on some sort of psychoactive substance, there was something wrong with you," says Gamall Awad, who arrived in S.F. from England in 1989, lived with Sharp in the warehouse, and managed Reflective. "Everyone was on that [stuff]. It was *cheap*." A hit of acid cost less than five dollars.

The Bay Area was undergoing its biggest psychedelic explosion since the sixties; street availability of LSD, DMT, mushrooms, ever more intensive strains of marijuana, and of course ecstasy blossomed like details on a Mandelbrot set. "You wouldn't say 'ecstasy,'" says Sharp. "It'd be pure MDMA—one of the cleanest drugs that probably exist." This fine strain was sometimes referred to as "pure molecule," the pills as "mollies." "They were these empty capsules with a tiny bit of powder in the bottom," says Imri Jonas Merritt, then a traveling salesman in L.A. who attended parties throughout the U.S. "When I first saw it, I was like, 'What is this? I got ripped off!' But then you do it, and you're like, 'Whoa!' It was as pure as you could get."

The modern-shaman aspect of psychedelic culture was a perfect bed for the rave scene to feather—especially in the home of Ken Kesey's Acid Tests. "All those hippies loved seeing younger people taking psychedelics again," says Awad. "It was all happening again in the same time and the same place." Timothy Leary was one: "Raves are very much like high-tech Acid Tests," he said. "The difference is that the kids are a thousand times more sophisticated and worldly now than hippies were back then."

Maybe not a thousand times: Sharp recalls one chill-room gig being invaded by a group of DMT smokers. "I said, 'Go ahead, do what you want to do.' These guys got completely naked and were running around the room with bongo drums. They kept everyone out of the room." This was typical. "There was a lot of actual fucking going on," says Awad of the ambient rooms. "A lot of getting naked, a lot of dancing like trees, a lot of losing your mind."

Oftentimes that loss occurred outdoors. Early on, Golden Gate Park was the site of regular events. ("I've always had a good time— EvEn without hElp, if you catch my EXcEllEntly subtlE drift," an SF-Raver posted.) But the Full Moon parties typically took place farther out of sight, put on by a consortium that included the Gathering's Martin O'Brien; Wicked's Markie Mark, Garth, and Jenö; and another transplanted Irishman, Malachy O'Brien, an eco-activist who gave away inspirational pamphlets at Come-Unity, his party at Ten 15 Folsom, whose proceeds Malachy regularly donated to charity.

Jane Lerner, a Chicago native who attended UC Santa Cruz in the early nineties, had only heard rumors about the Full Moons when she accidentally stumbled onto one. Her photography class had taken a field trip to a beach near Highway 1. "We pull over, and there's dozens of cars on the side of the road at eight forty-five A.M.," she says. "It was a couple hundred people, and six or seven of us wandering around with cameras. This guy came up: 'Can you guys stop taking pictures?' They wanted us out. We were college photography students. What did we know?"

NORTH OF SANTA CRUZ and well south of San Francisco proper, San Jose, California, is the unofficial capital of the knot of towns dubbed Silicon Valley. There, telecommunications technology was being rapidly accelerated, shaping the Bay Area's futurist optimism as much as the drugs and the music. Ravers were as likely to find someone operating a "brain machine"—a small strobe pulsating inside a pair of goggles, "designed for meditation and relaxation purposes," as one operator put it—as they were someone selling tabs.

"We thought a big group of people jumping around together for hours on end, on high-quality mind-expanding drugs, listening to repetitive electronic music with positive messages, was taking us to new [places]," says Bullock. "It corresponded to other pursuits of the possibilities of consciousness in other areas, including electronics and foods." Adds Awad: "A lot of those ideas for what became the Internet started from these hippie ideas of community, like the WELL [Whole Earth 'Lectronic Link]"—a proto-Internet dating from 1985, with connections to *The Whole Earth Catalog* and the Grateful Dead.

Another component was *Mondo 2000*—the first attempt at a tech lifestyle magazine. "We were reading it a lot," says Awad. "It was written in almost this prophetic way." *Mondo 2000* focused as much on drugs, sex, and music as gadgets; its very San Franciscan theory was that technology was an *experience*, with its own aesthetic and ideology. (One of *Mondo*'s contributors, the English-born Mark Heley, was a Toon Town cofounder.) Though this viewpoint would eventually incur a generation gap even wider than the sixties', some psychedelic elders were all for it. "One day really soon this whole city is going to be connected—the world's going to be connected to the Internet," Timothy Leary pronounced to a surprised Jonah Sharp in April 1992, a month after Sharp's arrival in the States. "I had no clue about the Internet before I moved here," he says.

That futurist ferment spread all over the Bay Area. "There was this missionary sense of, 'You're inventing the future at your day job, and you're inventing the future at the stuff you do for play,' which is addictive," says Behlendorf. "It certainly led to a very porous boundary between work and play. A lot of people that I met at parties and the SF-Raves lists were also programmers I ended up working with."

Behlendorf grew up in Pasadena, a classic KROQ kid who gravitated to "Madchester" indie bands led by "Funky Drummer" samples and the plangent plastic fantasias of 808 State. He also began going to raves, including L.A.'s biggest yet, Magical Mickey's Holy Water Adventure, on June 20, 1991, at Wild Rivers, a water park in the Inland Empire: "We actually brought our swimsuits. The water rides were open until two in the morning."

That fall, Behlendorf enrolled at UC Berkeley, weary of the "festival atmosphere," the amusement rides and bouncy castles, in his hometown. Jacking into the college's e-mail system seeking local rave newsgroups, all he could find was club info. In 1991, online access was generally limited to university students, tech workers, government employees, military personnel, and the idle rich. There was no AOL, CompuServe, Genie, or Prodigy; BBS networks—the kind you dialed into to talk in real time with others—didn't yet exist. To communicate electronically, newsgroups and mailing lists were *it*.

Behlendorf began SF-Raves with a tentative list of five upcoming events sent to thirty-five people on March 4, 1992. To host it he built a server called Hyperreal (pronounced like "Hyperion," rather than "hyper-real")—as well as a number of other regional rave lists, beginning with NE-Raves, founded by MIT student John Adams that spring. Quickly, more Hyperreal lists sprouted, including—to stick with those whose available archives this book plunders—MW-Raves (the upper Midwest), NYC-Raves (merged with NE-Raves in 1996), PB-CLE-Raves (Pittsburgh-Cleveland—the Rust Belt), SoCal-Raves, 313 (Detroit and related), plus a dozen more.

Coinciding with SF-Raves was another interactive tool: a Telnet-based "Unix-CB" chat server called "Vrave"—the "V" stood for virtual. "Vrave was basically instant messenger for ravers," says Damian Higgins, a Pittsburgh college student who eventually became star drum and bass DJ Dieselboy. Through Vrave, Higgins made the ac-quaintance of out-of-towners like Todd Sines, from Columbus, Ohio, and Taylor Deupree, from East New York. "I was working in a com-puter lab all through college, '91 to '95," says Higgins. "Even on my spare time I'd go to the lab. Like these Korean kids at twenty-four/seven Internet cafés playing World of Warcraft, that was me talking about music and raves on Vrave."

BY FEBRUARY 1992, the *San Francisco Examiner* could list seven ongoing "rave" parties: Wicked, the Gathering, Housing Project, A Rave Called Sharon, Mr. Floppy's Funhouse, Sunnyside Up, and Out-rage. The paper's reporter attended a New Year's Eve party thrown by Toon Town that drew seventy-two hundred and netted some $125,000 in profit. The Nutrient Café, the event's juice bar, made five thousand dollars serving "smart drinks"—mainly fruit juices goosed with powdered amino acids and vitamins; the unspoken idea was that they would help maintain and extend an MDMA buzz, the way a cultish "smart drug" like 2C-D did. (Smart drinks sold for around five dollars apiece.)

"Toon Town felt like the first rave-rave," says Robbie Hardkiss (Cameron), an NYU grad who'd moved west in 1989. He'd begun attending the parties after his high school friend Scott Friedel sent a letter from Oxford, where he was doing a school year abroad. "You're going to love this music," he wrote, describing tracks like the Scien-tist's "The Bee." "It's got crazy noise. It's like fast hip-hop. You've got to look for this in San Francisco." Toon Town was where Robbie found it. To the *Examiner,* an older raver sneered: "Teentown."

"People in San Francisco viewed rave a little bit more stringent-ly as an anticommercial entity, even if it was always a moneymak-ing thing," says Behlendorf. It didn't take long for SF-Raves to start sounding the drum. "If you hear an ad for a rave on [FM radio station] Live 105, don't go," went one post; another vented about party flyers' "blatant commercialism," utilizing "eleven different font styles and every cliché in the book, [such as] '40,000 Watts of Turbo Generated Space Bass.'" For Sheffield native Awad, rave had been "an outgrowth of these ideals of communalism I experienced with postpunk, with Northern Soul and rare groove." In Brit-heavy San Francisco he was not alone—in that, or in being suspicious at the way three other pro- moters, who'd come from the East Coast, clearly aimed to be *stars*.

Gavin Bieber and Scott Friedel met as freshmen at the University of Pennsylvania, bonding over Prince bootlegs. Gavin joined Scott in Oxford in the summer of 1990, attending Glastonbury—where, by coincidence, they saw the Tonka Sound System in a rave tent. The two of them started throwing parties in Philadelphia—whose thriving rave scene was largely the work of a bright-eyed (and straight-edge) young DJ named Josh Wink (Winkelman)—and going to New York to buy twelve-inches from Frankie Bones at Groove Records and hit the clubs. A typical night in the city might involve taking LSD and seeing My Bloody Valentine at the Ritz, then dancing all night to Frankie Knuckles at the Sound Factory.

B.A.'s in hand, the two drove cross-country in Scott's dark-blue Saab to San Francisco in 1991. Gavin wanted to start a record label; Scott wanted to produce and DJ. "Robbie was already living in San Francisco," says Gavin. "We wanted to rope him into this dream we had created." A bass player without a band, Robbie was more than willing; the three moved in together to start a new DJ collective they dubbed Hardkiss, each taking the surname, Ramones style.

"We were lucky enough to find a basement of a studio that had fire damage," says Gavin. "It used to be a recording studio, fully soundproofed. We had this sound-reinforced room to learn how to DJ. Scott and I wanted to throw parties along the lines of what we'd experienced in the UK and along the East Coast." They met Mar- tin O'Brien soon after arriving in town, and within two months the newly christened Hardkiss Brothers were Saturday-night residents at

650 Howard Street, as well as throwing illegal parties outdoors by Candlestick Park and at Bonny Dune Beach, near Santa Cruz.

"We brought Frankie Bones to San Francisco for the first time in 1991," Gavin recalls. "In '92 we did a show at the San Carlos airport, an all-nighter in a warehouse there. We did an all-night party on a double-decker boat in the bay. We did some morning parties, six A.M. Sundays. One was called Splash, at a bathhouse with a swimming pool." Eventually, Gavin bowed out of the party-throwing side of things, selling the sound system and purchasing recording equipment. "It was a choice between putting it all on the line every few months, or buying studio gear and learning how to make music."

DESPITE ITS NAME, the Finale of the Gathering was no finale at all. Martin O'Brien had intended it as the going-away bash for one of the crew's regular DJs, Tony, who was moving to Sweden. O'Brien fully planned on continuing to throw events, albeit under a different banner. Instead, the Gathering came back on July 4, 1992, with Let Freedom Rave. The following month they threw another event, the same night, again, as Toon Town's.

On September 12, the Gathering threw an outdoor day party at the Golden Gate Park bandshell, noon to 7 P.M., five dollars for charity. Copromoters included Hardkiss, the Housing Project, Come-Unity, Full Moon Massive—and SF-Raves, which was now organizing parties as well as discussing them. In August, Behlendorf put together a list-oriented event called Connection on a beach in Santa Cruz. "We used the mailing list itself to crowd-fund a rave on a beach that was as epic as anything, I think personally, even though there [were] three hundred people on a Thursday night. It had lasers. It had projections. It had headlining DJ acts. It had an epic location. It wasn't permitted, but it did go all night. It gave people who were involved, I think, a sense of, 'Wow. We did that? We *did* that.'"

I may just be a screwed-up white kid jumping up and down to a beat I don't understand, but the altitude me and my friends, blacks and whites and yellow and green and straight and gay, obtain around 2:15 A.M. every Sunday morning is the beautiful truth.

—ANONYMOUS MALE CALLER TO *REACTOR* MAGAZINE
   VOICEMAIL, OCTOBER 1992

GRAVE

ONE OF THE SHOWS Brian Behlendorf mentioned in his first SF-Raves post was Primal Scream at the Warfield Theater on Friday, March 6: "I know this isn't exactly 'underground,' but it's being billed as a rave, and rumors exist that the Orb is gonna be there, too." The Orb's mastermind, Dr. Alex Paterson, did indeed DJ the show. Behlendorf went, but he wasn't impressed. David J. Prince went, too, and was—so much so that, having left Los Angeles that day to move back to his hometown of Chicago, Prince drove right back down to L.A. the next day to see them again at the Palladium.

Born in 1968 and raised in Evanston—the birthplace of the Women's Temperance Movement a century earlier—Prince was a budding experience junkie, perpetually sniffing out the next good time. The fast-flowering U.S. rave scene's ideology, nomadism, and taste in stimulants suited him perfectly. Prince had gone to parties in Chicago—mostly gatherings of three hundred or fewer in lofts along Milwaukee Avenue—but nothing like what he'd encountered out West. "I really had no idea that it was so big as it was in California," he says. Why would he? When Prince and his girlfriend took up a friend's offer to stay in Pacific Palisades in the summer of 1991, Chicago barely had a house scene anymore, never mind a rave scene.

IN LATE-EIGHTIES CHICAGO, house music was everywhere—on the radio, in the clubs, booming out of cars. One South Sider, Curtis A. Jones, religiously recorded Farley "Jackmaster" Funk's DJ sets off the radio. "I still have my tapes of those shows," he says. But he found himself dismayed when Chicago house music's popularity dwindled in its hometown: "House was the most popular form of music for a lot of the black urban scene here." That changed in the nineties, Jones says: "The original house audience left and went to hip-hop." Chicago DJ-producer Gene Farris adds: "Back in the day, blacks and Latins were all [into] house—the gangsters, too. When hip-hop hit Chicago, it separated those worlds really fast."

It didn't help that by the end of the eighties, many of Chicago's big names had departed for the coasts, beginning with Frankie Knuckles's 1988 departure to New York—a year after Larry Levan's Paradise Garage shut down. Steve "Silk" Hurley and Jesse Saunders both went to L.A.; Hurley worked full-time remixing pop and R&B big leaguers (Prince, Janet, Madonna). Ron Hardy, meanwhile, contracted HIV before dying of a heroin overdose on March 2, 1992. During his last few months, Hardy had moved to Springfield with his mother, partly to escape the noise of local celebrity; his funeral was small and quiet, attended by a mere eighteen people. Levan, too, died in 1992, of endocarditis, a heart inflammation made worse from years of heavy drug use.

The Muzic Box was long since closed. A city ordinance passed on April 1, 1987, forced Chicago's juice bars shut at 2 A.M., same time as the alcoholic ones. The culprit was Medusa's, a popular North Side teen spot with a punk, Goth, and industrial bent, which had been raided by police in late 1985, two years after opening, due to neighbor complaints. At Medusa's, says regular Jana Sackmeister, "You had to show a school ID—you had to prove that you were *under* eighteen. Fridays you went and lingered in the Dunkin' Donuts parking lot."

Medusa's DJs mixed Trax and D.J. International with the Cure and Pailhead; by the late eighties it hosted guest spots from Lil Louis (who broke "French Kiss" there), DJ Rush, and Julian "Jumpin'" Perez of the Hot Mix 5. "There were full-on jack parties up there," says Milwaukee native Kurt Eckes, who went every week, as did Laura Schebler Rammelsberg, who calls Medusa's "the incubator for the rave scene." For one thing, E was easy to access: "We were going with a guy who had lived in Dallas, where ecstasy was legal in the eighties," says Eckes. "He had worked at bars down there and had connections with people that were involved in that. Ecstasy was part of what made it so awesome."

Medusa's openness to dissolving the borders between industrial and house music wasn't appreciated by everyone. Vince Lawrence attempted an industrial-tinged album that Geffen Records shelved; Derrick May's protégé Carl Craig attempted without luck to shop a demo to Wax Trax! Records. "Someone bootlegged Front 242 and re-packaged it to look like a Chicago house record, and all these black guys started playing it that weren't playing it before," says Matt Adell, who worked for the label in the early nineties. "We were bummed. They probably sold more copies in Chicago than we did." (He declines to name the bootlegger.)

The curfew meant that house music migrated into the city's lofts and warehouse spaces. "Eighty-nine to '91, there were a lot of loft parties going on," says "Mystic" Bill Torres, who'd moved to Chicago from Miami in 1988, at age eighteen, to DJ house music. The lofts advertised with simple photocopied flyers. "It would just be text," says Justin Long, a longtime resident DJ at Lakeview's Smart Bar who came of age playing the lofts and, later, raves. "Party, name, address, DJs, that's it—very to the point, minimalistic."

Long began spinning in 1992, when he was fourteen; soon he was playing parties along Milwaukee Avenue, at venues referred to only by door number: 1355, 1471, 156. "Drugs weren't a factor," he says. "It would be two DJs doing their thing for hours, telling a story." Adell and David Prince—best friends since eighth grade—both fondly recall the three-story Reactor, at 1115 West Lake, where DJ Rush and Ron Trent played regularly. "It was pitch black except for a strobe light," says Prince. "It was a little bigger than somebody having a party in their apartment. The strobe would flash: A woman would be dancing with a bowl of fruit on her head, and then gone."

PRINCE HAD FIRST ENCOUNTERED house music in high school, when a job at Record Exchange got him into the Metro with an X on his hand. There, he first encountered, and was riveted by, Frankie Knuckles—whom Prince had heard of from friends who saw him at Medusa's. While Adell went to San Francisco for school, Prince stayed home and attended DePaul, DJing weddings and bar mitzvahs. "I wore a tux. It was hula-hoop contests, the whole nine yards."

Prince had long been fascinated with music writing as well as music since picking up *Ask: The Chatter of Pop* by UK rock journalist Paul Morley, a key architect of one of David's favorite groups, Frankie Goes to Hollywood. "That's what stoked my literary potential," he says. A class on the sociology of rock with professor Deena Weinstein, who wrote heavy metal reviews for *Rolling Stone* as Daina Darzin, cemented it.

Adell had grown up in a biracial family—on principle, he'd stopped listening to Steve Dahl following Disco Demolition Night—and had gone to the teen dance nights at Dingbat's, whose bouncer was a prefame Mr. T: "He was rocking the Mohawk, the cutoff denim jacket, the gold chains, feather earrings. He was super-nice to the little kids." Adell latched onto house music early through his siblings; when he moved back to Chicago in 1990, he began grad school at Columbia College and worked part-time for Wax Trax! in the warehouse (where, typically, Ministry's Al Jourgensen was passed out). By the time Prince returned from L.A., Adell had left Wax Trax! and started his own fledgling house imprint, Organico Records, signing his long-time friend and loft-scene fixture Derrick Carter.

In the summer of 1990, Prince and Adell laid hands on "a huge supply of really good, really cheap LSD," recalls Prince. "It would be Sunday morning at ten and I would be pulling my wrinkled tux out of the closet and showing up at bar mitzvahs, having no patience for it." Off-hours, he read Jay Stevens's classic LSD history *Storming Heaven*. It introduced him to the Beats, science-fiction writers Aldous Huxley and Robert Heinlein and—especially—Dr. Timothy Leary, who'd gone from Harvard professor to international outlaw after acid shattered his perceptions. "I started to feel we were part of something larger."

ABOUT THE TIME David Prince headed west, a Chicago DJ named James Johnson became the city's first rave impresario. He started in the fall of 1991 with a small party called Tropical Breeze, in a warehouse at Forty-sixth and Michigan. Doing business as E-System, Johnson next threw Enjoy, whose map point was on the El train's Blue Line—on Halsted Street between Harrison and Van Buren—and attracted 250. "When the rave scene first started, it was more hard techno [and] what they called 'breakbeat,' which turned into drum and bass and jungle," remembers Torres. "There was a lack of house music in those parties."

"There was two different scenes going on," says Davey Dave (Mason), another loft regular. "The loft scene was Derrick Carter, Lego, Spencer Kincy, Diz, all those cats. Then there was the rave scene, which was Hyperactive, James Johnson, Miles Maeda, Josh Werner. The two scenes weren't interacting with each other." The first time Doc Martin came to Chicago to play the Shelter, he thought, "Chicago house—I've got this in my sleep. I got there and it was Speedy J and Amsterdam techno. I was really surprised."

Ravers were different from house heads—younger, whiter, greater in number. "Rave brought a whole new crowd of people into the music scene—at first, mainly white kids from nearby suburbs," says Torres. Rammelsberg was one of them, attending an E-Systems party in the fall of 1991: "It was a nasty warehouse. There was trash and broken tires. It was the first time I'd ever seen prostitutes walking along the street in person." Nevertheless, the parties' size grew exponentially: E-Systems' third event, Journey into the Rhythm, brought in eight hundred. Ecstasy was in plentiful supply there, says Rammelsberg: "I had never done drugs before then," she says; she did them then because "that's what people in the UK were doing."

E-Systems' true coming-out party was Grooveyear, in early 1992. Torres, who knew the promoters, was on the lineup. "They had me play late, after all the real hard music." For the first time, out-of-towners were headlining: New York's Adam X and Minneapolis's Woody Mc-Bride (DJ ESP). "That was one of the first full-color printed flyers I ever saw," says McBride. "All the shows bit brands: Grooveyear looked like Goodyear Tires. It felt completely unchaperoned and unsecured and renegade. Anything, good or bad, could happen any moment—that was their style."

Another early Chicago promoter was Charles Little II, an old Mendel High regular. Like his friend Mike Dearborn, Little had left house music behind while at school, only to come back in on the ground floor of the new scene in 1992, putting on parties with promoter Wade Elliott of Core Innovations that mixed techno and house. "My theory was Wade would bring the rave kids, I would bring the adults, and that's exactly what happened," says Little. "Audiences never mix. You have to know how to mix them."

THAT MIXED AUDIENCE WAS ripe for someone like Curtis A. Jones, a South Side native who'd begun writing songs while studying chemical engineering as an undergrad at Urbana-Champaign. "My original intention was just to be a producer," he says. "Back then I was a shy person, so I wanted to do something more behind-the-scenes." After rejecting grad school at Berkeley, Jones returned to Chicago and began releasing twelve-inches on a local label, Clubhouse, in 1991, under the name Cajmere, sometimes working with veteran session singer Karen Gordon, a.k.a. Dajae.

One of their early songs together was "Keep Movin'." (On the record, Gordon is billed as Nané.) The single included the "Straight Up Drugs Remix," featuring a weird, wet, rubbery percussion noise. It passed without notice, but Jones heard potential. He kept messing with it, eventually releasing two additional tracks on Clubhouse that tweaked the same effect. When Jones started Cajual Records in 1992—like his performing alias, an extension of his initials, C.A.J.— he made its first release the fourth and final variation on that sound. This time the track was called "The Percolator." It was pure simplicity—a militant snare, Jones nonchalantly chanting "It's time for the percolator," and an elongated version of that noise, now revealed as a pitch-bent synth note. The track went nova in Chicago.

"When 'The Percolator' came out, it was like a tidal wave," remembers Justin Long. "Around Chicago during that time, there was definitely a Percolator dance. When a dance is made after your song, you know it's something special—like the Electric Slide." Another Chicago-bred house jock, DJ Sneak, adds: "It was a track that everybody could play. Not just the ghetto South Side kids, not just Bad Boy Bill on the radio—*everybody* came for that record."

"The Percolator" and its follow-up, Dajae's soulful "Brighter Days" (which peaked at number two on the *Billboard* dance chart), were both instant Chicago house standards; the latter was later given remixes by both Masters at Work and Todd Terry. ("I did it for no money," says Terry. "You always want to be on a hit record, no matter what it takes.") Together, the first two Cajual releases announced the city's next wave of house music talent.

"Cajual, Relief, and Prescription Records created a whole new scene," says Traxx (Melvin Oliphant III), another scene veteran. Relief was a Cajual spin-off; Prescription was founded and run by Ron Trent and Chez Damier, late of the Music Institute and KMS Records' longtime A&R man. Prescription specialized in deep house— moodier, jazzier, more late-night melancholy than the fist-pumping anthems fast becoming the house norm. The Chicago producers were learning from their Detroit peers. They were stepping out on their own.

NO ONE IN DETROIT was more militantly do-it-yourself—more *militant*, period—than Underground Resistance (UR). Together for just over two years, the trio of Jeff Mills, "Mad" Mike Banks, and Robert Hood remain America's most important techno group ever, with all three moving into equally brilliant solo work.

Mills was a Detroit legend long before he started the group. As the Wizard, he was a radio rival to the Electrifying Mojo, crafting fleet-fingered hip-hop mixes that sliced well-known tracks into confetti, and never speaking on-air. He was also in the industrial band Final Cut, and met Banks, a former session musician who'd served in the army, in the studio. The two hit it off and decided to make a Public Enemy for techno, staring their own label after Juan Atkins didn't move quickly enough to put them on Metroplex.

Hood was the last to join—a Music Institute regular who grew up on Mojo and got involved with techno despite tough odds: "Detroiters are fickle to begin with. It's not a game, and they'll let you know quick it's not a game. Around 1990, my first DJ partner was beaten half to death, his equipment smashed up, because he wasn't playing the right records. He was in the hospital for two or three months: Detroit don't play."

Neither did Mad Mike, though his militancy had a tinge of sci-fi: "I feel that there is only one law in underground music, especially in

experimental music, and that's to 'go where no man has gone before,' "
he told Brad Owen of the Milwaukee zine *Quadrasonic* in 1993. "Captain Kirk laid down the law and motherfuckers ought to follow it."
That allusion was no accident: The first time Hood saw Mills's studio,
he was amazed at all *The Wizard of Oz* posters. "I see this small guy—
it was like meeting the Wizard of Oz! He didn't appear to be what I
had imagined. I can't say Jeff was outgoing. He was very energetic, to
the point, driven. He would laser-point specifics."

Hood had come in to rap but wound up producing—solo as the
Vision, with the others as UR as well as X-101 and X-102. The latter
pair were often the work of Hood, Mills, and Banks jamming out ideas
in real time: "Maybe Jeff at the 909, me at a Juno 106 [keyboard],
Mike at the 303—just going for it," says Hood. As titles like the *Riot*
EP (1991) and Mad Mike's solo "Death Star" (1992) implied, the
UR sound was swarming, swaggering, and hard, just like that of the
Bomb Squad, Public Enemy's producers.

UR's politics were every bit as incendiary as PE's. Banks, especially, interpreted techno as a natural outgrowth of political radicalism,
embedding the larger critique—common in Detroit techno—that
gangsta rap's commercial rise was modern-day Uncle Tomming, the
ultimate in big business mocking the race for fun and profit. "You're
not gonna see fuckin' Mad Mike eating chicken wings on a fuckin'
Kentucky Fried Chicken commercial," he told Owen, alluding to an
MC Hammer ad campaign. Banks, instead, saw himself as "the Ho
Chi Minh of the underground."

Pressure cookers tend to boil over. "It was Mike and Jeff's mutual
understanding that it was best they broke up," says Hood, who says
things came to a head while he and Mills were working on X-103's
Discovers the Rings of Saturn. "It imploded on itself. Emotions and
ideas were starting to clash. I saw it coming and I was preparing for
it, but still, it was sad when it happened." By all accounts Banks and
Mills remain close friends. Mills moved for a while to Berlin, which

UR had fit like a leather glove. The Germans loved UR's conceptual leaps; with the help of former Motown mastering engineer Ron Murphy, the fourteen tracks of X-103's *Discovers the Rings of Saturn* weren't just named for Saturn's rings and moons, but featured music designed so the vinyl grooves *looked like* those rings and moons. Top that, Roger Dean.

NICK ANDREANO—frat-party DJ Nick Nice—transferred from the University of Wisconsin, in his hometown of Madison, to Paris for junior year. It was 1990, and he got there on time for the rave explosion. "They were a couple of years behind England and other parts of Europe," he says. "They would say, 'Meet in front of Bercy Stadium and someone will lead you to the party,' and you literally would." His first party was in an abandoned Metro station: "Everyone had masks to keep the dust from getting into your nose. They also did events on industrial boats that I'm sure were not up to code."

In summer 1991, Nice hosted his old friend Michael Vance, who'd been studying in London. "We spent that summer going to clubs and parties," says Vance. When Nick returned home in August 1991, he says, "There wasn't a lot going on. I had all these records that nobody had: Belgian labels like R&S and MusicMan; the British bleep stuff." He decided to "do a couple of small parties and then build to a big warehouse party on Halloween—the natural night to do it."

Nice calls these early parties "pre-raves": "We were trying to introduce people to the concept. We had to start out with hip-hop to get people dancing." The MDMA just making its way into town helped: "You'd get a hundred people on ecstasy, two hundred people drinking." His second party ended after twenty minutes, when the cops arrived. "It created this hype for our Halloween party that we couldn't have planned for." Halloween took place at a loft above a futon shop. "A perfect party—no problems, went all night, even though it was literally two blocks from the Central District Police Dispatch."

Nice was resident DJ at the Cardinal Bar; Vance was the lighting director. Nick's mixtapes were reaching across state lines: "We had people road-trip in to hear the music." In spring 1992, Nice "found a space just outside of Madison—a friend of mine had done some fraternity parties there. This guy would rent the barn out, all empty, and the second level was perfect for a DJ setup." This was the location of Ravee (May 15, 1992), the upper Midwest's first serious rave outside of Chicago and Detroit.

Nice returned to the same barn on August 28 with the even bigger Alice in Raveeland, featuring out-of-towners like Woody McBride. Tommie Sunshine (Thomas Lorello), a Medusa's regular from suburban Chicago, was equally impressed by the music—"Full-on, 160 [BPM], banging," à la Aphex Twin's *Xylem Tube* EP—and the décor: "Every time that party would get crazy they would lower this big plastic cow from the ceiling. Woody had sound effects cued up: *Mooooo!* What would you rather see on acid than a cow descending from the ceiling of a barn in Madison, Wisconsin?"

McBride had grown up in Bismarck, North Dakota, before attending the University of Minnesota. His journalism studies fell to the side when he discovered DJing, specifically the House Nation parties being put on by Kevin Cole—long-standing resident of downtown rock palace First Avenue—and Thomas Spiegel, every Thursday at First Avenue's side room, 7th Street Entry. McBride and Vance bonded at Alice in Raveeland, along with a fellow U of M student named Bobbie Reiss and Milwaukee artist Robin Bott. Each wanted to throw a party like this of their own, so they decided to pool their resources and do it in Bott's hometown. "Chicago would have never [worked]—it was too risky and scary," says McBride. "Milwaukee was a big city with a lot of warehouses. It didn't seem like anybody was really paying attention."

McBride was getting involved with Twin Cities events; a Milwaukee scene had kicked into gear thanks to roommates Kurt Eckes and Patrick Spencer, doing business as Drop Bass Network. "Every weekend, you had something happening," says Nice. "There wouldn't be competing parties. There was one party to go to"—not per city, but for the entire region. "It was like a counterculture circus—a diverse age group, a lot of older hippies, not the youth phenomenon that it became."

That changed as the upper Midwest solidified into a road-trip party network—Minneapolis native Chris Sattinger (Timeblind) recalls being "strictly an I-94 raver," after the interstate highway that starts in Billings, Montana, and runs through Minneapolis, Madison, Milwaukee, Chicago, and Detroit. A routine established itself: Friday night was the pre-party, Saturday the rave, Sunday the after-party. "You'd just party all weekend," Vance recalled.

"At that point, we didn't even think it was a culture," Sunshine said. "It was just something we did: 'Oh, it's Saturday night, let's get in the car and drive to a rave in another town.'" Usually, Sunshine's partner in crime was Eckes, who'd introduced himself by tapping Tommie's shoulder at Alice in Raveeland, pointing to another kid wearing a FUCK ART, LET'S KILL T-shirt, and shouting: "That guy has got it right." "The following weekend we started traveling together to parties: Cincinnati, Columbus, Detroit," says Sunshine. "We started doing the circuit."

GRAVE WAS SET TO TAKE PLACE at a warehouse on 710 West Virginia Street on Saturday, October 31, and Vance, McBride, Bott, and Reiss spared little expense, enthusiastically tricking out the building. "Milwaukee and Madison and Chicago had big shows, but they had four speakers," says McBride, who rented twenty-four for Grave. When Vance walked the outside to test the system, he says, "The roof was vibrating. It was almost subsonic."

Vance had outfitted Grave with digitally controlled strobes and a handful of Intellibeams. "Intelligent lighting started to come out, and it was pretty inexpensive," he says. Intellibeams could be programmed for all sorts of patterns, shapes, and colors—far beyond simple disco lighting—but they were also heavy, "a good eighty, a hundred pounds: We had to build stage scaffolding around some of the columns, and hoisted them up—suspended on this rickety ladder, twenty feet up, with this massive piece of equipment." They also had cameras everywhere to effect the classic L.A.-scene trick of telling warehouse owners their building was being rented for a film shoot's wrap party.

The organizers of Grave provided plenty for a roving camera to capture. Bott had done set design, so the party's haunted-house façade, which occupied one of the warehouse's corners, looked realistic. They surrounded it with dead leaves and a white picket fence that Vance had found discarded in a Madison field. Two spigots jutting out from the façade poured Gatorade and Kool-Aid, and volunteers handed out Halloween candy from a false door. "I don't think I slept for three or four days—we were grabbing all this stuff and getting it ready, or building it, or painting it, or putting up lights, or speakers," says Vance. "The plan was to set up and then just crash out in there, then start tearing everything down" once the party was over.

One disconcerting thing about the setup: "It was a warehouse that shared a common wall with a Milwaukee Sheriff's training ground," says Vance. "There was a fake jail next door where they would stage fake jail riots and breakouts to train officers." Vance had already rejected a space where Drop Bass Network threw a rager called Tempest: "There were gaping holes in the floor that went down two or three stories. The cops had come to that party. They just didn't have enough people on staff that night to shut it down." Kurt Eckes had asked the police to intervene while things got hectic inside—gang members were running riot through the place—but to no avail.

Nevertheless, local police were keeping their eye on Drop Bass, presuming that any similarly styled party was probably Eckes and Spencer's work, whether it was or not. Eckes went to Grave—and shouted it out on Drop Bass's telephone info line—in part because, he says, "We wanted to be there in case the cops shut it down, so we would not be blamed." (Rumors were beginning to float around town that a bust might occur.) Eckes and Spencer were also friends with Nice and McBride, and fellow Cardinal regulars.

LESS THAN A WEEK before Grave, on October 23, Tommie Sunshine took a road trip to Detroit to attend Journey Through the Hardcore, at the Majestic Theater on Woodward Avenue. In the upstairs bowling alley were mostly house DJs; the main floor featured a sprawling lineup from Detroit—UR, Blake Baxter, Kevin Saunderson, D-Wynn, Juan Atkins, Richie Hawtin, Claude Young, Alan Oldham—and beyond (Manix, whose "Feel So Real" was one of the big UK hardcore anthems, and Moby).

Journey was one of a handful of parties KMS Records had put together; another was Panic in Detroit, at the State Theater on September 6. Saunderson was Detroit's most fecund producer, eager to try out every new style as it emerged and usually mastering it. "My goal was to get people out and educate the scene. It was important not to miss the boat. I wanted to bring something that would cross over to the whole audience. I didn't agree with all the music coming out—but in principle I thought there was a connection that was important." Saunderson got out of the party business within a year. "I could never commit to it. It was very hard to handle."

The act everyone wanted to see at Journey was UR. "They came out with UR bandannas over their faces, with aluminum baseball bats at the front of the stage," says Sunshine. "I turned to my friend like: 'We're gonna die here.' It was in the scariest fucking ghetto on earth. This is the craziest shit I've ever seen, and here we are running around taking drugs. We came to this rave to have a good time and UR steps onstage and we're like, 'Oh, no!'" By comparison, Grave—whose headliner was UR's Robert Hood, billed as DJ Rob Noise—looked to be a breeze.

. . . .

LATE AFTERNOON ON OCTOBER 31, Grave's hotline number was updated with directions to XLC Hair, a short drive from the warehouse. Bott knew the salon's owners and oversaw ticket sales. The voice mail stressed that weapons would be searched for at the door and that gang colors weren't allowed: "Peace, love, and we're gonna Grave your world."

Tickets went on sale at 11 P.M.; the warehouse opened its doors right afterward. "There was a pretty sizable line right away," says Nice, the party's opening DJ. Quickly, a thousand kids were dancing. "The vibe was awesome," says McBride. "We were set to reach capacity." Sunshine showed up in a twelve-person caravan from Chicago. "The music was crazy," he said. "Very hard European techno. We were pogoing to it. There was a station where kids were doing graffiti. Then they moved the station, and it turned into a body-painting thing, like a Grateful Dead show. It got very psychedelic very fast."

As Nice was spinning, the Milwaukee Police Department was being issued a series of search warrants. An officer had bought a ticket to Grave at XLC Hair, then went to Judge Jeffrey Wagner and got permission to raid both the salon and the warehouse on suspicion of underage drinking. Around 1 A.M., as Nice handed the decks over to Hood, the police seized the map point and took the promoters' tickets and money for evidence; then a larger team trekked to 710 West Virginia Street. About eighty officers took part. By the time word reached the warehouse of the impending sting, the police had arrived.

At 1:30 A.M. Vance heard that there were cops at the door. He'd handled it before at Alice in Raveeland: "They came in, looked around, and were happy with the way it was being run," he says. "So I went to the door, and *bam!*—full-on riot gear. There were fifty or sixty cops, with shotguns, like they were expecting us to shoot back. I was shocked. One of them planted the butt of his shotgun against my chest, shoved me up against the wall, and said, 'Get the fuck out of my way.' They were there to make a statement."

From the decks, Robert Hood was watching, agape. "I couldn't believe what was happening," he says. "That was a full-on raid. I've been at raves when they come in, talk to the organizers, and come to an understanding—someone got paid off or whatever. I've been to raves where they'd been shut down. But that was the only one I'd been to that was completely violated by law enforcement."

"A lot of people just split," says McBride. "I wish I could have, but I had a sound system to look after." Eckes was in the middle of the dance floor, high out of his mind: "It was really confusing. You think, 'We're being robbed.'" Vance ran to the back, clearing out the haunted house. The luckier kids ducked out through the officers' training station in the rear, where Vance had opened a door: "It must have freaked people out who were trying to get out, and they're running through a fake jail."

So many of the kids were carrying drugs that they did the only thing they could—swallowed or stashed. "Everybody ditched their drugs on the floor," says Milwaukeean Brad Owen. The hay from the haunted house made for both easy cover and plausible deniability. Nice watched as people threw their goods into a "big plastic tub of Bazooka gum. It makes you wish there were cell phone cameras back then because, boy, that would be a funny thing to watch right now." Spencer adds: "A lot of drugs got in the drinking supply."

A cop yelled at a startled Hood: "Stop everything. Take the records off." He turned to the crowd: "Everybody, get down; guys, go over here; girls, over there. Everybody's going to be processed one by one."

"It was like getting arrested in Mayberry," Sunshine said. "The first thing I saw the police do once they'd busted the place was to bring in a big coffee table, a giant coffeemaker, plug it in, and start brewing coffee." The kids groaned loudly, says Nice: "They knew they were in it for the long haul."

The Milwaukee PD zip-cuffed the kids, sat everybody on the floor, and demanded quiet. "You can't keep nine hundred kids on drugs quiet," Sunshine said. "We had to endure them arresting us, but they had to endure someone muttering 'doughnuts' and cracking everybody up every few minutes. You had a bunch of kids running around with their bodies painted, unable to look anyone in the eye when you talked to them. They must have thought it was some kind of pagan ritual." The promoters were taken to a separate area and zip-cuffed as well.

The police set up a processing station in the middle. It took between two and three hours for processing to begin. Rumors of police harassment abounded. "Everybody's dressed up in Halloween costumes," says Nice. "There were stories from women who were in French maid outfits: 'You've gotta undo your top,' ridiculously offensive things."

Police Chief Philip Arreola later reported the bounty to the Associated Press: "Forty-four marijuana pipes, eighty-one small cylinders of nitrous oxide, assorted pills and admission tickets," marijuana, and fewer than ten cans or bottles of alcohol. And what were they being charged for? According to the stamp on the $325 citation the Milwaukee PD handed to 973 people early the morning of Sunday, October 29, 1992: "Subject was on unlicensed public premises where person in charge was permitting the consumption of alcoholic beverages."

"The only alcohol that was around was for the DJs," says Nice. "There was a six-pack of beer and maybe a bottle of vodka. It was our beer. The ironic thing about this party compared to the [earlier] ones, where there was a fair amount of drinking going on—this party, there was *no* drinking going on." Arreola's report doesn't mention MDMA, just "assorted pills," and the police didn't ask anybody about it, in or out of zip-cuffs. "The police didn't know about ecstasy," says Nice. "They had absolutely no idea what was going on."

MICHAEL VANCE WAS THE LAST of the four organizers brought to the county jailhouse: "By the time I got to jail, Woody was already in. I didn't know what was going on until I got to the police station for holding. They were convinced we were drug dealers." Eckes and Spencer had also been arrested.

The cops kept asking Vance: If the organizers weren't selling drugs, why were people paying ten bucks to go to a party? "I was like, 'They pay twenty, thirty bucks to go to a rock concert. You understand that, right?' 'Well, what are they getting for their ten bucks?' They'd confiscated the money at the map point and thought it was pure profit. I said, 'It's not. We spent money on the DJs—Rob Noise came in from Detroit. We put them up in a hotel, we paid for their flight—it ain't cheap.'"

Vance was eventually taken to a block cell with McBride and Bott. "Ninety percent of the other people there were in for spousal abuse," he says. One approached Vance: "Were you that guy that threw that party? Damn, how many people?" Nine hundred or a thousand, Vance responded. "Damn! And that was at your *house?*"

Vance's stay was helped along by a hit of E he'd secreted away. "We didn't want to go into jail with those," he says. "At that point we hadn't been searched." It was hardly the only substance being ingested on lockdown. "There were guys in the cell smoking crack," says Vance. "There was one place they could stand, on the back of the toilet, where the camera couldn't see them." The cops didn't seem much better organized than at the warehouse. "At one point they opened the door and this guy, mentally disturbed, just wandered out. An hour later, they brought him back in the cell. He was just out there wandering around that police station."

Eckes recalls that when he went to talk with the police, "They had a whole file where they had been monitoring our parties and keeping track of things." Only this wasn't a Drop Bass party, so Kurt and Pat were off the hook. Grave took a bullet for Drop Bass Network. As for the "film crew" cameras: "Everything got confiscated, so there may be footage out there somewhere," says Vance. Grave's DJs did get their records back, though. "I didn't pay any fine," says Hood. "I just went on home, trying to forget about it." Nice did the same thing, only to turn on the TV after driving back that morning and seeing the event on the news: "My friends spent the night in jail for throwing a party."

ONE OF THE KIDS arrested at Grave, Melissa Musante, was the daughter of a policeman-turned-lawyer, and knew her rights. She got home and called the news; a TV a crew interviewed her and her father together. Soon his phone started ringing—kids from the party who wanted representation. (One was Steven White, now married to Musante.) The city backed down quickly, dropping several charges, including the building's alleged fire code violations as well as a "one-for-one" which would have made the promoters responsible for not just their individual fines but those of the entire group—into the middle six figures. "They didn't have very much," says Vance. "A $350,000 fine for ten bottles of beer would have been hard to get to stand up in court."

The promoters paid their fines in full. McBride was in the stir three days, eventually borrowing bail money from his girlfriend's parents (he repaid them a year later), and signed an agreement with the city not to promote parties in Milwaukee again. Bott lost some twenty thousand dollars; the incident is still something of a sore spot. Vance threw a couple more parties, then was finished with promoting.

A few days after Grave, Vance went back to clean up the warehouse. "They had police tape over everything," he recalls. He was relieved to find that it was basically intact: "The lighting was right where we'd left it. We had to sweep up leaves." What they found under them, and wedged in the walls, were pills galore—thousands of dollars' worth. "They must not have done a very good job of sweeping through there. It was pretty obvious." Adds Nice: "You have to remember, the drug gangs were moving into the rave scene at this point. For them, a huge Halloween party—*bam*. They were going to clean up. When the police came, everybody hid what they had. It just didn't seem like they knew what they were looking for."

Later in the week, four hundred arrestees met at the University of Wisconsin's Milwaukee campus. Once the charges were dropped, Waukesha civil rights lawyer William Pangman filed a fifteen-page class-action suit against the City of Milwaukee, citing police mistreatment and sexual harassment. The suit fell through, though, when few of the ravers agreed to commit themselves to it. "We understood that only a handful would go the distance," said Pangman. "They were young people who wanted to move on with their lives, and a lawsuit just drags on mercilessly."

DAVID PRINCE WAS BECOMING a rave evangelist. During his year in L.A. he'd attended a handful of instant legends: Double Hit Mickey (September 14, 1991), in Long Beach, headlined by 808 State and surprise guest Björk; Technoflight, at Spruce Goose Dome, two months later with the Shamen (whose "Move Any Mountain" had made the U.S. top forty, the first "rave" track to do so) and the opener Moby, who stole the show; and the wild multiroom Shiva's Erotic Banquet (April 24, 1992), which featured Prince's hero Timothy Leary in the chill-out room.

Prince had also been picking up issues of the L.A. dance zine *Urb*, and when he returned to Chicago and saw a similar scene taking shape, he went into action. He'd already learned QuarkXPress out West; his best friend Matt Adell's father was an Apple VP, barely touched Macs littering his house. They used these machines to produce their own rave zine, named for their favorite loft: *Reactor.* "We had a lot of naïve urgency," says Prince. "I wouldn't even say I knew how to write; if you read some of the stuff I wrote at the time, you would say I *didn't* know how to write."

Nevertheless, Prince looked for stories as well as gazed at his navel, and when he heard about Grave he drove straight to Milwaukee. "I felt so incensed—'This is wrong,' " says Prince. The cover headline of *Reactor*'s long, detailed report: "YOU CAN STOP THE PARTY, BUT YOU CAN'T STOP THE FUTURE." Prince saw it as an analogue to a May event in England: At Castlemorton in Herefordshire, at a rave thrown by itinerant travelers ("crusties") who'd claimed Castlemorton Common as a communal party space—for a week. Some twenty thousand people joined in. The impromptu festival prompted a Home Office minister to declare it "a direct assault on the structure of social life in the country," and soon a bill was enacted to prevent its like from happening again.

In Milwaukee, Prince met, and instantly liked, Eckes and Spencer. "They seemed like the most together of everyone I'd met on the rave scene—the most organized, the most fair, and also into the most extreme music. What they were listening to was not what I was going to listen to in Chicago." Prince became a regular at the events Kurt and Pat were throwing in barns. "There were cows there, and more drugs. It was just more extreme. It was Wisconsin—not glam in any way, shape, or form. From meeting them I was like, 'I want to throw a party. I should do it with these guys because I don't really know what I'm doing.' "

Personally, I'd like to see all of this talk of past raves and old records put aside because what we should be about is the future and forward thinking. Once the glorification of the old replaces the celebration of the new, we might as well all pack it in and go to a Beach Boys concert.

—MOBY, LETTER TO THE EDITOR, *UNDER ONE SKY* #7, OCTOBER 30, 1992

> 6

STORM RAVE

Staten Island, New York
December 12, 1992

NOT COUNTING HIS gates-down, E's-up get-acquainted bash on Avenue U, Frankie Bones's first renegade party in his hometown was deliberately small-scale. "We were doing fifty people in a gutted-out apartment on Coney Island Avenue," says Adam X. But word spread rapidly. "It happened so quick. By '91 we were doing generator parties in the junkyards down by Foster Avenue, by the freight tracks, with four hundred people showing up. By winter of '92, Staten Island: fifteen hundred. By [fall] '92, we're doing five thousand people on Maspeth Avenue. That's how fast it grew." In late 1991, Bones formalized his parties' structure, dubbing them Storm Raves.

The Storm crew would gig at clubs and bars, Bones acting as an evangelist for the new style that moved away from both freestyle and the house music starting to rule Manhattan clubs. Oliver Chesler, a SUNY Purchase political science major in the early nineties, remembers seeing Bones, Adam, Heather Heart, and Jimmy Crash DJ for a hundred people on Long Island. "They were all going crazy. And the music was starting to be techno." Not just when Bones's crew played it, either: "I would go to this club called the Building. They only played industrial and new wave—but suddenly, T99 would play, or [DHS's] 'House of God,' and it was just so much stronger than the other music at that time. It's not that it was better. It was just so much different that everyone knew something new was happening."

For Storm Raves, Frankie deliberately scouted out-of-the-way locations: "You've got to be able to put your party somewhere where you're not drawing a lot of attention," he says. "We would go up by Sunset Park, or by the docks. If it looked like something we could rent, we would try to rent it, and if we could break into something we'd break into it." They'd test a likely locale by cutting off the gate's lock and replacing it with their own: "In two weeks, if nobody took your lock off, you knew you'd be able to do something."

Storm was structured like a small business. "I had three partners: My boy Dave Lights, my boy Joe Fax, and this guy named Mr. Hyde—nobody went by their actual name, obviously," says Bones. Frankie conceptualized the parties and handled the talent; Fax was in charge of sound and lighting; Lights drove the talent around; and Mr. Hyde had a family member close to John Gotti's family. "Because we were in Brooklyn, at some point somebody had to be able to take care of any Mafia stuff that happened. If we didn't have him, I would have been in a lot of trouble."

He was anyway. Once, a couple of thugs came into Groove trying to force Bones to add a Joker Poker gambling video game to the store. "The guy was like, 'What, are you afraid of gangsters?'—trying to pull that card," says Bones. "I walked right up to them, drill sergeant style: 'I *am* a fucking gangster.' Never seen those guys again." Nevertheless, Bones began making thousand-dollar donations to policemen's charities and hiring rookies for event security: "Until the police caught on to what we were doing, we were good for a year and a half." He printed up phony permits to proffer if the law showed up anyway.

Mr. Hyde, says Adam, "wasn't your typical guy. He was really nice and into the music and making the parties good. But if something went down, things could be handled very easily." Once at Groove in early 1992, he recalls, "These two Italian mafioso guys come in: 'Where's Frankie Bones? You tell him that if he doesn't come to our party in this club in Staten Island this weekend, it's going to be a big fucking problem,' blah-blah-blah, whatever. Bones was like, 'Fuck 'em.' Couple months go by. Party gets busted in Manhattan. As the party's getting busted these two guys walk up again. My brother is like, 'We're dealing with the police right now.'" Bones pointed them to the club's owner. "They had a little sit-down, like out of *Goodfellas*," says Adam. "Next thing you know, the [mafioso] guys own the club. Took the club from them in Staten Island—straight out *took* it. That was the level of what was going on. *Everything* was controlled."

Everything, that is, but the parties. "It was completely new—the volume, the no-rules, the no-security," says Maria 909 (Rotella), who attended the early break-ins. "We would set up speakers and turntables, and bang! *Everybody* danced."

"ALL THESE PEOPLE I KNEW were talking about this Storm event they went to in Brooklyn," an NE-Raver posted, remembering mid-1992. "From what they described it sounded like the warehouse parties I used to go to in west Philly—just on a larger scale."

One of NE-Raves' regularly scheduled posts was called "Hook-up-o-matic"—a long list of ravers in search of rides, locally and interstate, to parties all along the East Coast. A December 1992 post features requests and offers from Washington, D.C.; Philadelphia; New York City; Hoboken; Boston; Grafton, Massachusetts; New Haven; Pittsburgh; Providence; Cambridge; southern Maine; College Park, Maryland; and the University of Delaware.

Raves began happening down the coast as rapidly as in New York—in Washington, D.C.'s case, even more rapidly. The capital's first promoters were siblings Fernando and Jorge Baez, working as

Catastrophic Productions—probably the East Coast's first dedicated rave promoters. "They did the first party in D.C. that was referred to as a rave—in fact, the name of the party was literally The Rave," says D.C. native John Selway. "By the end of 1991 it was getting a lot bigger. It was packed all the time." The early D.C. parties, remembers Damian Higgins, brought out two thousand a shot. By the time Selway left the District for college at SUNY Purchase in the fall of 1991, he'd been going to raves in his hometown for a year.

Catastrophic's analogue in Baltimore was Ultraworld, run by Lonnie Fisher. The two cities' promoters tended to be friendly. "There wasn't an us-versus-them thing," says Michael Meacham, then a DJ in D.C. Ultraworld would gain a reputation for wild events; one October 1992 warehouse party, Ultraworld Excursion, allowed patrons to bring their own alcohol.

THE PHILADELPHIA SCENE was essentially the work of one person: Josh Wink, born in 1970, who'd begun apprenticing with Captain Jack's Mobile DJ Company at thirteen. Three years later he became a bar back for the club Memphis. "I got to see adult playgrounds when I was sixteen. I'd open up the door of the bathroom and see people passed out in their vomit: 'This is the glamorous life?'" (Though he drinks occasionally, Wink is a lifelong abstainer from drugs.) Eventually, he began playing fill-in DJ slots at Memphis, moving to a residency at the after-hours spot the Black Banana. Acid House Wednesdays, which began in 1988 at the Bank, were particularly inspirational: "That's really the kind of music that made me want to produce, instead of just DJ."

In the fall of 1989, while working at the Black Banana, Wink and his friend Blake Tart—they met working as bike messengers—rented a punk squat called Killing Time and threw Philadelphia's first warehouse rave. Wink taught his roommate, Tower Records clerk King Britt, how to mix for the party, which Wink describes as "not necessarily illegal, but not necessarily legal." The firetrap drew eight hundred. "You couldn't let any more people in—you couldn't move. The floor looked like it was going to cave in." Why not? The roof already had.

In 1990, Wink and Britt sold their first track together, E-Culture's "Tribal Confusion," to Strictly Rhythm in New York. As Wink's production career took off in 1991–92, it took him out of Philadelphia with greater frequency, to guest-DJ gigs at clubs and raves around the East Coast. At home, Wink and a crew of locals threw a rotating, occasional Monday party called Vagabond: "We'd go to the natural science and history museum." One popular locale was Silk City Diner, a half-eatery, half-nightclub in the Northern Liberties neighborhood. "It was originally at the bar, but it got big enough that we opened the diner," says Wink. "People were dancing on the countertops."

The early raves in Pittsburgh, five hours away, were the work of Joel Bevacqua (Deadly Buda), who'd spent time in England as acid house waned and worked briefly as a club promoter while at school in New York. There he'd met Englishman Neil Keating (Controlled Weirdness), a DJ whose sister ran a small record stall that sold "white labels"—unmarked promotional twelve-inches, ahead of official release, from UK hardcore labels XL and Double Helix. Bevacqua's first event took place at a boutique called Slacker on December 13, 1991. Keating headlined; nearly one thousand attended.

Bevacqua set up the record shop Turbo Zen (a nod to his DJ moniker) in an empty room of an indoor-mall comics shop—it was the only way he could buy direct from Watts, America's main dance-music distributor. "The only way I could get good records was to start a store account," says Bevacqua. The shop became a ready-made map point for Bevacqua's Power Rave (November 13, 1992), featuring Richie Hawtin and Adam X: "No alcohol and no attitude," the flyer trumpeted. It was one of the first Pittsburgh parties to be promoted via NE-Raves as well as flyers. "I actually reapplied to Pitt just so I could get an e-mail account so I could get on the rave boards," says Bevacqua.

Bevacqua's fellow NE-Raver Damian Higgins (Dieselboy) had moved to Pittsburgh in 1990 to attend Carnegie-Mellon. Higgins was converted to techno when a DJ at a Front 242 show dropped T99's frantic Belgian hardcore track "Anasthasia" (1991). Higgins spent thirty dollars for an English import CD containing it: "I didn't even have a CD player—my roommate did. I felt if I didn't buy it then, I'd never see it again."

After a few college-radio sessions where he "mixed" his import CDs, Higgins got his first residency Sundays at the Metropole: "It went from a couple hundred to fifteen hundred people in a year." Higgins also began hawking his mixtapes on the mailing lists. "I capitalized on the fact that I was deep in these communities. I'd charge five dollars just to cover shipping and to make a couple bucks, because I needed it for [new] music."

The UK hardcore Higgins began to specialize in had germinated—much the way Chicago house had at the Warehouse—at the London club Rage. Beginning in 1990, residents Fabio and Grooverider would play breakbeat-driven house records at 45 rpm instead of 33. Gradually, they moved onto tracks purpose-built with those elements as well as system-wrecking sub-bass, in particular the releases of London's Shut Up and Dance, the production duo of PJ and Smiley (Philip Johnson and Carlton Hyman). By 1992, the sound was becoming darker and more panicky—and more dexterously put together with software such as Digidesign Pro Tools, an all-in-one digital audio editing system, multitrack recorder, and mixer that cost one-tenth the price of the Fairlight sampling keyboard, the previous decade's industry standard. With Pro Tools, UK hardcore's breakbeats subdivided into baroque shapes while keeping dancers moving.

THOUGH NEW YORK'S techno crowds were growing, at the center was a rather small group of DJs and producers. "If you look at flyers from early-nineties New York, there were between ten and thirty people actually making music and releasing records," says Oliver Chesler. John Selway, who met Chesler while majoring in music composition at SUNY Purchase, adds, "Everyone used to go to each other's studio—or there was *one* studio, because not everyone could afford the stuff."

Selway and Chesler had both been playing with synths since they were kids, and began collaborating on techno tracks of their own— and showing them to the class. "We came in and played an epic rave overload—Euro-ravey, big chords, that early hard, dark sound," says Selway. "It completely blew away the whole class. There weren't actual letter grades, but I got a lot of props for that. I don't know how much they liked it, but they were pretty impressed by the advancedness of it." Jimmy Crash's label, Direct Drive, released the track as "Schizophrenic," credited to Disintegrator, in 1991.

It was a fecund time for New York techno producers. The biggest hit was Moby's "Go," but the most musically important New York producer by far was Queens-bred Joey Beltram. His *Volume 1* EP (1990), on R&S, featured "Energy Flash," one of techno's most iconic records— bleeps like flashlights shining out of a dark swamp, a groove full of muscle and sinew, whispered chants of "Ecstasy, ecstasy" promised a chill as well as a tingle. Shell-hard, it beckoned the future.

"Energy Flash" may be techno's greatest single, but it wasn't even Beltram's most impactful track. That was "Mentasm" (1991) by Second Phase (co-produced by Mundo Muzique—Mike Mundo), which forced the genre to reckon with it for a good eighteen months. At its center was an infernal sonic exhaust, informally dubbed the "Hoover," because it sounded like an animatronic vacuum cleaner. (In a clean, round-edged, wireless world, it's easy to forget that technology was once assumed to evoke black tar and burnt wiring.) "People were making different sounds by fucking with the waveform and the attacks on 'Mentasm,'" says Adam X. One copycat track was "Tingler" (1992) by Smart Systems—an alias of British snoozeballs the Future Sound of

London. Adam then turned around and sampled "Tingler" for his own "Lost in Hell" (1992), cheekily bringing things full circle.

Beltram was relentless, but Lenny Dee, as he puts it, "was on the pursuit of making it harder and more-more-more-more." Already a music-biz veteran by the time he met Bones, Dee had engineered for Nile Rodgers and Arthur Baker right out of high school. By 1990, he was tired of house music: "'That shit's just boring disco crap.' I was young and had a bit more attitude. I was like, 'Techno is what we're doing, and fucking right, it is another level.' I stopped looking at my old influences and started looking at rock. It really made sense that I could fuse this music with metal and punk. Next thing you know, I discovered the Netherlands and Belgium and Germany."

At a party in the Frankfurt airport (long story), Dee met Marc Acardipane (Trauner), who shared his ideas. "I said, 'I'm going to start this label—if you have anything, I'd love to release it.' We sat down, fucked up on pills and everything else, like any other night at that time, and I heard Mescalinum United for the first time." Mescalinum United was one of several Acardipane aliases—in this case, for a track called "We Have Arrived," which made "Mentasm" sound like "Mary Had a Little Lamb." Distorted 909 kicks and claps make the track sound like it's drilling into your skull, an impression given weight by a "tune" like an air-raid siren. Dee was floored: "I said: 'This is it. This is the future. This is where it ends and where it begins.'"

"We Have Arrived," backed with "Nightflight (Nonstop to Kaos)," which Acardipane had issued as the Mover, became the first twelve-inch on Dee's Industrial Strength Records. "I will make this fucking music work," Lenny told Acardipane. "If I release this, it's going to change." Later that year, when Dee dropped "Arrived" at the giant German techno festival Mayday II, he says, "I've never seen ten and a half thousand people in one room raise their hands all at once, ever." This was a different sort of hardcore than what the UK dished out—not breakbeats and sped-up vocals, but a hard solid-four stomp with minimal coloring and maximal menace. In Holland, they were starting to call it by a new name: *gabber*, which means "friend" in Dutch.

"Everyone was in awe when that record came out," says Dee. "It was the birth of something completely different. You get a guitar and it was totally acceptable to distort it and make rock records. Why wasn't it totally acceptable to distort all the electronic instruments? It's like a kid hearing rock and roll for the first time, back in the fifties. It took off and I never looked back."

It was also a definitive middle finger to house music's vanguard. The New York house world could feel like a fraternity, complete with spring break in Miami—the site, every year since the mid-eighties, of the Winter Music Conference, an annual confab for dance professionals headquartered at the Fontainebleau Hotel. "They weren't into it, man," says Dee. "People like David Morales have a different perspective, from the seventies, of what DJing is about. All of a sudden, there's another kind of music that's not ripping off disco. It already did that—faster—in the early part of the nineties. This is *our* thing. These are *our* sounds. These are *our* influences. [Instead of] saying, 'I want to make an analog record with an analog drummer, as opposed to using a drum machine,' back then it was like, 'Fuck that. I want the drum machine.'"

RATHER THAN BEING rough-and-ready like Todd Terry, by the mid-nineties New York house music was a whole lot smoother. Much of that was due to its state-of-the-art studios, which offered a more professional sheen than what came out of Chicago. It's also where Frankie Knuckles and David Morales cemented their working partnership. "We used to rent Quad Studio, back-to-back," says Morales. "If we weren't mixing records together, I was programming his drums on his records. Frankie always took care of the orchestration. I took care of the groove, and Frankie was the embellishment. We were the modern house version of Gamble and Huff."

Knuckles' new partner had a CV nearly as extensive as his own.

Born and raised in Prospect Heights, Morales had been a resident DJ at Brooklyn's Ozone Layer when he began to fill in for Larry Levan at the Paradise Garage. Morales then went to Zanzibar, an equally revered club in Newark, New Jersey, to play alongside Tony Humphries, who had a Saturday night mix show on KISS-FM, at the time one of New York's premier black radio stations.

As Def Mix Productions, Knuckles and Morales changed the face of remixing. "Before us, when you did a remix, you worked with what was available to you," Knuckles said. "By the time we got started, we were bringing in musicians and completely overdubbing everyone's songs, reworking the music and the tracks, everything." Knuckles, a consummate professional, found he liked working with the big guns: "[When] you've got someone as big as Luther Vandross and Michael Jackson sitting there saying, 'Whatever you want, however you want it, I'll stay here as long as you need me,' that's the reward right there."

Eventually, the artists themselves got in on the act, as when Mariah Carey rerecorded her vocals from "Dreamlover" for Morales's 1993 remix. "The arrangement was done all on the desk using an automated console," says Eric Kupper, a keyboardist and programmer who worked extensively with the Def Mix crew (and produced RuPaul's first album in 1993). "'Dreamlover' was nothing but two to four bars with keyboards, and we just opened up this and that. We would play the desk." In 1995, Morales netted eighty thousand dollars—the highest remix fee to date—to rework Michael Jackson's "Scream."

In early-nineties New York, house DJs were more apt to mix in big techno tracks along with the divas, says Larry Tee: "Things like the Prodigy and [Fortuna's] 'O Fortuna' went over incredibly well for gay crowds—they would literally scream with delight." Nevertheless, a retrenchment was setting in. "In 1991 techno and rave and early jungle were entirely new genres that were really exciting," Moby said in 2008. "The house guys kind of reacted against it. They got slower and even more song oriented."

The principal New York house producers of the decade, Masters at Work—Little Louie Vega and Kenny "Dope" Gonzalez—could traverse both sides: Vega might drop Plastikman's Detroit anthem "Spastik," as might mid-nineties club king Junior Vasquez. Plenty of MAW-affiliated tracks banged in warehouses filled with glow-sticky teenagers as well as in the city's superclubs like Twilo and Tunnel; their big crossover hit of 1993 was Hardrive's spare, spooky diva dub "Deep Inside." Vega guesses this might be because "a lot of those keyboards on those records were more minimal—it was a more naïve sound."

For others, house music's (not to mention techno's) increasingly abstract, increasingly instrumental direction chafed as the decade progressed. "Everywhere I go, all I hear is house music," Timmy Regisford, founder and resident of New York's Shelter, complained in 1995. "I don't hear no lyrics or songs and it's the same everywhere that I go—I may hear two songs in an hour and a half, but that's not satisfactory." The same year, disco-era DJ vets François Kevorkian and Danny Krivit joined with the younger but equally classic-minded Joe Claussell to start Body & Soul at Tribeca's Vinyl (formerly Area), where soulful vocals were the order of the day.

Techno snuck in here and there—usually slowed way down. That's how Danny Krivit would play the Aztec Mystic's "Jaguar," an Underground Resistance track, in 1999. Krivit later told the *Village Voice* that he'd play it "pitched down as far as the turntable goes. I remember going to play it and the DJ put it back all the way—'What are you doing?' I said, 'That's how I play this record.' 'Really? Oh, you're losing all the energy.' 'No, *you're* gonna lose all the soul.'"

DRUM MACHINES TRUMPED SOUL at the Limelight. A huge deconsecrated Episcopal church on Manhattan's Twentieth Street and Sixth Avenue, Limelight was one of a quartet of mega-clubs owned by Canadian impresario Peter Gatien—the others were Palladium, Club

U.S.A. (the smallest, it held twenty-five hundred), and the Tunnel (the largest, holding five thousand). For many, Limelight was a touristy no-go zone, derisively nicknamed "Slimelight." But unlike the hipper Area or Mars, awash in free drink tickets for the in-crowd, Limelight actually made money.

As Bones's parties gathered steam, Limelight promoters "Lord" Michael Caruso and Michael Alig began to feature techno. "We made a decision not to play house on the main floor, because Michael wanted the latest, newest sound, and he'd heard techno," says Larry Tee, who put on Disco 2000 every Wednesday with Alig. The latter reveled in nightlife's most depraved aspects—from handing friends glasses of his own urine to drink to holding a "pool party" in the flooded Tunnel basement—and made them his parties' centerpieces. "It was Limelight and it was us—there were no other organizers doing raves in '92," says Adam X.

Though it featured DJs from Doc Martin to Jeff Mills, the stars of Disco 2000 were Alig's coterie of "club kids," who dressed as outrageously and behaved as provocatively as he did. Together, Alig and the club kids made regular appearances on *Donahue* and *Geraldo*, parlaying them into paid gigs around the United States. "You'd have drag queens in nurses' outfits, barely able to stand, ping-ponging on the walls drunk, and you got to have cutting-edge music as well," says Doc Martin.

Ravers were vocal in their disdain. "The Club Kids are way stupid and take too many damn drugs," an NE-Raver posted. The sentiment was returned in kind: After Bevacqua referred to one of his own Pittsburgh parties as "a refreshing break from the fake birthday-party Club Kid stuff going on in New York" in the Toronto dance mag *Streetsound*, he says: "Michael Alig and four or five other club people left a voice mail—'We will take over your rave scene! We will do our birthday party there!' They were really worked up about it."

Pietro DeMarco (RePete) became a Limelight resident in 1991, playing Thursday nights in the Chapel Room until 1996. Like Bones's crew, he was an outer-borough kid (born in Brooklyn, raised in Staten Island), but he mostly avoided the Storm parties. "There was a lot of friction between Lord Michael and Storm Rave—a lot of politics involved," says DeMarco. "Everyone wanted the gold, so everyone was bad-mouthing one another. They would try to sabotage one another's events. When you grow up in the streets you learn that the less you know the better off you are." Nevertheless, he says, "I knew something bad was going to happen sooner or later—something really bad."

RAVERS MADE FOR EASY criminal pickings. In October 1992, a warehouse party in Newark ended with two people beaten and three stabbed. In Philadelphia that summer, a party on North Fifth Street culminated with a mugger shooting a twenty-seven-year-old woman. She soon recovered—and, she told a reporter, was ready to rave again.

That was the case behind the scenes as well. Lord Michael Caruso, a stocky kid from Port Richmond, Staten Island, had palled around with thugs and sold drugs since he was a teenager. "Lord Michael [was] very Mafia connected," says Adam X. Caruso had thrown parties at Staten Island discos and met Lenny Dee, who'd briefly fallen out with Bones. Dee invited Caruso and future Limelight DJ Anthony Acid (Caputo) across the pond to party, promising: "I'm going to change your perspective." Dee recalls conspiratorially: "I took them to England and turned them on to the music, and brought them back with the *love* that they soon shared with everyone else in that club." In addition to an MDMA supplier, England provided Caruso with his nickname: "Lord" referred to the way he flaunted his money. At the Limelight he ran Future Shock on Fridays, whose crowd was outer-borough macho Italian tough guys taking a vacation from punching one another out in order to feel better than they had in their lives. Caruso, meanwhile, began robbing his associates and hiring wise guys as club security.

When Bones took the Storm Raves to Manhattan in July 1992, on Ninth Avenue near Thirteenth Street, someone called the authorities, who then shut it down. "I showed up at eleven P.M.," says Adam X. "There was literally a line all the way down to the West Side Highway. And the fire department showed up and the police came. I didn't even get to walk into the venue to see the setup. It was always suspected that the Limelight pulled the plug. We stepped into their turf. Whenever we did a party when they did their club nights, we would empty their club out." The fire department fined Bones twelve G's. "They wanted me to be an informant, and I wouldn't," says Bones. "The party got moved in secret to a beach down near JFK," says NE-Raves regular Laura La Gassa. "I packed up people in my car and we drove down and waited for the sound system to show up." It never did. "I remember DJ Sandra Collins sitting there in her rental car with the doors open wide, blasting her own mixtapes."

Shortly afterward, Bones was carrying a brown bag of groceries up the stairs of the new condo he'd moved into with his girlfriend in Canarsie. He'd just thrown a party in a park called Field of Dreams. "We had some trouble with gangs, and I had my people take care of it. But the kids that had started the trouble assaulted some kid out on the street, and somebody said that it was my people that did it." Caruso's crew caught wind of this and saw an opportunity to teach Bones a lesson.

Two men blocked Bones's path on the stairs: "Just like the scene out of *Saturday Night Fever* where he gets jumped. I noticed something was wrong, and screamed out my girlfriend's name." Two others emerged from bushes brandishing Louisville Sluggers; the men in Bones's way used gun butts. "I tried to duck. Four guys all took one shot, and all connected—all to the head." The second-floor neighbors ran out to the patio as the thugs scattered. "My ear was hanging upside down, backwards. If I'd went unconscious, I wouldn't have woke up." It took 290 stitches to patch the four holes in his head. Bones still isn't sure how Caruso's crew got his address. (Lord Michael boasted about ordering the attack the next night at the Limelight.) For his next DJ appearance—Deliverance, at Long Island's Warehouse on August 7—the flyer declared: "Going back UNDERGROUND."

THE NEXT STORM RAVE, on September 19, took place at a truck loading dock in Queens. "It was a really awesome spot," says Bones. "You could fit maybe fifteen hundred people in the building." On the other side was "this big-ass yard, like a cemetery—no houses, nothing. There were five thousand people there; it was definitely our most successful night ever." The music that night was 100 percent hardcore, aside from a 6 A.M. set by Long Island's Dante, who massaged everybody's bruised eardrums with a set of hard trance. Trance was intensely repetitive music deeply indebted to the acid house 303, intended to zone you out as much as pump you up, its bellwether recordings being Age of Love's "The Age of Love (Watch Out for Stella Club Mix)" and Hardfloor's *Hardtrance Acperience* EP (both 1992).

Around 1:30 A.M., a number of drunken partiers, who'd brought in their own cases of Bud, began a mosh pit in the middle of the floor. "I think what fascinated me about the Storm Raves [is that] the music was just so ferocious and intense and macho," says former *Spin* editor Charles Aaron, then a Brooklyn resident who attended many of the Storm parties. "It's so much about this wound-up energy. Brooklyn, Queens, Staten Island—those guys wanted to go crazy. They didn't feel like they wanted to express it through the preexisting music. They didn't give a shit about rock and roll. They were too young to know about the history of house music. They just wanted to go forward. They wanted the most intense, crazy music. It was the same exact thing as seeing Bad Brains in [D.C. club] the Basement—crazier, or as crazy."

Watching Lenny Dee, one of La Gassa's posse asked, "What is he on—speed?" somebody asked. John Adams responded: "No—*rave*."

Out in San Francisco, Brian Behlendorf was alarmed by NE-Raves' party reports. "*Moshing*? At a rave? YOW," he wrote. "People on E don't mosh!" He was even more flabbergasted by the BPM counts being thrown around: "Er—I find this hard to believe . . . 180 bpm means *three beats per second*." Nobody spun anywhere near that fast out West.

FRANKIE BONES NEARLY MISSED what turned out to be the last Storm Rave. "The night of that party there was two feet of snow. We had a nor'easter." On Thursday, December 11, 1992, Bones played a gig in Toronto. The next morning he went to fly home. "At the airport, the lady tells me, 'Maybe you want to try Greyhound,'" says Bones. "Then I thought: Amtrak."

He caught a 9:30 A.M. train to Albany, arriving with no one to meet him. "I was going to maybe try to hotwire a car—call my friend to tell me how. Then, as I'm walking down the platform, the train next to us, I heard the conductor go, 'Yo, Mike! We're bringing this one into Penn Station.'" Bones jumped on just ahead of the doors. An hour later, a motorman came across Bones, the car's only passenger, on a routine sweep. "I'm like, 'I've got to be in New York. I'm a stowaway. I hope I'm not in trouble.' He laughed, gave me a Pepsi." Bones arrived on Thirty-fourth Street at 11 P.M., took the 1 train to Manhattan's lower tip, and ferried to St. George, Staten Island. He arrived at 12:25 A.M., five minutes before his scheduled set.

The turnout heartened him: "There was twenty-five hundred people there. There was no way that many people should have showed up in a major snowstorm like that." He got on the decks and picked up the microphone: "I started traveling at eight in the morning, and I just wanted to play this record," he shouted, and started his new track, the Public Enemy–sampling "Show 'Em We Can Do This." "The place went bananas," he recalls.

That place was a Staten Island horse stable. "We got it for a really good price," says Bones. The assembled partiers danced on a dirt floor, mud and manure everywhere. It stunk even in the cold—and there was no heat inside. "When it would get too hot in there, i.e. so hot you couldn't even see your breath anymore, they helpfully opened the three truck-access doors, bringing the temp back down to a more comfortable –5 degrees C or so," an irate NE-Raver posted. The house lights occasionally brightened for no apparent reason.

"It was so goddamn freezing," says La Gassa, who led a NE-Raves contingent in a caravan to Staten Island from her place in Hoboken. "That did not put anyone in a good mood at all. You have [an] indoor arena for horseback riding—that tarmac is nice and soft for the horses, so it's dusty and dirty and nasty. That didn't help. And we weren't really into the DJ we were hearing. The kids looked a little weird. I don't think I was at that party for more than an hour. We couldn't take it."

A HARDIER CARAVAN came from the Midwest, led by Kurt Eckes and Tommie Sunshine. To them, barns weren't novelties; they were where parties always happened. But there was still something exotic about it for the Eckes and Sunshine. "It was really the first time I'd ever been that far away from home [that was] not a family vacation," says Sunshine, then twenty-one.

The two of them were used to long car trips—not to mention excess. "We would be halfway to Indianapolis," says Sunshine. "He'd be driving, and I'd grab the wheel while he'd be doing whippets—in the car. We were crazy. If there was ever Hunter Thompson and his lawyer in the Midwest, it was me and Kurt." Eckes had been a clean-cut professional working for a Milwaukee design firm, but it didn't last. "He'd started growing his hair when we made the pilgrimage to Storm Rave."

The drive took fourteen hours. "We met up with a second minivan full of kids from Cincinnati," says Sunshine. "We actually arranged to meet them at, like, exit 256 in Ohio—no idea how we were going to get there. We pulled into the exit and there they are, ready to go. We had a Rand McNally atlas. That's terrifying to me now. If I had to do that again, you couldn't pay me enough money."

Rather than the starry-eyed tomorrow children of their loved-up dreams, Sunshine and his pals found a crowd that slam-danced. Sunshine had candy-flipped—taking equal doses of LSD and MDMA simultaneously, alternating between acid's heavy psychological carnival ride and Ecstasy's gush. At the party, a pipe was passed, and Sunshine, without realizing it, was smoking angel dust, sprinkled with cocaine.

The speakers were placed twenty feet behind a chain-link fence that also walled off the DJs. "It was a baseball field-type fence," says Bones. "It was already there and we decided to put the booth behind it—utilize what we had to make it work for the party." Upon the fence were frothing dancers. "People were climbing it, losing their minds," says Bones. "It was the craziest thing I've ever seen," says Sunshine. "I remember hiding out in a porta-potty for a good solid hour because the drugs were just too much—and the worst place you could go in a loud warehouse was a porta-potty, because then you've got the echo off the walls times two. It makes everything even worse."

During Lenny Dee's set, the DJ would finish spinning a record and then, with a flourish, shatter it against the wall. Sunshine said he received a further jolt during Dee's set when the New York ravers screamed, "Faster! *Faster!!!!*" But according to Eckes, the biggest maniac in New York that night was the one who'd driven from Naperville. "Tommie was just freaking out while Lenny Dee was playing, wanting to get near the speakers and security wouldn't let him," says Eckes. "He was screaming for Lenny to play faster and harder."

The party turned the wheels inside Eckes's head. "It was decadent and hard, everyone is moshing. I felt like, 'This is where I belong': All the darkness of the heavy metal and punk rock I was into, culminating in a horse barn in New York. I was like, 'Fuck, why am I doing parties in warehouses? From here on out, we are going to be hardcore, and we're doing our parties out in the country.'"

Bones made a decision of his own that night. Upon finishing his set at 2 A.M., he told his confederates: "This was a sign from the heavens. We're never doing another Storm Rave again."

"STORM RAVE SUCKED and I'm never going to another one of their parties again," La Gassa fumed to NE-Raves. But it had catalyzed a good time anyway: La Gassa had some two dozen NE-Ravers over for a holiday party, including Damian Higgins and John Adams, and they wound up partying all weekend together. "Damian e-mailed and asked if he could spin at my house so he could get exposure," says La Gassa. "It was hilarious. We put a piece of plywood on top of my oven and turned off my oven at the breaker so there'd be a place for the tables to be. People were spinning in my kitchen." La Gassa's bedroom, outfitted with a soft magenta light, acted as a de facto "chill-out room."

The group quickly began planning its own event, with Behlendorf's encouragement: "I think NE-Raves is ripe for a rave at this point," he posted. "You're all beginning to act like a family, which is the most important aspect. . . . You have a lot of work ahead of you—but it will be worth it in the end, trust me. Do it! Do it! Do it!" Still, many on the list were wary of the *wrong crowd* finding out. "Invite as many people as possible," one of the list's DJs stressed, "as long as you would feel comfortable bringing [them] into your own home, 'cause the freight yard is your home that night."

A friend called me from L.A. and said
she just heard my song "Go" on the
radio. I said, "That's impossible; no one
plays music like that on the radio."

—MOBY, 2001

RAVE AMERICA

Los Angeles, California
December 31, 1992

HOW HEEDLESS WAS early L.A. rave? Brian Behlendorf was a good kid who got home by 3 A.M. He spent New Year's Eve 1990–91 at a break-in at the Burbank airport: "It involved a map point and a certain degree of subterfuge. But once you walked into this hangar, it was madness. There were people dancing all around directly underneath corporate jets. It definitely felt like somebody had a key to the hangar and didn't quite tell their boss what they were going to do on New Year's Eve." This was *par* in Los Angeles.

The city teemed with competitive, over-the-top promoters. "One of the marketing terms they would always use was 'virgin location,'" says Daddy Kev, a DJ-promoter who got his start handing out flyers for Double Hit Mickey, one of the biggest L.A. crews. A rave might be at a water-slide park (Grape Ape—August 10, 1991); a casino on Catalina Island (Gilligan's Island—August 31, 1991); a Hollywood storage unit with a basement full of nitrous oxide; a Native American reservation near the Compton freeway; or the high desert north of L.A. "These dry lake beds—that's nature's dance floor," says Aldo Bender, who played several times at New Moon Gatherings there.

After years of DIY shows, big L.A.-area promoters like Avalon Events were catching on, producing an 808 State show. "They were concert guys," says Pasquale Rotella, then an L.A. teenager. "Avalon rolled up L.A. [raves]. They knew how to put on a concert and happened to put on a dance one because it was blowing up."

A big reason why was at the bottom of the 808 State bill. Gary Richards's father was a local radio promoter who knew people at Tommy Boy, 808 State's label, and pulled some strings for his twenty-year-old son—DJ Destructo—to help Avalon promote the show. Among the most popular and credible British dance acts, 808 State also carried the built-in imprimatur of their hometown. "We were trying to emulate the Haçienda in Manchester," says Richards. He'd been initiated into acid house at the Mayan in the late eighties, and he started his own Sunday-morning after-hours called the Sermon. "Me and my two buddies would dress up like priests and tell people: 'Don't be excommunicated. Come to the Sermon.'" Five hundred people showed up every week, so Richards tried a Saturday-night event, Midnight Mass—and from there, because why not, a water-slide park.

Mr. Kool-Aid had already created the Double Hit Mickey imprimatur—named for a type of LSD—and put out flyers featuring Mickey Mouse with acid on his tongue, part of the prevalent trend for "logo bites": pop-cultural figures or corporate logos reconfigured for party flyers, after the style of Freshjive, L.A. graphic designer Rick Klotz's T-shirt brand and flyer company. "Mr. Kool-Aid could not mix records to save his life," says Jason Bentley. "This is not objective. This is absolutely crystal clear on large sound systems. But it didn't seem to diminish him as a leader in the scene. He had this rock-star status." That was common in L.A.: Daddy Kev, who worked with and admires Richards, asks rhetorically: "You know *why* they called him Destructo, right?"

Richards became Kool-Aid's marketing man. He'd budget for a one-thousand-person turnout, then draw three or four times that. "Back then you'd get away with paying dudes just a couple hundred bucks," says Daddy Kev. "Gary gave me really good advice: 'The venue is more important than the talent.'" So was having a good mailing list; Kool-Aid's was one of the biggest in Los Angeles, and so was that of Daven "the Mad Hatter" Michaels, who'd been involved with one of L.A.'s major early parties, LSD (Love, Sex, Dance). "Back in those days, guys would pay Daven to use his list for other parties," says Daddy Kev. "At the height of that, I was getting an invitation every two weeks. Those were the best parties."

Michaels, Kool-Aid, and Gary Blitz went in on Magical Mickey's Holy Underwater Adventure (June 20, 1991) with Richards. "I wasn't a full promoter but I promoted it and got a piece of the action," says Michaels. "We'd do a lot of stuff together." Initially, the location was Monsoon Lagoon in Redondo Beach. With a week to go, the park manager caught wind of the event's nature and handed back the deposit. "Kool-Aid was going nuts," says Richards. "I didn't even know the guy, and he was like, 'What are you going to do? We've been planning the water park this whole time.' So I came up with Wild Rivers in Irvine. I cut a deal with them on Tuesday and the show was on Saturday."

The short lead time was part of why the park agreed. "They thought, 'How the hell is this kid going to get people here this week?'" says Richards. Kool-Aid kept panicking, but Richards told him: "Trust me, they'll drive if it's good." As added incentive, "We had them go about halfway, get off the freeway, and gave them free gas." A DJ was set up at the gas station, which functioned as the second map point. Along for the ride was future *Please Kill Me* coauthor Legs McNeil, profiling the promoters for *Details*. "I didn't know who he was," says Richards. "He wanted to come and hang out and see what I do. So we let him follow us around."

Magical Mickey's Holy Water Adventure drew two thousand. "Me and Mr. Kool-Aid became partners because it was so successful," says Richards. "We went on to produce one event a month for two years." To keep things in-brand, they used names like Double-Up Mickey, Magical Mickey's Electric Daisy Carnival, and Magical Mickey's Mind Arcade. McNeil's feature appeared in *Details*'s December 1991 issue. "That got the word out to people in North Carolina and Phoenix and all around the country," says Richards. "It really spread the scene."

The issue was on stands concurrently with the November 14, 1991, episode of *Beverly Hills, 90210*, "U4EA," in which the show's high schoolers visit (gasp) a rave. "People in L.A. were really pissed when that episode came out," says Tamara Palmer. "Everyone was like, 'It's dead! It's over! It's done! It's mainstream!' I was watching the show because I was a teenage girl. I was rolling my eyes because it was so cartoonish. The drug of choice was called 'euphoria,' or 'phors,' so there was a guy with a giant '4' T-shirt. Even though it was a show I enjoyed, it was like, 'This isn't underground if fucking Brenda and Brandon are here.'"

AMONG AN AVALANCHE of Generation X think pieces, raves were a perfect journalistic sell—kooky enough to titillate squares, chewy enough for amateur sociologists. "The air is highly charged with sexual energy, but nobody's thinking about getting laid," wrote the *San Francisco Examiner* in February 1992. "Faces bathed in sweat and bliss—blank, glazed, open, innocent. Is it rapture? Or is it the drugs?" In April, *Newsweek* upped the ante with a scare-the-parents classic that began: "It's a scene that could send a kid into years of intensive psychoanalysis. . . . What's that, Mother Goose? You want me to dance?"

Press dedicated to dance music on its own terms was far thinner on the ground. For Americans with access to import magazines, slick

English titles like *Mixmag* (est. 1983) and *DJ Mag* (est. 1991) mostly covered the disco-derived diva-sung house music played at the big UK clubs, often by the people (Danny Rampling, Paul Oakenfold) who'd helped start the acid house craze—music with little traction in the U.S. rave scene. "*Mixmag* was aspirational: 'Imagine if we had clubs like this,'" says Detroit-bred writer-editor Joshua Glazer. "But musically it wasn't much."

That's where the zines came in. There were loads of them throughout the U.S.: in New York, DJ Moneypenny's *Brand X* and Heather Heart's *Under One Sky*; in Detroit, Alan Oldham's *Fast-Forward*; in Minneapolis, Woody McBride's *Disco Family Plan*; and many others. These were mostly tip sheets, full of DJ top-tens, simple Q&A's, scene reports, and third-generation-Xeroxed graphics. L.A.'s *Urb* was the first to seem even semiprofessional. Founded in December 1990 by local photographer Raymond Roker, *Urb*'s HQ was Roker's studio apartment in Hollywood.

"Raymond was avidly documenting the scene, and I was a journalist and DJ," recalls Jason Bentley, who became the magazine's managing editor after he saw an ad seeking a staff writer, and stayed on for two and a half years. "The magazine became closely aligned with the culture as it grew," says Bentley. "Streetwear lines, nightclub events— these parties were generating a lot of money, so they in turn would advertise in *Urb*." Bentley also made biz connections through the magazine: Neil Harris, London/FFRR's A&R man in New York, paid him two hundred dollars a month to tape his favorite new twelve-inches. By 1992, Bentley was hosting a nightly dance program, *Metropolis*, for KCRW-FM.

Shortly after Bentley came aboard, so did Daddy Kev, who began interning for *Urb* as a high school senior. "I was an avid *Urb* reader; it was my bible, basically. We were sitting at the edge of Raymond's bed, doing magazine stuff. Raymond started using this place as a map point as well. One of the parties got busted, and some kid came back and broke a window, pissed because he couldn't get a refund." Gary Richards promoted that party: "There were gunshots. We'd had gunshots at our events before—at that time, a lot. I was like, 'Okay, you can have the cash. I don't want to die.' We were always in bad neighborhoods. It was the underground—anything goes."

DOUBLE HIT MICKEY WAS a younger crew than the earlier L.A. organizers with roots in the underground. "It was all pretty much twenty-one-and-under; our scene was very much twenty-one-and-over," says Steve Levy. "It wasn't kids who necessarily were from L.A. They were coming up from Orange County. They were coming up the 5 Freeway and going to these parties that they couldn't down in Orange County."

The O.C. promoters' brashness wasn't limited to party décor. "In the early days, all us promoters were totally on the DL," says Michaels. "Everybody was behind the scenes, because nobody wanted to go to jail." Then, on a visit to New York, Michaels spotted a top hat in a haberdashery window and impulsively bought it. "I said, 'From now on I'm going to be known as Daven the Mad Hatter.' I created this persona, walked around in this tailcoat. It was risky. We weren't illegal anymore, but the cops were always looking for me, always looking to make an example of me. But I felt it was the only way to take it to the next level: Now I had this brand."

To imprint the brand, Daven the Mad Hatter put on a party at Union Station in downtown L.A. called Under the Paw Paw Patch. "In old movies, whenever they show the train station in L.A., that's where he did the party. It was all 1940s décor in there," says Doc Martin, who spun alongside Frankie Bones and Adam X. Tamara Palmer, then a high school senior in San Francisco, was in town to look at UCLA and visit Brian Behlendorf, whom she'd met on a Prodigy music bulletin board. She attended Paw Paw Patch with him. "It was super full," she says. "I was completely sober, but I found the experience completely disorienting. It was just darkness and music and people in Cat in the Hat hats and Mickey Mouse gloves. Literally."

Paw Paw Patch's success was license for Michaels to "get bigger-bigger-bigger." On June 24, 1991, came Paw Paw Ranch. "It was out in the middle of the wilderness—the desert, actually," says Doc Martin. "One of the biggest challenges was, how are we going to get people to drive two hours outside of L.A.?" says Michaels. "The way we did it was, we had to trick 'em! We had a map location that took them to another map location that took them to another map location. I remember, as we got close, we found a blank billboard. We projected on the billboard: 'Paw Paw Ranch,' fading into 'You're Almost There.' People were cheering as they drove by."

AROUND THE TIME of Stranger Than Fiction, Richard "Humpty" Vission, a fledgling rave DJ interning for Power 106, got a weekly program showcasing the new music, *Power Tools*, and Ken Roberts, who'd owned KROQ from the late seventies until 1986, purchased two easy-listening stations—KDLD in Santa Monica and KDLE in Newport Beach—which both resided at the 103.1 FM signal, and simulcast them, the first American FM station to do so. The combined station was dubbed MARS. Roberts hired his old KROQ DJ Freddy Snakeskin—who'd helped break Billy Idol's "Dancing with Myself" and New Order's "Blue Monday," among others, and was getting fed up with KROQ's direction—as his new program director. "KROQ was going in a more guitar-driven direction. So the idea was, 'Give them the guitars. We'll take the keyboards.'"

Snakeskin hired Swedish Egil (Aalvik) as music director. Freddy wanted New Order–style dance-rock; Egil, who came aboard six weeks before the new station went live, wanted to embrace techno. They settled on a mix: Madchester bands like the Charlatans UK and Happy Mondays, "the dancey side of Siouxsie and the Banshees" (Egil), Del the Funky Homosapien and De La Soul, a spoonful of

Madonna. "We were very aggressive about going after new music," says Snakeskin. "Actually, MARS played Nirvana several weeks before KROQ."

Nevertheless, the station's remit was to present the pop-friendly side of underground dance music: Eon's "Spice," Moby's "Go," and—most newsworthy at the time—Dutch techno group L.A. Style's "James Brown Is Dead," a Belgian stomper that essentially scolded dance producers for using breakbeats instead of a hard four-to-the-floor. In the summer of 1992, a San Antonio, Texas, shop owner reported that "James Brown Is Dead" was selling twenty times more than a competing Michael Jackson single; it eventually sold 325,000 copies in the U.S. and scraped the Hot 100 (a symbolic number ninety-nine), making it the first track to actually break the *Billboard* charts through the rave scene. The media and the biz were now watching.

But most adults simply couldn't hear it. Rather than hypnotic, they found the repetition irritating; instead of hearing the way the grooves built and crested, they wondered why there wasn't any chorus. One day, one of the station's general managers drove down to San Diego listening to MARS in the car and told Snakeskin, "Wow—it seems like you only played one song."

Others were even more irate, for different reasons. *"I did not give you permission to mention my event!"* an anonymous promoter screeched into the MARS voice mail after the station did a roll call of upcoming parties. "I'm going to sue your ass! You're ruining the scene, motherfuckers!" Snakeskin was amazed: "It just disintegrated into a tirade of obscenities." Naturally, the station used it as an April Fools' Day promo.

Still, plenty of L.A. kids played MARS on the way to parties. "One thing that was really great about it was that the playlist was limited, but you would hear tunes that you would hear out and you might want to know what they were so you could go get them," says Tamara Palmer. "It was really educational in that way. It was also something for people to bitch about too, on the other hand: 'Oh, look how mainstream the scene is getting.' A lot of people didn't like the songs that were on the air. You're not going to please everybody, especially when there are a lot of people who wanted to keep a lid on it."

The boom came for MARS-FM on Wednesday, August 19, 1992. "I was prepared for it because they called a big meeting for six o'clock, which is unheard of," says Snakeskin. "There were security guards that we never saw before hanging around the parking lot that [the general manager] hired to escort us out. But the big giveaway was after I signed off the air at six o'clock, she had one of her pet engineers come in and remove all the microphones from the studios."

"I think what it did was legitimize the scene," says Steve Levy. "It certainly put what we were doing as promoters on the radar of the traditional promoters." Exhibit A: Avalon grabbing the 808 State show out from under him.

BORN IN GLENDALE and raised in Eagle Rock and the Pacific Palisades, Pasquale Rotella ended up in Hollywood. The son of small restaurateurs—his father also did construction work—Rotella was fifteen when his friends brought him to his first rave, in 1989. "My friends were getting dressed up for it, putting on giant top hats and wearing overalls, pinning rubber daisies to their clothes. They told me, 'We're going to an underground.' That was about it for details." He hooked instantly into his surroundings. "It was very different than the culture I was around growing up: break dancing on the Venice boardwalk, a little bit of exposure to gang culture in passing, hanging out in Westwood Village as a kid into graffiti. People were able to be individuals and friendly with one another." He laughs. "I filled my backpack full of lollipops."

Early in 1992, Rotella spent a month in London, checking out Rage and hearing UK hardcore there for the first time. By the time he got back home, everything had changed. "In '92, raves became really uncool to people," he says. "I called the crew up and they were like, 'What are you talking about? We're not going to *raves* anymore.' It was a bad word—like, 'You're a nerd.'" The gold-rush excitement of the early scene was turning into territorial warfare—the by-now-usual call-the-cops-on-each-other routine. Rotella was in the crowd when the police shut down Magical Mickey's Haunted Mansion (October 26, 1991). "It was getting old."

THE VERDICT WAS HANDED DOWN on national television at 3:15 P.M. Los Angeles time. Within an hour, five young men on Florence and Dalton, in South Central, smacked a Korean American deli owner's son upside the head with a glass bottle and said, "This is for Rodney King."

On April 29, 1992, the city's smoldering racial tensions—a corrupt police department that constantly harassed blacks, a surge in street gangs, tensions that had been aired for years on records by L.A. rappers—went on national display. A year earlier, Rodney King had been videotaped being beaten and kicked by a group of police officers—full on, no mistaking it—and his assailants had somehow been found not guilty. Much of black Los Angeles went up in smoke. (In 2003, South Central was renamed South Los Angeles in hopes of destigmatizing the neighborhood.)

"There were some parties scheduled during the L.A. riots, and people had to be in by a certain time, so that affected everything," says Rotella. "The whole city seized—in that spasm of violence we were not able to mount the events for some time. The city was on lockdown, probably nine months to a year," says Jason Bentley. DJ Dan immediately noticed a new paranoia at the parties: "L.A. became a dark scene, and very violent." Additionally, the LAPD was taking notes. "There'd be a task force within the police department focused on these events and trying to shut them down by '93, '94," says Bentley.

"They came down on us like a ton of bricks," says Aldo Bender. "It went more mainstream: You had to pay for venues. You had to do it legal or don't do it at all. The hardest-hit areas were downtown L.A., with the warehouses, and the dodgy neighborhoods"—i.e., where most of the parties were. "If the cops weren't cool with the landlord, we would go to the Indian reservation, because [the cops] couldn't do anything on an Indian reservation. You'd park outside and talk to the sheriff on the way in and way out, but once you're outside, you're cool."

The parties also began to travel farther out to the suburbs—and the Eastside, which was relatively unperturbed by the disturbances that had rocked L.A. after the King verdict. "It was a weird time," says Steve Levy of 1992. "The crews started battling against each other. A lot of events were getting shut down because one promoter called on another. Nitrous started stepping into it. It was horrible. You had the Eastside guys, the Latin rave scene coming in and running against the Orange County guys." Latin Underground was the big company, putting on parties that attracted crowds on par with the Double Hit Mickeys and Moonshines. "They were very different than anything going on in the L.A. rave scene," says Rotella.

For one thing, says Eastside dance-scene historian Gerard Meraz, East L.A. parties were "never a hundred percent" house or techno: "There was a whole sub-scene called the Rebels—really into hard house, specifically the Abstract label. [The DJs] would throw on the Stray Cats or Billy Idol. They wouldn't leave the dance floor. One kid would play everything from hard house to gabber, and *boom*—you'd hear a reggae song. They weren't purists."

For Rotella—briefly a member of Eastside party crew Latin Pride as a teenager—the most important differences weren't musical. "Girls would stand up on stages and show their asses. There were cholos fighting." Eventually the Eastside parties began booking popular L.A. rave DJs like Barry Weaver, and the crowds began to mix. "Ravers

would be getting jacked," says Rotella. "You'd have these happy ravers with big hats on and these cholos would come up like, 'Give me
your wallet.' If you express your individuality among cholos you get
clowned. That brought me back to the whole reason I wanted to get
out of that whole thing—it was dark and negative. By '93, it was a
wrap. There was nothing going on."

IT WAS TIME TO GET OUT, decided Gary Richards. From McNeil's
feature to *Newsweek* and the *Wall Street Journal*'s sneering features to
TV-newsmagazine exposés (*Inside Edition, 48 Hours*) to *90210*, raves
were attracting more attention from adults and younger kids in the
crowds. "A lot of people dropped their age limits," says Doc Martin.
"That was the kiss of death for a lot of promoters. You have to have
some quality or crowd control or you're going to lose everything."

"I felt like the scene was getting rinsed out," says Richards. "It became a place for little kids to party—it really wasn't about the music." His solution: "A mega-sold-out" New Year's Eve bash called Rave
America. What else?

Richards was still interning at Power 106, so he asked the general manager about locations. "What kind of location are you looking for?" the GM asked. "An amusement park would be great." The
boss delivered Knott's Berry Farm. A short time later, he asked Richards: "When do you want it?" He wanted it December 31, 1992—his
twenty-second birthday.

Richards wasn't going to mega-sell-out alone. He gathered in as
many promoters as he could "so there was no competition." (Well,
there was another party called What?—but this was Knott's Berry
Farm.) "The big thing that got the bodies there and got the word out
was we had Power 106 involved, too. They were promoting it."

"That was very *not cool*," says Rotella, still audibly irritated by
Rave America's existence after all these years. "The cool kids went
to What?—I mean people who were searching for good vibes. The

Knott's Berry Farm rave had all the DJs that played for the gangster raves"—the Latin Underground events. "That was one of the demises of the scene as well. They didn't care that they were promoting on Power 106, knowing that would draw gangsters. There was no long-term thinking. It made it difficult, years later, for the culture to recover from all that."

RAVE AMERICA FEATURED seven stages with thirty-seven listed acts, plus four hosts. The bill was topped not by a house or techno artist but by rappers Black Sheep, who'd hit that year with "The Choice Is Yours." In addition to a heavy number of locals were New Yorkers Joey Beltram and Keoki (from Limelight), and Messiah, the Belgian act behind the MARS-FM hit "Temple of Dreams."

The party sold out in advance—around eighteen thousand tickets. "I'd never done an event where we sold tickets in advance," says Richards. "All my kids were walk-ups. So if we sold eighteen thousand tickets, another eighteen thousand are going to show up." He warned the park's staff to prepare for an onslaught. "They were like: 'You're just some kid. We've been running the park for forty years.' They saw how many tickets we sold, so they're like, 'We're gonna do a rave every weekend,' and put a big 'K' in front of the 'rave' to have their brand on our poster." (Many people still refer to the party as K-Rave.) A Knott's exec boasted: "We are leapfrogging into the nineties."

One of the partygoers was fourteen-year-old L.A. native Vivian Host. She'd been converted after seeing the Prodigy at the Palladium in the fall of 1992. "I was in the front row, dancing, and Keith [Flint] from Prodigy saw me dancing and started doing the same dance as me. I died, basically. I decided I was going to be a raver." For New Year's Eve, Host's mother rented a motel room near Knott's Berry Farm for her and a friend—her mother's idea. "She didn't want to have to pick me up forty minutes away at two or three in the morning. I was totally a good kid—that's how I was allowed to have a motel room."

Host and her friend arrived at 9 P.M. and were handed "passports" to be stamped at each of the park's seven stages, with directives such as: "Find someone who looks like the Mad Hatter." Says Richards: "We divvied it up into styles of music—a trance area, a house area, a techno area—so we made it a fun little scavenger hunt." Host saw right through it: "It was a mission for people on acid—something you invent for people who are tripping."

Not that there wasn't plenty else to do—the park left the rides running all night long. "I remember my friends from high school being on acid and going on the roller coasters," says Host. "They were like, 'It's so awesome!'" Some kids were doing Special K—the street name for ketamine, a hallucination-inducing horse tranquilizer starting to make its way into coastal nightlife—and getting sick on the rides. Others wandered into the gift shops and played with the toys, irritating staff.

They had enough to deal with at the gate. Richards had tried to warn them. "It was complete chaos," he says. "You've got the eighteen thousand [with tickets] trying to get in, and another eighteen to twenty thousand trying to *sneak* in. All of the freeway ramps off the 5 and the 90 were completely backed up. Everyone descended. They'd never had that many people at their park at one time. There were fights. There were people jumping fences. It was crazy. I'd say ninety-nine percent of it was solid, but there was one-to-two-percent element that was just getting wild, and they weren't prepared for it. They're used to families."

At 11:50 P.M., Richards watched from the upstairs balcony as a troupe of African drummers made their way to the main stage. "Right at midnight I made a five-minute snippet tape of all the hit songs from the past year with just ten seconds of each song, and they did a firework show piped into all seven areas. The place was just going nuts. I was standing on the top of this DJ booth on the main stage with my brother and he was like, 'We're gonna die!' The whole thing was bouncing." *Literally* bouncing. The staff panicked. "To try and get control of the park, they turned the electricity off in the entire place for, like, an hour to try and calm everybody down." Many people left, including Host. Knott's Berry Farm opted not to pursue the rave business. It was Richards's last party for fifteen years.

Amid the hubbub, Richards managed to hang out with Rick Rubin—not for the first time. They'd met when the Def Jam and Def American Records founder had shown up to a Double Hit Mickey map point wearing a purple boa and squiring Sofia Coppola. At K-Rave he'd come with ZZ Top's Billy Gibbons and Anthony Kiedis of the Red Hot Chili Peppers. Rubin especially enjoyed Messiah. At one point, says Richards, "He threw it out there that he was looking for someone to sign this kind of music. I said, 'I'll do it!'"

When Rave America was over, Richards was broke: "I never got a penny on it. I don't know who made the money." But he managed to take a meeting with the head of Creative Artists Agency—one of the top talent companies in Hollywood—before Rubin finally called. "The recruitment came," he says, "and I went into the record business."

Warning: Do not expect a rock concert.

—SEE THE LIGHT TOUR FLYER, 1993

> 8

SEE THE LIGHT TOUR

Thirteen North American cities
October 29–November 14, 1993

GARY RICHARDS'S FORAY into the record business was not immediately fortuitous. Arriving at American Recordings (formerly Def American) his first day—where he was to head up Rick Rubin's new techno venture, WHTE LBLS—he found out that the boss worked from home and was never around, because a middle-aged exec greeted him: "Oh, you're that techno faggot Rick was talking to me about. Just stay out of my way. I've got real shit to do."

"Rick thought that this was going to be like hip-hop and take over the world—that everyone's going to love this music," says Richards. But no one else did. "[Rubin] started to make noise that this was the next hip-hop," says Dan Charnas, American's hip-hop A&R man. "He liked the fact that techno was extremely edgy and used very angular sounds, and [that] he could play it super loud. The chaos of it really hooked him. Suddenly Rick is throwing all these resources at techno."

But resources weren't enough. "None of them between 'em had a damn song," says Charnas of the WHTE LBLS roster. "How could Rick forget that? How could he forget that? Even hip-hop at its hardest hardcore was producing three, four-minute pop songs. It didn't matter if the group was N.W.A or Fresh Prince. The song structures were there. And I wondered how you could claim [it was the new hip-hop] if rave wasn't producing that."

The acts Rubin and Richards signed—Awesome 3, Digital Orgasm, Lords of Acid, and Messiah—had had rave hits in Europe, but in the U.S. they didn't translate. Like punk or hip-hop in its early days, electronic dance music was evolving at lightning speed, and those acts' days were over. Rubin paid well for his bungle. "I'm sure it went up into the millions, all told," says Charnas.

Ironically, Rubin let slip through the one act that went on to substantial success. American issued *XL Recordings: The American Chapter*, a compilation of songs from the hit-making English label run by Richard Russell, which included the Prodigy's "Charly." Richards had licensed the collection in hopes of wooing XL's star act, and brought Rick Rubin to see them play at L.A.'s Palladium in the fall of 1992. The Prodigy—on record, the work of producer Liam Howlett—was dissatisfied with Elektra, its U.S. label: "They were always trying to get shit remixes done by people we didn't like." Howlett welcomed American's overture: "We were like, 'Shit, man, Rick Rubin is here!' I wanted his autograph. I grew up on the records he produced." But Richards left American before he clinched the deal, and WHTE LBLS died on the vine.

ELECTRONIC DANCE MUSIC lived on vinyl. One-off twelve-inches that eventually touched radio, like "James Brown Is Dead," weren't how the big biz rolled. When an underground label put out a CD, it didn't usually get distribution into major outlets. And DJ mixtapes were almost exclusively local, tiny, and technically illegal. Enter the rave compilations—dozens of them, mostly awful, but for many the first way to not only have in hand but also *identify* what they might have heard the previous weekend—or, by the time the comps hit the stores, months earlier.

New York's Profile Records had made its money on hip-hop (Run-D.M.C., Rob Base and DJ E-Z Rock, DJ Quik). In 1991 Profile hired London transplant DB Burkeman—DJ DB—as its new dance-music A&R man. "We started doing the *Best of Techno* series, which no one was doing yet," he says. "We were just throwing our favorite tracks on these albums. The first one [sold] a hundred thousand copies because nobody could buy techno yet in mainstream shops. It was crazy." Soon compilations from majors and indies alike flooded the racks. "It [was] a way for labels to test the market relatively risk-free," says Peter Wohelski, then editor of Tampa rave zine *Trip*. "It didn't cost them anything."

DB MOVED TO NEW YORK in 1989, and in 1991 started a London-style rave night called Brilliant. "It didn't work—it was a year too early," he says. NASA (Nocturnal Audio + Sensory Awakening), a Thursday copromoted by lighting director Scotto (Scott Osman), began a year later, in July 1992. "Everything clicked. It was a moment in time. Those Manhattan kids had something of their own and went for it; they were feeling like it was theirs. I've never seen energy, before or since, like some of the nights at that club."

NASA benefited from the growing interest among young teenagers in the music; the Shelter opened at 9 P.M. A small army of rotating DJs—including many Storm and Limelight regulars—played till 7 A.M. The vibe was all-inclusive; territorialism was for scenes not built on P.L.U.R.—"peace, love, unity, and respect," a tenet Frankie Bones had been throwing around for a while that had caught on as a kind of unofficial rave-scene slogan by 1993. Unlike Limelight, where the vibe was druggy in a teeth's-edge way, NASA was euphoric. Scotto's lighting enhanced this—he was one of the first in New York to utilize Intellibeams.

An increasing number of DJs coming into the ranks meant that hour-long sets were the norm. That fit a music that seemed to splinter every month. In early January 1993, Laura La Gassa and her NE-Raves posse arrived in time to hear Scott Henry switching from rough looping breakbeats to groovy house and then trance, finishing with local boys Disintegrator's "Dark Black Ominous Clouds," harder but still somehow congruous. That's how DB played as well—whatever caught his ear—even as those styles were increasingly legible as separate things.

The L.A. scene was outlandishly styled, but NASA codified the U.S. raver dress code. "The kids at NASA were taking their wide jeans, cutting upside-down V shapes, then sewing in their own fabric to make them even wider and cover their whole shoes," says Scotto. "The club kids had platforms; so did the rave kids. There was 555 Soul with funky sock hats—more of a hip-hop thing, to hold back your dreads. The rave kids—mostly suburban white kids—could adapt and merge all those together." NASA was even the font of the "liquid dance"—arms cutting nonstop shapes in the air, like human lava lamps: "There was this drug dealer, Philly Dave. He wore these white Mickey Mouse gloves, tripping, doing his thing, and that's how that dance started."

NASA was immortalized in Larry Clark's movie *Kids* (1995), a film that crystallized the picture of New York rave life as crazy and decadent. (The film's screenwriter, Harmony Korine, and lead actress, Chloë Sevigny, were both NASA regulars.) "Somebody told me that [in *Kids*], the drugs were accurate and the sex was not," DB says. "That sounds about right—I think the sex might have been accurate for a few as well. They definitely had raging hormones, an appetite to fill any crevice or orifice. They were just pilling it. Shrooms were very big. I think a lot of it was because they were so young they didn't realize the difference of what they were taking. A lot of kids got hooked on heroin out of that scene, and they didn't even know the difference between Special K and smack. It was just total crazy innocent scariness."

NASA's music was far more playful than Storm's. "I love hardcore,"

La Gassa posted a few days after attending NASA, "but it is stagnating as a musical form . . . how many saw-tooth waves can you take?" DB favored UK hardcore's breakbeats, pianos, and helium voices— the result of speeding up samples to make the breaks go faster, giving the music an ominous cartoonishness both fetching and menacing, like NASA's 3 A.M. anthem, NRG's "I Need Your Lovin'."

"I played at NASA so many times I honestly can't count the number," says Moby. "It was completely out in the open and it was fantastic, really fun and celebratory. Kids would do one hit of ecstasy—maybe on a big night, two hits. It was that halcyon period before people became aware that there were consequences to that level of degeneracy. I felt by '93 it had become a little more factionalized." NASA itself ended in July 1993.

WITH STORM RAVE OVER, Adam X and Heather Heart were throwing smaller parties under the name Mental. "We wanted to scale the parties down because the police were starting to crack down on [large] events," says Adam. "On Kent Avenue [in Williamsburg, Brooklyn], people were living in abandoned warehouses, so we did a party in one of them. It was fucking incredible: five hundred people, the cops didn't show up or nothing. You could just do whatever you wanted." Bones fondly recalls a Mental "boxcar rave—we put eighty kids in a parked train."

A number of new promoter crews popped up in all five boroughs: the McMuffin Family, Infinity, Guaranteed Overdose, Uptown Underground, the Caffeine Crew, Park Rave Maddness. Several found breaks with one landlord in particular. "There was a really popular area on the Brooklyn-Queens borderline, under the BQE in Greenpoint," says Adam. "There was an old guy, a real estate mogul, renting all these spots. One of the Mental parties was in a parking garage in this area—a thousand people. Kids that wanted to try to do parties were going to him—five hundred, six hundred people, a lot of really good parties. Bones played at some of these parties, but he wasn't involved in promoting or throwing them."

By the end of the summer of 1993, Bones wasn't equipped to even play them. "I got caught up in angel dust," he says. "I was reckless. I didn't care if I lived or died. I was really partying—and basically lost my mind." A car crash alerted his mother, who made him check himself into detox. Bones wound up spending six weeks in a mental hospital; he calls it "one of the worst times of my life. You'd never want to be in that situation." He recuperated at his mother's home. Within a year, he was back on the road, no longer a kingpin but still indefatigable.

A FEW DAYS BEFORE a party in suburban D.C. called Future (June 27, 1992), one NE-Raver posted: "I heard Moby DJs and uses keyboards at the same time." Another responded: "As I remember, he only had one keyboard and possibly a controller of some sort. He was playing a lot of the lines, [and] either had a DAT or a sequenced backing. Then he shouts things like 'Get your hands up in the air, motherfuckers!!' This sounds stupid, but it was GREAT."

Future was the brainchild of Michael Meacham, then spinning Goth and industrial Monday nights at the D.C. gay club Tracks. He'd been friends with Moby since high school. A few months earlier, Moby stayed with Meacham—he was in town to perform at the 9:30 Club. "I'm going to do this warm-up set," Moby told him before a perfunctory sound check. "I'd never seen him perform live," says Meacham. "He hit the keyboard a few times. I thought, 'This should be kind of boring.'" After dinner, Moby walked onstage a changed man, one prone to stage diving. "Holy shit—I could not believe the energy he put out at that show. We were throwing shit—the highest compliment you can give somebody is when you pick up a chair and throw it across the room, because there's nothing else to do. All the D.C. people that were techno heads? Lost it—lost their fucking minds."

BORN RICHARD MELVILLE HALL in New York City on September 11, 1965, Moby got his nickname at birth, a joke on his diminutive size and family history: Herman Melville was an ancestor. The son of a chemistry professor killed by a drunk driver when Moby was two, he was raised alone by his mother in Darien, Connecticut—a hippie with a peripatetic communal lifestyle. Drugs were around, and so were his mom's scary boyfriends, like the one who pulled a knife on her in front of him. Moby took classical piano lessons early and played hardcore as a teenager. He experimented with everything he could lay hands on, followed by an extended period—ongoing during the rave years—of abstinence from alcohol and drugs.

He moved to Manhattan in 1989, after landing a full-time DJ gig at Mars, on the west side. Late that year, he became the first signee of a tiny New York indie, Instinct Records. "At the time the label had neither a name nor a location, nor employees," says Moby. "I was the only artist. We started putting out these records that would sell around five hundred copies." The first, in September 1990, was "Time's Up," credited to the Brotherhood; shortly after came the *Mobility* EP, his first recording as Moby. On the B-side was "Go"—title word sampled from Tones on Tail, another of Jocelyn Brown sighing "Yeah," undulant synth lines that filtered Detroit through London.

Moby decided he could like it better: "Remixes in the eighties had been simply taking a Depeche Mode song and beefing up the drums so the DJs could play it. In the late eighties, suddenly the remixes started to sound a lot less like the original." Kevin Saunderson had started it, replacing the entire track of British rap duo Wee Papa Girls' "Blow the House Down" with his own; by the early nineties, this was standard. "Even when a record came out, you would always think, 'Maybe I'll go back and try this,'" says Moby. "I had my own studio, it didn't cost anything to do remixes, and I didn't have a girlfriend at the time. So I would just keep remixing things."

The version of "Go" that stuck bore an appropriate name, the "Woodtick Mix"—it layered in the chord sequence from Angelo Badalamenti's *Twin Peaks* theme, both ominous and warm. This "Go" made the English top ten in the fall of 1991, prompting Moby's appearance on *Top of the Pops*. "Ninety percent of it was rave based: Me, Altern-8, 808 State, Dream Frequency"—and Genesis. "I remember Phil Collins watching the rave acts do their sound checks and he had such a look of baffled horror on his face."

"You have to remember, he was one of the first artists to come out of the U.S. that actually crossed over in Europe," says Doc Martin. "That was a big deal—we finally had one of our own making noise in that market. It wasn't a major-label star deciding to do a techno mix. It was actually someone who came from within our scene. When Jam & Spoon"—the German duo whose "Watch Out for Stella Club Mix" of Age of Love's "The Age of Love" was trance's defining early anthem—"did a remix [of 'Go'] for *him*, that validated the whole thing."

Moby was invigorated by the emergent U.S. scene: "It was this perfect hybridized version of all these different musical genres I loved—hip-hop breakbeats with disco vocals, new wave bass lines, and big orchestral strings on top of it—thrown together in a sped-up, exciting way." He was equally impressed by its DIY underpinnings. "The rave scene reminded me of the hardcore punk scene of the early eighties. It was completely self-generated."

Rave was also largely apolitical—not a description of Moby. "What inspired me performance-wise was seeing Black Flag with Henry Rollins, that idea that you presented yourself as directly and confrontationally as you could." That was the model for the live shows Moby began to stage shortly after "Go" became a hit. "If I'd grown up a few years later and been obsessed with Curve, Ride, and My Bloody Valentine, my performance would be a lot different." But his shows' forcible interaction fit rave's frenzied energy. "Everyone was jumping around. The rave scene was all about energetic drugs."

REVIEWING MOBY IN EARLY 1993, Charles Aaron described him in *Spin* as "techno's crazed youth minister." The analogy wasn't an accident. After briefly studying philosophy and comparative religion before dropping out of SUNY Purchase, Moby took a friend's advice and picked up the New Testament, putting it down "blown away and frightened," he said. In Christ, Moby found a fellow iconoclast. He soon renounced drugs and alcohol, despite working as a full-time club DJ. When raves began in New York, Moby found deep commonalities between them and religion: "Raves are basically people getting together in a dark place dancing together with lights in their eyes. Forty thousand years ago people banged on logs in front of a fire and it was basically the same thing."

Nevertheless, Moby was beginning to feel uneasy about the way things had become in the rave scene. "NASA was where I watched it go from idyllic to quite dark. It went from, in '92–'93, people taking ecstasy, throwing their hands in the air, and dancing until six o'clock in the morning, to '94, when it was really dark jungle music—which I loved, but it was definitely very dark. It became seventeen-year-old kids sitting on the floor in K-holes." Saying so in interviews, for many kids, seemed too close to the kind of lecture they were going to raves to avoid. He told an interviewer something else in 1993: "I intentionally do things to antagonize people in a very ambiguous way."

NASA WAS ONE OF THE SPONSORS of Rave New World, a six-date U.S. tour in February 1993, headlined by the Prodigy, Moby, and Cybersonik. Marci Weber helped organize the tour for Elektra, who'd hired her to look after the Prodigy's U.S. interests. On record, Cybersonik were the two men behind the Plus 8 label, Ontarians Richie Hawtin (from Windsor, five minutes from Detroit) and John Acquaviva (from London), plus Detroit producer Dan Bell. They'd broken out with the hard-riffing "Technarchy" (1990), which sold fifteen thousand out of the box. Along with "Mentasm" and Underground Resistance, "Technarchy" was a key U.S. blueprint for Euro-hardcore. Bell recalled that Derrick May chided him: "You guys are responsible for all this rave stuff."

"We couldn't afford to take Dan with us," says Acquaviva. "Hawtin and I were basically DJing on that tour." They traveled on a fourteen-person bus. European touring is very different from U.S. touring, and the Prodigy had never spent so much time driving. "It was completely alien to them, getting on a bus from Rochester to San Francisco, and back to New York the next day, all within a forty-eight-hour period," says Weber. "Every day for an hour, I talked to every single member on the phone to discuss why we were doing this."

The Prodigy's full-dress show (matching track suits and choreography) didn't impress many U.S. rave kids, who wanted things stripped down. Keith Flint, wearing his hair long and blonde, "runs around, makes weird faces, sticks out his tongue, and basically has an epileptic seizure," an MW-Raver shrugged. Moby complained that the Prodigy's weed smoke got into the bus's air-conditioning vent and made him sick.

Moby recalls the tour fondly: "We were all friends, we were all young kids, and it was celebratory. It felt like we were all in it together." Nevertheless, after the stop in Montreal on February 4—which climaxed, as all his shows were beginning to, with Moby standing atop his keyboard, arms aloft in a Christ pose, while his track "Thousand" battered away below—the ravers there started referring to the tour as "The Moby Show."

John Acquaviva was Moby's tour roommate: "By the end I was spoofing Moby and his track dates at sound check. Moby was starting to take off, so he stopped traveling with us because he couldn't be bothered being a team player. By the end of the tour he was flying around and would just show up and do his shows and not hang out. He just couldn't get along." The bouncy castles several promoters had provided along the way grated as much as what the Plus 8 guys disdained as showbiz. When Hawtin got home, he decided to throw some parties of his own. One thing he did not want was to call them "raves."

MOBY HAD CRAFTED NOT JUST a string of tracks, but a string of anthems: "Go," "Rock the House" (as Brainstorm), "Voodoo Child" (as Voodoo Child), "Drop a Beat," "Next Is the E" (he swears it's not a drug reference, that the title vocal sample was a "happy accident"). This, he says, is because he was a shameless magpie.

"Honestly, during the rave era, ninety-eight percent of my records were inspired by other people and were really naïve, enthusiastic homages to other people's records—everyone from Derrick May to Joey Beltram. I did a few 'Mentasm' homages. I would listen to something like Rozalla's 'Everybody's Free' and write 'Move.' There was this one record by a band called Dream Frequency called 'Feel So Real.' My homage to that was so blatant and obvious: 'Feeling So Real.' I just added a syllable." After seeing Sven Väth play "a record that went from 130 BPM to 160 BPM, I went home and made a record that went from 130 BPM to 1,200 BPM"—"Thousand," his traditional show-closer.

Moby's gift was for taking dance-music production tricks and turning them into pop songs—shorter, tighter, more classically structured with each release. "Joey Beltram was coming at it from the perspective of a DJ, and I always came at it from a perspective as a musician. So mine were, unfortunately, a little too song oriented, which I actually saw as a detriment. A lot of records were being made by DJs who had no songwriting background—yet they were making the interesting records."

The rave scene's deliberate anonymity was wearing on him anyway. Early in 1993, he signed with Elektra in America, much to the consternation of Instinct. (He's been on Mute in Europe his entire career.) "They didn't want me to go. It was hard because they had been friends of mine and we'd built things up together, and there was an unfortunate amount of acrimony that existed while I was trying to leave." (All fences have long since been mended.)

Moby's first major-label release, the *Move* EP, came out August 31, 1993. "If I go back, I'm really happy listening to the songs, but none of them really worked on a club level. The way it was mixed, it was really hard for DJs to play." Instead of a clean, loudspeaker-ready mix of heaving lows and piercing highs to punch it across the room, *Move* was all midrange, like it had been mastered for radio; one DJ refers to the EP's sound as "gluey."

"KEEPING IT REAL" was the watchword of mid-nineties popular music. Independent or "alternative" rock in the wake of Nirvana and Lollapalooza struggled with it; so did hip-hop once Dr. Dre's *The Chronic* turned gangsta rap into the new radio pop. Both styles' core fans embraced rougher music that wore their unfiltered aesthetics on their sleeves—liver-than-live Steve Albini–type production and/ or Sebadoh-style lo-fi for the former; unblinking lyricism and grimy, minimal beats for the latter.

Alt-rock and hip-hop both had mass American audiences, though; electronic dance music did not. Labels looking for quick dollars could put out all the compilations they wanted—they weren't going to get much back unless this music could produce a real star. That's how the record business had worked since Caruso. Moby, with his ingratiating tunes, outspoken worldview, and energetic live show—and, let us not overlook, alabaster skin—was, many figured, the one with the best shot, especially in a country that took fifteen years to finally get to grips with punk.

Techno's penchant for futurespeak was alienating to most Americans—many of whom still believed Disco Sucked—but it was thrilling to a burgeoning class of kids whose interaction with advanced technology was fast becoming not a quirk but a necessity, deeply entwined with their everyday activities. Moby, then, was perfect for bizzers, writers, and kids whose primary interest in rave was as a diversion rather than as a scene. The rave scene wasn't necessarily looking for a pop version of itself—it wanted to go further out. Unearned knee-jerk snobbery ran rampant on the mailing lists, but electronic dance music was mutating quickly, creatively, and in many directions at once.

Moby was generally modest, but he could also be a diva, and his righteousness could grate. He wanted to be a star in a scene that consciously rejected glamour. His show made mesmerizing, exciting theater, the spectacle of a man changed by electronic dance music reenacting the Damascene experience to a loud backing track—everyone knew the music was mostly on DAT. Moby claimed authorship over the total work as proof of his DIY ingenuity. But increasingly, party flyers around the U.S. were promising "live PAs" from artists. Being able to *bring it* onstage with a bunch of gear and no traditional instrumentation was starting to matter. Maybe it's surprising that a scene so frequently flaunting its rejection of the human touch would vilify him almost overnight for miming his performances. But that's what happened.

FOR FALL 1993, WEBER put together a thirteen-city North American package called See the Light. Moby topped a formidable undercard: Orbital, Aphex Twin, and Vapourspace, with local DJs all over. The NASA crew was involved again—Scotto lit the shows, and DB and Tim from Utah Saints flew in to spin at many.

Vapourspace was Mark Gage of Rochester, New York, an industrial fan who'd moved in with a club DJ in 1991 and got inspired. He already owned much of the equipment need to make it—gear that the techno explosion had forced a run upon: "The prices I paid in the eighties were cheaper than the used prices in the nineties, because all of this stuff became vogue. A friend in the eighties bought a brand new 909 for five hundred dollars. I sold my 909 for a thousand dollars in the nineties."

Gage sent his demos to Plus 8; eventually Acquaviva signed him. In January 1993, Gage recorded a quickly conceived one-off performance to DAT and edited it into a track he called "Gravitational Arch of 10." London/FFRR picked it up for wider release after the Plus 8 release; they paid Gage's tour support for See the Light. He'd only done a couple of local performances beforehand; still, he wrangled his gear afresh every night: "I never had tape to back me up. If something was really going well with your set, you could milk it for all its worth."

London had also issued the first two albums by Orbital—brothers Paul and Phil Hartnoll—though they weren't quite sure how to promote them in the U.S. "I did get the feeling, when we went into the meetings on how we were going to market this, there wasn't really much of an idea," says Phil. So the company sicced Orbital on the road: "It was down to touring and touring and touring. That's when we came up with packages with other electronic artists. Otherwise it was pretty difficult to do a tour individually."

The Hartnolls wrangled gear unsexily onstage, but had a visual advantage. Phil calls them "the torch glasses": Two miners' hats outfitted with small Maglites so they could see their gear in the dark. They'd picked them up at Space Age Gifts, a novelty shop across the street from a New York Tower Records, in 1992. Gage, who toured twice more with the Hartnolls, was impressed: "Their setup was so complex that I couldn't believe that they were capable of pulling it off the way they did, but they were brilliant." Orbital typically finished the night, after Moby was done.

THE FOURTH ARTIST on the bill was See the Light's most critically revered figure. Richard D. James had grown up in Cornwall, an isolated city on England's southwest peninsula. An inveterate tinkerer who was pulling apart pianos at age ten, then making his own circuits not long after, James was ready when rave hit town; he and his friends threw their own on the beach. On tour, the alien tones and haunting tunes he'd made with rebuilt instruments attracted cadres of quizzical young men who'd peep his gear, looking for clues. In addition to Aphex Twin, James also recorded as Powerpill, AFX, and Polygon Window—the latter's *Surfing on Sine Waves* was one of four albums on the English label Warp Records that Wax Trax! licensed for U.S. distribution in October 1993.

Founded by Sean Booth and Rob Mitchell in 1989 from a Sheffield record shop, Warp made its name quickly with a pair of fluke British chart hits. One early release, Nightmare on Wax's "Dextrous," grazed the top seventy-five almost by accident; a pair of 1991 tracks, LFO's "LFO" and Tricky Disco's "Tricky Disco," both made the top twenty. "The Warp material is less brutal than the Belgian techno: still using crunchy industrial sounds, but more minimal, more playful," Jon Savage wrote in 1993. A deluge of "bleep tracks"—a different way of making Kraftwerk funky—followed in the wake of Warp's first few, including Orbital's "Chime."

By mid-1992, Warp had largely left bleep behind, finding its next signature sound by issuing a compilation of mellower tracks (including cuts from non-Warp artists like Richie Hawtin—as UP!—and Dr. Alex Paterson of the Orb) titled *Artificial Intelligence* that July 9. (A second volume followed in 1994.) It was an announcement of a new aesthetic wrinkle—electronic dance music didn't have to be for dancing at all. Years later Booth said, "We imagined a small audience of kids like us tripping in their bedrooms." But that audience was scattered around the globe, something the nascent mailing lists helped achieve.

In fact, the Warp collections inspired a mailing list. In August 1993, Hyperreal began hosting IDM, which stood for "intelligent dance music." The list's name came from *Artificial Intelligence*, and its focus was anything Aphex- or Warp-related. But "intelligent" is a term loaded with class snobbery, particularly in England, where faster, giddier UK hardcore, just merging into jungle, was ritually disdained by collegiate techno snobs. Ironically, the Polygon Window album—Richard James's first full album released in America under any name—was one of the few he's made to consist mainly of straightforward dance tracks.

UNLIKE JUST ABOUT EVERYONE else in mid-nineties U.S. rave, Marci Weber was a music-biz veteran, having spent the eighties with the powerful William Morris Agency. A short list of her clients includes the Clash, Billy Joel, George Benson, the Cure, David Bowie, and Peter Gabriel. She was tough—she had to be: "At that time there were maybe three women agents in the entire business," she says.

Weber always loved dance music; her first biz job was with the Miami disco label T.K. Records. In 1990, she attended a rave at England's Castle Donnington, where she was swept up but also a little confused. "I must have looked like an idiot for even asking: 'Why are you chewing on a pacifier?' 'You mean me dummy? It stops me from chewing me mouth.' I didn't realize that was a drug thing." It didn't matter. "It was ten thousand people having the best time of their lives. I was looking at a new culture emerging. This was right up my alley."

After leaving William Morris, Weber and partner Barry Taylor began MCT Management, signing Kevin Saunderson, Joey Beltram, and Altern-8. Weber heard Moby spin at Mars without knowing who it was. "I think LFO was playing. Morrissey was there, throwing spitballs." Later she heard "Go" on a friend's mixtape and was promptly introduced to Moby; soon they were working out a management deal at a Thai restaurant. "We didn't know he was vegan. He had water." She got him tour support to open for the Shamen in 1991 and buttered up the headliners' crew. "I was giving them extra money to [light] Moby's set. It was their dinner break."

American raves were a slipshod proposition; many promoters were high schoolers. "I would ask if they had workers comp," says Weber. "Do they have insurance? I wanted to see the permits. I tried to do as much due diligence as I could, right down to the safety of the stage. I know what it means to see a stage fall down. If you're the only adult in the room, be the adult." At Future, Michael Meacham's partner, a hip-hop promoter, took every penny from the door, stuffed it in a trash bag, and rode off in his Mercedes, never to return. Meacham was forced to drive home and to an ATM to grab whatever cash he could. Many DJs were paid fifty dollars—"Gas money," he says. Weber's clients were paid in full. She made sure of it.

WRITING UP AN ANNOUNCEMENT for See the Light to be distributed to the newsgroups, Moby decided to respond to some of the more suspicious questions about his stage show: "now, regarding this whole live vs. DAT debate," he wrote, in all lowercase,

my shows in the past have relied on dat for drums, samples, etc. this show will be more live, but basically, who cares? would you rather watch a totally "live" and totally boring act that doesn't even break a sweat or an act that puts things on dat and puts on a good show? . . . people who make an issue out of "is it live?" techno are dangerously reminiscent of people who can describe eric clapton's guitar solos in depth and who dismissed punk, techno, hip-hop (and jazz and rock and roll for that matter) as not being valid because you didn't need a masters degree in music theory to appreciate them . . . my keyboard's not made of cardboard, it's a fully functioning multi-timbral yamaha sy35 capable of receiving eight midi channels simultaneously for sixteen-note polyphonic playback . . . stop smoking, moby.

"Back then he either wrote in all lowercase or all caps," says Meacham, who'd first shown the computerless electronic musician the mailing-list debates about him. "He just was not a good typist."

Instead of shutting down debate, Moby's post opened it up wide. "If it is all on DAT there is no live performance," Joe LeSesne* responded, not insensibly; LeSesne was the alt.rave member who'd first joked that Moby's keyboard was made of cardboard. "So it shouldn't be advertised as such. Moby, I'd be happy if say only fifteen percent of your 'live' show was live." Others fanned the flames: "Stage presence is worth nothing. I don't go to raves to watch some guy dance around on stage." Meacham tried arguing the merits of showmanship; list members wanted transparency. Neither side gave.

In 1993, this sort of endless, no-winners back-and-forth—a wearying cliché of electronic communications—was actually new. For Meacham, the posts' tone was unsettling. "If you were drinking the Kool-Aid back then, it was about love and humility and peace," he says. "I couldn't believe it: 'Wow—people hiding behind the anonymity of a computer will say anything.'" Part of it, he sensed, was personal. "There was a phrase that came out of Vrave, more than SF-Raves or SoCal-Raves: 'Go away, Moby,' a total pre-meme meme," says Tamara Palmer. "People turned against him. There was a definite backlash."

SEE THE LIGHT KICKED OFF on October 29, in Washington, D.C., at the 9:30 Club. From there it went to New York, Philadelphia, Boston, Montreal, Toronto, Detroit, Chicago, Indianapolis, Denver, El Paso, and Los Angeles, finishing in San Francisco on November 14.

At the 9:30, Moby debuted his new band—a drummer and keyboardist, both standing, both far taller than the diminutive performer. In fact, they'd been picked as much for their height as anything.

. . . .
* LeSesne, a.k.a. drum and bass DJ 1-8-7, became Jordana LeSesne in 1998.

Both sidemen went unmiked; keyboardist Jim Poe later wrote that his job was to "look cool." Though Moby sometimes soloed on keyboards, most of the show ran off a DAT. During "Thousand," Moby's techno-Jesus pose inspired deep backstage ridicule. "Why stop there?" Richard James snorted. "Why not just program it to be a million BPM?"

James's live presentation was the diametric opposite of Moby's—he barely appeared at all, choosing instead to crouch over his boxes conjuring his fractured, beguiling beat-scapes at the very back of the stage, almost off it, while his friend Paul Nicholson—who'd designed the Aphex Twin logo—danced loonily around to the music. Many attendees thought the dancer was James himself. It wasn't the only time James would offer a show of this sort, but in the context of See the Light it functioned as a parody of the headliner's performance. It also put a Zappa-like smirk on the insecurities, never far from the surface, of American ravers hearing from all sides that what they liked wasn't "real."

On Halloween, the tour went to the Trocadero in Philly, with local guest Josh Wink, followed by a day off—Wink took members of the tour party out to see *The Nightmare Before Christmas*. At the Troc, Moby began to play a little guitar in his set—something he'd do for the rest of the tour. They stopped in Toronto on November 4, John Acquaviva driving up with a Plus 8 posse to see Gage, but the real news happened between the wires. That day, Moby responded to the gathering mass of alt.rave posts, again through Michael Meacham. Instead of all lowercase, this missive was in all caps. "He [didn't] know what he was doing was, to this day, 'yelling' at people," says Meacham:

I THINK THAT JUDGING A PERFORMANCE SOLELY ON THE BASIS OF WHETHER THE MUSIC IS BE-ING GENERATED 100% LIVE IS PARTICULARLY AR-BITRARY . . . CAN'T YOU JUST RELAX AND ENJOY YOURSELVES? DANCE/TECHNO/RAVE CULTURE IS

NOT JUST ABOUT SITTING AROUND AND BEING UP-TIGHT AND JUDGMENTAL. IT IS ABOUT DANCING, BEING UNINHIBITED, AND BEING OPEN TO NEW THINGS, WHICH IS WHAT I TRY TO PRESENT IN MY PERFORMANCES.

The answer, of course, was that rave was now "about" any number of things. Moby's intersection with the wants and needs of the American rave massive had gone awry, and they didn't want to be lectured—yelled at—by someone bound to a moment just past.

IN CHICAGO, WEBER had long been friendly with Metro booker Joe Shanahan, who in turn brought David Prince and Kurt Eckes in to co-promote. They filled every room with DJs. "It wasn't like a rave-rave," says Eckes. "It was more like a concert, but it was cool." Same thing next night at Industry, in Pontiac, Michigan—Detroit's analogue to Medusa's in Chicago, mixing industrial and techno for underage crowds. "The artists were set up in balcony areas," says Patrick Russell, a budding local DJ and Industry regular. "Orbital played behind us, under the stairs." The after-party, he says, was at "a super-small little coffeehouse-pizzeria" down the street: "Orbital said, 'Can we sit with you?' Of course! DB had flown in and was playing house records. D-Wynn got behind the counter and was spinning two pizzas around like records."

The next show also involved fast food. On November 7, like a knob-tweaking *Spinal Tap*, See the Light played the food court of an Indianapolis shopping mall. "That was a weird show," says Gage. "The audience was sparse." Many tour principals were vegetarians playing to chain eateries few could have ordered from even if they'd wanted to. Backstage, Jim Poe was taken aside and reprimanded for gabbing with fans in Detroit about his un-plugged-in keyboards—it was all over the mailing lists again.

Poe wasn't alone in feeling frustrated. "Moby was Joe Celebrity," says Gage, still irritated two decades on. "He got flown from city to city. Everybody from Richard James to Phil and Paul Hartnoll carried equipment. In every city, we were the ones unpacking Moby's equipment. He wasn't even using this equipment to perform—they were just fucking stage props that weren't even plugged in."

What a splendid time for a magazine reporter to show up on the bus. Erik Davis, later author of *Techgnosis*, was covering the tour for *Spin*. As the bus rolled through to Denver, Davis hung out in the front (the back, "Aphex Twin-land," was not for visitors). He found the company congenial, particularly Gage and the Hartnolls. James was harder to access but not unfriendly; when Davis finally caught up to him, in an El Paso hotel room, James was both lucid and decidedly off: "There was this distant church bell going off. He instantly started to break down the waveform of the church bell. He was trying to explain the way he processed reality fundamentally differently than other people."

So, Davis asked, where's Moby? Off the record, several people on the bus confirmed the tension that Davis says "was apparent right away." He adds: "People were not ragging on him as a topic of conversation on the bus. There was a sense that Moby was moving to take advantage of a space that put him above a bunch of musicians who were not being rock stars but were just playing music. The basic vibe was: 'He's sensitive. He wants to control the situation.' Moby never put on any airs for me. He was smart, and I genuinely like smart people."

Other kinds of tension were afoot. During sound check in Denver, says Weber, "One of the roadies broke a bottle and threatened Moby with it. I think Moby might have said something smart-assed— sarcastic, funny. I think he might have been suffering [from]: 'These guys are not musicians. They're jumping around and dancing. They're not like a real rock band.' They resented it, because it would shake their status quo."

Despite the fact that, according to Denver native Charlie Amter, the city had raves dating back to 1989, See the Light brought out only about two hundred people, mostly rockers as put off by the presentation as the roadie. The tour took the next day off, sightseeing in Carlsbad Caverns, New Mexico, where Davis did formal interviews. "Of course, Aphex Twin wanted to trip while he was down there," says Scotto. "I advised him not to in case he never came back."

James seemed like he was consistently on *something*—Davis noticed a lot of weed being smoked back in Aphex Twin-land, but adds: "He didn't seem out of it. At Carlsbad Caverns he just looked like a happy tourist, just enjoying [himself] and chatting." But not everyone was happy there. Gage recalls confronting Moby on the bus in New Mexico over a request, conveyed by management, for him not to talk badly about Moby to the press. "I don't remember arguing with anyone," says Moby.

THREE DAYS LATER, on November 13, Moby and Marci Weber were returning from lunch near the warehouse in Marina Del Ray where See the Light was to take place—as part of a larger party called Circa '93. "We were walking toward the venue," says Weber. "Everybody was walking toward us—the whole crowd; it was sold out. Moby and I looked at each other: 'Shouldn't they be walking with us, not toward us? *Uh-oh.*'"

"We pulled into town, set up the entire stage, people started gathering outside—hundreds of people," says Mark Gage. But before the doors even opened, the fire department had shut the building down, leaving the kids stranded. "The venue turned out to be a warehouse that made prefab wood-bay windows," says Weber. "The dressing rooms were made of giant black bin bags. They'd taped them together, put them on a string and made curtains." In short, it was a firetrap: "One kid, smoking, could light up those trash bags—it's a disaster," says Weber. Gage recalls: "They literally called in riot police, who had to back the crowd up down the street so that the tour bus and the equipment buses could get out of the venue."

Circa's producers were Philip Blaine (of L.A. concert promoters Goldenvoice) and Tef Foo, who'd brought in Art Parent, a notorious L.A. rave promoter reviled by many, including Weber: "He seemed more interested in the financial gain," says Weber. "I didn't like working with him, or particularly care for his style. I was working with Tef Foo and Philip Blaine, but I didn't know they'd brought this guy on behind my back. He was monopolizing all the raves."

Pasquale Rotella recalls Circa as "another idiot bonehead move" on the part of the fast-dwindling L.A. scene. "They threw it in Marina Del Ray, the worst place you could ever throw it. It was a catastrophe. It was just the same old shit again. It was probably the nail in the coffin. It seemed like the people running the scene—you did have some cool people, for sure, but there was definitely more people just trying to make money."

SEE THE LIGHT came to an end in San Francisco at La Galleria. The scene there had been hit hard that March, when Malachy O'Brien, the most personally beloved promoter in town, was paralyzed following a Full Moon Rave. He'd been in the back of a van full of equipment when the vehicle's driver fell asleep at the wheel, went off the road near the Candlestick Park exit and into mud, and sent the equipment on top of O'Brien, breaking his neck. "I tried moving my hands, but it was like I was in thick oil, or underwater," he told journalist Amanda Nowinski. There had been a cathartic benefit party copromoted by Wicked, the Gathering, Full Moon, and Come-Unity, featuring a Zen monk and a shaman leading a healing ceremony, as well as Malachy himself, watching over an early Internet hookup and receiving messages and well-wishes in real time.

La Galleria was, by all accounts, the best show of the tour—even Moby's. ("It's as if even the DAT tape was inspired to sound better,"

Poe wrote.) Still, one San Franciscan remained unimpressed. "Moby seemed to be the one individual, this almost iconic person, to be noticed on a national or international level," says Gavin Hardkiss. "And musically, I wasn't that thrilled. It seemed to me like he didn't really embrace that opportunity. I remember going home and writing this shit down. Like, 'Whoa—he's the guy that everybody's jumping on? He's kind of a nerdy cynic.'"

A couple of months later, in early 1994, Poe ran into Moby at a small club. They started talking about music, and Poe's old boss told him he'd basically lost interest in the rave scene. "The music's gotten too esoteric," Moby said.

Richie Hawtin and Dan Bell are innovative musicians. So what if they don't wear Fresh Jive or baggy pants? Just cause they don't look like ravers doesn't mean they aren't cool people.

—SPECIMEN, "RE: THE DEATH OF STORM" (NE-RAVES POST, DECEMBER 14, 1992)

SPASTIK

Detroit, Michigan
August 13, 1994

CARL CRAIG WASN'T MUCH of a sports fan, but in late January of 1994 he found himself watching the Super Bowl. As Dallas trounced Buffalo 30–13, Craig fiddled with a bass line sampled from Loleatta Holloway's Salsoul classic "Hit and Run," which he'd chopped to the nub—one galloping, insistent bar, looped and ceaselessly drawing sparks. Craig kept playing hide-and-seek with the drums and bass line, layering thin strings between them to relieve the tension and organ chords to nudge things along. At one point he decided to sing, in a cracked falsetto: "I want to see your haaaaaaands in the air!"

"It was almost like I made it without thinking," he says. "By the time I even thought about it, it was something that was really working." The track was nearly fifteen minutes long; Craig assigned it to his alias Paperclip People—what he used for his "crazy loopy disco madness" tracks—and called it "Throw." Shortly after, Craig was playing a party (he no longer recalls where) and threw on the acetate. "The minute I put it on, the whole club went nuts—the *first* time. It was like, 'What the fuck?' That was like, you put a nickel [in the slot machine] and ten billion nickels come out." It didn't take long for "Throw" to become a staple for house and techno DJs alike.

Craig had become a DJ out of expediency. "I wasn't playing guitar in a band. I was making records with nobody else, so that's how you tour—you DJ." Growing up on Detroit's west side, his sharp wit and easy charm helped him navigate past the notorious violence of his alma mater, Cooley High. He'd gotten booted from Cass College after skipping classes in favor of video games. "I was probably training myself to become a DJ," he says. "The nineties was the time when gaming really got big; people started make millions of dollars skateboarding, BMX, dirt-biking. I'm part of a generation that made a fortune off of things that were considered child's play."

Craig initially recorded for Transmat, but quickly elected to make his own space. "The spirit of Detroit is that you take control of your destiny. The [United Auto Workers union] was so strong that you worked for Ford, but UAW was the boss. UAW could walk in and say, 'We don't like what you're doing. We're going on strike today.' That's some serious power. When I'd take music to Derrick and he didn't like it—and I liked it—I wasn't interested in making arguments about why he should put it out." In 1990 Craig and his colleague Damon Booker cofounded Retroactive Records; then, on his own, Craig started Planet E Communications, giving himself as much creative license as he could afford.

A 1992 release demonstrated just how far out he could get. "Bug in the Bass Bin"—off-kilter brushed drums and organ swells, an organ trio jamming on First Choice's "Let No Man Put Asunder," synth-strings tracing its lines—wasn't precisely house or techno; no one was sure just *what* it was at first, including Craig: "I was working on something else, and came up with the bass line. I was like, 'It's not really working for the track, but it's working.'"

Craig put "Bass Bin" on a twelve-inch that accompanied Planet E's compilation CD, *Intergalactic Beats*, but not the comp itself. When

London DJs Fabio and Grooverider got their hands on it, they'd play it at 45 RPM rather than 33 and slot it between the UK hardcore they were massaging into jungle at Rage. The track's skittering beats also presaged another UK club sound, "broken beat," heavily steeped in seventies jazz, that bubbled around 2000. Like much of Craig's music, "Bass Bin" didn't initially fit in—and then, suddenly, it did.

BERLIN HAD BECOME a techno mecca following the Berlin Wall's collapse. Vanessa Daou recalls a German friend telling her how New York DJ Bobby Konders's "The Poem" (1990)—which sampled Jamaican vocalist Mutabaruka's a cappella spoken-word track "Dis Poem" (1986)—became a Berlin anthem almost in spite of the vocals: "What people were taking from 'The Poem' was the bass. A lot of people [heard] that track as an expression of this freedom that was new to so many people—purely musically."

"Techno never developed into anything much in terms of a business anywhere until Germany started to take it in," says Milwaukee techno musician Mark Verbos. "Berlin became a home of all the Detroit techno guys for business, rather than Detroit, where they were all making records but not selling them."

Tresor, the record-label adjunct to the Berlin club, had established itself with a slew of Underground Resistance–related titles. By the mid-nineties it was issuing records by much of Detroit's technocracy: DJ T-1000, Blake Baxter, Eddie "Flashin'" Fowlkes—not to mention the godfather, Juan Atkins. He'd come to the label after befriending Berlin producers Thomas Fehlmann (originally from Switzerland), Mark Ernestus, and Moritz von Oswald, who'd traveled to Detroit.

"They would go to all these pawnshops, buying up old analog gear," says Atkins, who mentioned to Fehlmann that he had seen England but not the rest of Europe. "Thomas said, 'Why don't you come over and we'll get Tresor to book you for a night, and do a record deal to offset some of the expenses?'" Atkins recorded with Fehlmann and von Oswald as 3MB (Three Men in Berlin), and on his own as Infiniti, though he saved the latter alias's "Game One" (1994), coproduced by Amsterdam's Orlando Voorn—one of Detroit techno's loosest, most playful recordings—for his own label, Metroplex.

Another Berlin label, Hard Wax, spun off from a record shop, issued Robert Hood's recordings as the Vision. With Underground Resistance broken up, Hood had been cautious about reemerging on his own. "I didn't want to be left without any idea of who I am musically," he says. "You don't want it to be, 'A Tribe Called Quest broke up and I'm Phife Dawg.' I just couldn't see myself going out like that." He resisted leaving Detroit, despite Mills's urging. "I didn't want to depend on standing in the shadows of Jeff Mills in order to make it. I had to stand on my own."

Any doubts about Hood's ability to do so were ground to dust in 1994—with Mills pushing in the background. "We had this phase where we'd have weekends [of] making tracks. We were constantly calling each other, Friday through Sunday: 'Listen to this.' It became almost competitive. I later realized he was still training me to develop my own sound." That sound was stripped down, polished, and rubbery, its timbres undulating in and out of focus. "That's your signature sound," Mills told Hood: "It's a Detroit sound. It's a cross between house and techno—neither one of them, but all of them at the same time."

The title of the first of Hood's two major 1994 releases was also the result of a telephone call with his old mentor. "We were having a conversation about how rave was shifting into minimal," says Hood. "Between myself and Dan Bell and Robert Armani, this new sound was developing. It was a departure from the rave scene, from Digital Boy and Speedy J and Joey Beltram." Rather than swarming "Mentasm"-style riffs, these new tracks—Bell's "Losing Control" (as DBX, 1994) and the Hardfloor remix of Armani's "Circus Bells" (1993), as well as

Hood's—utilized a handful of sounds and were hypnotically repetitive, with tiny shifts in tone, timbre, and rhythm making floors erupt. "I told Jeff, 'The minimal nation is rising.' He said, 'That's it! That's what it should be called.'"

Minimal Nation (1994) was the first album—or double-twelve-inch, take your pick—on Hood's own M-Plant Records. These tracks weren't *trax*, in the old Chicago sense—they were skeletal and raw, but carefully worked over. The follow-up, *Internal Empire* (1994), on Tresor, expanded *Minimal Nation*'s palette and knotted it up: the central one-bar keyboard line of "The Core" distorts shape every time around. "I wanted to do something just to show I'm not just this stripped-down rhythm-track dude," says Hood. "I wanted to show there's an experimental side, a melodic side. I'm a forward-thinking dude, and I want to move forward."

So did his old partner, albeit in far different fashion. The B-side of Mills's *Cycle 30* EP (1994) consisted of seven locked grooves—endless loops you had to drop and remove the needle on manually. Hood accompanied Mills, once again, to visit Ron Murphy at National Sound Studios. "I remember Jeff first asking him, 'Can we lock the grooves? What BPM does this need to be?' Ron did the calculations: 140-something. It was like scientists comparing notes."

RICHIE HAWTIN WASN'T the only person around Detroit soured on the idea of "raves." So was Marke Bieschke, born in Southfield and raised in Detroit. A clubber from age fourteen—the Liedernacht, Boogie's, Todd's, Heaven, the Music Institute—who'd worked the door at Industry, Bieschke had caught the Summer of Love in London and, in late 1991, read Legs McNeil's feature on Double Hit Mickey in *Details*. Compared to Derrick May's black-box-and-a-strobe, all those bouncy castles looked like some *bullshit*. "We were like, 'Hell no,'" he says.

Bieschke and his friends decided to take action "before this tacky-

white-people thing happens. We wanted to start something underground first, so we could make sure it preserved the quality and intel-
lectualism and fine love of detail and community that we thought was
unique to Detroit. We didn't want some outside promoter, or some
kid from the suburbs, to start all this candy-raver, liquid bullshit. Plus,
we had access to these great buildings that no one was using. We could
be as intellectual as we wanted—and also as druggy as we wanted."

The group called itself Voom, and had a large, amorphous membership that included, at various times, Bieschke, Alan Bogl, Mare
Costello, Sam Fotias, Brian Gillespie, Meredith Ledger, Dean Major,
Steven Reaume, and Jon Santos. Reaume designed the flyers; the early
parties were small: "Like loft parties in New York," says Gillespie.
The group squatted together in an abandoned building Major says was
"bought from the city for a dollar" by a benefactor who intended to
turn it into a coffeehouse.

Voom's first party, Klonk, took place July 25, 1992, and featured
Alan Oldham headlining. "We filled 1515 Broadway with white Sty-
rofoam peanuts, waist-high, and turned on the black lights," says
Bieschke. "It was packed. There was a line half an hour before we
opened our doors. We tried to keep it as quiet and underground as
possible, but people got excited." Clark Warner, then a graphic designer and DJ, calls the Voom scene "creative and edgy—younger skaters, people into hip-hop, people into design, gay, straight, black, and
white. It was really a mixed, liberal crowd."

Gillespie stresses that Voom parties weren't called "raves"; Warner calls them "straight-up raves." Bieschke leans toward the latter,
though he resisted the term for years. "There's definitely a stigma
against the word," says Bieschke. "There was also a tricky racial divide: Raves were this thing for white people. I felt like we constantly
had to be proving our Detroit authenticity because suddenly there
were all these white suburban kids who wanted to come in."

In October 1992, the Brooklyn zine *Under One Sky* ran an irate letter from a Detroiter about a feature on UK hardcore label Suburban Base. "This ain't *Schoolhouse Rock!*" fumed the letter: "Suburban Base could never produce *real* techno music—hardcore or otherwise—because it takes *heart* along with the *art.* . . . Suburban Base, in the name of true techno—go back to the drawing board—oh! Excuse me, the blackboard." Emphasis, clearly, on "black."

Accordingly, the parties' reverse-white-flight was received badly by many of downtown's everyday citizens. "It really used to piss me off," says Carl Craig. "These raves were being thrown in serious hoods. You and your family won't live in Detroit—why are you coming to party in Detroit? I saw it as slumming. And I didn't take drugs, so I didn't realize that maybe people were looking at me weird because they were completely off their faces. I took it as an insult: 'What the fuck are you looking at me like that for?'"

Things came to a head at Voom's November 21, 1992 party, Cindy's Cat, held in the basement of the Bankle Building. One of the party's DJs, Paris the Black Fu (Mack Goudy) wore a blond wig and a T-shirt that said NIGGER. "It was an art project for him," says Bieschke. "Part of it was a comment on a white crowd watching a black DJ, even though our crowds were very mixed. It had resonance. But that was also the party Underground Resistance happened to check out."

It didn't help that Goudy's best friend at the time, the white Gillespie, made his own shirt that said HONKY—and as Gillespie recalls it, the shirts' wearers were reversed. ("The fact that it's a word don't make it racial," he insists.) The party's security staff stopped them: "You need to take those shirts off *right now.*" Shortly afterward, Mike Banks called Bieschke at home. "Honestly, it helped inform my worldview a lot," says Bieschke. "Basically, they were concerned: 'They come in and see this and it's their worst fears confirmed.' The Black Muslims were getting upset. I talked out of my ass and spent a lot of time listening. I think we reached an agreement that we were doing this for the right reasons. But it was a little scary."

· · · ·

RICHIE HAWTIN UNDERSTOOD. In 1991, his label Plus 8 issued its first compilation CD, *From Our Minds to Yours, Vol. 1*, its booklet proclaiming: "The future sound of Detroit." This raised eyebrows, and ire, among some of the city's African American producers, already unhappy with the way European producers were messing with the music and leery of an out-of-towner (minutes away, but still), much less a *white* out-of-towner (one who'd championed the music from the beginning, but still), claiming their provenance. "We had a lot of backlash," says Plus 8 cofounder John Acquaviva. "We took it hard, because Rich and I cared about the community." (They quickly abandoned the slogan.)

Hawtin was born on June 4, 1970, in Banbury, Oxfordshire, England, two years before his brother, Matthew. The family moved to Windsor, Ontario, in 1979, so their father could work as a General Motors robotics engineer. "My dad always had a high-end hi-fi," says Matthew. "There was always music playing; it was hard to get away from." Richie and Matthew became attached to techno and acid house over the radio in the late eighties. In addition to messing with synths and drum machines as a teenager, Richie ran a *Star Trek* BBS called Starfleet Command, through which he met Karl Kowalski, another aspiring DJ who was going to the same all-ages clubs, like Windsor's Masonic Temple.

Richie and Matthew ventured frequently into Detroit—their parents weren't afraid to take them there as kids, unlike many suburbanites—to hit clubs like the Shelter, on the bottom floor of the three-story St. Andrews Hall, for their Friday-night teen dances. One Shelter resident, Scott Gordon, eventually took Richie under his wing, showing him tricks and letting him spin warm-up sets. Spinning as Richie Rich (a blond kid with money—*touché*), Hawtin began attracting a steady base of fans, including an aspiring Detroit DJ-producer named Kenny Larkin, who became a close friend, bonding over Derrick May mixtapes.

Like Craig, Hawtin's magnetic personality impressed even his heroes. "I met him at the radio station in his university in Windsor by sheer accident," says Derrick May. "I went to do an interview and this blond kid walked up to me with big glasses on and said, 'Hello, Mr. May. My name is Richie. I'm gonna make music one day.' I remember how he looked me in the eye. My meeting with him was three to four minutes long. He didn't give me a cassette. I didn't meet him again until he became somebody. But he was so impressionable that I just couldn't forget."

Another older DJ was equally impressed. Born Giovanni Acquaviva in Italy in 1963, John Acquaviva immigrated to Canada as a child and began to DJ in 1980. Within two years he was spinning "full-time, six days a week" at a large London disco, mixing in Detroit techno as it emerged. He also worked at an Ontario record chain, Dr. Disc, where he met Kowalski, who brought him to the Shelter in 1989. "I liked Richie's energy," says Acquaviva, who had recently purchased a sixteen-track MIDI studio. "We hit it off right away. When I went to Detroit, I was going to see who I could work with. Richie and Kenny Larkin [were] the first guys I really hit it off with."

Though Acquaviva had studied guitar, the records he and Hawtin began making together required him to "throw my classical training out the window." Using an early Akai S-900 sampler, with a scant two seconds' memory/playback time, they recorded eight pieces and put them on *Elements of Tone*, credited to States of Mind, on their new label, which they dubbed Plus 8 as a joke—both DJs liked to pitch records as fast as they'd go. Already intensely media aware, Hawtin boasted to Alan Oldham that the EP was "number one on Evil Eddie Richards's chart, number nineteen in *Jocks*, number one in *Brand X*'s Motor City Top 10, and we got good reviews in *Record Mirror*."

Dan Bell, another Shelter regular, gave Plus 8 his demo, which led his collaborating with John and Richie as Cybersonik. "Technarchy"'s popularity led to European dates. When journalist Dan Sicko asked how many of the kids at those shows were on drugs, Bell snapped: "Come on, Dan—it's like ninety percent!" But following Rave New

World—Bell didn't go since there was only room for two—and a meeting with CBS Records that made both Hawtin and Bell queasy, Cybersonik quietly disbanded.

Hawtin was also worn down from Cybersonik's teeth-gritting intensity—and techno's generally. He liked what the Voom guys were doing, playing several of their parties. On April 18, 1993, shortly after Rave New World ended, he went home after Skylab 5, at the Bankle Building, headlined by Derrick May, and messed around on his 909, 808, and 707 drum machines, jamming for some twenty-three minutes before pressing stop on the recorder. A nine-minute edit of the session became "Spastik"—slower and more deliberate than Cybersonik, but no less intense.

After going through a few aliases—Circuit Breaker, F.U.S.E., Robotman—Hawtin seemed to settle on the moniker for this track, and for big projects going forward: Plastikman, whom he made flesh with a rubbery illustration by California skateboard designer Ron Cameron.* The Plastikman logo became an icon in ways both myth and business related—an early example of electronic dance musicians moving from techno's early radical anonymity toward nascent image management. "This was before the word 'brand' was ever used," says Jason Huvaere, who began promoting in Detroit in the fall of 1993. "None of us had marketing training."

VOOM'S SIZE AND UNSTRUCTURED configuration made it ripe for "spinoffs and fractions," as Gillespie puts it. The same was true of Detroit's other party crews. "Three guys would work together and we'd call ourselves Big Three," says Huvaere. "Then we'd bring this guy in and move this guy out, and it was called Bent Fabric. Those two guys over there were called the Lollipop Kids." Dean Major, who promoted

....
*Hawtin was initially unaware Cameron had drawn it—a third party who'd scanned the image sold it to him. When Cameron got in touch, Hawtin happily squared things with him.

as System, says that at the Detroit scene's height, there were upward of ten active promoter teams at a time.

Whether you got in trouble with the law or not depended. "Cops weren't really a problem until 1995," says Huvaere. "In fact, some of the events we worked on, the cops would keep an eye out for us, to keep the transients and troublemakers away." But Major says the fuzz regularly rooted out his System parties: "We would build up [to] four hundred people over a year, and then the police would start raids and that would knock it back down to two hundred."

None of these promoters had much in the way of budget—a typical Voom party, says Bieschke, cost "fifty to a hundred dollars—it wasn't really a moneymaking proposition." (Packing peanuts, for example, were cheap décor.) But Hawtin had "a single-event budget that probably surpassed all the money that passed through my hands through some forty or so events," says Ed Luna, cofounder of Columbus, Ohio, party crew Ele_mental, which consistently featured top Detroit talent. "Compared to the skin-and-bones productions in Detroit at the time, it was a big difference," says Kowalski.

That was particularly true of the audio systems. "Rich was one of the few guys that we knew that could pay for top sound," says Gillespie; in the Midwest, only Woody McBride's Minneapolis-based Wall of Bass setup compared. "We had a sound system that was specifically used every time, and we didn't deviate from that for a long time," says Matthew. "It was the one that had the most power. It wasn't the cleanest sound, but it was the most real."

No one handed out candy or glow sticks at a Plus 8 party. "We never thought of them as raves," says Matthew. Nevertheless, they featured the same drugs; at one point, Richie began marking them out in MW-Raves posts as "'A'rts & 'E'ntertainment." "Acid was the main one at the time," says Matthew. "Ecstasy didn't really hit Detroit until 1994. With acid, obviously, the environment is very intense for the music and it makes you focus. I think with ecstasy you become a little unfocused—you tend to wander a bit. Maybe the music isn't important, but the environment is."

One reason System's parties did so well, Major freely admits, is that he kept them stocked with favors. "I had seen great lineups at parties—and there would be no drugs, so the party would be over by two in the morning. That's frustrating as a promoter—a headlining DJ in an empty room. You still broke even, but it reflects badly on the city. I decided that would never happen to me, and that's how I got into selling ecstasy."

It's how a lot of promoters and DJs got into selling ecstasy. One of the era's open questions is just how many. Some of the people interviewed for this book discussed it forthrightly (like Major); others did so off the record. Many pointed to parties' moneymen as dealers looking for a large, controlled sales floor; others went with the reliable chestnut that "the lighting guys always had it." Like the scene itself, this differed from city to city, state to state, scene to scene. It was (is) not uncommon for promoters to be friendly with suppliers who can help create the right vibe—such as Drop Bass Network providing *mandatory hits of acid* at the door (only Brad Owen abstained) for a private all-night Mixmaster Morris performance in a Milwaukee warehouse in late 1995.

One of the places Major sold his wares was at Hawtin's events: "I was pretty much in charge of supplying the drugs to Rich's parties," he says with a laugh.

HAWTIN ANNOUNCED HIMSELF as an event promoter with a trilogy of 1993 parties: Hard (Bankle Building, April 10); Harder (Capital Street Warehouse, June 19); and Hardest (Roma Hall, October 16), all put on in collaboration with Voom. Or nearly all: Harder got busted before it began. "We took it in stride: 'You're going to shut us down here? We'll just go somewhere else,'" says Kowalski; the party relocated to "a big studio outside of Derrick May's place."

Rather than six to twelve DJs playing for an hour apiece, Hawtin booked a handful of DJs playing long sets, always with himself as headliner. Harder (before it was shut down) and Hardest were two-room affairs—a main dance floor and an ambient room, the latter helmed by Matthew Hawtin, renamed the Acid Guru for Hardest. "It was never my intention to DJ," says Matthew. "I can't say I was listening to Brian Eno when I was twelve or something. We always tried to have a contrast. We tried to make it as comfortable as possible, a place where people could just go and just hang out, talk, listen, freak out—in good ways. We had some live goldfish in that room, which someone tried to eat throughout the night."

Hardest was the release party for *Sheet One*, the first Plastikman album. (Not Hawtin's first—he'd issued *Dimension Intrusion* as F.U.S.E. a year earlier.) Issued by Novamute—the pure-techno spin-off of England's Mute Records, which issued a series of Tresor compilations in the U.S.—*Sheet One* didn't contain "Spastik," which came out as a stand-alone twelve-inch. But it did contain a CD insert that was perforated to look like an LSD sheet, as well as tracks like "Plasticity" and "Glob," which utilized the 303 for a slow-winding menace.

The CD cover would earn Hawtin further notoriety the following summer. On July 27, 1994, a young man in Rockwell, Texas, near Dallas, was pulled over for speeding; searching the car, the policeman found a copy of *Sheet One* and arrested the driver for possession of a controlled substance. The insert looked like blotter acid; therefore it must *be* blotter acid. The young man faced two to twenty years and a ten-thousand-dollar fine; he was released after five days in jail on a fifty-five-hundred-dollar bond. Novamute sent his parents a sealed copy of the album to use as proof in court. Hawtin was amazed: "I've heard of people pretending the blotter was real and selling it, and I know people who made it real, so I guess it's ironic that he got picked up and it wasn't." It was gossip fodder that managed not to invade Hawtin's personal life. Even when he wasn't trying, Richie's brand management was impeccable—especially when the charges were dropped.

THE *SHEET ONE* ARREST was made right ahead of Hawtin's biggest party yet: Spastik, on August 13, 1994, at the Packard Plant, a crumbling, sprawling, five-story former auto factory. It's long since been condemned: "There's no reason to go back there," says Gillespie. "There's so much security now, it's a danger zone." But the unguarded Packard was one of nineties Detroit's go-to spots for everybody from suburban upstarts to Kevin Saunderson, who threw one of his 1992 KMS parties there—in part because the building was so big that you could throw multiple parties there without utilizing the same space twice.

Wherever they were, Plus 8 parties took you into a full-scale, senses-heightening environment, accomplished simply as possible: Richie wrapped the rooms, floor to ceiling, in black plastic. "Controlling the ceiling was always a big thing for Rich," says Warner. "Both me and Matthew spent many times crawling around warehouse rafters. [We'd] turn to Genie lifts to make our parties happen." Richie hung plastic along with everyone else. (Acquaviva didn't: "I was managing the label, so I wasn't going to manage the parties.") All that stood between the dancer and the sound was others' bodies, plus whatever the dancer might put into hers.

The older Detroit crowd gleaned this strategy's lineage in the Music Institute. "I saw it as a way of going back underground," says Saunderson. "Back in the day, the walls were painted black, you had strobe lights—but that was mainly urban kids. You went from that to rave, which was really bright and colorful, then back to the underground, but in a different way: You'd get this building and make it look unique." In Spastik's case, the long black-plastic tunnels leading to the dance and ambient rooms weren't just for decoration, but for safety—take the wrong turn and you could fall to your death down an abandoned elevator shaft.

At Spastik, the winding, twisting journey from front door to main dance area took a good ten minutes; only an occasional pin-spot lit the way. The black plastic walls were both sci-fi creepy and a controlled environment for an oncoming chemical rush (no surprise). One didn't enter a room so much as become deposited into one. Team Hawtin had spent a week preparing. "We went all out with that one," says Matthew. "We blacked out everything; there was no fire escapes or exit lights." None of it would have passed fire code. "It would have taken a flame somewhere to cause this stuff to go up in smoke. I can't even imagine how much we used. We certainly weren't the most environmentally friendly, because all that stuff just got thrown away. We think back and cringe."

Others look back and smile. "There was really good E there," says DJ Terry Mullan, who'd befriended Hawtin at a party in St. Louis and become tight with the Plus 8 crew. "People were in control. There was nobody really freaking out." But even the perfectly sober might have felt like they were melting. Earlier that evening, it had rained heavily, with several sections of I-94 flooding and backing up traffic; one MW-Raver complained that the cavernous space was like "danc[ing] in a godawful hot plastic bag."

Upstairs was a different story. Like Hawtin's previous party, Heaven and Hell (February 5, 1994), at 1315 Broadway—the original Music Institute—Spastik's chill room was covered entirely in six inches of white foam. A pair of oil-wheel projectors decorated the walls with shifting color patterns. "We were using layers of camouflage netting, which you could get in white—you can project onto it," says Matthew. It wasn't all you could do: "I'm sure there were a few children conceived in the chill-out room," a MW-Raver posted.

Downstairs, speakers were placed in clusters dotting the room, rather than against one or two walls. There was a small concession area with a smart bar, a table selling large water bottles for a dollar (an affront to several MW-Ravers, who felt fountain water should have been provided with admission), another with T-shirts. In the corner sat an industrial fan.

JETSTREAM, KARL KOWALSKI'S DJ alias, began playing when the doors opened at midnight. At the beginning of 1994 Kowalski had gotten a job as the pit boss of a newly opened casino in Windsor. He took the night off to spin at Spastik; within two years, he was out of the scene entirely. He counts the party as his favorite ever: "I played as well as I had played up to that point," he says. At about one thirty, Chicagoan Terry Mullan took over. At one point, he played a track by a rising producer named Daniel Wang, who issued disco-flavored tracks on his own label, Balihu, prompting Wang himself to come to the booth and say hello.

Around three forty-five, the Hawtin brothers wrangled a table full of gear for the first-ever Plastikman live show. "They weren't trying to do anything the way it is now, where the light show is the star and you're in a frickin' cage in the middle," says Kowalski. "All that mattered was that it sounded good." Their concession to stagecraft was a video projection of the rubber guy dancing around, put together by the local company Sigma Six. "They would be considered very crude animations now," says Matthew.

The set went over big, and not just with Richie's regional base. In addition to the usual Midwest road-trippers, "There were a lot of UK journalists over for it," says Matthew; reps from Novamute also flew in. Mullan was impressed by the many English accents backstage: "I realized then, 'Wow, Richie's going to be huge.'" A young local named Eric Haupt followed Plastikman. "He was incredible," recalls Kowalski; MW-Raves agreed, naming him the top up-and-coming DJ of 1995 and second-best Detroit DJ (after Claude Young). Naturally, Plastikman won favorite Midwest live act.

Mullan followed Haupt, but around five thirty, the party stopped—someone in the main room had opened a can of pepper spray. "They had to clear the venue to settle everything down," says Kowalski. As the

tear gas spread through the main dance floor, several hundred cough-
ing, gagging kids straggled either outside or into the chill-out room.
The industrial fans blew the smoke out of the building. Within an hour,
the room was clear enough to reenter. Richie thanked everyone who
stuck around—about half the crowd, still—and his crew handed out
free bottles of water to partygoers for their troubles. "Almost because
of the disturbance, it seemed like the energy was better after," says
Kowalski. "Everybody was like, 'Man, I don't know who the hell tried
to fuck up our party, but they failed, so let's *give it*.'"

Hawtin got back on the decks and stayed all morning. "I thought
Richard played the best set of music that he's played before or since,"
says Kowalski. "His absolute peak as a DJ was that night." A MW-
Raver agreed: "The vibe was so thick you could taste it—at several
points he [Richie] would just let a song end and people would scream
and *clap*. It was amazing. In fact, people were screaming most of the
night." The loading bay door that had been opened after the pepper
gas came out was shuttered as the sun rose.

Hawtin leaned over to a confederate and asked: "Think they're ready
for some 'Spastik'?" He began working double copies on the decks. ("He
played 'Spastik' at every party," says Ectomorph's Erika Sherman with
a laugh. "You probably couldn't go to a party without hearing 'Spastik' for three years—multiple times.") By 9 A.M., a few hundred people
were still dancing; by eleven, the number had dwindled to seventy-five.
The man who'd put the whole thing together was giddy, but even his
staunchest confederates were wiped out. "At the end of the night I was
like, 'Dude, I can't even stay awake anymore. We need to stop this
party,'" says Kowalski. "He's like, 'Fuck that, man. This is a great party!
I'm not stopping.' I think I went out to the car and slept after a while—
which to this day I regret, because it was so good."

TWO DAYS PRIOR TO a New York show called Voyager 2 (April 22, 1995),
Richie and Matthew packed up their gear and headed for the Detroit

airport. "It was just us two—we were the only people coming from Canada," says Matthew. Nothing was unusual—people crossed over from Windsor to Detroit all the time. "There was no security at the border," says Major of those days. "I was the king of losing my ID and crossing the border and never getting stopped." But the day before, on April 19, Timothy McVeigh had masterminded the bombing of a federal building in Oklahoma City, killing 186. "The border was a little more on high alert," says Matthew, who was stopped.

Typically, the Hawtins would say they were visiting a friend, not making a hefty chunk of their living and bringing the proceeds back over the border—working in the States without prior disclosure, punishable by permanent barring from the country. "They pulled us over and separated us and asked us many questions," says Matthew. "They actually went through our car and they found a piece of paper with some of our dates on it. We weren't legal to work in the States. That was our downfall."

Neither was arrested; they were simply sent back home. "I got off lucky," says Matthew, "because my name wasn't on the papers they found." But Richie's was. "They found my brother working without a visa—and he lied to U.S. customs. Rich was given these papers [saying] that he wasn't allowed back in, and that he had to do these things to gain admittance again." It would be a year and a half before Richie was allowed back into the United States. "He had to hire a good lawyer. You just don't lie to the customs people, because if you get caught, you get screwed."

Matthew could travel, so he went ahead to New York the next day. Voyager 2 was the second part of a two-day party (the first was Voyager 1.5) that featured an entire Detroit-themed "Fuk" room. Though the venue had a sign stating a capacity of 1,580, an MW-Raves post guessed the crowd as closer to thirty-five hundred. Irony of ironies, they were treated to a DAT recording of an earlier Plastikman performance.

We were then turned on to none other than Daft Punk. You know, the last song on Mullan's *New School Fusion 2* tape . . . "Meow, meow meow meow meow, meow meow meow meow, meow meow meow meow, meow meow, meow . . ."

—BRENDA BEAN, EVEN FURTHUR '96 REVIEW
(*bEAN* #6, SUMMER 1996)

EVEN FURTHUR '96

Blue River, Wisconsin
May 24–27, 1996

DESPITE THE MILWAUKEE POLICE department's intentions, the Grave bust galvanized the upper Midwest rave scene. "It weeded out the on-lookers," Michael Vance said. "You had to really want to be a part of it." The bust also left Drop Bass Network—the team of Kurt Eckes and his roommate Patrick Spencer—at the top of the Milwaukee rave heap, though for years their parties took place everywhere in the region except Milwaukee proper. Eckes's trip to Staten Island with Tommie Sunshine determined its course. "I can't wait to bring this back to the Midwest. This is the new way," Eckes told Sunshine. Tommie recoiled: "Oh God—please don't."

The next year's worth of parties were *full on*. "Really, the Midwest scene was like the hardcore punk scene," says Chris Sattinger. "After the UK decided punk was over, the Americans made rootsier, more honest, and much louder and nastier punk. Hardcore techno, especially in the Midwest, was *really* hard. Drop Bass parties were an endurance test." The most notorious Drop Bass event of 1993 was Mideon, on September 18—pronounced *median*. "It was in a barn with two sound systems in the middle facing opposite ways—one side was all hardcore, one side was all house," says Eckes, who cranked the hardcore side several magnitudes louder than the house side, drawing ire. "There was something to be said about people who were fans of that sort of thing," says Spencer, whose role within Drop Bass decreased with time. "Kurt looked at it more as a concept. I think the concept fed upon itself."

NEAR THE END OF 1993, Eckes read Ken Kesey's *The Electric Kool Aid Acid Test* for the first time. "At that point, we were over doing E and were taking acid instead," he says. "This book was all about these people doing this every day. I was like, 'Holy shit, we're thinking we're on ten, but we're only on five or six—these guys have it turned all the way up to eleven. We need to kick this into high gear. What is the next level?'"

"The next step is, obviously, you have to camp," David Prince told him over dinner at a Milwaukee restaurant. "You have to go for a whole weekend." Mystic Bill Torres had attempted this in rural Illinois; Prince had been one of exactly three people who'd shown up. "We were going back and forth," says Eckes. "Neither of us would have had the balls to do it, but we were telling Woody about it, and he was like, 'Let's do it.' We were like, 'Are you sure?'"

"We were pretty excited about the idea," says McBride, who was now producing hometown parties on his own as M.O.R.E. (Minneapolis Organization of Rave Enthusiasts). "Kurt really had a vision, and the mechanics of how to get things done. He had big balls; he was smart. He had an attorney. He knew how to deal with police and how to negotiate with business owners, and how to break the reality of what was going to happen to them in a gentle, professional way." As Prince puts it: "He had his shit together in a world where a lot of people had their shit falling apart."

THE FIRST EDITION of Furthur took place in rural Hixton, Wisconsin, from April 29 to May 1, 1994. It was the first serious attempt at a U.S. rave gathering-of-the-tribes. "People from all over the country made this pilgrimage," says McBride. Aphex Twin headlined—McBride signed him on for five hundred dollars plus airfare; Woody also brought in a trio of German DJs, Hoschi, Roland Casper, and Spectral Emotions, a.k.a. Thomas P. Heckmann. From San Francisco, Scott and Robbie Hardkiss, as well as their manager, Wade Randolph Hampton, now promoting events Chicago, San Francisco, and Los Angeles. From L.A., Barry Weaver; from Brooklyn, Frankie Bones, Adam X, and Micro; from Philly, Nigel Richards; from Pittsburgh, Deadly Buda and Dieselboy; from St. Louis, Terry Mullan and the outlandishly disco-outfitted Superstars of Love. Not to mention plenty of the usual I-94 suspects.

The first Furthur was magical, if freezing. "I don't think it stopped raining for three days," says Bones. "It got real muddy and unforgiving, as far as setting up and camping, moving speakers around. I remember digging speakers out of a foot of mud, and having to scrounge up wood to set speakers on," says McBride. Recalls Terry Mullan: "I was surprised at the scale of it. You'd come back to your tent and somebody would be sleeping in it you didn't know. It dawned on me: 'Wow—we have a *movement* here.'"

By Saturday night, the weather was getting to people. "I spent an embarrassing amount of time during the first Furthur curled up in a tent with my girlfriend just trying to stay warm," says Matt Bonde, editor of the Milwaukee rave zine *Massive*. "I'll say it right now: I missed Aphex Twin. It was just too damn cold." The music wasn't all he missed. "I remember going around, hyper-aware but definitely high, and said to Kurt, 'This party needs some nudity,'" says Prince. "He's like, 'Yeah, sure.' Then I climbed up on the speaker." Just then, McBride walked back in from a gas run: "I look up, and David Prince is raging in his birthday suit."

The cops shut it down after Aphex's set, but one partier was still raging. Tommie Sunshine, who'd arrived wearing an iron-on T saying BIG JUGS & HARD DRUGS, had approached the party as a last stand: "I was going to OD, or I was going to move out of the Midwest." He was already looking at moving to Atlanta, where his brother lived; why not take it all the way? "I can't imagine any human being doing more drugs than I did in those three days," he says. In a video made by another partier, Laura Schebler Rammelsberg, Sunshine talks calmly while wearing a giant pair of shades. "I'm on nineteen different drugs," he says. "You can see them fighting in real time."

THE PLANNING FOR EVEN FURTHUR (May 26–28, 1995) was a lot more ad hoc than the first. "Woody and I had a falling out over the record label at the time," says Eckes. He and Prince didn't start working on the festival until January, though, sensibly, they changed the dates to Memorial Day weekend. "I don't think they came out of the first one sure that it was ever going to happen again," says Prince, who himself wasn't certain he'd participate again. "But the reputation of the first went much farther than the number of people there. The legend spread through the rave scene for a year."

The space was a ski lodge in northern Wisconsin—"inasmuch as Wisconin has ski lodges," says Prince. "I mean, it looks like a toboggan hill." No snow—that was unusual for Wisconsin—but, says Mark Verbos, "There was a hill from the main area and a chairlift that went up." The weather, again, was far from idyllic. "It was really messy," says Prince. "Everyone was camping on these slopes, and it just poured." Frankie Bones made the mistake of bringing his girlfriend. "That wasn't a pleasant weekend," he says. "We wound up sleeping in a Winnebago. My girl was not happy."

Headlining were Kurt's heroes, Spiral Tribe, and most of the core Midwest regulars (Terry Mullan, DJ Apollo, Mark Verbos) reappeared, as did Bones. "I don't think the DJs being booked for raves had discerning agents that were able to weed out the semi-shady raves at that point," says Prince. "But Drop Bass had a great reputation. Kurt wouldn't book somebody before there was a space." Even Furthur did "roughly double" the business of the first one, says Prince, but its momentum didn't come near its predecessor. "We definitely came out of the second one going, 'Next year is going to kick ass.'"

IN 1989, A PARISIAN DJ named David Guetta began promoting a night at Paris's Rex Club called Unity. "The Rex was more of a rock club," says Guetta. "The night was a combination of American house music and hip-hop. It was called Unity because I was playing two types of music. At the time, no one was playing house music in France. It was super-small—in a gay club for three hundred people. If it was small in the U.S., imagine how small it was in France."

In 1993, Guetta became the artistic director of Le Queen— formerly Le Central. "It established itself as the number-one trendy gay club when it opened, early nineties," says Martin Solveig, the Parisian DJ-producer who began playing Le Queen in the mid-nineties. One of the DJ residents Guetta hired was Nick Nice, who'd moved back to Paris that January. "I got a tryout in April," says Nice. "It's funny, the fact that David Guetta is a pop star. No one of us could have predicted that at the time."

Having watched the rise of the Paris rave scene in the early nineties, Nice had returned to see the city stratifying the way it had in the States. "There would be people who'd go listen to house music in the clubs, and people going to listen to hardcore and trance in the raves," says Guetta. "I was part of the house music people, even though I actually played and organized some of the first raves in Paris. But very soon it started to sound not very musical. I didn't like it anymore, so I went back to the clubs." Other spots were popping up as well: Le Palace, for example, which attracted more of a straight crowd, was where Solveig got his start.

Paris's new taste for house, particularly Chicago house, put Nice at a distinct advantage—he'd drive east to visit Gramaphone Records, Chicago's twelve-inch mecca. "Some records never made it to France because they were at the mercy of Watts distribution," he says. "It's nothing like picking up some test pressings that only Gramaphone has. Green Velvet was something I was on before a lot of people: 'Preacherman' was a sensation. I got to DJ at the Queen during the week, which was more of a get-down party. All the French producers—people still making music today—would come out, because you didn't have tourists."

Among those producers was a Mutt-and-Jeff duo—one short and unsmiling, the other tall and goofy-looking—of well-off Parisian kids who'd met in eighth grade and started making up songs together. Guy-Manuel de Homem-Christo (short) and Thomas Bangalter (tall) were the sons, respectively, of advertising executives and a writer-producer of French disco hits. By high school, they had a band called Darlin', after the Beach Boys song. The *NME* called one of their recordings "daft punky thrash."

Thomas and Guy-Man hit the Paris raves as they began. Bangalter was particularly taken with house and techno music; he invested his eighteenth-birthday money in equipment. They quit university in order to pay explicit homage to the music coming out of the Windy City. "There are producers who are spending . . . too much time [on their tracks]," Bangalter told *Massive* in 1997. "There's kind of a spontaneous feel when you have a production in Chicago . . . but it's the shit, and they leave it like that and do the thing in five minutes."

"Thomas would hang out more," says Nice. "Guy would be at the office. He didn't seem like the social type. Thomas was more outgoing. He would come out to the Queen and you would see him dancing. They'd be working on tracks, getting ideas." One early recording of Bangalter's was a remix for fellow Parisian Manu Le Malin, for a twelve-inch on IST Records, the less frenetic sublabel of Lenny Dee's Industrial Strength. The remix was credited to "Draft Ponk": "Dave, the guy working for me, fucking misspelled it," says Dee. "I apologized profusely for it."

DAVID PRINCE MADE A LOT of new friends from Furthur, including the Rephlex crew. "I would go to England for two-, three-week chunks," he says; once, walking on the street, he ran into Richard James, who was wearing headphones and making beats on a drum machine. He and Adell had ended *Reactor* (and, briefly, their friendship), and Prince had become a full-time freelance writer (*Urb, Request, Option, Rolling Stone*). "My goal was, 'How do I get an assignment that they'll send me overseas, or to California?'"

Around Halloween of 1995, Prince visited Manchester. "There was a Warp Records party in the city. Richie Hawtin, as F.U.S.E., was the closing DJ." What stuck with Prince was Hawtin's final song—a track with an acid line that the British dance mag *Muzik* described as "the bastard son of Queen's 'Another One Bites the Dust' and Hardfloor's 'Acperience.'" This was "Da Funk," the first release—on the Glasgow label Soma—by Bangalter and de Homem-Christo's new alias, Daft Punk. No one in the room had heard it before. "He played it in its entirety, and it was like, 'Holy shit, what is that?'"

Prince and his friends next hit a party at the former Factory Records office, now a nightclub. "Downstairs was the Back to Basics party, which was Ralph Lawson and Derrick Carter," says Prince. In another room was Daft Punk, playing live. "They had all this crap on the table," says Prince. "I remember coming back like: 'We should get these guys for Furthur.'" But McBride—back in the fold again—beat him to the punch: The duo had opened for him earlier in 1995 at the Rex Club. Woody was already telling Eckes about "this badass acid group from France."

McBride made the overture to Bangalter and de Homem-Christo to play Even Furthur '96. "I think we paid them two flights, accommodations, $700 to $1,000, and a good time." McBride had done live

PAs for years and knew how difficult they were to pull off at Daft Punk's level. "Woody was really into a raw live setup where people were actually doing everything," says Eckes. "He was super-hip to the way they were making music."

Before "Da Funk," French producers occasionally hit with underground tracks—particularly techno DJ Laurent Garnier, who'd scored with "Acid Eiffel" (1993), as Choice, with coproducers Shazz and Ludovic Navarre. But "Da Funk" was a bombshell: not merely a French house record, but one that sounded and felt French, even as it was clearly indebted to Chicago. It was the emerging "French touch" DJ style—the club-based house approach of DJs like Solveig, Guetta, and Nice, full of disco loops going in and out of aural focus after being sent through whooshing low-pass filters—manifested on a recording.

"Da Funk" worked like a pop record, building and cresting and layering with verse-chorus logic far beyond the simple "filter-disco" of much mid-nineties house. "It was so *indie*—that was really a shock," says Solveig. "They were from a different scene from us. I didn't even know they were French at the time. They have definitely opened a lot up for a lot of French accents—all of them. Daft Punk got radio play." Nineteen ninety-five is "the year Daft Punk made it possible," he says, for him to have an international career. Just as important in the Midwest was the B-side, "Rollin' & Scratchin'," which Eckes calls "totally what Drop Bass was—driving, hard acid." Verbos agrees: "The acid and hard techno guys would play it all the time."

DURING HIS TIME IN L.A., David Prince had become friends with Timothy Leary. In the early nineties, Leary had found a new career as the Southern California rave scene's unofficial guru-in-chief. Their friendship deepened through the mid-nineties, and now the doctor had been diagnosed with prostate cancer. Leary took the news with aplomb, telling the press he was looking forward to the great beyond. Right after locking down the space for Even Furthur '96,

Prince moved back to California, to be with his friend. He stayed part-time in L.A. with promoter/DJ Wade Randolph Hampton and his girlfriend Stephanie Smiley, then a publicist for the Levy brothers' label Moonshine Music, and part-time in Leary's mansion.

IN CHICAGO, ALL-HOUSE RAVES caught on fast with kids who'd grown up listening to house on the radio. "The house DJs were the most popular DJs," says Dan Labovitch, a suburban Chicagoan who turned sixteen in 1995. "Boo Williams, Paul Johnson, Justin Long—those guys would headline a party all day long and draw people."

By the middle of the decade, ravers who'd cottoned onto the music's rootless futurism were beginning to revisit techno and house music's beginnings. Like rock music looking back to blues and country in the late sixties, returning to root styles like Chicago house and Detroit techno was proof that you weren't just at the party looking for the next hit of E. "We were hearing more and more: 'Chicago is where house was from,'" says electronic musician Kate Simko, a native Chicagoan who went to her first rave in 1995. "We realized [from] the magnitude of people that were playing [at events] how important Chicago was. We definitely had a sense that history was being made. I couldn't believe that this shit was going on, that we're going to a roller rink and it's full of fifteen hundred or two thousand kids and it's going until six in the morning."

As the parties grew, part of their allure was a general good-naturedness. "You've got to remember, Chicago to this day is the most segregated city in the country," says Labovitch. While rave attendees were largely white suburbanites, the parties were open to anyone. "The thing I loved about the rave scene was it was extremely diverse—black, white, Latino, Asian, whatever," says Curtis A. Jones. "By '95, that was pretty much the peak of the rave scene."

A subculture built on partying is bound to go overboard sometime, and that boiling point was the subject of Jones's greatest record,

"Flash" (1995), which he released as Green Velvet, a nickname from a girlfriend's dad. It became his alias for harder-hitting tracks that blurred the lines between house and techno on the Cajual sublabel Relief. "It was really raw," Jones says of "Flash." "It didn't have any structure to it. I did it live, totally improvising off the top of my head. I thought it had too many vocals for the techno heads and was too hard for the house heads. It turned out that both of them played it. When it was played in the raves, the kids just loved it."

They should have—it was about them. "Flash" takes place at "Club Bad," a party gleefully presented as a den of sin. Kids huff nitrous oxide from balloons as Jones chortles through menacing distortion, "Laughing gas—but this is no laughing matter." The crowning touch in the song's sick-joke structure is that Jones is narrating the entire thing to the kids' parents, who are presumably looking on, horrified.

Jones calls "Flash" "an accumulation of all the things that I was seeing and experiencing in the rave scene." In the beginning, he says, the scene was all about the music. But the pervasive drug use began to bother him. "You would see teenagers, young kids—some of them looked like they were twelve, thirteen—doing very serious stuff," he says. "As fifteen-year-olds, acid was easier to get than weed," says Labovitch of the mid-nineties. But the drugs grew harder at the same time that the crowds grew younger.

CHICAGO HOUSE'S KEY mid-nineties label was Dance Mania, established in 1985 by Jesse Saunders, but run from the beginning by Raymond Barney, owner of West Side distributor Barney's Records. It issued late-eighties classics by Farley "Jackmaster" Funk (House Master Boyz' "House Nation") and Marshall Jefferson (Hercules's "7 Ways to Jack"). By the mid-nineties, Saunders had moved to L.A., and around the time of "The Percolator," Barney began signing new South Side talent as well—notably, Paul Johnson and DJ Funk.

The wheelchair-bound Johnson (he'd accidentally been shot by a friend in 1987) created a sound both raw and versatile, like genre exercises by a good low-budget filmmaker—from an airy disco cutup like "Welcome to the Warehouse" to the dirty-mouthed, dirty-drums ghetto house of "Feel My M.F. Bass" (both 1994). His most famous record is 1999's "Get Get Down," with a piano part that amounts to a distillation of every piano riff from every house hit ever.

Born Charles Chambers, DJ Funk was raised by his grandmother, moving around Chicago neighborhoods, mainly on the West Side; he spent some of his adolescence in Detroit as well. Chambers began break dancing as a teenager, paying attention to the differences in the two cities' DJ styles. In Detroit, he noticed, DJs cut faster, but in Chicago they rocked the party better. He vowed to do the latter.

If much of house's original black Chicago audience switched allegiance to hip-hop in the nineties, Chambers did the opposite. He'd started as a rap producer, working with Do or Die, a Chicago hip-hop act whose "Po Pimp" went top twenty-five pop in 1996. When Do or Die signed to Rap-a-Lot/Virgin, Chambers felt unacknowledged. He decided to switch course. "I was a young adult in my twenties, thinking, 'Gangster music is cool now. This is where I come from. But I don't see it lasting long for me.' I played the curve." He initially made his own album, pressing five hundred copies and bringing them to Barney's for distribution. The owner made Chambers an offer: "We'll sell tons more if you do it on my label."

Chambers became Chicago house's Luther Campbell—a blunt-talking auteur (DJ Funk's song titles include "Pussy Ride," "Move That Mother Fucker," and "Bitches!!!!!") with beats fortified by trunk-rattling Roland 808 and 909 drum machines. "I like to make my music mostly for girls so they can get down," he says. "If the girls are getting down, the guys are getting down."

Chambers was a prime mover behind both ghetto house and booty house—and yes, they are different things. "In the ghetto house scene there was a separation of 'ghetto' and 'booty,'" says Mystic Bill Torres. "Ghetto was reminiscent to a lot of the eighties stuff—raw beats with little samples. [In] booty, they got a little nastier with it." Clarifies Chambers: "We took it to the booty style because that made girls dance more. It's more about, 'Bitch, get yo' ass on the floor,' 'Shake that ass, let me see what you've got,' 'Where them hos at?' It's more of *that* style than the regular ghetto style." In ghetto, he says, "You don't have to be talking about girls. You could just have music playing. It can sound more techno. It [gives] you a little bit more room."

Still, this was not exactly a music of fine gradations, and that was central to its appeal. "A lot of cats were running around with ghetto-house music booming out the trunk," says J. R. Gibson, a house DJ (under the alias Julius Romero) and late-nineties rave promoter from St. Paul, Minnesota, who frequently hosted Chicago DJs at his Twin Cities events. Gibson grew up in the sketchy Frogtown area. "I think about Chicago house from a gangster perspective—like New York hip-hop, Chicago house had attitude. Funk and those guys were just illustrating stuff out of what I grew up with in my neighborhood: black culture, maybe even borderline stereotypical, where everyone's running around saying 'Bitch' that, 'Fuck you,' 'I'll kick your ass.' They put a four-four beat behind it and just rocked it."

OVERSIZED T-SHIRTS AND JEANS had long been commonplace at raves, but the latter were optimized, for better or worse, in 1994, thanks to a Vancouverite named Noel Steen, who was traveling frequently to Seattle parties. One day at the Salvation Army he was looking for bell-bottoms. "Before rave really had its own costume, it borrowed from a bunch of other preexisting things, [like] disco. I came from a hip-hop background where they're baggy pants but they taper really around the ankle, so you've got this falling-off-the-back-of-your-ass thing. I didn't want that, but at the same time I wasn't ready to give up the looseness around the thigh."

Steen designed an alternative that quickly became called "phat pants." "The phat pants as I designed them ended up having a nice fitted bum—not so baggy or falling off—and then, from the thigh, wide straight legs that would ultimately, hopefully, cover your entire shoe." Steen teamed up with a small Vancouver western-wear factory called Laramy to manufacture them. Within weeks he'd dropped out of university "to continue designing these pants."

The design caught fire—not least because their design gave ravers plenty of places to stash their drugs. "I had a pocket full of pills at the time, so that, you know, brought in some revenue," says Steen. "You were either paying for it or you were selling it." But like the money he made dealing E, the phat-pants revenue dried up, with Laramy merely paying him by the hour: "I didn't do a very good job of negotiating my position."

ONE OF CHICAGO HOUSE'S prime disseminators was Terry Mullan—MW-Raves' favorite Midwest DJ of 1995.* Mullan was the region's mid-decade mixtape king—the rave-scene heir of Bad Boy Bill (William Renkosik), a onetime Hot Mix 5 member who issued dozens of tapes during the late eighties and early nineties. As another DJ says of Bill, "The RIAA would have sued him out of existence" if they'd been aware of how many tapes he'd sold. (A not-unreasonable estimate: one million.)

Mixtapes were the lifeblood of the scene, its ongoing soundtrack outside of the parties themselves—and many times the mixes were recorded at those parties. "Mixtapes were the only way people I knew listened to music once they got into rave," says Minneapolis drum and bass DJ Brandon Ivers, whose first party was in 1994. "When you jumped in somebody's car, you were going to listen to a mix-

....
* He was also named third-best Chicago DJ—less contradictory than it sounds, since in scene terms, "Midwest" merely meant region (and Mullan still had St. Louis ties), but "Chicago" connoted the Cajual/Relief/Dance Mania axis. Hence, Paul Johnson was named best Chicago DJ.

tape. You weren't going to listen to a CD." For popular DJs, mixtapes were a reliable source of income that, like the largely cash-in-hand world of party promoting, could elude the IRS. Some DJs, like L.A.'s Huggie, just handed them out to fans, as thank-you gesture and self-promotion. But for others they made a serious dent in the bottom line.

In the mid-nineties Mullan put out a flurry of tapes, full of sharp selections and mixing and—rare for a house DJ—effective hip-hop scratches. "I would spend a lot of time on it," he says. "I wanted it to be as perfect as possible. Each one I'd spend a week on." The most popular, by far, was spring 1995's *New School Fusion Vol. 2*, a sequel to a title from late 1993. *Vol. 1* had sold six thousand; *Vol. 2* sold some ten thousand—regional-mixtape platinum. (That's not counting all the dubbed copies and bootlegs.) "I could not have been more into music in my life," says Mullan. "I lived down the street from Gramaphone. I was in heaven."

He'd just finished *Vol. 2* when he made a return trip to Gramaphone. "I was about to send it off that day. Daft Punk's 'Rolling and Scratching' b/w 'Da Funk' had come out on [Glasgow label] Soma. Soma was almost a buy-on-sight label. I'd always loved acid. It had this gnarly, crazy bass sound. The tape was already done, so I just spliced it on at the very end: 'I have to put this on here. I don't care if it's not mixed.'"

"Everybody in the Midwest had become familiar with Daft Punk through *New School Fusion Vol. 2*," says Brad Owen, by then a *Massive* editor. "That was the biggest-shit mixtape of that year." Adds Matt Bonde, "I can't speak to the rest of the country, but he broke that song here. People called it 'that Terry Mullan song.'"

ECKES SECURED A CAMPGROUND called Eagle Cave, in southwest Wisconsin. "They have a cave there, and they do a lot of Boy Scout retreats, BMW, Vintage motorcycle campouts—nothing like what we did." It was deep in the woods—"in the middle of a cow field, literally," says Will Hermes, then arts editor of Minneapolis's *City Pages*.

"I remember driving there in a torrential downpour, fearing for my life the entire time," says Nice, who'd just moved back to Madison after three years in Paris. "It was pouring, pouring, pouring rain. It felt like *Night of the Living Dead*. It was already dark. Everybody was fucked up on God knows what. They were all swarming my car—coming close enough it was making me uncomfortable, but not enough to run them over." There were showers on site, but there was so much mud, few bothered using them. A lot of clothes were ruined; an MW-Raver posted that following Even Furthur '96, "I drove home covered in filth (head to toe), walked in [the] shower with everything on, and undressed there."

"This is the difference between the festivals now and the music back then," says Davey Dave. "The rave scene was built on music and people's camaraderie between each other. We took away the rockstar aspect of it. You were there strictly for the music. It was hard to put up a stage in mud—dangerous, too." Prince recalls "people being afraid to touch their microphones because they were standing in a pool of water. Any outdoor [systems] tried to block the wind out of the turntables and [were] taping quarters to the top of the tone arms."

"The site was really inconvenient," says Bonde. "A lot of my friends had to camp up on top of a hill. There was a valley, but you didn't want to be down in the valley because it was raining. There were people who'd wake up and there'd be a creek running through their tent. A number of friends injured themselves. One fell with his leg down a pipe and basically skinned the front of his leg. He was walking around with a flap of skin. My friend Ray was walking in the dark and got his scrotum attached to a barbed-wire fence and was rushed off to the hospital. In the end it saved his life because they figured out he had testicular cancer."

"No injuries that I know of," says Chris Sattinger, "but I do remember they were selling drugs out of the ambulance."

"CANDY-FLIPPING—remember that term?" says Minneapolitan Jana Sackmeister, referring to a simultaneous dose of LSD and MDMA. "They were doing Special K, huffing balloons. There'd be kids just standing there and holding a balloon, not being able to move. I remember walking up to someone: 'Are you okay?' They couldn't move: 'I'm stuck in the mud.' I can see!"

"The drug use was off the fucking hook," says Hermes. "Those of us who were a little older were moderate in our consumption. But there were young kids there. And frankly, I don't remember it being so much a musical experience. I remember it being kind of a war zone. People were fucking high. I mean, *really* high." Among the revelers were members of the Rainbow Family, a post-Deadhead tribe, selling acid. "It started to be that element, because Jerry Garcia had died," says Sackmeister. "They couldn't follow the Dead anymore, so they started going to raves."

"It was totally out of control," says Eckes of Even Furthur '96. "By then people had figured it out: 'I am going to be somewhere for three days. I am going to go freaking nuts.'" Sometimes literally—among the "fucked up shit that happened" bullet-pointed by the Chicago zine *bEAN*: "Guy wigged out next to us on some crazy Kentucky E"; "Guy wigged out in upper campsite, and busted some windows, and claimed he was God."

"We tried to go to sleep around five," says Hermes. "At six we heard this thumping and yelling—somebody going around the tents, yelling, 'Who's got speed? I need speed. Who's got acid?' Walking through the tent city at dawn yelling for drugs. It became clear we weren't going to get any sleep. I came out of the tent and saw this young guy who was clearly off his nut. People were trying to calm him down. At one point this guy jumped up on a car, denting the hood, deeply. Then he started jumping on the roof to the point where the windshield shattered. The top of the car crushed. Somebody grabbed him, pulled him off, pinned him down, and held him. [An] ambulance came. They took him away. It was like: 'We've had enough. We're going home now.'"

But for Furthur's regulars, this was part of the routine. "The fact that there were lots of people on drugs at the Furthur parties was not a negative aspect at all," says Sattinger. "There was a sense of total freedom. This was not a club or even a warehouse. *This was not civilization.*"

"HOUSE MUSIC IS DISCO'S REVENGE," Frankie Knuckles once said. That was the prevailing sentiment of mid-nineties house, from Paul Johnson's "Welcome to the Warehouse" to Paperclip People's "Throw" to "The Bomb! (These Sounds Fall into My Mind)" by the Bucketheads, an alias of Masters at Work's Kenny "Dope" Gonzalez. The omnipresent track at Even Furthur '96 was Gusto's "Disco's Revenge," featuring an irresistible eight-note riff that sounds like it's being exhaled by a video game monster, capped by a sleazy little guitar lick. "God, I heard that everywhere," says L.A.'s Huggie (Hector Merida), who spun a trance-heavy set late Friday night and partied for the next two days.

One DJ who mixed "Disco's Revenge" in was Boo Williams, one of two Cajual-affiliated DJs on the bill. The other, Glenn Underground, didn't show. "Glenn didn't want to play to a bunch of fucked-up white kids," says Prince—hardly an uncommon sentiment. "Being put in the second room, or playing the four A.M. slot, they felt they were second fiddle to these headliners who were playing a different kind of music—and they were," says Prince. "The true house DJs, a subset of them were antidrug and weren't into crossing over."

Yet many Chicagoans were in the tent on Saturday night. "There was definitely a contingent that came up from Chicago that was more of the Shelter club scene that wasn't really into the raving, definitely wasn't into the camping—but they were like, 'I gotta go see Daft Punk,'" says Prince. "They were a draw in our tiny little subset of the world, even back then." Adds Nice: "Everybody knew that was the show."

It took place in the main tent, at the bottom of the hill. "It was a green-and-yellow-striped circus-looking tent, maybe a hundred twenty by sixty [feet]," says Minneapolis drum and bass DJ Graham Ryan. There had been hard rain on Saturday afternoon, but it had stopped by evening; the grounds were a jungle. By 2 A.M., the floor was filling up. "It was one of those things where everybody's racing to the tent," says Nice.

Davey Dave was one of them: "Once I heard them play 'Da Funk' live, instantly I knew exactly who it was, and that's when I rushed the stage." "People were just going bananas," says Frankie Bones. An MW-raves poster noted: "The main tent was packed like a rock concert and people kept cheering at every song and buildup." Davey Dave adds: "There was no stage show. There was no huge LED lights or anything. It was a basic laser light show and a decent sound system. But I'd put that moment over any moment that happens at any festival, any day."

"You didn't have everybody focusing on the stage. In that tent, everything was level," says Nice. "Unless you were at the very front, you couldn't even see them. Watching the video on YouTube—that's more than I saw them that night." That footage—of the complete, half-hour show—has been online for years, with the duo's tacit approval. "Even now, people go on YouTube to get videos from that night—it was true energy," de Homem-Christo told *Stop Smiling* in 2007. "We were twenty-year-old kids, and I thought it was really one of the best festivals we'd done. . . . We have great memories of it."

But what you see on YouTube isn't from Paris. "The center frame through nearly the entire video—almost more important [visually] than Daft Punk—is Mark Verbos's older brother, Matt," says Bonde. "He did security for Kurt. If you get your hands on *Homework*, that's him, printed inside the album cover. On YouTube I've read comments like, 'Is that one of the guys?' It's funny how much they've obscured things by going into this masks thing." Even on-site, people mistook them: "DJ Slip was hitting on one of them because I guess dude looked like a lady," says Sattinger.

"What they were doing was so completely at a higher level than what anybody was doing with live gear, especially people who made music back then," says Nice." The way they put it together, made it flow—it was like a DJ set. It wasn't, 'Here's a song,' stop, 'Here's an-other song,' stop: The way that they segued it all together, in and of itself, was revolutionary." Adds Prince: "It was really dicey to set all that up in what was really bad weather. The whole thing about tour-ing back in those days—shit would get stolen or broken. That stuff's not meant to travel. Those machines were not made for live perfor-mance. There weren't flight cases built for them. People would come with their shit in suitcases, duffel bags."

"I remember when they performed we all had cups, because the rain was leaking," says Frankie Bones. "Everybody was holding cups to catch the rain." Prince kept his clothes on this time, but this felt even better. "When I saw Daft Punk at Even Furthur, I was pretty damn sure that this was going to be the biggest band in the world."

BONES WENT ON right after Daft Punk. He almost didn't play—a kid tripping on acid grabbed his records and ran. "I just knocked him down. The tent almost fell—he tripped over the knot holding the tent down. But it was back to normal once I got on the turntables." Bones started slow and built up to a gabber frenzy.

Starting at 6 A.M., Mixmaster Morris spun a five-hour ambient set. Later he played in the Freebass tent—one of the site's many DIY systems—spinning ambient jungle, the mixture of wafting bird calls, dolphin noises, and soaring gauzy female coos over drum and bass rhythms gone through an aural desalination. That April, the style's pioneer, LTJ Bukem, issued *Logical Progression*, a double-CD showcase of artists on his Good Looking label; it was heavily touched by fusion jazz—occasionally gorgeous (especially "Music," 1993), but an utter inversion of UK hardcore's giddy thrills. So were the increasingly straight beats that had followed the path of Alex Reece's "Pulp Fiction" (1995), which smoothed out the kinks in jungle's knotty groove just enough to cross over with house and techno fans.

If anything, Sunday night was even better musically than Saturday. Nick Nice kicked the evening off. "Even more so than Daft Punk, for me as a DJ it was like, 'Clearly this is what I want to do for the rest of my life. Nothing's ever going to be as good as this'—just start-to-finish, so much good energy," says Nice. Boo Williams followed, mixing Martin Luther King's "I Have a Dream" speech over jazzy disco-house.

Around 4 A.M., Scott Hardkiss went on. He'd been commissioned to remix Elton John's "Rocket Man," but the record never came out officially, so he had an exclusive. "People were really crying during the Elton John remix," says Nice. "Anybody who was there for that moment remembers it. It was the end of the weekend; you had this communal vibe with everybody that's gone through a torrential downpour. People knew something big had happened, but nobody could grasp just how big." When Hardkiss finished, McBride got on the microphone: "This is the set Scott wanted to do two years ago at the first Furthur. He had played one record when a screaming naked man came running in and said, 'They're shutting us down! We're all going to jail!'"

THAT NAKED MAN (who, to be fair, had dressed again within minutes at the first Further) was getting ready for the next phase. "I had a couple of disturbing encounters at Even Furthur," says Prince. "One was hanging out with these kids who were shooting up their ecstasy. I was like, 'Whoa, that's crazy.' And I remember Saturday night being twice offered heroin to buy. That made me really mad. I wasn't putting out all this effort and risk to create a zone where people could do smack. I was very uneasy about that. That seemed super dark to me."

The first night of Even Furthur, Prince had been in an altercation with a county fire commissioner, irate that they were shooting fireworks over a lake. "I was in his face: 'This is totally legal, I have my permit,' almost belly-to-belly with him—very fucked up on drugs, a lot of money in my pocket, and probably a lot of drugs, and just being fearless about it: 'We're not shutting this down.' Reflecting on that a month or two later, I felt that I might just be a little too reckless to put myself in this position. I was almost grandstanding. It was poor judgment."

The incident would haunt Prince in the wake of his mentor's death: Timothy Leary exhaled his last on May 31, four days after Even Furthur finished. Prince had gotten to tell him the party had been a roaring success.

The stars in this music don't look like rock stars.

—GAVIN HARDKISS, 1996

Frankie Knuckles, c. 1988.
(Al Pereira/Michael Ochs Archives/Getty Images)

D-Wynn in the mid-
nineties. *(Todd Sines)*

Tommy Musto and Frankie
Bones, April 1990.
(Steve Pyke/Getty Images)

A Full Moon Party near Highway 1.
(Jane Lerner)

Lenny Dee spinning in Dayton, Ohio, 1994. *(Todd Sines)*

Dieselboy. *(Todd Sines)*

Moby in Germany, 1993. *(Martyn Goodacre/Getty Images)*

Carl Craig in Ann Arbor, Michigan, 1994. *(Todd Sines)*

Some of Detroit's anti-"tacky-white-people brigade" chilling at the Packard Plant, 1994. Left to right: Steven Reaume, Mark Biesche, and Eric Lynch. *(Todd Sines)*

Brian Gillespie and Paris the Black Fu (Mack Goudy) in Detroit, mid-nineties. *(Todd Sines)*

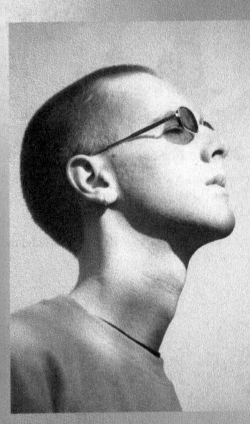

Richie Hawtin, 1994.
(Kevin Cummins/Getty Images)

The Packard Plant in the mid-nineties. *(Todd Sines)*

TECHNO
IS THE
DEVIL'S MUSIC!
<u>BEWARE</u>
the hypnotic voodoo rhythm,
a reckless dance down the Devil's road
of sin and self-destruction,
leading youth to eternal damnation
in the fiery depths of hell!

Pre-flyer for Even Further '96.
(Courtesy of David Prince)

Flyer for Even Further '96.
(Courtesy of David Prince)

Paul Johnson spinning at an Ele_mental party in Columbus, OH, 1995.
(Todd Sines)

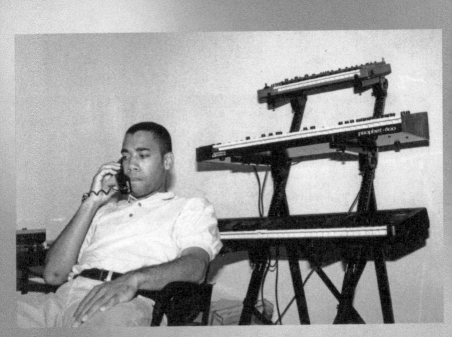

Carl Craig doing business, mid-nineties. *(Todd Sines)*

Detroit Grand Pu Bahs' Paris the Black Fu rocks the Motor Lounge stage in Hamtramck, Michigan, 2000. *(Todd Sines)*

Detroit Grand Pu Bahs at
Detroit Electronic Music
Festival, 2000. *(Todd Sines)*

Tommie Sunshine and Disco Donnie Estopinal at the premiere of *Rise*, the documentary about Estopinal's trouble with the law, at WMC 2002, Miami. *(Julie Drazen)*

Adam X playing The Bunker, New York, 2006. *(Seze Devres)*

Dave Turov playing
The Bunker, New
York, 2008.
(Seze Devres)

Steve Goodman (Kode9) playing
The Bunker, New York, 2011.
(Seze Devres)

Untold playing The Bunker, New York, 2010. *(Seze Devres)*

Steve Aoki at Hard Festival, Los Angeles, 2008. *(Jared Milgrim/Corbis)*

Random Access
Access
Memories

PLEASE JOIN DAFT PUNK FOR A NIGHT OF CELEBRATION.

SUNDAY, JANUARY 26, 2014, 10:00 PM

THE LEGENDARY PARK PLAZA HOTEL.
607 South Park View Street, Los Angeles, CA 90057

GUEST LIST ONLY - NON-TRANSFERABLE - PLUS ONE ADMITTED
RSVP REQUIRED TO RSVP@DAFTARTS.COM

The Random Access Memories after-party invitation.
(Courtesy of Tommie Sunshine)

>11

ORGANIC '96

GERRY GERRARD HAD figured concerts were easy. In late-seventies San Francisco, the London-born Gerrard was studying electronics and waiting tables when he made the unused space attached to his restaurant into a club. Punk had revitalized the city; finding bands was a snap. Soon Gerrard was putting on shows four nights a week. Eventually he became the U.S. tour manager for a number of English acts, booking "teabag tours" of the largest U.S. markets—New York, Chicago, Los Angeles, and San Francisco—for audiences of Anglophiles and expats. By the mid-nineties, he'd worked his way into the big leagues with Nine Inch Nails.

Gerrard's tastes led him to the first spate of British post-acid-house dance acts—especially those with headliner potential. He'd fly overseas to meet prospective clients, typically to a secondary market rather than a primary one, cornering the Shamen in Livingston, Scotland, rather than London or Manchester. Gerrard saw the Prodigy on the Rave New World tour, but didn't think they were ready for the big time quite yet. "It didn't matter how much I loved the act: If they didn't make it in Europe, they wouldn't make it in America, either. American or English, they have to be discovered and established there before America pays attention. It's been that way from Jimi Hendrix onward."

Gerrard knew how different the markets for dance DJs and rock bands were in the States, so whenever he'd put on a dance act in the States—including, eventually, the Prodigy—he made sure to cross-promote. "Dance promoters did parties. Rock promoters did concerts. Parties, you think about who invited you, what's likely to happen, and that's how you decide to go. When I would try booking these acts, some of the best venues in the country would say, 'Are you telling me it matters who gives somebody a flyer?' 'Absolutely.'" Still, he adds: "If you'd asked then: 'Want to come to this club and see this DJ?' ninety percent of us would have said: 'Oh, I don't do DJs.'"

WHAT "RAVE" HAD BEEN to compilations in 1992, "ambient" became in 1993–94. Ambient music had something of a pop moment in England in the early nineties, thanks to the Orb and the KLF (whose 1990 *Chill Out* was their first U.S. release after Matt Adell licensed it to Wax Trax!). But what brought on the deluge was U.S. labels figuring out that collections like Warp's *Artificial Intelligence*—not to mention Aphex Twin's *Selected Ambient Works Volume II*, released the same month as the first Furthur—were likelier to sell to non-ravers than blaring Euro-hardcore.

One of the best-liked comps was *Excursions in Ambience*, assembled by Brian Long and issued in March 1993 by Caroline Records. In the late eighties, Long had worked for SST Records: "I was all about 'real guitars and drums.'" That changed after Long spent some time working for the indie-biz trade mag *Rockpool*, where he was educated by the communal office stereo. "When you're exposed to a genre you don't know about, you start crystallizing: 'That's good, that's bad.' And New York is such a dance town. Going to clubs, being exposed to it in the right environment, I started getting it."

In 1992, Long moved to Caroline Distribution as product manager and A&R man in charge of the English label Play It Again Sam (PIAS) and Antler-Subway, the pop-savviest of the emerging Belgian labels. The prize act there was Lords of Acid, whose debut, *Lust* (1991), featured the smutty novelties "I Must Increase My Bust" and "I Sit on Acid," and sold a hundred thousand copies. "Lords of Acid broke because it was kitsch," says Long. (The same group would sign to Rick Rubin's WHTE LBLS under another alias, Digital Orgasm.) Long followed up *Lust* with two quick compilations of Antler-Subway tracks, *Technomancer I* and *II*: "I was hating life," he says. "It was just such bad, generic techno music." *Artificial Intelligence* inspired him to try "something that's capable of being an album."

Excursions in Ambience sold twenty thousand copies in a few months and got written up in the *New York Times*. The follow-up that October appeared on a new imprint, Astralwerks. *Excursions in Ambience* ended after four volumes. "As they started getting credibility, we started going after original tracks," says Long; by the series' end, about half the tracks were previously unissued. They helped make Astralwerks a rarity—a credible American electronic-dance label sired by an established imprint, rather than a homegrown operation à la UR or Plus 8.

BY THE MID-NINETIES, drum and bass had largely replaced ambient in the parties' second rooms. But the style of electronic dance music that caught the typical collegiate Yank's ear tended to be what *Mixmag*, in 1994, dubbed "trip-hop": "Slow and crunching hip-hop beats, no vocals, just strange swirling noises over the top . . . a deft fusion of head-nodding beats, supa-phat bass, and an obsessive attention to the kind of other-worldly sounds usually found on acid house records. It comes from the suburbs, not the streets, and with no vocals you don't need to be American to make it sound convincing."

Trip-hop was an arty, bohemian version of rap music minus the ghetto-bred personae and lyrics that made much of the audience (not just whites) shift uncomfortably. It was also very English—even the American most associated with it, DJ Shadow (Josh Davis), from college town Davis, California, recorded for the London label Mo' Wax. Bristol was the home of trip-hop's other top producers: Massive Attack, Portishead, and Tricky. The three-man production team Massive Attack's debut, *Blue Lines* (1991), was like a cross between Isaac Hayes's *Hot Buttered Soul* and Marley Marl's back-to-basics production of L.L. Cool J's *Mama Said Knock You Out*, with the songs sung blue by Shara Nelson and rhymer Tricky (Adrian Thaws), among others.

That combo of moody breaks and singer-songwriter fare—on *Blue Lines* and its follow-ups *Protection* (1994) and *Mezzanine* (1998)—inspired a lot of toothless music by similar configurations: synths and samples by one or two (usually) quiet men; up front, persona and hooks by (usually) a sullen-sounding woman. That was Portishead's shtick—and its DJ-producer Geoff Barrow was a tea boy at the studio where *Blue Lines* was recorded. With musician Adrian Utley and the baleful-voiced Beth Gibbons, Barrow made the most melodramatic music of the bunch, without tipping into self-parody; their "Sour Times" reached number five on the Modern Rock chart in February 1995. Tricky, by contrast, ran his alienated mutterings—like a bad joke he'd been seeing through since before puberty—beneath the more languid, haunted croon of Martina Topley-Bird. His 1995 bow, *Maxinquaye*, featured music flintier, more ragged, and more resonant than his Bristol mentors'—a distinction that vanished from his records well before the decade was up.

Trip-hop held sway with dance music's more doctrinaire quarters, particularly in Detroit. But by 1996, the phrase was falling out of favor among cognoscenti—not "serious" enough, apparently. They were calling it "downtempo," a colorlessly literal term that radiates palms-up-shrug consensus, imbued with, in Pauline Kael's words, "the solemnity of a horse's ass."

"SOLEMN" WASN'T THE WORD for the Levy brothers' label. "When Moonshine first started, we were just doing compilations," says Steve Levy. "The real key for us was that we started out with national distribution. We went through Indie, the first independent national distributor—they merged three regional distributors." The first Moonshine release, in October 1992, was titled *Techno Truth*—a reference to the siblings' Truth nights at the Park Plaza Hotel. Then the label began throwing out new titles every few weeks. "I think we shipped a couple-hundred thousand units in two months."

Moonshine had no trouble stoking demand, issuing three volumes of *Speed Limit 140 BPM Plus* in 1993 alone. Levy's English contacts, such as Tall Paul (Newman), the resident at Turnmill's, London's first twenty-four-hour dance club, greased the path for superclub house and trance collections from UK labels such as Cleveland City, Tomato, and Hooj Choons.

Moonshine was the earliest U.S. company to put out DJ-mix CDs. In 1993, the Levys licensed the British series *Journeys by DJ*, beginning with a set by Londoner Billy Nasty. "It didn't really connect, because no one fucking knew who Billy Nasty was," says Steve. Moonshine distributed DMC's *United DJs of America* series, including volumes by Frankie Knuckles, David Morales, Scott Hardkiss, and Josh Wink. One of Moonshine's best-loved mid-nineties titles was the two-volume *FunkyDesertBreaks* (1996–97), mixed by John Kelley, who'd come up playing the Moontribe parties on the outskirts of L.A. in 1993; Kelley went on to mix three more Moonshine titles, including a *United DJs of America* edition.

Nothing divided opinion like Moonshine's artwork. The CDs looked unapologetically like party flyers, with either old-school product-biting (the pseudo–Campbell's Soup *Cream of Tomato*, 1993) or full-on candy-rave color splotches and Photoshop cartoons (the early *Speed Limit* covers). Levy stands by it all: "I'm looking at the *Ravin' USA* cover and it looks good today," he says with a fond laugh. Many of the DJs on his roster disagree: Damian Higgins, who issued four Dieselboy mixes for Moonshine between 1996 and 2000, compares them to Cheeto's cheese puffs.

"The Levy brothers were smart businessmen," says Jason Bentley. "If they saw a trend in the scene—happy hardcore, for instance—they would be the first ones to put a compilation together, [or] distribute and rebrand compilations that existed in England. Their market wasn't interested in digging through record crates." Within the dance scene, such brazen appeal to the nonce was frowned upon. "If it made it to a Moonshine compilation, it was passé already," says Bentley. "There wasn't any subtlety."

By contrast, Bentley's compilations were almost ostentatiously subtle. After leaving *Urb* in 1994, he met Bruno Guez, who ran an imprint called Quango and had sent him his first collection, *A Journey into Ambient Groove.* "I don't think he had distribution yet," says Bentley, who became Guez's partner in 1995, leading to a deal with Island Records. "Chris Blackwell really liked it," says Bentley. "He saw the potential for opportunity."

Quango, in a sense, was "downtempo" to Moonshine's "trip-hop," its artwork and concepts far more tasteful, though just as time-bound. The best of Quango's collections was *Pop Fiction* (1996). "The idea was to draw from the downtempo tracks that felt very soundtracky," says Bentley; one track, Grantby's "Timber," essentially retools John Barry's *Diamonds Are Forever* theme. But despite the garish packaging, Moonshine's output could be strong. The *Speed Limit* series' eight volumes (1993–96) were a useful For Dummies guide to UK hardcore's ongoing splinter into jungle, drum and bass, and happy hardcore.

JOHN KELLEY'S *FunkyDesertBreaks* mixes showcased a breakbeats-and-303s sound that shuffled more than it rocked out, with a heavy New Age overlay that marks it as pure Cali. By contrast, a similar style coming out of Orlando, Florida—"funky breaks"—was closer to Bambaataa-style electro. Orlando was the hardest-partying city of a state not light on competition; one of the scene's founders, DJ Icey (Eddie Pappa), would basically slow down piano-driven UK hardcore anthems to 136 BPM. "It was feel-good breakbeat," says Orlando native Dave Minner (AK1200).

Funky breaks was swirling, ingratiating music, often feather-light—huge in Florida and California, ritually disdained on the East Coast and in the Midwest when they acknowledged it at all. "It could be about the climate," says Minner. "There's a lot of hotels and beaches and theme parks. It's hard to write dark music in a happy place." Orlando was also inundated with MDMA.

Minner, on the other hand, went for the "crazy breakbeat stuff" that began arriving in droves on import, which took UK hardcore past itself. "It became my passion—the vibe of the music; the hip-hop and ragga samples; sped-up breaks and rewinds and little glitchy tricks." This emerging style got its own nickname, too: jungle. Nineteen ninety-three was jungle's bonanza year, with labels like Suburban Base, Movin' Shadow, Urban Shakedown, Reinforced, and Ram tossing out great records like firecrackers—often, the records sounded *like* firecrackers, haphazard but irresistible. The harder-hitting, more minimal tracks got a nickname as well: drum and bass. Eventually, "jungle" fell out of favor, just like "trip-hop," and the duller nickname became the go-to.

Jungle required active DJing. "I was constantly on the cross-fader," says Minner. "The other side of that coin was progressive house, which was very melodic and long journeys and slow mixes. You let the record speak for itself." One huge 1993 progressive house hit was a double-A-side, "Rez" b/w "Cowgirl," by Underworld, formerly a New Romantic band called Freur, who'd added a younger DJ and beat maker, Darren Emerson, to craft long tracks that rambled and shimmered.

Underworld's record was on Junior Boy's Own, the premiere prog-house label—apart from its other major 1993 title, licensed from a couple of guys in Manchester who'd put out their own tiny pressing the previous summer. One of them, Ed Simons, had borrowed three hundred pounds from a friend under the condition that if he didn't pay it all back within six months, the friend was to earn 10 percent of Simons's future royalties. The tune was called "Song to the Siren." The DJs called themselves the Dust Brothers. Ed paid his friend back.

Simons had met Tom Rowlands studying history at Manchester University; they'd started spinning together, playing hip-hop to warm up for a night of house music—then decided to fuse them. "Song to the Siren" set a sample of Goth band This Mortal Coil's cut of the same name over dramatically paced rhythm. Over time, they'd discover that the more they fussed over the breakbeats, the better the result.

"Song to the Siren" was massive in Orlando, so for Fourth of July weekend in 1993, DJ Icey brought the Dust Brothers to the Edge for their U.S. debut. Tom and Ed got five days at the Travelodge, two meals per day, and a planned visit to Walt Disney World. They hadn't packed converters for their gear, so Icey snagged some from Radio Shack within five minutes of closing time. To their utter surprise, the Dust Brothers filled the Edge. "They were like, 'We'll go to Disney World. It'll be a good laugh,'" says Wohelski. "They show up, and they're playing to [twenty-five hundred] kids going absolutely bonkers to 'Chemical Beats'"—a new track they'd release the following year.

BY 1994, WOHELSKI WAS in New York as Astralwerks' new A&R man. He put on the duo's demo. "I listened to a couple songs, handed it back to Brian Long, and said, 'If we don't pick this record up, we're stupid. We'll [sell] twenty thousand without blinking. If we get a few breaks, we'll do fifty thousand.'" Shortly before the album came out, L.A.'s Dust Brothers, hip-hop producers Mike Simpson and John King (Tone-Loc's *Loc-ed After Dark*, Beastie Boys' *Paul's Boutique*), threatened Rowlands and Simons with a lawsuit if they didn't change their name. Tom and Ed were now the Chemical Brothers.

Exit Planet Dust (1995) retooled the duo's earlier singles into a cohesive piece of work—something few dance acts had accomplished. It was an immediate critics' hit—not just with underground tastemakers like *Massive* but also with pop and rock writers. Astralwerks built on that momentum with aggressive marketing. "It started with college radio specialty shows and then snowballed," says Errol Kolosine, who ran Astralwerks in the late nineties. "Modern rock radio was changing," says Wohelski. "It crossed between the dance-music thing and the rock thing."

The Chems' live show helped. There were no dancers, no costumes, no "real instruments"—just audiovisual sensationalism. Their mate Adam Smith, a.k.a. Vegetable Vision, looped forceful abstract imagery behind them—explosions, riots, clocks spinning out of control—while the Brothers triggered gear in real time, including five samplers and several vintage guitar pedals. "It's not pretty music we make; it's quite rough and abrasive," Simons said. That made them easy to sell as next-gen rockers.

For Kolosine, weary of the "willfully dissociated people looking at the ground plucking out the same four chords" then littering college rock, the Brothers' live show offered salvation. "Black people, white people, gay people, straight people, frat boys, you name it—everybody in here is equal, and the music is what is bringing everybody in here together. It occurred to me: 'If I get enough people to experience this, we can't lose.'"

Not every radio programmer understood at first. House music, after all, appealed largely to urban gay audiences; wasn't this just another version of that? "The reactions ran everything from 'We don't play gay stuff' to 'If I play that, I'm going to lose all my white males fifteen-to-twenty-one because they want to hear Korn or Limp Bizkit,'" says Wohelski, who credits Nine Inch Nails' crossover for paving the way. "If you have a station that plays a lot of industrial stuff, you

[say], 'Listen to the beats. It's heavy as fuck.' Then you talk to a rock station: 'It's a song: it has a chorus, it has a verse—play it at night, see what happens.'"

"The next step was getting these big programmers down to come see the Chemical Brothers," says Kolosine. "I wouldn't sit at the back or at the bar with them. Me or my staff would bring them down onto the dance floor, or down the front. They looked around like, 'These are all of my listeners.'" Within a year, the Chemical Brothers—and eventually Orbital and the Prodigy—began receiving regular rotation on KROQ.

Exit Planet Dust was a turning point in a few ways. For one thing, it redefined how an electronic-dance album *looked*—specifically, nothing about the album's packaging resembled Moonshine—no floating gobs of color, no video-game-reject graphics, no winky-winky references to MDMA (except, of course, the Chemical Brothers' name). "I felt like that put a barrier in front of the music: 'Here's a kid in phat pants and a pacifier in his mouth and glow sticks,'" says Wohelski. "Yes, that's part of our culture—but it shouldn't be a barrier for you to enjoy the music."

Wohelski refers to the Chemicals' packaging—and subsequently, that of Astralwerks' cannier groups—as "scene-neutral." "The cover [is] these two hippies seemingly hitchhiking down the road with a car driving by," he says. "It doesn't necessarily tell you what the music is. But you take notice: 'What's this all about? Is it hippies? Is this a rock record? They're wearing bell-bottoms and suede. Is this a folk record? What *is* this?'"

"I ALWAYS THOUGHT the formula of big beat was the breakbeats of hip-hop, the energy of acid house, and the pop sensibilities of the Beatles, with a little bit of punk sensibility—everything I came up on, all rolled into one," says Norman Cook, the Brighton-born DJ better known as Fatboy Slim. Cook supplied not only its definition but its moniker: "The name came from our club, the Big Beat Boutique, which I'm tremendously proud of." Cook founded the Boutique with Damian Harris, the owner of Skint Records, Fatboy Slim's label. "House music was named after the Warehouse. Garage music is named after the Paradise Garage. And big beat was named after our club."

Brighton gave big beat its name, but the style first germinated in London, where Cook, Rowlands, and Simons were regular DJs at the Heavenly Social (held at Turnmill's). Cook had spent the eighties playing bass with hit-making indie rockers the Housemartins, then switched to dance music. DJs sopped up the tracks he put out as Beats International, Freakpower, Pizzaman, and the Mighty Dub Katz; the latter's "It's Just Another Groove" (1995) cuts up Cloud One's 1977 nugget "Disco Juice" into high-street filter-disco. Cook's debut as Fatboy Slim, "Santa Cruz" (1995), was simplicity itself—a (literally) one-note guitar riff over a cranked hip-hop break. It slotted right into funky breaks DJ sets on America's coasts; it was also perfect for rock-club DJs who wanted an update without alienating their base.

Different as big beat was from rave, it too was chemically dependent. "In the way that it was a mixture of house attitude and hip-hop attitude, it was a mixture of ecstasy and cocaine—more ecstasy than cocaine, though," says Cook. Fatboy Slim was rumored to have a contract rider requiring specific amounts of vodka, orange juice, and cocaine to perform. "A certain amount of vodka, definitely," he admits. "But it wasn't a demand in writing—[more like] 'It's Norm, give him his usual.'"

Cook initially dismissed the very idea of conquering the U.S.: "I'd seen too many bands try to break America and had it broken them. Also, I didn't think you'd like it. I just thought America liked rock and country and western." But he figured things out fast enough: "People like the Prodigy and the Chemical Brothers—we saw it as very similar to the Beatles and the Rolling Stones, who grew up listening to soul and blues records and then sold an English version of it back to America," says Cook. "We were listening to obscure records from Detroit and Chicago, giving them an English pop sensibility, and sending them back to you."

MOBY ISSUED HIS FIRST "real" album—there were three on Instinct he hadn't supervised—on Elektra on March 14, 1995. *Everything Is Wrong* was a bold declaration of mastery of every genre he attempted—be it blues-punk ("What Love"), programmatic minimalist composition ("God Moving Over the Face of the Waters"), or happy hardcore ("Feeling So Real"). Rock critics were in awe—*Spin* named it the best album of 1995—but the dance underground was far less enamored: "When the title of *Everything Is Wrong* came out," says Tamara Palmer, who'd become an editor at *Urb*, "it was like, '*Yep.*'"

That summer, Moby toured on Lollapalooza's side stage, where his show revealed a new wrinkle—roughly half was three-piece punk, the kind he'd played as a teenager. Moby was also performing corny rock covers ("Sweet Child o' Mine," "Sweet Home Alabama," "Purple Haze") for no discernible reason—except that he clearly wanted out of his old scene, pronto. But the jack-of-all-styles bid didn't take; by mid-1996, *Everything Is Wrong* had stalled at sixty-nine thousand copies. By contrast, *Exit Planet Dust* was at one hundred thousand and rising.

The Chemical Brothers' sales arc made the industry take notice, because 1996 had the record companies worried. Things had gone stagnant. Modern rock, which had skyrocketed on the back of Nirvana and Pearl Jam, audibly deflated after Kurt Cobain's April 1994 suicide. Hip-hop's East Coast–West Coast rivalry was turning deadly. "The gangsta-rap nonsense just alienated a lot of people in the music industry, and fans," says Charles Aaron. "Rock was getting boring—really boring. It was the fake grunge era."

For a decade, things were flush thanks to compact discs, which spurred older listeners to repurchase old LPs on the new format. The early nineties saw a steady stream of blockbusters from all corners of pop. But things were flattening. In 1996, catalog sales fell by a quarter. By year's end, some five hundred record shops shuttered nationwide. Having sold a combined twenty million copies of their first three albums, Pearl Jam's fourth, *No Code*, sold "only" a million.

If the Chemical Brothers' sales were climbing, maybe it pointed to a solution. Or maybe not: Alternative had germinated slowly. The Sex Pistols were never huge in the States; they just never stopped selling, until enough kids had heard them to assume they'd always been part of the American rock firmament. The path to Nirvana's *Nevermind* was long and gradual—groups like Depeche Mode and R.E.M. and the Cure had moved from clubs to halls to stadiums over a decade. No one had expected those bands to take a faltering biz out of its slump.

TRYING TO BREAK electronic dance music to live audiences in America, Gerry Gerrard consistently got the same response from other promoters: "It'll never happen." But sometimes one would take a chance. Woodstock '94, in mid-August, vaulted Gerrard's prize client, Nine Inch Nails, into rock's upper echelon; in addition, Gerrard was put in charge of the dance tent, dubbed Ravestock, along with NASA's Scotto. The DJs included Doc Martin, Frankie Bones, Kevin Saunderson, and Little Louie Vega; the live acts, Orbital, Deee-Lite, and the Orb. But the event was pulled together last minute and announced only two weeks beforehand. There was also a kerfuffle involving Aphex Twin, who had the plug pulled midshow after signing a false name to a contract that would have given the event's corporate backers, PolyGram Records, the right to release the performance.

It convinced Gerrard that a large-scale electronic-dance Lollapalooza—not a club tour, like See the Light—could work. He understood concert-industry realpolitik, and he had the talent: By

1996, he took commissions from Underworld, the Orb, the Chemical Brothers, and the Prodigy, as well as Meat Beat Manifesto (Jack Dangers), who'd come out of industrial music but happily courted the dance crowd. But Ravestock wasn't a working model. "I thought: I'll do a one-off just to test the concept and figure out what it's really going to cost." The event would feature four stages and plenty of DJs, but Gerrard wasn't throwing a rave. This was about live acts. The working title was Chaotica, after Gerrard's agency.

Though based in New York, Gerrard stacked the deck by setting the prototype in Southern California, still the States' healthiest scene, despite a number of mid-decade busts and nonstarters. His team included Philip Blaine, who'd started L.A. punk promoters Goldenvoice in 1981; Sioux Zimmerman, Orbital's New York publicist; and Paul Tollett, formerly of Los Angeles's Palladium.

To book DJs, Blaine brought in Pasquale Rotella, with whom he was doing business as Insomniac, L.A.'s top rave promoter—they threw Nocturnal Wonderland and other parties as lavish and fanciful as their names. "It was mostly Pasquale who did the legwork on that event," says Gary Richards. Rotella calls Blaine "my investor—he was supposed to be my silent investor, but he didn't do that, necessarily. I was doing more parties; my investor was doing more concerts."

Blaine came up with the show's new name: Organic '96. The flyer depicted a ladybug. Says Vivian Host, who attended: "You can't sell a huge concert with Mickey Mouse with acid on his tongue."

GERRARD ATTEMPTED to bring his prize act aboard to headline Organic '96, but the Prodigy was busy recording. Harder, slower, and more authoritative, their second album, *Music for the Jilted Generation* (1994), had been a British number-one, spawning four top-twenty hits; it came out a year later in the States but still didn't make the Billboard 200. "I remember seeing Rick [Rubin] at Tower Records," says Gary Richards. "I was like, 'Dude, did you hear the new Prodigy record? It's unbelievable.' We went out to his car and were listening to it in the parking lot. He was like, 'Shit, I think we passed on this.'"

On March 30, 1996, the Prodigy's first post-*Jilted* recording went straight to number one in England, staying at the top of the singles chart for three weeks. Liam Howlett had always made records alone, but "Firestarter" featured onstage dancer Keith Flint on vocals. It was a breakthrough: "Keith can perform it onstage, and the way he does it, the way he gets his energy across, that obviously helped the track sixty percent," Howlett said. So did the way he looked: Flint had cut his long blonde hair into a reverse Mohican—shaved down the middle, the sides colored multiply and sticking up like a crust-punk crown.

The black-and-white video for "Firestarter" made Flint seem deadly. Two years on from *Jilted*, the Prodigy now sounded hungry for blood. The song's video hocked a loogie at the Chemical Brothers' "the art is the star" approach: Flint's menacing do, accentuated with kohl-black eyes, antic mien, and a harder-than-thou lyric, were electrifying. "I thought it was dope," says Dan Charnas. "All hell broke loose. The crazy-ass white dude was like Flavor Flav, only for techno. They were stars. Of course, Rick never mentioned it again." But Howlett still had a lot of work to finish the next Prodigy album; headlining Organic was out of the question. "If it didn't do well, they didn't want the industry to think, 'Oh, the Prodigy doesn't draw,'" says Gerrard. "So we went ahead and did it without them."

ORGANIC '96 TOOK PLACE on June 22, 1996, at the off-season Snow Valley Ski Resort, in San Bernardino National Forest, a mountainous site east of Los Angeles. The grounds opened Saturday afternoon at four and closed at 8 A.M. Sunday; tickets were twenty-five to thirty dollars. Steve Levy's old friend Phil Blaine got three Moonshine bands onto the foot of the bill: Oversol 7, Cirrus, and Electric Sky-church. Then:

Loop Guru (7 P.M.)

Meat Beat Manifesto (8 P.M.)

Underworld (9:30 P.M.)

The Chemical Brothers (11 P.M.)

Orbital (12:40 A.M.)

The Orb (2:30 A.M.)

Organic was a press showcase as well as a biz one; Zimmerman and her three-person team arrived in California two weeks early to coordinate dozens of interviews. One of the most interviewed groups was Underworld—largely because they had a key song in a highly anticipated film. *Trainspotting*, English director Danny Boyle's adaptation of Irvine Welsh's tale of heroin addiction, theft, vomit, feces, and raves, opened in America a month after Organic—well after it ran in England—and became a cult smash. The climax—Renton's (Ewan McGregor) final escape—is amplified by ten yammering, propulsive minutes of "Born Slippy (Nuxx)," which anchored a soundtrack album as iconic as the movie. "We really had to piggyback off *Trainspotting* to get people to pay attention to Underworld," says Charlie Amter, then TVT's PR man, who attended Organic.

For much of the English lineup, staying at the same hotel, the show meant missing the Euro '96 football (soccer) quarterfinals. "A bunch of us wanted to see England play," says Underworld vocalist Karl Hyde. "[The Orb's] Alex Paterson had his colors on. We expected to see it on ESPN, and it wasn't on. We were just cut adrift then. We didn't know what to do." Not so Darren Emerson, the band's DJ: "A big, pink, old drop-top Cadillac pulled up with a guy in a cowboy hat—a hairdresser Darren knew, with this broad Essex accent: 'Jump in, mate! Come off with us and have an adventure!' And Darren disappeared in this Cadillac with the cowboy."

AMTER WAS WOWED by Snow Valley's size. "We didn't really have a sense of how massive it would be until everyone showed up. There were a lot of walk-ups, and it definitely swelled as the night went on." John Kelley—not yet signed to Moonshine—showed up around five, thinking, "*Wow: This seems like a real event.* It seemed so official, so un-underground."

The crowd was better mixed both racially and age-wise than an average rave, with a number of drag queens and plenty of candy ravers. Acid and E were easy to access; Jason Bentley, who DJed between bands, recalls "being so high I saw two tone arms" on one turntable. But the vibe was more adult than kiddie. "It was a really rich cross-section of people, diverse and well educated," says James Lumb of Electric Skychurch. "It almost had a Silicon Valley vibe." By six, the collective mood was exuberant.

Backstage was like a convention, swarming with scenesters from around the world. Kurt Eckes and David Prince were there a month after Even Furthur's mud-bath spectacular. Prince was both unwinding after that bender and reeling from the loss of Timothy Leary. But otherwise, says Zimmerman, "It was very chillax. There was none of that festival stress." Performers used to being treated like second-class citizens were particularly impressed. The sound was first rate; Gerrard had hired a Turbo system. Lasers cut geometric shapes in the nighttime air.

Steve Levy held court inside a large trailer with his roster and some English reps: "By '96 there was certainly an impression from the UK that there was business to chase in the U.S." Ditto his home turf. "At one point I looked around and said, 'These guys have signed up the West Coast,'" says Lumb. Moonshine was issuing mixes by Kelley, Doc Martin, and DJ Dan, and had a pressing-and-distribution deal with Hardkiss. "Everybody had a different role," says Lumb of the roster. "Cirrus was the funky breaks [group]; we were their ambient-spiritual band." In addition, Moonshine distributed another L.A. imprint, City of Angels, whose stars were Las Vegas natives the Crystal Method (Ken Jordan and Scott Kirkland), who'd scored two club hits, "Now Is the Time" (1994) and "Keep Hope Alive" (1995), both with heavy Chemical Brothers echoes.

Electric Skychurch went on at six. Lumb had moved to L.A. in 1991 after a half-decade as an indie rocker in Athens, Georgia. As Skychurch took off, their growing notoriety cost Lumb his day job at Imagine Films. "Brian Grazer and Ron Howard backed me up to the wall and said, 'Hey! You're on *acid*!' " He wasn't (though being told so by Richie Cunningham must have felt like it), but Lumb was ready to move on. "What I was experiencing in the clubs on weekends was a lot of joy and camaraderie, and a real lack of misogyny and douchebag dating situations—refreshing to get away from, high up in the film industry."

Loop Guru's set ended about the time the sun went down—no joke, at 8:08 P.M. "People started moving together—it started to pack up front," says Lumb.

UNDERWORLD, SCHEDULED FOR nine thirty, began closer to ten. Introduced by KROQ's unctuous Jed the Fish—the station had just begun broadcasting the show live—the trio charged into their set, the thirty-nine-year-old Hyde traversing the stage like an agitated Mick Jagger. "It reminded me of seeing *Woodstock* on TV," says Hyde, who was amazed by the lack of a stage back wall. He acclimated to the thin mountain air by gulping oxygen from a tank. "I remember other bands taking the piss that we'd ordered oxygen, but they didn't move around and dance like I did."

"I loved Underworld," says Prince, "but I do remember being like, 'Oh, this is just some old-dude rock star.' " Even so, Hyde felt everything work that night: "Gerry really got it. It wasn't somewhere you could go and see a rock band next week. We were a frontier town that made this step into a new territory." The climax, of course, was "Born Slippy." "They lit the hill up," says Levy, who watched from the motor-home roof. "Remembering it still sends shivers down my spine."

Everyone else was just shivering—the temperature fell to the forties. Zimmerman's crew had to head back to the city for jackets. Campers felt like they were in fucking Wisconsin or something. "It wasn't really memorable in any way other than that I was freezing," says Host. "We were all in sleeping bags up to our eyes, huddled together."

PEOPLE POGOED AT Chemical Brothers shows, and Organic was no exception. "Someone once said to us, 'Why don't you get a live drummer?'" Rowlands said. "And we said, 'No. The drums we use are not physically reproducible.'" That was the effect at Organic, undoubtedly aided by the sheer need for body heat. Zimmerman, who'd been up since 7 A.M., was jolted back awake by the Chems—her first time seeing them. (Brian Long, who'd just left Caroline, skipped Organic to backpack for six weeks in Thailand.) Orbital were old pros used to playing at peak time, their mellifluous intensity perfect after the Chems' clobbering. An SF-Raves audiophile singled out Orbital's sheer *sound* as Organic's highlight. The Orb played through the dawn, and during "Little Fluffy Clouds" the lasers spelled out ORGANIC overhead in green.

By the time the Orb were finished, the sun was up, and a lot of people thought the show was over—including backstage. "The Orb had run so late that Dennis the production manager pulled the sound and everything," says Gerrard. He'd left the main stage's final act in the lurch: Michael Dog, who'd flown in from England to play. "I ran out: 'What the hell are you doing?'" recalls Gerrard. "Oh, it's only the DJ, let's go home," the stage manager, an old U2/Nine Inch Nails hand, told him. Gerrard had to set him straight: "It's not *just a DJ.*"

James Lumb had a great time, but he was a realist. "We were driving back at nine in the morning. I remember all these radio people in limousines. We had our little pickup truck full of stuff, and these A&R guys from Moonshine are taunting us as they blow past in the limousines. I turned around to everybody [in the truck] and said, 'You just paid for that.'"

ORGANIC '96, SAYS Gerard Meraz, who attended, "was totally more concert than dance. It was more set up to stare at a stage rather than be part of this ritual. It was the first one that was more like, 'Let's come and watch this, rather than dance and be a community.'" And the community, says Rotella, skipped it: "The ravers didn't really care about Orbital playing. People who loved the music would rather have a DJ play it. All that event did was satisfy people that didn't support the culture anymore, that don't go out, and journalists that gave the scene a chance for a night. All it did was push the real people out of the way."

Organic's final attendance—sixty-three hundred, plus a guest list of over a thousand—was only one-third of Rave America's three years earlier. Rotella says that the same night, another L.A. party, Endor, put on by some of his friends, sold out and took bodies away from Organic. "I was trying to tell [Gerrard] we shouldn't run that day. No one would have shown up if I was not on the ground promoting that thing. We only had four weeks. We killed ourselves getting the word out about that. But we lost money. No one got paid." It wasn't a rave at all, but Organic got the U.S. concert business semi-seriously interested in dance music for the first time.

ON JULY 13, "CHILDREN," by Italian producer Robert Miles (Roberto Concina), which had already sold more than two million copies overseas, peaked at number twenty-one in the U.S.—better than "James Brown Is Dead" ever did—thanks to an instantly grabby piano hook, both perky and dewy, an effect only enhanced by the synth strings. This shameless melodicism had become a trance hallmark— far from the head-down, gridlike body music it was early on. "Trance is written the way your sixth-grade teacher taught you to write short stories or essays: with a beginning (intro), a middle (climax), and an end (denouement)," Tricia Romano wrote in the *Village Voice*. "Ready, set, go—can't you just *feel* the emotion?"

Romano didn't just mean on the radio—she meant in clubs. That September, DJs Sasha and John Digweed issued *Northern Exposure*, a double-CD mix of trance and progressive house that solidified the hands-in-air rep they had been building in the UK. (It came out in the States a year later, in two separately sold parts.) "Sasha and I did a mini-tour of the States in 1996," says Digweed. "New York was one of the dates, at Twilo. The night went incredibly well, and the owners came to us both with the idea of playing each month. That night went on to last five years." Sasha fondly recalls "three thousand people cheering us Friday nights."

Still, the effect of that celebrity status could be unnerving to long-time dancers. "It was, rather unfortunately, the first place that I saw people just standing and facing the DJ booth—maybe moving around a little bit, but not dancing with each other, certainly," says Bruce Tantum. "They were just looking at the guy playing the records."

I am completely prepared to allow corporate
America to drop their money into our scene. I think
it's a big waste on their part that will net zero
results, other to exhaust their advertising and P.R.
budgets.

—MATT BONDE, MW-RAVES POST, DECEMBER 1, 1996

>12

WOODSTOCK '99

Rome, New York
July 22–25, 1999

ON SEPTEMBER 6, 1996, MTV premiered an hour-long pilot for a new show called *Amp:* electronic-dance videos from all over the spectrum, from Sun Electric and Aphex Twin to Orbital and Tricky, "segued" together, DJ-style. A poster on the 313 mailing list noted that some of the show's bumper music came from Astralwerks' recently issued *Detroit: Beyond the Third Wave* compilation, including electro producer Will Web's "Life on Tek." Web—formerly Mr. Bill, who'd played the first Furthur—replied on-list: "Oh no. Does this mean I've gone commercial?"

Kidding or not, a lot of people on the lists were getting itchy that their grassroots scene could turn upside down. "The best thing we can do is guide the expansion of the rave scene into its mainstream direction with as much positive influence as possible," an SF-Raver posted. "If we do not make our presence known, the mainstream will eventually [phase] us out completely."

Some of the best conversation about this came from PB-CLE-Raves—the industrial Midwest had more at stake. There, parties would top out around five hundred, and they ran heavily on true belief. If the cops decided they didn't like it, down it went, period. "I've heard about people getting arrested for just being at an illegal party," posted a PB-CLE-Raver. "That really scares me, especially since if I get anything at all else on my record (besides a drinking misdemeanor), I can't go into the military, and then I would have no idea what to do with my life."

Still, the noise could be overwhelming, and excessively whiny, inviting well-earned derision. "Oh no!" chided a PB-CLE-Raver. "Our scene isn't going to be 'underground' anymore. Uncool NORMAL people are entering our once private domain . . . Fucking grow up . . . This is starting to sound like Usenet." On MW-Raves, Chris Sattinger was even more to the point:

> Underground? Co-opted by the mainstream? All of these artists [on *Amp*] are fucking Europeans. These artists have been *in the mainstream for years*. No one makes any distinction between techno and rock as far as marketing over there. They advertise in different glossy magazines, they play venues on different nights. They have overlapping audiences. The artists remix and guest on each other's albums across genres. . . . Please don't put all of techno in the same boat. It's been going on for *twenty fucking years now*. It is old enough to look after itself.

"Still," Sattinger added in a later post, "bleeping noise and repetitive beats aren't going to fly in Peoria."

BY 1996, MW-RAVES HAD five hundred subscribers, SF-Raves four hundred, and NE-Raves three hundred. In this, they mirrored the rise of interactive technology. In San Francisco and Seattle, especially, Internet cafés were popping up, renting terminals at anywhere from six to ten bucks an hour. You could listen to music at them, thanks to the 1995 debut of two audio-compression systems. Though the MP3 would eventually change the music business (and the world) as we know it, the first format to gain favor—particularly among ravers—was RealAudio.

Jonathan Golub began working for *HotWired* in 1995—the first Web magazine, an interactive sister to *Wired* magazine but a separate editorial entity. *HotWired* was top-heavy with electronic-dance insiders—downstairs were Web developers Organic, led by Brian Behlendorf, who'd been part of *HotWired*'s launch staff in 1994. "A bunch of those people were putting on raves," says Golub. "When Burning Man happened, the whole office would be empty for a week."

At the office, Golub began producing *Feedback*, a weekly program streamed via RealAudio. "The beauty of RealAudio was, you were recording to a file. As soon as the broadcast stopped, people could immediately access the archive." A year later, Golub and coproducers Ian Raikow, David Goldberg, and Zane Vella started the first DJ-centric Webcast, Beta Lounge, in Vella's space. "We used *HotWired*'s equipment, like a DSL router. Eventually we pulled in Brian Benitez, an audio engineer from *HotWired*."

HotWired's attitude toward moonlighting was laissez-faire: "People were using equipment and bandwidth with the blessing of the company. There was no paperwork. It was an unwritten policy: 'If you're going to go out and invent something, have fun.' Yahoo! was still hosted on Stanford's servers; it had been a noncommercial entity. There was no Google. Apple was making computers, but they weren't involved in any of this stuff."

Beta Lounge's first-year guests included Derrick May, Stacey Pullen, Doc Scott, Ed Rush, Gavin and Robbie Hardkiss, Kevin Saunderson, Alton Miller, Moodymann, and Goldie. "Basically, any DJ in town would get booked at Beta Lounge," says Jane Lerner. "I thought I was in heaven when I found Beta Lounge," says DJ-producer Jeff Samuel, then in Cleveland. "I'd sit around listening to mixes. They had great taste. And they presented it pretty professionally." San Francisco journalist Philip Sherburne cut his DJ teeth at Beta Lounge. "There was obviously a lot of processing power going on, and there was often someone in the back fiddling with some obscure black box," he says. "Someone from the crew would always get on the mike to announce the DJ, which reinforced the idea of broadcasting out to the world."

OF COURSE ASTRALWERKS wanted Daft Punk. They were used to cherry-picking Virgin's European roster unimpeded; that's how they got the Future Sound of London and the Chemical Brothers. But Virgin America muscled in. "At that time, we were still of the mind that grew things fairly organically: 'Let's let the underground have just a little bit longer. Let's not totally pimp them out to doing cheesy shit,'" says Peter Wohelski. "Virgin said, 'We're going to spend a shitload of money.' That record was in some ways a no-brainer. All you had to do was throw enough money at it and it was going to happen."

Bangalter and de Homem-Christo were still steeped in the underground aesthetics of rave even as they made the jump to a major label. "We even tried not to be on Astralwerks, and be on Virgin Records America, which is more like Smashing Pumpkins and Lenny Kravitz, and try to change their view about it," Bangalter said. "Even if Virgin America didn't get it at the beginning then maybe it's a good thing that they get it now and change their view about the whole thing." In short, Daft Punk wanted to be pop stars—but do it similarly to the way Underground Resistance *refused* to be pop stars, by wearing masks, or blue face paint, or helmets, and not actually starring in their videos. The riffs and tweaks were the stars; the visuals were the star; the logo was the star. Daft Punk just wanted to do it on a massive scale. To them, there was no contradiction, even if America insisted otherwise.

"THE ELECTRONICA REVOLUTION," trumpeted the top strip of the cover of *Spin*'s October 1996 issue. The record world needed something to tag all this music with, and with "rave" over, "acid house" too old, and "techno" too severe, "electronica" functioned the way "new wave"—Sire Records president Seymour Stein's less-scary substitute for "punk"—once had. The *Spin* cover solidified it as a convenient catchall.

The term baffled some of its beneficiaries. "It surprised me when I went to America that they were describing me as 'electronica,'" says Norman Cook. "In England, it means something more serious, like Warp Records; also, what I did was made by samples rather than synthesizers." Liam Howlett of the Prodigy is more dismissive: "We soon disowned that silly tag." With retrospect, electronica has become—à la new wave—a convenient term for commercially minded late-nineties electronic dance music, usually with block-rockin' breakbeats.

In October, the Prodigy's "Firestarter" was added to MTV's regular rotation; within six weeks, it joined the Buzz Bin, the network's next-big-thing anointment. Just before Christmas, Maverick Records, Sire/Warner Bros.' Madonna-run imprint—having just sold fourteen million copies of Alanis Morissette's debut—announced they'd signed the Prodigy; the next album would be out by spring. The track was having a tangible effect—sales of the second Prodigy album, *Music for the Jilted Generation*, had jumped.

On December 23, *Alternative Nation* (not *Amp*) aired "Firestarter" back-to-back with the video for another new single: "Setting Sun," by the Chemical Brothers, also a Buzz Bin clip. Part of the Chems' U.S. audience, says Wohelski, was "that anglophile kind of rock kid who follows *NME* religiously. He's curious because Oasis is talking about the Chemical Brothers, and the Chemical Brothers were talking about Oasis." "Setting Sun" made it more than talk: Oasis guitarist-songwriter Noel Gallagher sneered over the top of careening drums and woozy backdrop. It sounded a *lot* like "Tomorrow Never Knows"—appropriate for a guest star who'd risen to fame pilfering the Beatles.

"It didn't hurt timing-wise," says former Astralwerks exec Errol Kolosine. "Imagine that on the radio today. I mean, it's an air-horn strung together with these pummeling beats and this psychedelic stuff going on. It still amazes me how well that did." That Christmas, New York was plastered with posters for the single that blared, loud as the song: AS HEARD ON K-ROCK.

ON NEW YEAR'S EVE 1996–97, the L.A. crew Go Ventures threw a party called Seventh Heaven on the seventh floor of an office building. Wade Randolph Hampton—a veteran DJ who'd put on parties in the Midwest, California, and his native Dallas—was one of Seventh Heaven's promoters, as well as playing the party: "There was already a bad environment going up to that. The religious look of the flyer, a *National Geographic* cover with a hand reaching out, felt eerie to begin with." Outside, says L.A. native Bonnie Chuen, who did street promo for the event, "a drink company was handing out test tubes of the initial form of energy drinks—a combination of ginseng and high doses of caffeine and sugar. People had a bad medical reaction. They had to shut down the doorway of the party to get people out into the ambulance."

It was, in essence, a smart-drink overdose—more than thirty people unwittingly wacked on a kind of larval-stage Red Bull or Monster Energy Drink. "Right out of the gate a bunch of kids hit the ground," says Hampton. "Everyone was trying to get in before the countdown at eleven o'clock," says Chuen. "It was a party for fifteen hundred people. You had maybe four hundred, five hundred people on the seventh floor. The party never stopped. You had eight hundred people downstairs trying to get upstairs for the countdown. They had to shut off the entrances to get people out into ambulances. The people outside rioted—there were riot police."

"It escalated and escalated," continues Hampton. "That riot was far worse than in 1992—we're talking fistfights in the streets with

LAPD. Rubber bullets were flying everywhere—I've still got one in my shin. My mother had been brought in from the Midwest. We were finally going to show her what all those years of backing me up on all this meant. She was watching my baby at a hotel room down the street at the Biltmore, had watched the whole thing live on a helicopter cam. She was mortified."

It made the news, of course—with "electronica" on the rise, the media's interest in the parties, and their illicit goings-on, was renewed. By 1997, Fox News outlets around the U.S. were sending hidden cameras into the parties, and even Barbara Walters presented an exposé on *20/20:* "They call it a rave, and it's the latest kid craze. Millions of youngsters, as young as age ten, flock to secret locations to party and dance through the night—that's all night long—often till eight or nine in the morning."

People in the scene cried "scare tactics," including Chuen: "The [reports] were not necessarily indicative of what was really going on. You'd have all these different groups from all these different walks of life. You had gangbangers with club kids; the rich, affluent kids from Orange County with Hollywood scenesters. In no other environment were these people around one another. They would go into a party and there'd be no friction."

ON JANUARY 21, 1997, Moonshine issued *Happy 2B Hardcore,* mixed by DJ Anabolic Frolic, whom the Levys signed on the back of a demo tape (and their Canadian distributor's urging); Jon, particularly, was a fan. "[Frolic] was throwing these parties up in Toronto called Hullaballoo," says Steve. "It was clear he absolutely knew the scene and was really in touch with it. The *Speed Limit* series had got to nine [volumes]. We were looking for something different, so we jumped on it." He cackles. "We weren't subtle about it." *Happy 2B Hardcore,* eight volumes long, became one of Moonshine's bestselling series.

Seasoned ravers *hated* happy hardcore, *despised* candy kids. (Often the kids spelled it "kandi"; this book doesn't.) "If you were a candy raver, you were entry level," says Tricia Romano. "You didn't know Richie Hawtin." The candy look took the blissed-out cartoonishness of early-rave totems—Cat in the Hat hats, Mickey Mouse gloves, rainbow-colored outfits—as a first principle, and the kids wore actual candy necklaces and bracelets—especially gross after a sweaty night on the dance floor. "You're sucking on a binky?" fumes Maria 909. "What's next, you're going to wear a diaper? Why would I revert to being a child again?" The torch had passed from rave's original claque—hipsters who couldn't wait to move to the city—to déclassé suburban kids who didn't want to grow up, dressed like cartoons.

"The most jarring part was the age difference," says Charm Stadtler (Gabber Girl), a Minneapolis gabber DJ who moved to the Bay Area, where she cofounded the Beta Lounge–style streaming Web station Technostate. "The people I was dancing with in San Francisco were all twenty-five and up. They're all business professionals. Whereas in Minneapolis, at twenty-one years old, I was one of the oldest people there."

"The candy kids were the ones that did the most drugs," said Brandon Ivers. "They were the ones that had the weirdest sexual things happen at the parties. They were definitely the most deluded." Frequently, they'd engage in E'd up group gropes known as "cuddle puddles." In Minneapolis, Ivers knew two sisters who sold ecstasy at parties. "These drug dealers would sponsor them and get them high, and have these two girls run around and sell drugs to the party, under the premise that maybe you would be able to go back home with them later. And they would make out for you. They're *sisters*."

THE ASTRALWERKS STAFF PLACED BETS on where *Dig Your Own Hole*, the second Chemical Brothers album, released April 8, 1997, would land on the *Billboard* album charts opening week. "It's all we thought about, are you kidding me?" says Kolosine. "I didn't go to sleep that night. I was waiting for my boss to call me with the numbers." *Dig* debuted at number fourteen, selling forty-eight thousand copies. "I knew all this airplay we had, and it seemed like we connected the dots. But it was pretty magical. People believed that it was an album that they needed to own, because it rightly got unbelievable reviews, in a time when reviews mattered."

"Setting Sun" had been merely an appetizer: *Dig Your Own Hole* was even more expansive than *Exit Planet Dust*. "It Doesn't Matter" throbbed like the dankest underground house; the sitar-driven, nine-and-a-half-minute finale, "The Private Psychedelic Reel," had the sweep of a classic-rock epic. (Upon hearing this track, Apple Corps inspected the tapes to see whether or not Rowlands and Simons had sampled the Beatles. They hadn't.) "The only people who can [make good albums] are the people who are the best at the music," says Charles Aaron. "You would listen to eight to ten Chemical Brothers songs, whereas you would not listen to eight to ten Crystal Method songs. The Chemical Brothers were the smartest and the most talented. They gave you a real kick in the teeth. And it wasn't, 'They made it rock and roll.' That's the rote language that ended up being in stories, 'cause that's how the editors wanted it to be. They were the most important rock band of that era, if you want to use *Spin*-speak."

For all the critics' positivity, many American reviewers remained deeply suspicious of the Chems' background. "Electronica's appeal is, let's face it, inherently limited: Synthesized bleeps set to rigid computer thwacks will never have the mass appeal of pop songs with singers and hummable choruses," *Entertainment Weekly* harrumphed—hardly the only write-up of the album to reduce an enormous amount of widely variegated music to "synthesized bleeps" and "rigid computer thwacks." (Rock and roll, by the way, consists of pentagrams and Satan worship.) Nor was *EW* alone in conveniently ignoring that America was an increasingly rare place that electronic dance music *wasn't* pop.

Naturally, the mailing lists, once agog over "Chemical Beats," contorted trying to pretend that *Dig* wasn't any good. *Urb* put the Chemical Brothers on the cover, but agonized over it first. "There was a big debate whether we should feature them or not," says Tamara Palmer. "But it made sense at the time that they were really nailing this."

"THERE WAS NO MASTER PLAN of trying to crack America ever," says Liam Howlett. "We were just happy to be there." But "Firestarter," and a clutch of similar songs, made them the subject of a bidding war. "Madonna made a point of coming to a few gigs and was keen," says Howlett. "The fact that she actively went out to get us always had my respect. I also liked the fact that she didn't try and schmooze us. She was just like, 'We want to do this. I love the band and believe in you. We are here, ready to go, if you want.' So we went with Maverick. [Those] guys did a great job. I mean we had done most of the hard work, to be honest. They weren't breaking a new band."

The week their third album, *The Fat of the Land*, came out, in June of 1997, Howlett received a call from XL's Richard Russell, who'd negotiated the band's U.S. deal. "Richard was like, 'I think we will do well with the album. It's going top twenty,'" recalls Howlett. "We were happy with that. The next call was [that] we were number one. It was important to us and to the UK, 'cause it doesn't happen very often with a band like ours. The record was number one in twenty-six countries, I think. But the U.S. made everybody sit up and say, 'What's going on here? We have to open our eyes to this.' It was mad."

The Prodigy appeared on *Spin*'s September 1997 cover—according to Aaron, among the magazine's bestsellers: "That issue was a monster for us. It hit right at the perfect time. But there weren't other groups like that, because that wasn't what it was about. Groups wanted to be respected and be popular, but they didn't want to change to the point where they had to have Keith Flint."

"We were really enjoying ourselves," says Kolosine of this period. "It was like we had slipped the plot on the business: 'Who are these fucking people? Why do they have all this airplay? Why do they have all these videos on MTV? Somebody go out and sign some of these types of bands immediately before I have to kill someone.'" Soon the majors began hiring people to do just that, starting up electronica subsidiaries like Kinetic (Reprise), Outpost (Geffen), 1500 (A&M), and F-111 (Warner Bros.). "I think people saw the opportunity," says Aaron. "Some people sincerely wanted to fill the void with the dance music they loved, and some people sincerely wanted to exploit the shit out of it."

"I fielded my share of phone calls from major-label A&R and marketing guys trying to pick my brain," says Wohelski. Once, he got a call from an exec at Columbia Records, which had signed on to distribute Josh Wink's label, Ovum. "Oddly enough, the guy who did the deal came from the scene. In hindsight, it's weird that someone from Sony was calling me when there is a guy in [his] building who knew what was going on."

Warner Bros.' F-111 was run by DJ DB and former Astralwerks A&R man Andrew Goldstone. "They gave us a really crazy wage and believed we were going to find the next Prodigy for them," says DB, who discovered the perks of a major-label expense account: "You can eat amazing lunches. You can, if you hear somebody's playing somewhere, justify getting on a plane and going to hear them. You can take artists to all kinds of expensive restaurants—the way the record business used to be."

GERRY GERRARD'S TOUR—he was calling it Chaotica again—was off the table by the time *Dig Your Own Hole* landed in the charts— the Prodigy, Orbital, and the Orb all joined Lollapalooza that year. "We played after Tool," says Phil Hartnoll. "We sold ourselves to try to get on those tours as the disco bit at the end. We didn't mean to undermine ourselves as a way to explain to people how it could work as actual fact—and it did sort of work in places." But only "sort of"; it was the last touring Lollapalooza for several years. Equally unsuccessful was the Philip Blaine–helmed Organic '97, on September 20 in Running Springs—a fire in the mountains had moved the party to flat land. The odd-couple headliners were Aphex Twin and Sneaker Pimps. Gerrard stayed home in New York.

With Chaotica off the table, summer-fall 1997 became open season on electronica tours. Daft Punk had a string of September club dates; the widely liked British electronic and downtempo label Ninja Tune did a pair of package tours. More ambitious were Electric Highway, sponsored by *Spin* and BF Goodrich tires and headlined by the Crystal Method; Moonshine Over America, starring the Levy brothers' roster; and Big Top U.S.A., the brainchild of Marci Weber's MCT Management and its marketing arm, Bold—another attempt to make her prize client a star.

Moby seemed hell-bent to throw it away. If *Everything Is Wrong*, with its piano rave anthems and metal guitar, had jackknifed away from the rave scene's direction, Moby's follow-up spit in its eye. The title of *Animal Rights*—issued in the U.S. in February 1997—put Moby's loud-and-proud veganism on the table, and the music was equally divisive. No one expected, or wanted, him to make a full-on rock album—especially his management. "It was one of those hiccups that hurts inside," says Weber. "You're chewing the inside of your mouth, going, 'Why are we doing this?' I thought that it could hurt him. I was very vocal about that. And it did. It hurt a lot."

Moby did himself few favors when Elektra asked him to alter the lyrics of "That's When I Reach for My Revolver" for MTV and radio's sake—it was just after the Columbine high school murders. "My first response, of course, was 'Absolutely not.'" For one thing, it wasn't his song—it was a cover of Boston post-punks Mission of Burma. But Moby asked Burma's Clint Conley, who "grudgingly gave his permission" to alter them. "I've made countless mistakes in my professional life. That was certainly one of the bigger ones."

ELECTRIC HIGHWAY AND BIG TOP were misfires from the off. "There was this corporate presence that weirded me out," says Terry Mullan, who spun at about half of Electric Highway's dates. "The corporate folks would come, and I got the feeling they were let down by the turnout. It didn't live up to their expectations." Tommie Sunshine, in Atlanta, was incensed at not being invited to play Electric Highway's House of Blues date, and showed up with the words FUCK CORPORATE RAVE written across his forehead. "It was the first time we had ever seen corporate branding in a club," he says. "Those tours were the first time targeted marketing came into the picture."

At least Electric Highway's headliners wanted to be there. Moby was clearly, visibly unhappy throughout the Big Top tour. "Going into it I knew they were going to have a really hard time trying to sell tickets, especially because they booked it into larger venues," says Moby. "It really was the wrong tour with the wrong lineup at the wrong time." At Boston's World Trade Center (September 1), the room was so hot he started handing sluggish fans soda and bottled water from his dressing room.

On August 31, Concerts East, Big Top's copromoter in Asbury Park, New Jersey, first threatened to pull out, and then, without telling MCT, called the venue and canceled. Outside the venue, a cardboard sign apologized for the inconvenience; full refunds were given. Nearly as bad was Dallas on September 9: Trance producer BT (Brian Transeau), one of MCT's up-and-coming acts, was too sick to leave his hotel room, and box office fell so far short that, says Weber, "We didn't have enough money to pay one of the bands and some of the crew. Moby gave me back his guarantee, the whole thing. I started to cry, I was under such stress. He just said: 'Don't worry about it.'"

Worst of all was San Francisco—well, it was supposed to be San

Francisco, but then it became Oakland's International Event Center, with three huge rooms. Everything looked great; the West Coast had always done well. On the way there, the tour bus received the news. "I remember being in tears," says Sheneza Mohammed, from MCT-affiliated Bold Marketing: "'What? There's a BART strike?!'" Some twenty-five hundred Bay Area Rapid Transit employees had walked out five days earlier over a salary system that underpaid new hires, leaving more than a quarter-million San Franciscans without a way to work—and hundreds of ravers without a way to Big Top. Moby's performance was peppered with complaints about the way the dance scene had changed, as well as the evening's ticket prices (twenty-five to thirty dollars). When Moby returned to San Francisco two months later to headline the Edge, he lambasted Big Top from the stage.

But L.A. was a triumph: MCT had partnered with Insomniac's Pasquale Rotella and Philip Blaine, who absorbed the lineup into their annual blowout, Nocturnal Wonderland. "We basically saved that tour," says Rotella. "Big Top landed on my date. I was going to kill it, so they gave me the talent for pretty much nothing."

Of the mid-nineties in L.A., Rotella says, "No one else was doing parties at that time." Many of his events were break-ins, leading to a pair of arrests and a subsequent decision to go legit. In East L.A., Rotella's first Nocturnal Wonderland (February 11, 1995) attracted between thirty-five hundred and four thousand. "That was a part of it that wasn't legit—the first Nocturnal Wonderland was way too crowded," says Rotella. "But we were in East L.A."—with far fewer police around—"so we got through it." Though Nocturnal '97 moved location three times, there was little sense it was endangered.

Insomniac still did things like it was 1992. "In that market, that's what the kids expected," says Mohammed. "They had carnival rides. They set up everything from sumo wrestling to a Ferris wheel. And it was perfect weather." Nocturnal Wonderland 1997 drew fifty-five hundred—fewer than Organic '96, but clearly the Big Top tour's best stop.

"Big Top was too much too soon," says Mohammed. "All of them were too much too soon. There wasn't enough infrastructure." Even the Nocturnal audience sensed defeat. "I felt like something was compromised," says promoter and manager Danny Johnson, then an L.A. teenager. "It's obvious now—in the process of corporate [sponsors] coming in, and losing what was so independent and so detailed and about the music and the fans. I remember being in this tent and [feeling] a lack of vibe."

"They were nothing but flops," sniffs Rotella about 1997's electronica tours. "They did not get it. It was people in offices that got inspired by the wrong event, and it led them down very costly roads. Organic did not spark anything but a series of unsuccessful shows."

The exception was Moonshine Over America—the most scene-centric lineup, the smallest ad budget, the least amount of press, the furthest removed from the rock-concert biz's prevailing ethos, and the one that lasted; it returned to the road three more times. "They used to look at SoundScan—the layout shows where your top markets are," says Dave Minner. "Naturally, if my top markets [as AK1200] are L.A., New York, D.C., Miami, Denver, then those are the dates he wants to have me on. If we were booked six months prior in the same market, there's no reason to be on that show. A lot of things factored into it. They were doing that with every artist."

The exception was Superstar DJ Keoki, who had come to Moonshine in 1994, after spinning an edition of *Journeys by DJ*—the title altered to *Journeys by Superstar DJ* for the occasion. The tour was a relief from the circus that had enveloped the Limelight, which was on the verge of closing. Worse, Keoki's ex, Michael Alig, with his friend Robert "Freeze" Riggs, had murdered drug-dealing club kid Angel Melendez, dumping his dismembered body into the Hudson River. Alig was sentenced to ten to twenty years in prison for manslaughter a week after Moonshine Over America ended in New Orleans, on October 24.

IN SPRING 1998, Norman Cook was spinning in Brighton to his home crowd at the Big Beat Boutique when he decided to test a new track. A rapid-fire syllable shot out of the speakers, then cohered into the voice of Lord Finesse: "R-r-r-r-right about now, the funk soul brother / Check it out now, the funk soul brother," over and over again—then a clattering breakbeat and a bouncy surf guitar line. "I put it on and everybody just looked up, mouthing, 'This is you, isn't it?'"

It couldn't have been anyone else. Fatboy Slim's "The Rockafeller Skank" was Cook's big beat formula *in excelsis*. "The first album, there were little glimpses of how we could make it radio friendly, putting hooks on it—making it less to do with acid house and more of a pop approach," Cook says. "By the second album, I'd really refined the ingredients." The ultimate big beat track, "The Rockafeller Skank" was impossible to get out of your head and nearly as difficult not to move to. "'Rockafeller Skank' came out the week I finished the album," says Cook. "An anticipation had built up, and a feeling that what we were doing was the right thing at the right time—less 'The album is almost finished' than 'We've got to get this album out, quick.'"

"The Rockafeller Skank" was issued in the States on June 16, the leadoff track on *Amp 2*, Astralwerks' second collection of cuts from the MTV show—which was barely being watched. Electronic dance music wasn't going to save the music business after all—teen pop and nü-metal and hip-hop were. "You had the rise of the Korns and Limp Bizkits and Sugar Rays," says Dan Charnas. "Hip-hop really showed that sampling could be the backbone of a postmodern way of making music." That meant for dance music to cross over, it usually needed a breakbeat. Take *Amp 2*: Besides "Skank," there's the Prodigy remixing Method Man, drum and bass forefather Aphrodite remixing the Jungle Brothers, and rappers Chuck D, Kool Keith, and KRS-One sitting in with, respectively, Ticc-Tacc, Hardkiss, and Goldie. Cook was the hookiest of any of them, and the second Fatboy Slim album, *You've Come a Long Way, Baby* (1998), turned him, briefly, into a pop star.

• • • •

A MONTH AFTER BIG TOP ended, Elektra had issued *I Like to Score*, a collection of Moby tracks that had been used in movies, and didn't renew his contract. Shortly afterward, Moby was visiting a writer friend who was dumping some old promos, and took home a copy of *Sounds of the South*, a box set of blues, gospel, and folk music recorded in the field over the summer of 1959 by the great American folklorist Alan Lomax. Moby fell quickly for it, not least as a trove of a cappella vocals—a DJ is a DJ—and he asked MCT to clear his samples of them. "We were like, 'Huh?'" says Sheneza Mohammed. "It was such an interesting get. Once we heard that source material, we were all like, 'This is so accessible.'"

Moby still didn't have a U.S. label when he issued his first track in this new vein, "Honey," as a British twelve-inch in the summer of 1998. A college-radio spin of the track in upstate New York led Kate Hyman, the head of A&R for V2 Records—Richard Branson's new venture following his departure from Virgin—to hear it. "V2 had already passed," says Weber. "She called us the next day and said, 'I want to hear the rest of the record.'" V2 issued *Play* in the U.S. on June 1, 1999. Moby began to promote it with a handful of springtime DJ appearances. "When I made *Animal Rights*, I wasn't trying to alienate anyone, and by DJing again, I'm not intentionally trying to *de-alienate* anyone, either," he said at the time. Nevertheless, the appearances helped bridge the gap back to the club audience.

At Chicago's Smart Bar, Moby's set veered toward the kind of glassy trance then blanketing clubs. Mohammed had left MCT by then to work for Kinetic. She recalls a pandemonium-riddled Virgin Records in-store in April 1999 for Sasha and John Digweed, upon the release of *Expeditions*, the final mix in the *Northern Exposure* series. "Maybe three thousand kids showed up," says Mohammed. "It was insane: line out the door, kids trying to get in, fans throwing flowers up onstage, making posters for them to sign. I don't think I've seen an in-store, ever, that well attended. John Digweed looked at me: 'Now I know what Ricky Martin feels like.'"

No one expected Moby to attract that kind of hubbub again. The exception, as ever, was Weber. Leaving his studio shortly after No Doubt's Gwen Stefani had laid down a vocal track for the new wave rocker "South Side," Marci turned to Sheneza and said: "I think we might actually go gold with this record. If everybody sticks with this, we might just sell half a million." It was like aiming for the moon. "No electronic artist was selling those kind of numbers," says Mohammed. "Not even the Chems—nobody."

THROUGHOUT THE COUNTRY, one-time renegade party throwers were starting to go legit. In Minneapolis, Woody McBride worked with rock promoters Compass Entertainment to put on large-scale raves in sports arenas. The live-show landscape was changing other ways, too: In the aftermath of the 1996 Telecommunications Act, nearly seventeen hundred radio stations traded hands to the tune of thirteen billion dollars in 1998; a year later, one radio conglomerate, Jacor, would turn into an even bigger one: Clear Channel.

Drum and bass DJ Dara (Darragh Guilfoyle), a New Yorker originally from Ireland, recalls a late-nineties booking at a venue he'd played several times already, always for the same promoter. "I went and played, same as I always did, and this guy showed up in a suit and handed me my envelope. This venue and this promoter had been bought out by Clear Channel. The Clear Channel guy was giving me my money. Everything else remained the same: same promoter, same venue, but now somebody else was in charge."

FOLLOWING EVEN FURTHUR '96, David Prince had gotten into band management; he was done by 1999. He found a job in New York fact checking for *Spin*, where he became the go-to festival guy: "Everyone who worked there just wasn't interested in getting in the mud."

Prince wound up with tickets to Woodstock '99, which featured a

Rave Hangar—half-indoor, half-outdoor—headlined by Fatboy Slim and Moby. The dance acts were a damn sight better than all the leaden boomer worship (Bruce Hornsby, Rusted Root, Sheryl Crow) and nü-metal (Godsmack, Korn, Limp Bizkit); the lineup like eating tar before you even got there. Nevertheless, Prince was game: "I was not on assignment. I was just there." Once again, he car-camped.

John Scher, one of Woodstock '99's promoters, was the head of Metropolitan Entertainment, whose corporate owner, Odgen Entertainment, sold the festival's vendors their food and set the prices high. "Suburban amphitheaters—sheds—often pay the talent ninety-five percent of the door income," says Gerry Gerrard, who booked the Chemical Brothers on the main stage. "They make their money on the food, alcohol, parking. I've never liked it. It feels to me like, 'Get the audience in, take them by the ankles, and shake every penny out of their pockets.' John Scher told me, 'Well, Gerry, you're fighting against the whole of the concert industry in America.'"

Concert prices were skyrocketing. "Three years ago, ticket prices of $50–$70 stood out like a sore thumb," Pollstar editor Gary Bongiovanni told a reporter. "In 1998, those prices are not at all surprising." Tickets for Woodstock '99 were $180 at the door. When you arrived, there was no comfort to speak of—a former airstrip with nowhere to sit, no shade, and no free water anywhere but on the far perimeters—in the middle of constant July heat. More then ten thousand people received medical treatment that weekend, mostly for too much sun.

"The photo pit from day one was like a M.A.S.H. unit, people constantly being thrown over and carried out on stretchers," says Prince. "It was chaos. The crowd was ugly. You could feel the security disappearing. Nobody was in charge." The sanitation staff—underage, undertrained, underpaid, underfed, under-watered—was walking out en masse by midafternoon, after the porta-potties began to leak. "There were these gross mud puddles," says Prince. Gerrard, with his wife and kids backstage in a motor home, recalls that the VIP camp-ers' tents "were in the runoff of the overflow from the porta-potties."

The mook-rock that dominated the lineup had brought out a simi-larly boorish crowd—*Lord of the Flies* with backward baseball caps and cargo shorts. Everywhere, beefy men surrounded smaller women and chanted, "Show your tits!" until they were too intimidated to say no. Eight women reported being raped; eyewitnesses recounted more. It was even dangerous backstage. "The dressing room trailer was on [the end of] a scaffold," says Marci Weber, there Friday for Moby's performance. "It was a mini-RV. There were two doors, and the door to nowhere wasn't locked."

Moby played to a crowd of twenty-five thousand; an NYC-Raver, presumably familiar with the city's club excesses, posted that the tent had "the most open drug usage I've ever seen." Many shed their clothes entirely; cuddle puddles turned to outright orgies. The fol-lowing night, with Fatboy Slim headlining, was even crazier. "It was truly one of the more wild things I've ever seen, especially for those kids," says Prince. "They had never seen anything like it. People went fucking apeshit. It was great."

But outside the tent was also an all-too-real demonstration of what people were starting to resent about big beat—its easy thrills and heavy whiff of testosterone made it a soundtrack to something far removed from the beat-geekery that set it in motion. "There were lots of jokes about 'Frat-Boy Slim,'" says Cook, who concedes: "I suppose 'Rockafeller Skank' became an anthem for that sort of beer-boyish mentality. The whole big beat thing got out of hand. It *had* got a bit frat-boy: 'Wheee! Let's all get drunk and party!'"

At Woodstock '99, the bonhomie that fueled Fatboy Slim's DJ sets was in short supply, leaving only the aggression. "I [went on] the mo-ment after the main stage was shut down," says Cook. "It had been quite peaceful during the day. I didn't notice any undercurrent." That changed once he got on the decks. "It pretty much kicked off during my set, from what I can gather." Early on, a fourteen-foot U-Haul carrying a half-pipe—intended as a skateboarding ramp elsewhere on the site—barreled in. "Somebody drove [it] right into the middle of the crowd," says Cook. "The suspension collapsed. It was one of those proper Woodstock moments, like the brown acid [in 1969]." His voice switches to perfect American loudspeaker: *"We have to get the van out. Fatboy Slim cannot play till we remove the van from the crowd."*

Typically, a post-show Cook was a garrulous Cook. Not at Woodstock. "When I got off the stage, they put me straight into the car, straight to the airport: 'Don't talk to anyone.' It was very unusual. I figured they were telling me to get out of there because they just figured I'd stay there about another thirty-six hours and get lost in some field. My American agent could see what was going on and said, 'Look, we've got to get out of here.' I flew straight back to England. By the time I got home, I saw footage on the news of my dressing room on fire."

When you prefer tomorrow's technology to yesterday's heroes, you'll let technology decide what is going to happen, and you forget that it still has to come from human souls.

—SERGE OF CLONE RECORDS TO 313 LIST, JANUARY 1998

DETROIT ELECTRONIC MUSIC FESTIVAL

Detroit, Michigan
May 26–29, 2000

JUST AS VOOM HAD FEARED, Detroit's rave scene grew steadily more formulaic. "It was always Terry Mullan or Rabbit in the Moon," says Hobey Echlin, a former Detroit *Metro Times* reporter. "The Midwest party kids were cultivated by trends. They got turned onto a more commercial side of it." The new kids were getting younger; DJ-producer Jimmy Edgar, from Warren, near 7 Mile and Woodward, went to his first rave in 1996, at thirteen: "There was a lot of shady shit going on, a lot of dudes selling drugs. The guys that threw the parties carried guns. It was normal—I didn't realize how fucked up it was until I left Detroit. When I was a teenager, it was glorified to have a gun."

A number of Detroit raves were funded by the Russian Mafia, which had taken root in the U.S. through the seventies and eighties. One group operated out of a Detroit chop shop that also did business as a party locale. "They were running the nitrous, a lot of the cocaine in the city," says Edgar. "They were in with the cops. A district attorney was trying to clean it up. Once you get political motivations involved, that's when the weird violence starts happening. You hear about girls getting punched in the face and people getting guns pulled on them—typical conspiracy shit. I didn't see that too much, but I was around a few bad situations."

The parties were turning into flagrant drug markets, says Edgar: "You'd turn a corner, and see people with bags and bags, hundreds of pills. Some of those parties that we did, the money was made by basically going into the gay bars and selling drugs. Once you started expanding, more drugs came, and it killed itself." A November 1998 Fox News report didn't help. Some promoters hired lawyers to man the door—to tell the police, "These kids are within their legal rights." That way, says Echlin, "Your party couldn't get busted."

"IT'S DAMN NEAR Woodstock for raves," an excited NYC-Raver posted when the lineup for the first Coachella Festival (October 9 and 10, 1999), in Indio, California, went live—meaning 1969, not 1999. Founded by Philip Blaine—one of the movers behind Organic '96—and promoted by his company Goldenvoice, Coachella featured reliable draws like Beck, Rage Against the Machine, and Tool. But the undercard had little in common with the headliners—and everything to do with L.A. Roughly two-thirds of the first Coachella lineup was, nominally or overtly, "electronic," including the Chemical Brothers, Underworld, Moby, Juan Atkins, Derrick May, Kevin Saunderson, Richie Hawtin, and BT. Goldenvoice wasn't putting on a rock show with a rave tent; this was closer to a rave with rock bands.

"There's so much crossover in California," says David Prince, who attended the first Coachella. "It's the same people, the same security crews, the same promoters." The grounds had hosted DJ parties, but for most of Coachella's crowd the venue was new. "That space is one of a kind," says Prince. "It's like a country club in the desert. You had free rein to walk around in this beautiful, perfectly manicured grass. The weather was really nice that first year. It was super easy to get everywhere because it wasn't that crowded."

Coachella flouted a lot of what the U.S. concert biz considered ironclad rules about how a festival is handled. "With Coachella, in the early days, you certainly couldn't bring in alcohol, but they weren't strict about bringing [food] in and out," says Gerry Gerrard. "They didn't have that many food vendors. They didn't really have camping; you had a thousand hotels [around] that were out of season. The neighborhood loved it, and still do."

"California just has a different attitude about large group gatherings," says Prince. "It's more European. It's more laid back. It's a cliché, but it's totally true: It's more chill. You can walk around in a bikini and smoke weed wherever you want. That's a lot more fun than being in a state park in New Jersey and having security breathing down your neck and it smells like shit. It felt like they had cracked a code: 'This is the antidote.' Coachella restored the balance." But it also didn't make much money, and its second installment came eighteen months later, relaunching Coachella not as a fall festival but a spring one, beginning in April 2001.

COACHELLA HELPED CLARIFY something in the air: With Lollapalooza out of the picture, European-style festivals were finally taking root in America. "It was brewing," says Rob Theakston, then label manager for Carl Craig's label Planet E. In fact, even while he was playing Coachella, Craig was quietly talking with Detroit officials about doing something similar in his home city's downtown—at Hart Plaza, a large open space right on the Detroit River.

The idea had developed out of the ashes of 1994's World Party, a disastrous event (about a thousand people showed up to Joe Louis Arena, which holds twenty times that many) organized by Carol Marvin, who'd started producing the Detroit International Jazz Festival shortly afterward. She still believed a showcase for local dance talent could be an international draw, and she started talking to Derrick May. "She tried to convince me [to] let her find somebody with money to back one of the old factory buildings here for Ford Motor Company," he says. "Over the top, totally ridiculous. But I was able to sway her from that to talk about some other opportunities."

One of them was a real-deal festival—not a rave—showcasing the city's homegrown DJ talent, an idea that had been kicking around Techno Boulevard's inner circle for years. "Derrick May, Carl Craig, Kenny Larkin, and I had an organization called CK DJ," says Kevin Saunderson. "It was meant to throw events, put out records, [and] one of those meetings was about a festival at Hart Plaza." But the inner circle was scattered around the world at any given time. "It was a community idea," says Craig. "Everybody wanted to see it happen— [but] Derrick and I had been more productive about discussing it. And then he brought in Carol." Saunderson recalls Marvin attending one of the meetings: "Derrick was like, 'She's connected. She can get sponsors.' But no progression happened from that meeting for a year, year and a half."

May got out before Marvin lined anything up—but she kept pushing on her own. The Detroit Electronic Music Festival (DEMF) was becoming Marvin's cause when she approached Craig. "At one point," says Theakston, "Carl and I produced a radio show for a local radio station called 'Detroit Technology,' and [we were] brainstorming how we could convince the sponsors of that show to give us a one-day festival—bring in Björk."

Early on, Marvin and Craig connected, with him DJing her charity fashion show for Absolut Couture. "They had a feel for how one another worked, for how well they would work together," says Theakston. "They had a good rapport." Marvin owned a PR company, Pop Culture Media; she had local government connections. In 1999, the idea was kicked upstairs, eventually reaching Mayor Dennis Archer; Craig nearly missed the meeting after Theakston forgot to remind him of it.

"I felt assured after the meeting," says Craig. "I knew we were going to make it happen." He and Marvin summoned Joshua Glazer, the

Real Detroit Weekly's dance-music columnist, who also booked the Hamtramck nightclub Motor. This was strategic, says Theakston: "If the city backfired, it wouldn't be because of us. Putting all this information out there forced their hand." Craig and Marvin told Glazer: "We signed the contracts with the city yesterday. You're going to break the story in next week's issue." At a Planet E party in Miami's Red Square during the 2000 Winter Music Conference, Craig announced the DEMF from the stage: "We hope that you'll be one of the quarter to one million people to come out."

CRAIG'S FAR-FLUNG CONTACTS came in handy when staging the first DEMF. "Carl was calling people in his Rolodex going, 'I need to work around your booking agents. I'm cashing in my chips,'" says Hobey Echlin. Craig's old friend Jonah Sharp (Spacetime Continuum) recalls picking up the phone and hearing: "Dude, showtime!" Another personal call went to Questlove (Ahmir Thompson), drummer-leader of hip-hop band the Roots. "Carl was adamant of the Roots playing there," says Questlove. "I was a little thrown off because I was a little worried that we would be the oddball out. I knew it wasn't a hip-hop crowd." Nevertheless, Thompson agreed. "[Craig] wanted a really good balance," says Theakston. "He wanted to have families come down that normally wouldn't go to an electronic music concert: 'Well, Mos Def—or the Roots—is playing for free down in Hart Plaza.'"

There was still a lot of skepticism from the locals. "Carl went through a lot of criticism and a lot of heat to do the DEMF," says Theakston. "But he also knew the reward if it was a success." Rita Sayegh, a local designer who'd done work for Planet E, was tapped to film a documentary: "Part of us didn't think this festival would actually happen. There were names we thought, 'My God, how is he going to get them here?' But it was, 'There's still more coming.'" That went for the audience as well. "We knew there would be [a tourist] influx," says Theakston. "Everyone and their brother on the 313 list were going to be there for the first one. But to what degree [it would go beyond that] was unknown."

Craig and Marvin were mooting a deal with the city to put on DEMF for three years. If a performer wasn't booked in 2000, they figured, there was always 2001 or 2002. "Carl never saw this as just a one-off thing," says Theakston. "When you're trying to do something of that magnitude, trying to have a diverse lineup, someone's going to be left out, and someone's feelings are going to be hurt." When Robert Hood wasn't invited, he says, "I remember feeling like, 'Wow—this ain't cool.' I got past it, because it made me realize, 'You're stronger than this. Deal with it and move on.' But it left a bitter taste." Alan Oldham aired his feelings on the matter publicly, telling an interviewer: "It's plain to see how I'm regarded by the people in charge of the festival, and we all know who's in charge of it."

THE WEEKS LEADING UP to the festival were, in Theakston's words, "a lot of hustle, a lot of drinking Coca-Cola and never sleeping." The team's one respite was Craig's thirty-first-birthday barbecue. Volunteers were rounded up; Tim Price, Richie Hawtin's long-standing aide-de-camp, was hired as production manager. The main issue was paperwork: As Memorial Day drew nearer the city hadn't yet signed off. "We hit a serious snag within two weeks [of] the festival," says Craig, who turned to a brother-in-law who worked for Lisa Webb, Mayor Archer's executive aide. Craig got a meeting with Webb the Wednesday before the festival's scheduled start.

He sweetened the deal by bringing along a CD-R of handpicked tracks by Herbie Hancock and Stevie Wonder, as well as Craig's peers. "The reality is, a lot of people think that techno music is weird. If I walked in there and played Human Resource's 'Dominator' and [Second Phase's] 'Mentasm' . . ." Craig trails off, laughing. "What Herbie was doing with 'Rockit' was electronic music. Stevie Wonder is electronic music. Hip-hop is electronic music." Even with Webb ramming it through, the final papers weren't signed until Friday afternoon, with less than twenty-four hours to go.

When Josh Glazer swung by Hart Plaza Friday evening of Memorial Day weekend, he says, "It was a total clusterfuck. Nothing was working. Every active person in the community was down there, trying to figure out how to help the union guys build a stage. The City of Detroit was paying for this—union crews, union sound, totally not right for this event. It was the same sound system they used for the jazz festival." He went to work at Motor, then headed south again to an after-hours to see a DJ Richie Hawtin had recommended. It was 3 A.M. "I decided to stop by Hart Plaza to see how things were going." This time he stuck around. "When all of your friends are there working, you can't just be like, 'See you guys later.'"

By sunup Saturday, nearly everything was done. "About six in the morning I was in a golf cart with Tim Price overlooking the Detroit River and said, 'You know, if we can get ten thousand people over the next three days, we'll have done our job,'" says Theakston.

"DETROIT ELECTRONIC MUSIC FESTIVAL," blared the entrance to Hart Plaza, through a series of cutout letters over television sets showing static. Walk past them and there were five stages, all pumping out a more or less continuous assortment of house, techno, breakbeats fast and slow, and more. Most of the lineup were locals who'd played plenty in their hometown, but not usually for the general public.

The question Saturday afternoon: *What* general public? "Hart Plaza is quite a large area," says Sayegh. "You can have hundreds of people there and they can all be different places and you wouldn't really fill the place up." "Because it was a free, open festival, for the first few hours [it was] just homeless people," says Glazer. Not that the staff was prepared for more. "Nobody had slept," says Motor's Jon Ozias—worse, "Nobody had commissioned a coffee vendor on the grounds." A late-morning drizzle didn't help, though Hannah Sawtell, Craig's wife, helped dispel it at the C-Pop Stage with mellow jazz-funk oldies "Give Me the Sunshine" by Leo's Sunshipp and "Wind Parade" by Donald Byrd. She got her wish—the sun appeared, though it remained windy all day, with some DJs struggling with jumping tone arms.

The festival streamed online via Seattle Webcaster Groovetech. "I remember the first day getting phone calls—'Dude, you've got to come down'—about two in the afternoon," says Detroit DJ Eric Cloutier. "I looked at the stream: 'But there's, like, two hundred people there.'" Gazing from the main stage during Spacetime Continuum's afternoon set, Jonah Sharp counted fifty punters: "It was really weird and empty." The festival itself, though, was a welcome change from the gold-rush mentality Sharp had watched creep over U.S. dance music; even with a sparse crowd, this was more like it.

Sharp was "blown away" later that day by the Berlin duo of Mark Ernestus and Moritz von Oswald—Juan Atkins's connection to the Tresor label, both of whom revered Detroit. They'd recorded as Rhythm & Sound, Basic Channel, Maurizio, Quadrant, and Phylyps, issuing a passel of lengthy, flickering, dub-drenched tracks that earned the Motor City DJs' approval. Ernestus and von Oswald's DEMF appearance following a joint performance by Tikiman (Paul St. Hilaire) and Scion (Peter Kuschnereit, René Löwe) was a surprise—the DEMF staff had forgotten to announce it. Rhythm & Sound played three and a half hours, from hollowed-out techno to a live dub set, when Isotope 217—a jazz-oriented spinoff of the amorphous Chicago band Tortoise—no-showed for its eight-thirty slot.

THE GAPS AT HART PLAZA were filling in—noticeably so. "The paper had been doing coverage on it in various degrees every single day leading up to it," says Ozias. "Half the people there had friends or relatives that were involved in it."

"That was a huge thing for nearly every veteran that played that festival," says Theakston. "At that point, a lot of the producers' and

DJs' families didn't understand what they were doing. Having this happen in their own backyard, where their families could come down, was a momentous thing for a lot of people. It was a huge point of pride. One DJ-producer who's been around forever, Delano Smith, actually hired a limousine to bring his family down, and gave them the five-star treatment. This was a validation for him."

One DJ was Theo Parrish, who'd grown up in Chicago, apprenticing with Larry Heard and Lil' Louis, then moved to Detroit and worked there for Ron Trent. He was steeped in house music fundamentals and outspoken about it, particularly as the Web began enabling younger fans to investigate the music's roots thanks to the likes of the Deep House Page site, begun in 1997 and featuring audio of vintage sets by Frankie Knuckles, Larry Levan, Ron Hardy, Tony Humphries, and Farley Keith. "There are so many people that were into other things when 'house' music was house music that I look at them and think, you're fraudulent!" he said in 2008. "The concept is not anything that you can go and learn online."

Parrish took the decks on the Motor Stage at 6, spinning a history lesson featuring Mr. Fingers, Black Ivory, Yaz's "Situation," Fela Kuti, Gil Scott-Heron, and ending, richly, with Prince and the Revolution's unambiguously patriotic "America." The middle stretch, though, was what stuck. First, Parrish tipped his hat to his family with the Intruders' "I'll Always Love My Mama." Then he went into Donny Hathaway's live version of "The Ghetto." "He was able to take it to this non-danceable thing," says Patrick Russell. "Then he just launches into this massive disco edit, and the whole place goes apeshit." (The edit, "Mustang 1," appeared on a white-label twelve-inch only for sale at the festival.) "There was this little old lady dancing nonstop the whole time, right in front of me," says Russell.

OZIAS HAD LEFT HART PLAZA that afternoon to pick up Josh Wink—Motor's headliner that night—from the airport; Wink wanted to see the festival, so back they drove. "Hannah comes running up to me: 'Oh my God! Have you seen it?' And she grabs my hand and she takes me over to the steps that lead to the main stage. Little by little I see that in two hours, this thing had turned into a solid sea of people all across the way. I get chills just remembering that moment."

"It takes a lot of people to fill it," says Sayegh. "You think it'll be the Detroiters, or supporters of electronic music in the area. You never think that it's going to be the variety of people I remember seeing." Black inner-city Detroit had turned out; white suburban metro Detroit turned out; European diehards who spent their free time fussing over Detroit matrix numbers on 313 turned out; people from all over the I-94 strip looking for the next killer (free!) party turned out. *Everyone* turned out.

Theakston, who'd been sent off to get some shut-eye after dropping a cinder block on his ankle, pulled up on a golf cart to Stacey Pullen DJing to a full bowl. "Dan Sicko ran up to me and gave me a head butt and kept screaming, 'Can you believe this shit?'" He adds that when Pullen dropped San Francisco DJ Simon's "Free at Last," featuring a prominent Martin Luther King sample, "It was this whole Woodstock togetherness vibe."

IT POURED EARLY AND STOPPED midafternoon on Sunday, just as it had Saturday, but the rain didn't deter anybody. "People were coming in droves," says Cloutier. "People did the same thing I did, but from much farther away: people from Chicago being like, 'Holy shit, let's get in the car right now. We're gassing up and going.' [Local] people were wandering around, crying their eyes out: 'I never thought this would actually work.'"

Most of the weekend's hip-hop was on day two, from small local acts on the Motor Stage (Lacksidaisycal, DJ Houseshoes, the Breakfast Club) to the main-stage troika of local heroes Slum Village—featuring rising DJ and producer Jay Dee, a.k.a. J Dilla (James Yancey)—the

Roots, and Mos Def. But what drew the dancers to DEMF were the city's two ascendant DJ styles, both with equal claim to techno and hip-hop: electro and booty.

Old-wave electro of the "Planet Rock"/Cybotron school had never lost currency in Kraftwerk-loving Detroit. But in the mid-nineties a new wave of regional producers worked to shear the style of cutesy Pac-Man associations. At the front was Drexciya (Gerald Donald and James Stinson), a duo even less interested in the press than Underground Resistance, who utilized a similarly conceptual framework—an underwater kingdom where the offspring of pregnant African women discarded during the Middle Passage gave "birth at sea to babies that never needed air," aquatic warriors who eventually rose to the surface to wreak revenge. (Stinson died in 2002.)

Donald also cofounded Ectomorph with Brendan M. Gillen (BMG), a former music director at Ann Arbor's WCBN, the University of Michigan's campus station; later, Erika Sherman replaced Donald. Gillen issued Ectomorph's sinister electro on his label, Interdimensional Transmissions, which also distributed similarly minded labels like Miami's Schematic and Detroit's Ersatz Audio. The latter was run by Adam Lee Miller and Nicola Kuperus, a.k.a. the highly stylized electropop duo ADULT., whose presentation borrowed as much from Kraftwerk, Gary Numan, and John Foxx as did the music. In 1998, Interdimensional Transmissions also licensed "Space Invaders Are Smoking Grass," by I-f ("interference"), a.k.a. Hague producer Ferenc E. van der Sluijs—an international underground smash.

Electro was also key in booty—the simplest term of many (ghettotech, Detroit bass, booty bass) for the hyper, electro-heavy, inner-city sound of local-hero DJs like Gary Chandler, Waxtax-N Dre, DJ Godfather, DJ Assault, DJ Polo, and DJ Fingers. Plenty of Detroit techno's old guard hated it. "I'm not gonna play a record at forty-five because they play it at the titty bar like that," Anthony "Shake" Shakir told Thomas Cox. "Go to the titty bar and dance." But it was ubiquitous. "Every major radio station—there were three of them—would broadcast booty live Friday and/or Saturday night," says Echlin.

It was also omnivorous, taking in jump-up jungle (heavy on vocal samples from dancehall reggae and hip-hop), Chicago ghetto (and, of course, booty house) house, Berlin minimal techno, Miami bass, and down-and-dirty hip-hop like Lil Jon & the East Side Boyz' "I Like Dem Hoes" and Project Pat's "Gel-N-Weave," all repitched to Detroit's jittery tempo. Brian Gillespie points out that "Groove La Chord," a crisp, gliding 1999 track by Swedish techno producer Aril Brikha, whose *Deep-arture in Time* album Transmat licensed in 2000, "crossed over to the ghetto crowd—it had that feel." Brikha and his Time:Space band played a heartily received set at DEMF's main stage on Sunday afternoon, after the rain ended, but the real party was at the Underground Stage.

"It was terribly unorganized and really fun," recalls Adam Lee Miller of ADULT., who played at 4 P.M. "We didn't get a sound check at all. So we brought each instrument in one at a time, starting with the kick drum, and would ask the audience to tell us if it was loud enough. Then we'd bring in the snare drum, and the hi-hat, bass lines, etc. It was actually a fun way to [fix the problem]; instead of being a prima donna and being mad, everybody became a part of it."

Gillespie's colleague DJ Godfather (Brian Jeffries) was up next. "As soon as Godfather started playing, there was a ton of ladies up on the fence shaking their asses," says Nicola Kuperus. "Up on the fences," adds Miller: "I mean, *up* on the fences—precariously, butts toward the stage." Theakston recalls "girls taking off their clothes—it was really uncomfortable to have to go up and tell them, 'Don't do that.'" Ectomorph followed at seven. "Everybody you knew was there," says Erika Sherman. "Everyone was getting external validation: 'This is real. It actually does matter.'"

Booty's biggest hit was "Sandwiches," by the Detroit Grand Pu Bahs, which Gillespie had first released in 1999 on his label Throw. Jive Records, swimming in teen-pop money, licensed it in 2000. The

Pu Bahs were enthusiastically received Monday evening on the Underground Stage. As the Planet E office recapped it, they "shocked an elderly couple who were happily grooving, when Paris the Black Fu [shouted], '*Let us see that thong.*'"

ANOTHER SURPRISE: French DJ Laurent Garnier didn't play the DEMF stage as planned. Instead, there was Moodymann: Kenny Dixon Jr., son of a Motown session player, whose first album, *A Silent Introduction* (1997), had grabbed attention as much for liner notes decrying white people sampling black music as for the distended, sample-heavy tracks that enacted a dialogue between the music's roots and its present. At DEMF, his set began boldly, with Gil Scott-Heron's "We Almost Lost Detroit," the spoken-word poet's harrowing 1977 recounting of a partial meltdown of the Fermi 1 nuclear reactor in Monroe County's Frenchtown Township.

"There were technical problems, so he had to restart it," says Theakston. "The wind was blowing the needle. He started singing along, and it was awesome." He also took a jab at the crowd: "Look at all these beautiful people driving through Detroit, having a good time. I drive *in* it." "It wouldn't be Kenny without making a slight political dig," says Theakston.

When Dixon dropped Parrish's "Summertime Is Here," Last Poets cofounder Umar Bin Hassan, one of Scott-Heron's contemporaries, got on the mike and offered an impromptu rendition of the Poets' "Niggers Are Scared of Revolution," while Dixon got off the decks and walked out front to dance with a woman. It was theater, a basement-party vibe with Dixon's just-another-cat-from-the-D persona writ large at the center. "His whole set was playing Curtis Mayfield records and talking on the mike to his buddies," says Sharp. "I was in heaven."

MAYOR ARCHER INTRODUCED Slum Village on the main stage. J Dilla—then known as Jay Dee—hung with dance as well as hip-hop producers, and had worked with Dixon and remixed acts for Planet E. He also hipped Questlove to the Thomas Bangalter twelve-inches on Roulé he was sampling, turning Quest into a Daft Punk fan. Slum Village's set was heavy on their upcoming album, *Fantastic Vol. 2*. As they wound down, Carl Craig came by and said hello to the Roots.

"The stage was set up weird—not a place that was ready for a band," says Questlove. Instead of a staircase, he had to step on a plastic milk crate to get onstage. "At the time, I was dangerously obese—about 420 pounds. I took one step on the milk crate and my foot went right through it. It went three inches into [my leg]. When you get stabbed you don't try to yank it out"—but he did. Then he got on the riser and played a two-hour set with blood pouring from his right leg. "Because of the adrenaline, it was painless. And of course, being mortified in front of thousands of people—and my idol, Dilla—I played it off like I wasn't hurt." When they finished, Questlove forewent a hospital visit because Dilla wanted to play him a new remix. "He said, 'What about your leg?'" That summer, the drummer began a diet, eventually shedding 150 pounds.

BY MONDAY, THE CROWD had metastasized so much that news crews were arriving. Clark Warner opened the DEMF Stage with a long ambient set, beginning with a track as pointed, in its own way, as "The Ghetto" or "Free at Last" or "We Almost Lost Detroit": Side A of Manuel Göttsching's *E2-E4*, all thirty minutes, with which Derrick May had sent people home from the Music Institute. Here, it welcomed everyone home.

But not everyone felt as welcome as they might. Juan Atkins didn't show up for his 4 P.M. Memorial Day slot—which he admits was a silent protest at his place on the schedule: "I felt like I had a lot to do with the creation of this whole sound. Why would you have me playing in the afternoon? I got there at the time *I thought* I should have been there"—e.g., prime time. Dan Bell, who'd missed Sunday due to faulty equipment, filled in.

The afternoon's most emotionally charged performance came from Anthony "Shake" Shakir—long one of Detroit's most versatile and talented producers, as well as one of its most fearlessly opinionated. "In the Detroit community, everyone tells it like it is, but Shake would have *no* brakes," says Theakston. "I remember him at Record Time talking to another guy: 'Who the fuck does Carl think he is doing this? He's going to bring all these white artists into Detroit.'" The fact that Craig pulled it off, Shake admits, left him "flummoxed."

Shakir worked a regular job and only occasionally took out-of-town gigs, and he rolled up to the stage in a wheelchair, having recently been diagnosed with MS. "I couldn't really move along a lot, but I was able to play," he says. Shakir didn't have insurance or benefits. "He was so proud," says Theakston. "He would never complain about it, not once." Kicking off with a molasses-thick D'Angelo groove, he was soon rocking Roulé doubles. "Once he got behind the decks it was like everything fell away," Bill Van Loo, a young Ypsilanti producer who'd played Saturday on the Underground Stage, posted to 313. A breakdancing circle formed. In the middle, an archetypal white suburban dad held his daughter: preschool-age, agog at everybody's moves. "Everyone was taking special care to see she had a good time," a 313 member posted.

BY ALL ACCOUNTS, DEMF's most ubiquitous track was the Aztec Mystic's "Jaguar," which Underground Resistance released in March 1999. Produced by Mexican American DJ Rolando (Rocha), from southwest Detroit, "Jaguar" became an instant standard, as immediately *right* as "Strings of Life." It became UR's bestseller, and Sony Music Germany asked to license it; Mike "Fuck the Majors" Banks said no. So an executive commissioned a trance version by a pair of producers calling themselves Don Jaguar, then advertised it as a "tone-by-tone" "remix-cover"—a plain claim-jump, aimed for the super-club trance market. UR's spokesman, Cornelius Harris, quickly issued a communiqué: "We urge all concerned individuals to flood Sony's offices worldwide with calls, e-mails, and faxes expressing those concerns. This kind of crap has to stop and it has to stop now."

Amazingly, it did—Sony dropped the release, which BMG picked right back up, this time crediting Type. So UR cut it off with a "Jaguar" remix EP, featuring, among others, Jeff Mills, and buried the remake. It was a victory for Detroit's techno cognoscenti, though eventually Rolando himself had to leave the fold in order to pursue the opportunities UR's hardline stance precluded.

Rolando played the DEMF Stage at six, right before Derrick May. After years of moving around Europe, May had recommitted to his hometown, expanding Transmat into Metroplex's old space after Juan Atkins moved his office to the Mike Banks–owned Submerge building. The Memorial Day sun—thankfully out all day—set behind him as he played. It wasn't his best set—meandering, without the focus May brings on a good night—but it did contain one resonant moment, when he pointedly cued up James Brown's "The Payback" just minutes in. "I love playing that record," says May. "I've never been afraid to play anything. It was really special. There was four or five generations in that audience."

Watching him from behind were Craig and Hawtin—Carl expectant but utterly at home, Richie's hands stuffed into his black Windbreaker, rocking on his heels. He was the weekend's final performer. "Rich was fucking terrified," says Theakston, who'd asked if he needed anything and waited ten seconds for a response. "He was so in his head about everything. He was polite, but he was so focused." Backstage, Hawtin paced as local percussionist Sundiata O.M. and Umar Bin Hassan joined May. "It was beautiful," says May. "It was not planned at all. There was no agenda."

. . . .

THEAKSTON WATCHED HAWTIN'S hands shake as he dropped the needle on his first selection. "The weight he must have carried for this—it was an unenviable position," says Theakston. "He couldn't win, in some ways—[it's] synonymous with race relations over the decades in Detroit." He opened with Vapourspace's "Gravitational Arch of 10," a record he'd put out but not made, a Detroit-identified track from somewhere else that went out to the world, from a time when people thought techno might stand a fighting chance at commercial success in America—an era, however recent, that now seemed as far away as the Music Institute.

But Hawtin was also reaching back to the MI itself. He'd promoted *Consumed* with live dates that advertised him on "tables/909 - fx/synth/controls," a hybrid recalling old-school Chicago-Detroit methodology, and rediscovered himself as a DJ in the process. In November 1999, he issued *Decks, EFX & 909*, a sizzling DJ-mix CD that stands as one of techno's strongest officially released sets. That was the setup, and spirit, Hawtin brought to the first DEMF. "He was phenomenal," says Theakston. "He had Carl and Kenny Larkin dancing. It felt like being in the locker room of a team that just won the Stanley Cup. Everyone was just hugging each other."

Backstage, Theakston got numbers backstage from a city official. The final estimated three-day total, he learned, was nine hundred thousand. That estimate would keep rising, unrealistically, to over a million. But everything felt possible right then. *DEEE-TROIT! DEEE-TROIT!* chanted the crowd. "It was dark out," says Glazer, "but I had my sunglasses on because I didn't want people seeing me get teary-eyed."

Disco Donnie Estopinal, asking a security guard
what "PLUR" stands for: And the R?
Guard: Rehab?

—FROM *RISE: THE STORY OF RAVE OUTLAW DISCO DONNIE* (2004)

>14

PHUTURE PHAT
HONG KONG PHOOEY

TOMMIE SUNSHINE FELL for Atlanta his first time there, visiting his brother, who owned a parking company. "I walked around Little Five Points and was like, 'Wow, I like this place,'" says Sunshine. "I went into Junkman's Daughter, a clothing store, and Criminal Records, and saw lots of rave flyers: 'Wow. They've got a scene down here? I could live with that.'"

Unsurprisingly, electronic dance music took hold more sporadically in the spread-out South than it did further north. Lexington and Louisville and St. Louis were part of the Midwest scene's southern tendrils, and Florida was a self-contained circuit. But even as southern cities such as Charlotte, Dallas, Nashville, and Atlanta all had thriving scenes of varying size (Charlotte parties drew about five hundred; Atlanta, several thousand) and musical provenance, they were too far-flung to be connected as intimately as the coasts and Midwest—self-sufficient cells within the scene's larger networks.

Sunshine needed the change. After making it through Furthur alive, he'd gone to another notorious outdoor party, Interstellar Outback in

Lexington (August 26–28, 1994), at which a twenty-three-year-old woman OD'd on heroin and flatlined for eight minutes before being resuscitated by on-site medical personnel. "The end of that party was literally the end of the party," says Sunshine. (The woman—whose chances of brain damage exceeded 80 percent—recovered fully, went home, and got on Vrave that night.)

Sunshine shaved his eyebrows every summer ("People can't figure out what's different: 'You look tired?' "), bleached his hair white, carried an American-flag satchel, and dressed like an extra from *Avenging Disco Godfather*. Quickly, he began getting DJ gigs, one of them at a boutique, Wish, in whose basement Scott Richmond, the owner of New York's Satellite Records, was getting ready to open another shop.

One day Sunshine cold-called Richmond: "Nobody in this city can run a record store like I can. Whatever you think you have set up, dismantle it." It was a bluff. "I had no experience," says Sunshine. "I had no idea how to run a fucking lemonade stand, let alone a record store. I did this completely on my music knowledge." It worked: Sunshine was the store's sole proprietor its first several months.

In 1999, the U.S. record business reached its zenith; compact discs alone earned $16.4 billion that year. There was capital aplenty for niche markets like dance vinyl. By 1999, Sunshine was supervising a dozen employees, all DJs: "They were worse than me, which is hard to imagine. I had to figure out how to get these twelve degenerates to show up for their jobs—that was the real job. The drum and bass guy was also a graffiti writer, so he was constantly getting arrested. Every day it was, 'Let's flip a coin and see if Haze is going to show up.' "

Sunday was reorder day. In the pre-digital era, Sunshine in Atlanta, Richmond in New York, and the buyer for the Boston store all got on speakerphone. "They would drop the needle and go, 'How many?' " says Sunshine. "From listening to it over the phone, through speakerphone, I would have to get whether or not that record was a fucking jam, and order it. If I got it wrong, I'd pray to catch it on the reorder. If the pressing sold out, sorry—that was that, usually."

Despite its future-forward iconography, compositional tools, and fan base, electronic dance music remained beholden to vinyl. Simply put, there was no other way to DJ effectively—you couldn't manipulate cassettes by hand, and the earliest CD mixers were too buggy. Whatever style you played, vinyl was a way of saying you were hardcore. "Back then most of this music was very limited release, a thousand [copies] worldwide not being uncommon," says John Kelley. "Maybe ten copies would roll through L.A.—maybe. A big part of DJing was hunting that stuff down, putting in the work, finding the good stuff, knowing where it was, and doing good with them—not just taking them home and putting them in your bedroom, but sharing them with the community."

SHORTLY BEFORE LEAVING Atlanta in 1999, Sunshine started going to New Orleans—for size and spectacle, the city that exerted southern rave's most magnetic pull. Parties with goofy names like Psychedelic Pimp Daddy Land (May 24, 1997) and Attack of the 50 Foot Raver Zombies (October 30, 1999) were held at the State Palace Theater on Decatur Street downtown and promoted by New Orleans native James Estopinal Jr., a.k.a. Disco Donnie, who was committed to turning a party into a Sensurround *happening*. Like Sunshine, Estopinal loved cartoony excess—the flyer for Attack of the 50 Foot Raver Zombies was a full-on comic book. By 2000, he was selling tickets in twenty states and copromoting events in Dallas, Atlanta, and Miami.

Sunshine—who'd been arrested at Grave, gone berserk at the final Storm Rave, and gotten so fried at Furthur that he lost consciousness even as he kept dancing—doesn't hesitate a second: "Donnie threw the craziest parties ever in America, no question. I have never been to a party like that outside of the State Palace Theater."

NEW ORLEANS'S PARTY KING started his ascent after moving back to his hometown in 1994. Estopinal was twenty-four, fresh from LSU, where he majored in accounting, his mother's profession. She'd been his only parent since third grade, when his father suddenly abandoned his job and family to become a nightclub DJ, taking the name Disco Jim. "He would say he was coming to pick me up for the weekend," says Estopinal. "I would sit by the window and watch every car that went by, and he wouldn't come."

Waiting tables and set to marry his college sweetheart, Estopinal became itchy: "I didn't want to be an accountant for the rest of my life," he says. He'd road-tripped to Athens, Georgia, for R.E.M. and Love Tractor shows, and put on themed events as his fraternity's president, bringing buckets of sand into the house for a Noah's Ark event ("We had two kinds of each animal in each room") named for the Grateful Dead's *Wake of the Flood*.

One night shortly after moving back home, Estopinal went with some coworkers to Ruby Fruit Jungle, a party at the now-shuttered Café Istanbul on Frenchmen Street, and got his first taste of rave culture. "It was such a mix of people you wouldn't put together now: drag queens and supermodels and hookers and fraternity guys—basically everything," he says. "They were very open to me. It was the first time I had been introduced to these groups of people all being together in one room, being friends."

That core was small—about a hundred people. "I was wondering why something so beautiful could be so poorly attended," says Estopinal, who that night volunteered to help promote the organizers' next event. He brought in such a big crowd that he demanded 50 percent of the door the next time, and got it. This new avocation broke up his engagement. Estopinal began wearing his father's clothes along with his own. The numbers he would crunch would be his own. He now called himself Disco Donnie.

By 1995, he drew fifteen hundred people to the first of what would become an annual Mardi Gras event at the State Palace Theater, bringing in Chicago's Mystic Bill and Terry Mullan. "We didn't know what the fuck we were doing, or anything about music," he admits. Instead, he read rave zines such as *Massive* and collected flyers from New York, Atlanta, and Washington, D.C., then tracked down the big names. He set up a voice mail line and answered every call, particularly the complaints. "I would call back and say, 'What can I do to fix this?' And they'd appreciate it."

A Disco Donnie event might feature *anything*, so long as it was sufficiently unique: "I was trying to change the setup every time." Once, he stopped the party at 3 A.M. to bring in a choir singing "Amazing Grace." Donnie would also book old-school rappers like the Sugar Hill Gang, or dance contests hosted by break-dancing pioneer Fred "Rerun" Berry of the seventies sitcom *What's Happening!!*

Donnie's Mardi Gras extravaganzas lasted up to four days in a row. By 1997 they drew twenty-five hundred people a day. "There was no dominant scene within a ten-hour driving radius of us," says Estopinal. "The attendance was going up every show. A show that was doing two thousand people in 1996 was doing five thousand in 1999." The parties grew so big the State Palace couldn't contain them. "We expanded into the buildings next door, so I had five areas, and built a deck on the roof," says Estopinal.

He also opened Heavyweight Records, a DJ shop attached to the State Palace and managed by John Larner, a.k.a. Cyberjive, who'd moved down from Indianapolis in 1996. A side door inside Heavyweight led to the State Palace's self-explanatory Jungle Room. During Disco Donnie's parties, the small shop stayed open all night. "We would sometimes do a week's worth of sales in one night when those parties were going on," says Larner. The shop's mixtape bestsellers were locals Stryfe (Daniel Millstein—UK-style hard house) and Trent Cantrelle (progressive house), as well as New Yorkers Micro and Frankie Bones.

The crowds in New Orleans were also *up for it*. Tampa's DJ Monk, another of Donnie's regulars—alone and with the trio Rabbit in the Moon—recalls playing one of Micro's late-nineties Caffeine parties in New York: "There was so much ketamine. People would come up: 'That was the best show ever!' We're like: 'Really? You didn't seem like it.' They loved it, but they were in their own little world." Not so in New Orleans. "He was not worried about anything other than every single person in the room having the time of their life," says Sunshine. "He was throwing a *party*." Robert and Brian Brunet, the State Palace's sibling owner-operators, stationed two ambulances outside in case things got out of hand.

SUNSHINE FIRST MET Estopinal in Miami, at a party Donnie threw during Winter Music Conference in 1999. "Laurent Garnier played all night, open to close—one of the best sets of music I've ever heard, and definitely the best Winter Music Conference party I have ever been to," says Sunshine. "It was industry only—every single motherfucker in the world who mattered at that moment was in that room." But what caught Sunshine's attention was the host's outfit: "I was like, 'Who is this lunatic in thrift store clothing with a feather in a fedora in South Beach?'" says Sunshine. "We bonded instantly. It was like we had known each other our whole lives."

By then, WMC was changing shape almost completely. Attendance tripled between 1995 and 1998. As major labels put money into electronica, the music opened up as well—there was a party for every style, every night. "We'd get to Miami and it was wheels-off, let's-go party time," says Wade Randolph Hampton. "Miami was all about the record business, almost no party [promoters]." Will Hermes, who went to WMC in the early 2000s as a *Spin* editor, adds, "It's not difficult to track down high-quality MDMA there. It was a little less common than exotic vodkas, but not much."

But the scene had lost its idealistic communalism. "I was very aware of this whole thing becoming big business," says Jonah Sharp. "It happened so suddenly. It ran off like a freight train." In 1999, Spacetime Continuum was scheduled to play Astralwerks's WMC party along with Fatboy Slim and Todd Terry; the latter had issued a drum and bass album with the label that year. Iggy Pop, a longtime Miami resident, showed up to hang out. Sharp was scheduled to play at 1 A.M. but ran into static from the other acts' managers. "I remember thinking: *'Fuck this. This is not how it used to be.'*"

ONE OF THE BIG DRAWS at WMC 2000 was Moby, who played Crobar on March 23. A month earlier, two major things had happened. One, the *Village Voice* put Moby on the cover—some five hundred critics had named *Play* best album of the year in the paper's annual poll. For many writers, *Play*'s embedding of old blues vocals into classicist pop structures, dusted and driven by technological means, represented a resonant stylistic bridging. And two, *The Beach*, Danny Boyle's follow-up to *Trainspotting*, starring Leonardo DiCaprio, opened in theaters, featuring *Play*'s "Porcelain" on the soundtrack.

For years, MCT had successfully lobbied the film industry to use Moby's music—in 1996, setting up a party for, Weber said, "every music supervisor in Hollywood" at Slamdance (Park City, Utah's indie film festival alternative to Sundance). *Play* was certainly user friendly, and film, TV, and advertising music supervisors—a newly ascendant role—were given the hard sell. In August 1999, ABC began using "Body Rock" in promos for the sitcom *Dharma & Greg*. "The request for *The Beach* was the transformational request," says Moby.

There would be, in total, more than two hundred promos, ads, soundtracks, and other placements for the songs from *Play*. "The Sky Is Broken" went to Galaxy, "Everloving" to Thorntons—both British chocolatiers. "Bodyrock" went to Rolling Rock and the BBC's *Match of the Day*. "Run On" went to Renault and Maxwell House coffee, "Find My Baby" to Nissan and American Express, "Porcelain" to Volkswagen, Bosch, France Telecom, Bailey's Irish Cream, and Nordstrom. By the time Moby performed at Crobar, all but one of the album's eighteen tracks had been licensed out. A month later, on April 20, a UK TV show faxed in a request for the eighteenth.

In November 2000, a year and a half after the album's release, Moby issued the version of "South Side" featuring Gwen Stefani and goosed its profile again. *Play* stayed in *Billboard*'s top one hundred for fourteen months, selling over ten million worldwide—the most successful album ever to emerge from the rave scene, and so ubiquitous it's nearly impossible to hear afresh.

ROUGH TREATMENT IN CLUBS became the norm in New York by the late nineties. Gone were the days when, as journalist Frank Owen recalls, you could tip your cabbie in cocaine and police were almost nonexistent on the street. Times Square was doing major business with the Walt Disney Company, the closest that place had been to anything resembling Mickey Mouse since the opening of animator Ralph Bakshi's X-rated *Fritz the Cat* in 1972. The seedier aspects of nightlife in New York, long able to run free, were undergoing a crackdown.

When Limelight was shuttered in 1997, many figured the cops would leave nightclubbers alone again. But the pressure ramped up. "You would endure a search that would be extreme even in a prison environment," says former *New York* magazine reporter Ethan Brown. "Your shoes had to be removed. They would actually put their hands in your underwear. They would sometimes open your mouth. It was just crazy and humiliating. If someone might be suspected of putting ecstasy in [his or her] mouth, that person would then be grabbed by the shoulders and picked up and literally, physically thrown out of the club."

It wasn't the Gestapo—nor, as Owen points out, was it anything compared to the treatment gays endured in the days before Stonewall.

But it was unsettling evidence that nightlife, a prime mover of the economy in the City That Never Sleeps, was shrinking in Manhattan.

THE MILLENNIAL NEW YEAR was a gauge of how much burnout was seeping into dance music culture. On the one hand, there was the horrific Twin Cities bacchanal that Brandon Ivers recalls: "People were eating drugs off the floor. The ecstasy didn't work for anybody anymore. Meth had come into the scene in a really big way. Everybody was angry. There's no way that could have kept going as a scene." At the opposite end of the scale, a consortium of San Francisco and Seattle partiers, led by Sunshine Jones and Moonbeam Jones of Dubtribe Sound System, chartered a plane to Hawaii to get away from all the amateurs. "A plane full of hippies went into a field on the south shore of Maui and just camped out," says Matt Corwine, one of the passengers. "There was DJ gear in the back. During the day we'd wander around the island." Even that milieu was a change of scenery from the West Coast's "druggy mysticism," which Corwine had become fed up with. Once, he'd overheard a conversation in a car on the way to the woods: "Tonight, what should I ask the mushroom?"

SOMETIME IN 1999, Estopinal had just returned home from an all-nighter when someone started pounding his front door. "I lived on Bourbon Street, at the end. I looked out the window [and saw] three guys with mustaches and mirrored sunglasses: [shouts] 'DEA! Come downstairs!'" He did. "Who are the drug dealers?" they demanded to know. Estopinal said he didn't know. The agents didn't believe him. "They basically read me the riot act. Then they switched tack: 'How much money do you make a year? We can double it if you want to work for us.'" Estopinal told them he'd let them know if he ever found out and took a business card.

Disco Donnie is adamant he didn't sell narcotics: "I could have gone that route, but I didn't, because I'm a big wimp." Besides, he didn't have to—it was New Orleans. Every February he threw a multiday Mardi Gras event because that's what everybody did. But after that DEA visit, he says, "I imagined that I was being, not followed, but watched—rave promoter paranoia." That November, he turned thirty with his mom in Amsterdam, part of a longer European trip. At the first train stop after leaving the Netherlands, the police came on board and sifted through his luggage—and nobody else's. Then they left. "When I got back to the States, [airport security] pulled me in a room and did the whole, 'Take off your clothes.' I was like, 'Okay, my suspicions are confirmed: Because I'm a rave promoter they think I went to Holland to buy drugs—with my mom.'"

By May 2000, the New Orleans DEA had become convinced that Donnie was a front—that the Brunet brothers were narcotics kingpins. Even Tommie Sunshine says, "As much as the State Palace Theater was a legitimate venue, what went on in that building was fucking unreal—kids laid out from the first floor to the top floor, on the stairs, everywhere." But the authorities had yet to shut down a Disco Donnie party.

PHUTURE PHAT HONG KONG PHOOEY offers a representative snapshot of the U.S. rave scene at the end of summer 2000. Phoenix trance DJ Sandra Collins recorded for Kinetic and regularly appeared on *Urb*'s cover (and back-cover ads). DJ Rectangle was a hip-hop producer and scratch DJ. Gene Farris repped Windy City house, even if progressive house paid the bills around those parts. Swede Christian Smith, based in New York, played supple techno half the year in America and half in Europe.

There were three drum and bass acts on the bill: AK1200 (Dave Minner), from Orlando, and two ascendant Brit groups, Renegade Hardware and Bad Company; the latter's rampaging sound was leavened with a deep bass glide, showcased to its fullest on 1999's "The Nine"—named drum and bass's greatest track by London D&B magazine *KMAG* in 2008. All three played hard, the way an audience bred by electronica's rock-crossover dreams liked it*—though it sounded little like the drum and bass that got American press: Roni Size/Reprazent's jazzy *New Forms* (1997), winner of the Mercury Music Prize in England, or the simpler dancehall and hip-hop-fueled "jump-up," epitomized by Aphrodite, who issued a self-titled compilation in 1999 on V2.

No one came with as full a package as DJ Monk, who'd played for Donnie numerous times, both billed alone and with Rabbit in the Moon. Monk had helped kick off the Tampa scene with a warehouse party at the end of 1991; one of his partners in that party, keyboardist David Christophere (Confucius), became his partner in Rabbit, along with performance artist Bunny (Steve Eachon, who'd acquired the nickname well before meeting the others), the group's bizarrely clad front man.

Every show, Bunny would go through a handful of costumes, from a "muscle suit" ("Striations and actual muscle fiber without the outer layer of skin, carved out of latex," says Monk) to an astronaut getup with bubble headgear to a full-on re-creation of Beetlejuice—each tailored to a specific number. During "O.B.E. (Out-of-Body Experience)," Bunny wore an outfit made of glow necklaces. At the track's first screaming climax, says Monk, "He'd push himself out onstage and stage-dive into the crowd. They would rip all the glow necklaces off his body."

Rabbit were among the most prolific American remixers of the decade, turning everything from Goldie's "Inner City Life" to Sarah McLachlan's "Possession" into a widescreen epic. The McLachlan track was a bootleg, à la the Scott Hardkiss version of "Rocket Man," but when her label Nettwerk caught wind of it, they sent the group the mul-

---

*Despite the cliché that women like softer music than men, a greater proportion of popular U.S. drum and bass DJs were female—from New Yorker Reid Speed to Seattle's Tamara (Weikel)—than in any other style.

titrack tapes and a contract. The official "Possession" remix was, says Tricia Romano, "a monster hit—hugely bombastic, the shit you pulled out at peak hour."

Bunny's outfits were the least of it—Rabbit in the Moon shows were audiovisual riots. They'd create homemade loops of time-lapse film of flowers blooming and project them onto "monitors we'd bought from school auctions." In 1996, they scaled way up, hiring one of the top party-visuals teams in the country, Chicago's OVT, cofounded by Columbia College alumni Brien Rullman, Brian Dressel, and Vello Virkhaus. "Vello was an unknown at that point," says Monk. "Later, everybody figured out he was doing the stuff behind the scenes."

"We had a huge collection of film loops: *Star Wars*, *Beetlejuice*," recalls Virkhaus. "I was using silicon graphics machines; we were using Alias Wavefront." OVT was a pioneer of projection mapping, or video mapping: animations that take the shape of the irregularly shaped objects onto which they're projected, like the weather balloons flanking Rabbit's stage. The total assault made Rabbit a top rave draw.

MONK ARRIVED EARLY SATURDAY afternoon with his visuals man Berkeley Meyer and two other performers for his show. Rather than go to the hotel to unwind, he headed straight to the State Palace Theater to set up gear—two projectors, a video mixer with two DVD players, and a laptop—to leave the evening free.

About 8 P.M., as Monk and his crew were finishing up, John Larner was behind the counter of Heavyweight, grabbing an armful of vinyl to restock for the night. The side door from the Jungle Room opened. "Three cops come in—I wouldn't say in riot gear, but they weren't just off the streets," says Larner. "I'm laughing to myself: 'Somebody's in fucking trouble!'"

"Put those down! Put those down!" the cops yelled. Then, unmistakably: *"You!"*

Larner set the records down.

"Grab the cash register, get everybody out of here, lock the doors, and come with us."

Larner followed them through the Jungle Room into the main theater. There, a few dozen uniformed officers had ordered about thirty people—mostly venue staff—into the first two rows of theater seats.

Monk's team was onstage when the DEA arrived, fine-tuning their video, when Meyer heard someone grab someone in his party. At first he figured it was staff security: "I'd just turned around to see them to yell at them, and a guy grabbed me and told me to get on my knees." He acquiesced after seeing "DEA" on their backs. "They were going through backpacks onstage, dumping everything out. I saw my toothbrush, my clothes, everything dumped. Plus I had a hard drive in my backpack; I was very upset that it was just dropped to the ground. They told us that everybody had to be processed—if you wanted to leave, you had to be processed first and you could leave. If you had to stay for any reason, you had to stay until they were done—it could be a couple hours or it could be a couple days."

Everybody was instructed to give their name, phone number, and reason for being on premises before the building was swept. "They wanted everybody to leave that building—that was obvious," says Meyer, who stuck around with a handful of other technicians. "I couldn't live without that gear. I had to stay to watch it. Younger kids who were helping out they went after right away. Then they took volunteers."

AS ROBERT BRUNET and an assistant led a claque of agents to the State Palace's off-site corporate office, where the agents grabbed armfuls of paperwork from the file cabinets, Estopinal himself was running late: With doors at ten, he figured he had time. He was stepping out of the house when the phone rang: "Don't come down here. It's bad."

Donnie went anyway, driving past the theater. Official vehicles festooned the entrance. He took a seat at a nearby Middle Eastern restaurant and watched the crowd gather: "There were so many people that had tickets already, just waiting outside." He told the staffer who'd phoned him to tell the kids: "The party's going to happen—just wait." Says Monk: "There was a massive line down the block for the show. People were screaming at the cops—cuss words, you name it—and throwing stuff at them."

The search itself took only a couple hours, start to finish: "They were done on the stage and in that main room within an hour," says Meyer. "They went through every single box and container of gear." The DEA was looking for evidence of drug dealing; they were convinced the raves were a front, despite Donnie's events selling tickets, through Ticketmaster, in 40 percent of the country.

Dave Minner recalls hanging with the Renegade Hardware guys at the hotel, waiting for updates. "I remember sitting in the hotel going, 'What the fuck's happening?' We started getting calls—and we waited and we waited and we waited."

Meanwhile, DEA agents engaged in impromptu pest control. "The State Palace Theater had these giant water rats called nutria rats—they're huge, almost the size of a beaver," says Meyer. "At one point they were chasing a rat around with their guns out, pointed to the ground."

The closest the DEA found to what they were looking for was the joint in the pocket of a State Palace bartender; off he went. Other than that: *Pffft.* The bored out-of-town agents began to mingle—"They were chit-chatting, asking about the music, the lights," says Meyer—while the locals gathered computers and other items they deemed evidence that Estopinal and the Brunet brothers were not, in fact, musical entertainers. "My gear bags were completely ripped through," says Meyer. "They grabbed my computer and said they copied the hard drive."

Some of the DEA's evidence was simply puzzling. "At one point they said they were taking all the water," says Meyer, who asked an agent what the DEA wanted with cases of bottled water. "I don't know," they replied. Also taken: specially made fortune cookies Estopinal had prepared for the party, and several hundred glow sticks.

There was one final flourish. "They had masks," says Meyer. "One of the guys came back in and said there were kids in line throwing stuff at them—empty water bottles—and yelling at them. So they basically all put on their masks so they could leave. They just dissipated—just put on their masks and left. We were like, Uh, OK." Donnie, meanwhile, was still stationed at the Middle Eastern restaurant. As midnight approached, he says, "These agents were getting tired." A number of them headed out for a bite—where Donnie was sitting. He slipped away unnoticed. On their way out, they told Robert Brunet: "Get a lawyer and call us on Monday."

THE STATE PALACE THEATER was a mess. It took about an hour to clean up; Donnie opened the doors at 1 A.M. Three hours after it was scheduled to begin, Phuture Phat Hong Kong Phooey was back on. "It was just jailbreak in here," Estopinal said in the documentary *Rise*—though the doorman searches were a lot more thorough than usual. With only a few people inside, says Donnie, "The light guy is hitting the strobes, and some girl has an epileptic seizure and drops, right in front of me. I'm like, 'Really?'"

The DJs adjusted their time slots to get everybody their turn, though a few people didn't play that night (Sandra Collins, who no-showed, and Larner/Cyberjive were two). The heat scared off a number of kids, but not enough: "State Palace was way over capacity, probably three thousand to five thousand people jammed in that place," says Monk. Outside, the remaining feds seethed. "They were pissed," says Estopinal. "They were *so* pissed."

At the party, if you didn't already know what had happened, everything seemed normal. Christian Smith arrived shortly before his set time after hitting a nearby strip bar with the Bad Company guys for a few drinks. Though he'd follow Donnie's subsequent troubles, Smith remained unaware he'd played the party the DEA raided until he was contacted for this book. Dave Minner claims that the raid didn't throw the room's vibe off—"If anything, it was more triumphant." Says Donnie: "The party went off without a hitch; we had no issues. It was a good night, but we had a feeling that it could be the last one."

To Larner, "It was the first jab in a long fight—that was how anybody who knew anything felt. It's all anybody could talk about. [It was] like going through an intersection and you realize somebody blew a stop sign. You don't get hit, but for the rest of the drive you're freaked out."

WORD OF THE RAID hit the scene grapevine like a sledgehammer. "I knew at that very moment that that was the end of the American rave scene, period," says Tommie Sunshine, at home in Chicago when he found out. "I didn't even need to think about it. If they got Donnie and shut down the State Palace Theater, that was *it*."

The raid reflected a rising moral panic. In 1997, U.S. Customs had seized a record 381,000 ecstasy tablets; that number vaulted to 3.5 million pills in just the first two months of 2000. Between 2000 and 2001, the number of reported ER visits related to MDMA rose by nearly 20 percent. Ecstasy was starting to look like an epidemic. "The more prevalent under-thirty crowd tended to use ecstasy much more frequently and in higher doses—as high as ten tablets a night, once a week for the past ten years," a Johns Hopkins study reported in 2000.

Law enforcement had been ramping up rave arrests. A June 1999 arena event in Morristown, New Jersey, ended with eighty arrests and fifteen hospitalizations, following forty medical calls. In September 1999, a Miami party had one death, ten hospitalizations, and thirty drug arrests. Chicago clamped down particularly hard: In May 2000, the city council added an ordinance to an omnibus bill fining unlicensed or uninsured venues up to ten thousand dollars, as well as instituting a 2 A.M. curfew.

A week later, Chicago police and prosecutors disclosed that a number of recent area drug deaths had come via an "ecstasy look-alike substance," reported the *Chicago Tribune*—stamped with a Mitsubishi logo, like a particularly high-grade brand of E that had been sweeping Europe—that actually contained the far more dangerous hallucinogen paramethoxymethamphetamine, or PMA. One eighteen-year-old girl died with a body temperature of 108 degrees, her organs shut down from the heat.

Out came the rhetoric. When a Tuscon, Arizona, rave called Transcend was canceled by the Southwest Fair Commission, a police captain told the *Arizona Daily Star*, "There's no such thing as a drug-free rave." On May 6, 1999, Texas attorney general John Cornyn suggested in a Houston community newspaper that most party promoters "meet the legal definition for a 'criminal street gang.'" That August, when a group of teenagers from San Bernardino County drove twelve hundred feet off a cliff on Angeles Crest Highway, a county supervisor told reporters that any rave, ipso facto, "promotes an outcome that is destined for disaster."

Not everyone rushed to the panic button. A police sergeant in Wicker Park told the *Chicago Tribune*, "The promoters don't push the drugs. What they push is the music and the experience. They put together a package. But then others come along and sell." And Melvindale, Michigan's police chief told the *Detroit News* that at the end of a party bust, "What you usually end up with is a pile of dope in the middle of a table. You have little to connect it to anyone."

COME MONDAY, the Brunet brothers sat down with Estopinal and their wives. Their lawyer had spoken with the U.S. attorney. The investigation had begun in January. DEA undercover agents had attended eight Disco Donnie events, buying drugs on premises each time. Donnie and the Brunets faced up to twenty years for those charges alone. In addition, the feds were charging them with a continuing criminal enterprise—another twenty-to-life. Twisting the knife, the feds promised to go after Donnie and the Brunets by wielding the Crack House Law.

Ratified in 1986, the Title 21 United States Code (USC) Controlled Substances Act imposes a half-million-dollar fine on any individual who is found to "knowingly open, lease, rent, use, or maintain any place, whether permanently or temporarily, for the purpose of manufacturing, distributing, or using any controlled substance." The idea was to root out slumlords letting their properties become drug dens. The DEA made no bones about what they were doing. The agents freely described it to Donnie as a "test case" for a larger rave crackdown that would reverberate nationwide. That's why they took the glow sticks and bottled water—they were "drug paraphernalia."

"At first I didn't understand the scope of it," says Estopinal. "They were like, 'We're going to bring a hundred agents from Washington to stop this rave scene.'" The agents offered them plea bargains: Estopinal would get one year, the Brunets two each. "They looked at them as bigger [game]," says Estopinal—the kingpins.

For months, Donnie wasn't at liberty to talk about the case. He couldn't even tell people *why* he couldn't talk to them. (Many figured he'd evaded his taxes.) Worse, his first lawyer didn't understand raves any better than the government. "He was like, 'Look, you don't want to risk this thing. I had this guy—he flew in a plane of cocaine off the Mississippi River and he got caught. I got him five years.' I was like, 'What does that have to do with me? I didn't fly in a plane of cocaine.'"

The ACLU's Graham Boyd took over, pursuing the case as a free-speech issue, telling *Rolling Stone*: "Performance of music to an audience is speech. And from 2 Live Crew to Marilyn Manson, when the government tries to censor music, they lose." DJ Dara recalls that the charges induced "a siege mentality. We felt that we were all in it together—Donnie's problems were all of our problems."

ESTOPINAL STILL HAD a living to make. On October 7, 2000, the State Palace was scheduled to host a Moonshine over America tour stop. "We'd always played for Donnie," says Carl Cox, the Londoner who'd run the sound system at Shoom and one of the UK's top DJs, who participated in a number of Moonshine tours. "I'd played State Palace probably ten times before, no problem. This time, the authorities said it's not happening. Donnie moved it to another club outside in the middle of nowhere called Pure Country. That didn't set too well with me. All I could think of was rednecks. The biggest night they had was line-dancing night. Does anybody understand why we're here?"

"It had fiasco written on it before it even happened," says Larner. "People were really thrown, and still leery of what happened at Hong Kong Phooey. The older kids that had been around a while, who didn't necessarily have to go to every party, all stayed away." When Cox got to the venue he took one look at the stage and saw "this enormous Confederate flag. I'm a black guy playing this type of music. I'm not playing; I'm going to stay on the bus." There he says, "I saw the police being mob-handed with all the punters. It was shocking. All the news crews were there, undercover police in the club, searching people out on the dance floor, pulling them up to the bar: 'What have you got in your pockets?' I'd never seen this type of behavior anywhere else in the world. It was a debacle."

"Police were stationed, not literally on the venue property, but right outside," says Dara, also on the tour. "They were literally pulling over cars, making everybody get out, and searching the cars, making it really uncomfortable for people to go to the show. It was total harassment, total intimidation tactics. A lot of people thought, 'This is more trouble than it's worth.'" Larner, curious, drove by: "I just remember the parking lot—a tour bus that said MOONSHINE, and all these cop cars: 'Nah, I'm not even going to walk in the door.'"

The next Disco Donnie show—Vampire Stripper Sluts from Outer Space—was scheduled for October 27 at the State Palace. Instead, Estopinal secured a warehouse venue connected to a restaurant that hosted Cajun bands. "I wasn't 100 percent honest with the owner," he said. "I told her it was a fraternity party. As soon as they released where the venue was, the police went there and told [the owner] that people were going to die," says Estopinal. "She called me saying, 'Donnie, please don't do this to me.' I said, 'Fine.' I had a contract, but I didn't sue. I was just trying to have a show. So it got canceled. I paid everyone, and that was it for trying to do a big party."

THE CASE AGAINST ESTOPINAL was quietly dropped in March 2001. The evidence was flimsy, the editorials mocking the New Orleans DEA embarrassing. (Monk had to send the ACLU written testimony that Bunny's glow-stick suit was a prop, not propaganda.) The Brunets were brought up on another charge, conspiracy to violate the Crack House Law; they pled guilty and were slapped with a hundred-thousand-dollar fine, less than the cost of a trial. They also agreed not to allow pacifiers, glow sticks, and Vicks inhalers—"drug paraphernalia"—into the State Palace Theater.

"Even not winning a conviction, by just bringing the case, it definitely made a lot of venues around that time cautious," says Estopinal. "There was a profound difference from July to October." But he found work, putting on weekly club nights for the local House of Blues. They weren't the blowouts of old, but they kept him, and what was left of the scene, going. They also helped him beat the DEA's case: "Basically, they were prosecuting me for something that I was doing every Saturday."

"It was like somebody knocked on their door and told them the bank was closed," says Tommie Sunshine. "I don't even think it took a month. The entire thing just crumbled. No matter your role—whether you were the soundman or the DJ or taking tickets—everyone at the party was getting a ten-thousand-dollar fine. Who was going to spit in the devil's eye and say, 'Let's see if they're serious'?" Adds Ethan Brown: "If you were involved in this culture, it was going to end up with you in federal prison."

Electroclash is escapism from today's uncomfortable world—a world that nobody feels they can change. Electro looks back on all the bad architecture, fat-faced politicians, faceless convenience, useless technology, and greed that still exists today. It combines all these things and makes it glamorous. It's the ultimate paradox.

—ALEX MURRAY-LESLIE OF CHICKS ON SPEED, 2002

>15

ELECTROCLASH FESTIVAL 2001

SOMETIME IN 2000, Josh Glazer was watching Josh Wink headline Motor when he noticed something odd. "There was nothing on the turntables—just a CD playing," says Glazer. "We thought that was fucking hysterical: 'You can't DJ without records—you look like an asshole!' It wasn't like, 'Fuck this dude,' but: *Really?*"

Really. The first Pioneer CDJs—a compact disc player that worked like a vinyl turntable, introduced in 1994—were buggy and unreliable; besides, most DJs wanted music that was available only on vinyl. But by 2000, CD burners cost less than $150, and aspiring producers wanting to play their tracks out—without having to cut acetate vinyl, pricy and only good for a couple of dozen plays—had warmed to it. After July 2001, when Pioneer brought out the CDJ-1000, its first fully successful model, vinyl-vs.-CD ceased to be an issue.

The entire apparatus of DJing was changing. At Motor early on January 1, 2001, John Acquaviva recorded a mix CD (*From Saturday to Sunday Vol. 2*) using the club's monitors and a laptop—to keep a track list, he said. Eventually Acquaviva's tech roadie confided to Glazer: he was actually using it to DJ. When Glazer cockily told Acquaviva he knew his secret, at Motor on St. Patrick's Day, the DJ eagerly responded, "Do you want to try it?" "I let everyone try it," says Acquaviva. "It was an epiphany—you could feel and see the future."

The laptop held a working prototype for FinalScratch, first developed by three engineers from Amsterdam in spring 1999. The system included a special vinyl record that played digital sound files generated from the laptop; the delay, one designer boasted, was "about twelve milliseconds." Acquaviva read about it, flew to Holland, and taxied to the office. He and Hawtin became investors as well as expert beta testers.

FinalScratch didn't hit the market until January 2002, but its publicity blitz was well under way by the previous fall. On September 18, Hawtin had released *DE9: Closer to the Edit*, a mix album featuring more than seventy tracks he'd broken down into some three hundred loops, between one and four bars long, arranged into fifty-three continuous minutes. The digital future was reducing objects to data, and storing that data in ever-smaller retrieval and playback systems. Not only was vinyl less necessary, so were CDs. "It had a lot of bugs, but I tried to fight right through it," says Kevin Saunderson of FinalScratch. "I was having back trouble, neck problems, from carrying records." By the mid-2000s, digital DJ systems and CDJs were the new global DJ standard.

Equally transformative was Ableton Live, which debuted in October 2001. Much of the time it is used as a composition and performance tool, its sequencing interface allowing enormous flexibility. Visual cueing is enabled with a waveform display pattern. "You can rearrange songs completely on the fly," says Darshan Jesrani of the duo Metro Area. In the nineties, says Stefan Betke (the Berlin glitch-dub producer known as Pole), laptops were solely "for playing back MIDI information. In 2000, it changed: The sampler stayed home and the laptop became more of an audio player."

Ableton Live was equally impactful on DJing, completely automating the matching of separate records' tempos in order to blend them seamlessly. Now, one didn't even need to know how to physically mix records—once the most important skill of the trade—to become a successful DJ. It also limited the physical performance aspect of live electronic music. Instead of wrangling tables full of gear, a live PA could become an inert experience. "Being hidden behind your laptop, you *do* look like you're checking your e-mail, and sometimes you are," says Jason Bentley.

Much new laptop music had a crisp, computery flutter—the seemingly true voice of the tinny, bright machines making it. Many producers embraced "glitches," bursts of static and other aural mistakes, as composing tools, and "glitch" became a de facto genre name. Naturally, the sound flourished in the tech-heavy Bay Area—particularly around the Tigerbeat6 label, run by Kid606 (Miguel De Pedro). Born in Venezuela and raised in San Diego, he'd made his name with an insolently oppositional, scene-critical stance (sample song title: "It'll Take Millions in Plastic Surgery to Make Me Black") that extended to source material, with which he took oft-violent liberties. His "MC DSP Remix" of N.W.A's "Straight Outta Compton" put Ice Cube's menacing verse through a mass of digital effects, playing simultaneously as *détournement* and homage.

LAPTOP RECORDING, and the new availability on file-sharing sites of a cappella vocals from big hits, meant well-known songs were increasingly grist for the electronic-DJ mill—a reaction to years of nameless, faceless music dominating dance floors. The cheekiest manifestations were dubbed bootlegs, or mash-ups. They'd been around for years—sound collagist the Evolution Control Committee's pairings of Herb Alpert and Public Enemy date back to 1987—but they exploded in the early 2000s. Dancers wanted songs again.

The sharpest bootleggers were 2 Many DJ's—Belgian siblings David and Stephen Dewaele of the band Soulwax, who plied incongruous-cum-ingenious pairings like "Magnificent Romeo" (Basement Jaxx's "Romeo" + the Clash's "Magnificent Seven") and "Dreadlock Woman" (Destiny's Child's "Independent Women Pt. 1" + 10cc's "Dreadlock Holiday"). On June 18, 2002, PIAS issued *As Heard on Radio Soulwax, Pt. 2*, an officially licensed DJ mix that included more than thirty head-spinning combinations, from the Stooges' grinding "No Fun" combined with Salt-N-Pepa's "Push It," to an impossible slide from Dolly Parton's "9 to 5" into the Norwegian house duo Röyksopp's dappled "Eple."

It didn't take long for mash-ups to become a tedious grind, with Girl Talk (Gregg Gillis) eventually running it into the festival-circuit ground (though 2006's *Night Ripper* is still a blast). But at the Tribeca Grand—a luxury hotel that showcased DJs—on Halloween 2002, 2 Many DJ's claim-jacking of pop history was a straight thrill. For the first time in years, "electronic dance music" felt like it could mean anything at all.

The conversation ran two ways: Mainstream pop and rock were brazenly copping moves from the dance underground. Madonna had worked with British producer William Orbit—the cofounder of Guerilla, one of the biggest UK progressive house labels—on 1998's *Ray of Light* and with Stuart Price (a.k.a. Jacques Lu Cont and Les Rythmes Digitales) on *Music*, which came out in September 2000. A month after *Music* came two albums: Radiohead's *Kid A*—an album heavily and unmistakably indebted to the Warp catalog—and OutKast's *Stankonia*. The latter's lead single, "B.O.B." (Bombs Over Baghdad), featured Andre 3000 and Big Boi rapping over a wild fusion of acid-rock guitar and jungle snare skids from Movin' Shadow circa 1994.

"B.O.B." missed the Hot 100 and barely charted R&B, but it sounded a challenge—finally met five months later, when Missy Elliott issued "Get Ur Freak On." The Timbaland-produced track (number seven pop, number three R&B) was easily identifiable as drum and bass, with the Asian-British electronic hybrid bhangra also audible. If electronic dance music wouldn't cross over to America on its own, maybe it could become pop's sharpest trace element.

THE SECOND YEAR OF THE Detroit Electronic Music Festival was considerably better funded than the first, in large part due to 2000's overreported attendance. "You can't actually put a million people in that plaza by any stretch of the imagination," says Glazer. (It was likely closer to one hundred thousand.) "But [they used] that number in getting a Ford sponsorship. All of a sudden, there were Jumbotrons."

But backstage, Carl Craig and Carol Marvin were clashing. On Thursday, May 10, Pop Culture Media terminated Craig's contract as the festival's creative director, Marvin charging Craig with not expediting artist contracts quickly enough. The following Monday, Craig filed suit against Pop Culture Media for breach of contract and defamation of character, stating that Marvin cut things too close for him to efficiently deliver final contracts. Rob Theakston was livid: "She was within her jurisdiction. But to terminate him so close to the festival, after all the favors he pulled in to make it a success, was cheap and thoughtless."

Shortly before the festival, Craig emailed the Planet E list: "Don't worry, because nothing will hold me back! I'm going to be there at the DEMF this weekend to support the music and the artists that I booked, and I hope that you will be there too!" But a number of allies—including Theakston, Rita Sayegh, and ADULT.'s Adam Lee Miller and Nicola Kuperus, among others—decided to make a public statement. At the Planet E booth, you could pick up hot-pink buttons and T-shirts stating I SUPPORT CARL CRAIG. Doc Martin, one of many who'd offered to cancel on Craig's behalf, arrived Sunday hoping for a button, but none were left.

On Monday night, as the protesters gathered in the Planet E booth to prepare their big statement, Craig and Theakston huddled. "Are you willing to get kicked off the grounds or arrested for this?" Carl asked.

"Are you going to post my bail?" Theakston replied.

Craig laughed and hugged him: "Absolutely." Then Carl disappeared.

It took "six or seven" people, says Theakston, to carry out the thirty-foot banner: DEMF = CARL CRAIG. The group marched to the back of the main stage bowl, hoisted it high, and circled the audience. They encountered some guff: "Volunteers from Pop Culture Media were visibly angry," says Theakston. "But we made the entire perimeter."

After they finished, Atkins began his set, but a hailstorm cut the program short. Derrick May, scheduled to close, didn't play until 4 A.M., at the club the Works, for an after-party. "Darryl Wynn and [fellow Detroit DJ] Mike Grant were playing," says May; when D-Wynn told him to get his records, Derrick didn't hesitate. "I brought everything inside: two record bags. I can do eight hours with two record bags." That night, he did five. "It was magical—one of my best performances ever. I played everything from Larry Heard to Underground Resistance to Donna Summer. I told a story. When you start the night it's 'Once upon a time,' and at the end, they either lived happily ever after, or they all got fucked up and died."

TOMMIE SUNSHINE first met Felix Stallings Jr. at Satellite in Atlanta. Within five minutes, Felix invited Tommie to Chicago: "Pack a crate of records and make some music with me." Born in Detroit and raised in the Chicago suburbs, Stallings had been making records from age fourteen, when he coproduced "Fantasy Girl" (1987) with DJ Pierre as Pierre's Pfantasy Club. By the time he met Sunshine, Stallings was recording under a plethora of pseudonyms: Aphrohead, Thee Madkapp Courtship, Felix da Housecat. Working with Felix helped prompt Sunshine's move back to Chicago.

For 2001's *Kittenz and Thee Glitz*, Sunshine wanted to amalgamate "all the musical styles from the late seventies leading up to house music": Kraftwerk, Moroder, new wave, electro. Felix took his demos to Geneva, embellishing them with engineer Dave "the Hustler" Jenefsky. Hanging at the studio with them was Miss Kittin (Caroline Hervé), a DJ (she'd played late-nineties Chicago parties for Mike Dearborn) and singer-songwriter from Grenoble who'd made her first record, "Frank Sinatra" (1999), with fellow Frenchman the Hacker (Michael Amato)—a dry, tongue-in-cheek rip on jet-set club culture. "To be famous is so *niiice* / Suck my dick, lick my ass / Every night in my limousine we have sex / With my famous *friiieeends*," she sang over stripped-back pings, alternating between icy hauteur and a delighted giggle—a photo from Warhol-era *Interview* magazine made audible.

Two weeks later, Sunshine got a call from Felix in Switzerland: "I'm in the studio with Caroline. We need a song." Stallings played the track over the phone—built on a sample of the Flirts' new wave nugget "Passion." Tommie's speakerphone-trained ear went to work. An hour later he e-mailed Felix a lyric called "Silver Screen Shower Scene," instructing Felix to chant along with the lines: "Hear the music, say the words, see the light, join the herd." The next day, Felix asked Tommie for a repeat for vocalist Melistar (Melissa Peralta); sixty minutes later Sunshine banged out "Happy Hour."

The title of *Kittenz and Thee Glitz* was initially planned as the name of the team that put it together—Felix, Kittin, Melistar, Sunshine, Dave the Hustler, Chicago DJ-producer Junior Sanchez. The idea was to perform it live, like a band. But City Rockers, Felix's English label, insisted it be a solo record. Sunshine, who'd been in the rave scene for years but was still new to the business end of things, didn't have a publisher, so no one collected his royalties on it, which were substantial: "Silver Screen" went top forty in England. "That song was on more compilations than any other track that year," says Sunshine. "That was the whole paying-your-dues part of my career."

The album briefly made Felix a star; the jet set his album mocked embraced him with zero irony. He'd remix Madonna's James Bond theme and collaborate with P. Diddy—who, after visiting Ibiza and being turned onto dance music mid-decade, somehow resisted the urge to switch monikers to P. Did E. And Sunshine parlayed the album's success into a new career as a remixer and producer.

LARRY TEE WAS SENSING a sea change. It wasn't hard to spot: NYC clubs were shutting left and right, and starting in the late nineties, much of the new blood coming into New York was bypassing Manhattan in favor of Williamsburg, Brooklyn. A short trip from Manhattan on the L, Williamsburg in the late nineties was abundant in big, cheap lofts and had almost no police presence—sometimes dangerous, but perfect for aspiring artists.

"All these creative people lived near each other on the same street," says Andy Salzer, who moved there from Seattle in 1999. "It wasn't any kind of a mean scene," says Jake Shears (Jason Sellards), another Seattleite who also moved in 1999. "Everybody was friends and supportive of each other." Most were multitasking—ever-faster Internet and ever-lighter laptops made it easy. Salzer could be a designer, run a tech company, and make music with the band Hungry Wives with equal facility. "You didn't have to be a craftsman," says Salzer. "Because of technology I was able to have it [all] taken seriously."

Born Laurence Thom in 1959, Tee had, in addition to cofounding Disco 2000 with Michael Alig, cowritten RuPaul's global hit "Supermodel (You Better Work)" (1993). By the late nineties, Tee and his DJ and promoting partner Spencer Product had 'ad it with superclub bombast. "People were really sick of going out, because nobody really liked that music," he says of ponderously vast Sasha and Digweed sets. "I started looking for electro, but there really wasn't a scene. We had to do little parties out in Brooklyn at Spencer Product's house." The turning point came when Frankfurt's DJ Hell (Helmut Geier) came to play Tee and Product's night at the Pyramid. Hell had issued "Frank Sinatra" on his label, International Deejay Gigolos Recordings.

The group that best exemplified Tee's vision was Fischerspooner—singer Casey Spooner and synth man Warren Fischer. They'd met as Chicago art students and reconnected in New York in spring 1998. Soon they were writing songs—campy, synth-heavy numbers that flew in the face of Fischer's musical past. "Warren studied classical violin and played in an orchestra and a math rock band called Table—very influenced by Slint," says Spooner. "For him to work in dance music was like sacrilege. He was a dyed-in-the-wool indie rocker, working in the crassest, most disgusting form of music that he had no respect for."

They made their debut August 25, 1998, at a performance night at the Astor Place Starbucks (really), mixing striking visuals with staging that, often as not, built in mistakes to wrong-foot the audience, befitting Spooner's experimental-theater background. Fischerspooner was an art project, but their brittle theatricality appealed to emergent electro fans not unlike the way another new local band, the Strokes, appealed to young rockers—a pared-down reset. Or pared down as their staging got: For their second show, around Halloween, Spooner "brought in a human-hair suit—super gorgeous, sewn custom. I was this very elegant beast. That was my first big look."

The duo cut its first few songs at Brooklyn's Rare Book Room. "That recording session, we started to really home in on the aesthetic," says Spooner. "We started picking up any shows we could get." At each one, the number of people onstage grew. John Selway, who saw an early performance, was so impressed with their song "Emerge" that he offered to put a twelve-inch out on his label, Serotonin. "We did some crazy contract where he had six months' license and he could release a thousand copies on vinyl." Soon, DJ Hell got in touch: "He didn't like the song, apparently, but he saw images of our performance and invited us to perform in Berlin." They went in summer 2000. "We were out at a nightclub at five in the morning and I heard the beat to 'Emerge' two blocks away. To be in Berlin for the very first time and to have your song be played in a nightclub—it was thrilling."

Fischerspooner was entrenched in the art world. "Through 1999, the goal [was] towards working with a gallery," says Spooner. That July, they were part of an installation at Gavin Brown's Enterprise. "It was this piece by Rirkrit Tiravanija called Apartment 21, where he had re-created his apartment in the gallery that was open to the public, twenty-four hours a day for three months. It had a working kitchen and a working bathroom. People were invited to have dinner parties. Someone shot a porn there." Fischerspooner made a memorable appearance. "It was insanely hot. It was like a pop sweat lodge. Gavin loved that performance and we started working with Gavin more seriously. He gave us a big New York show in March 2000."

For five nights, four performances per night, the shirtless, lip-syncing Spooner led a troupe of female dancers wearing military boots and corsets, chirping at the audience ("I want to see you work!") as Fischer cued up tracks. *Frieze* called it "part performance shtick, part queer cabaret tossed with glam drag, mock metal, torch song, and Eurotrash," and expressed mixed feelings about the way "what seems like ephemera one moment can seem indicative of a groundswell the next." To Elisabeth Vincentelli, then music editor for *Time Out New York*. "Fischerspooner was playing a dangerous role, because as soon as you start associating with the fashion industry, you're pretty much fucked. The fashion industry has nothing to lose."

HUNGRY WIVES' SOLE "HIT" was the tart electro number "It's Over," inspired by a dream Salzer had about vogue-dancing pioneer Kevin Aviance. In dream and song, Aviance looked around and clucked, "It's just one song, sweetie—*ovah* and *ovah* and *ovah* and *ovah*."

"In most house music at the time the beat didn't stop," says DJ-producer Armand Van Helden. "Listening to jungle, they would do those stops with no beats. I was like, 'I'm gonna throw that in house music.'" On tracks like his monster remixes of Tori Amos's "Professional Widow" (1996) and Sneaker Pimps' "Spin Spin Sugar" (1997), Van Helden became house music's bass king, looping a one-bar b-line into a walloping funk groove on the former ("Honey, bring it close to my lips, yeah," Amos yelps: "Gotta be big") and constructing most of the music on the latter, including the swampy, wall-caving drop.

Those tracks were replicated wholesale in England by records such as Double 99's "Ripgroove" (1997), which led a flurry of similar tracks dubbed "speed garage." This was in the lineage of something called two-step garage, or UK garage, which came from London DJs playing East Coast garage records—R&B-centric vocal house—at higher pitches, particularly remixes by Marc "MK" Kinchen, such as Nightcrawlers' "Push the Feeling On" (1992): vocal phrases cut into bright syllables and laid across percolating keyboards and deeply syncopated hi-hats and snares.

MK's great successor was New Jersey native Todd Edwards, a devout Catholic who turned Kinchen's cut-up technique baroque—a complex series of crosshatched samples, often a mere split-second long, creating uncanny patterns—as when Edwards snuck "It's all right, Jesus loves you," stitched out of a dozen voices, into his rapturous dub mix of Saint Germain's "Alabama Blues" (1995). In 1997, Daft Punk mentioned him as an inspiration in their "Teachers," then tapped him to coproduce and sing "Face to Face" on their second album, *Discovery* (2001). But the electro kids didn't care. "Two-step garage—I've never heard of it," Salzer moaned on "It's Over": *"It does not exist."*

SPOONER MOVED from Manhattan to Williamsburg in summer 2001, near Bedford Avenue. *"Everything* moved from Manhattan to Williamsburg then," he says. Spooner lived around the corner from the recently opened Luxx. "Luxx was a random Latin cowboy bar in Williamsburg," says Sheneza Mohammed, who knew Tee from Limelight. "A couple years prior I'd rented out that space for my twenty-fifth-birthday party." Spooner threw a housewarming party that spilled over to Tee and Product's new Saturday-night Luxx party, Berliniamsburg. "Casey's birthday party launched it," acknowledges Tee.

At that point in New York nightlife, partying in Brooklyn *wasn't done*. Berliniamsburg signaled a reverse-migration—more and more young Manhattanites were flocking to Williamsburg to live as well as party. Tee and Product took over Luxx's Fridays as well, calling that party Mutants. "It wasn't just straight or gay, even though the gay pickup thing kept it financially feasible," says Tee. "But everybody came because it was an exciting new happening."

There was little left in Manhattan anyway. Twilo shut permanently on May 24, 2001, after the state voted to allow the City of New York to not renew the venue's cabaret license. Authorities had discovered the club was sending overdose victims to the hospital using its own specially hired paramedic service—so as not to alert the police—after first attempting to revive them with ice water in a private back room. The day the club shut down, fans conducted a vigil. "People gathered around and took photos, hugging each other and bidding farewell," Tricia Romano wrote in the *Village Voice*. "A few cried and some danced to the music booming from a silver car parked at the curb."

Manhattan's early-nineties vogue for sit-down lounges, such as Spy, had introduced a queasy new concept: bottle service. "They were small places, initially," says Frank Owen. Club owners started doing the math: "You're not going to make a fortune if you have one hundred, two hundred people in there. Promoters said, 'Why don't we do this in a bigger club and we'll make a fucking killing? We can sell a thirty-dollar bottle of vodka for five hundred dollars."

BROOKLYN WASN'T the new Manhattan just yet. Tee knew that to properly showcase his scene he had to stick with the island. Luxx was part of the package of the October series he was planning, but the showcase gigs at its heart were at Exit (on West Fifty-sixth Street, one of the few remaining superclubs after the Giuliani putsch) on October 10, and Webster Hall on October 13. It also needed a catchy title. "I wanted a name I could trademark, because I wanted to be able to do the festival again without somebody stealing it," says Tee. "You couldn't really just call it 'electro,' because electro was eighties." "Electrowave" gave way to "electroclash." "It sounded very much like a genre name," says Tee.

Tee began guerrilla marketing the festival: "I put posters in every corner of the city in the middle of the night." "Electroclash" had its own slick logo, hot pink against black, the "E" tweaked into a quasi-"@." Many found this salesmanship rapacious. Soon after Tee's posters began appearing, an anonymous entity began covering them with stickers pleading: "ELECTROCLASH COULD BE THE NEXT 'GRUNGE.' DON'T LET BUZZWORDS AND MARKETING EXPLOIT AND DESTROY THE MUSIC YOU LOVE!"

DJ Hell, having championed electro for years, was not amused by Tee's trademark. "Hell felt like somehow we had just stolen it out from under him," says Tee. "We didn't, but he was definitely the first guy that was actually like, 'Oh, this has possibility.' We were more excited by the live aspects." Nor were many people who played Tee's festival pleased with the name. Detroit's ADULT., who played the Webster Hall show with Peaches and Chicks on Speed, found themselves lumped in with "electroclash" as a genre, rather than a show. "You don't play Pukkelpop Festival in Belgium and the next thing you're considered Pukkelpop," says Nicola Kuperus.

THE SUMMER OF 2001 was supposed to right the electronica touring disasters of 1997—starting with Big Top's headliner. Moby put together Area: One—his own tour rather than an MCT Management package that he was fronting. It was dance-heavy—Paul Oakenfold, the Orb, Carl Cox—but also eclectic: OutKast, Incubus, New Order, Nelly Furtado, and the Roots also appeared. "The dance tents were really well attended—Oakenfold—but I don't think people understood," says Hobey Echlin. Still, it made money, a rarity; industry-wide, show revenues from the year's first half were down 12 percent from 2000.

That downturn flattened both Toronto promoters Mekka, whose ten-city U.S. tour was canceled three days before touchdown in Detroit, and Creamfields—the latter a two-city (Las Vegas and Long Island) U.S. version of a major English dance festival. "We thought, 'Wow, here we go, Europe's coming over here, it's going to be a big thing,'" says Disco Donnie Estopinal. On August 2, Creamfields lost its Vegas venue and couldn't find a West Coast replacement. Six days later, the Long Island date, having sold only 6 percent of its tickets, flatlined as well. "When they canceled Creamfields, it was a big red flag," says Estopinal.

SOMEHOW, KURT ECKES HAD managed to continue Even Furthur every Labor Day weekend without a hitch. For summer 2001 he secured farmland near Lacrosse, by a "biker strip club in the middle of nowhere," owned by the son of the county chairman. Equipment theft had plagued the 1999 and 2000 Furthurs. "I was so bummed out," says Eckes. "All people wanted was to get drugs."

In 2001, he had a Burning Man replica ready to go: "We had a really big, elaborate ceremony planned. We hired all these fire dancers. Then some dumbass threw something on it, and it started burning down on Saturday." Next day, several Even Furthur participants went to the strip bar, where Sunday was Amateur Day: The bikers wanted to watch the raver girls pole-dance. "It just started getting stupid," says Eckes. A brief scuffle ensued: "Just a few punches, and it was over," says Eckes. But that was enough. "I was like: 'This is my curtain call.' I knew the shit that Donnie had gone through down in New Orleans. I was paranoid. I knew they were going to make an example out of somebody. I didn't want to be a martyr."

On November 2, 2002, Regroup, a fund-raiser to renovate Racine's Uptown Theater, was held down the street from where Eckes had thrown an event a few months earlier. The police busted it like they were taking revenge for Grave: kicking open bathroom stalls with guns out, cracking one woman's knee with a door and throwing her to the ground before she could pull her underwear up, forcing another to finish peeing as the cops watched. In the men's room, a policeman held a gun to an attendee's head for fifteen minutes and then locked him in a police car for three hours. "I had dodged another bullet, and I knew this was going to keep happening," says Eckes. He unplugged Drop Bass Network, moved to Lacrosse, and the man who'd thrown parties in barns became a farmer.

DOC MARTIN WAS HAVING a very good 2001. That February, he mixed his second edition of *Essential Mix*, BBC Radio 1's weekly DJ showcase; in August he celebrated the anniversary of his residency at the labyrinthine London club Fabric. Avoiding trance and hard house, the reigning UK superclub sounds, Fabric quickly became one of the most popular nightspots in the world. On Sunday, September 9, Martin played a New York boat party with Fabric resident Craig Richards, then the Tribeca Grand on Monday. He was due in Sacramento for a gig arranged only three days earlier, as a favor to a promoter friend whose headliner had canceled last minute. Martin was tired from all the travel, but was happy to help another promoter in a jam.

Martin pulled an all-nighter after the Tribeca Grand to make his America West flight to Sacramento; as usual, he'd sleep on the plane. Half awake at the Newark airport, Martin watched the passengers board United's San Francisco flight, one gate over. There weren't many—only thirty-seven of 182 seats—and they lifted off at 8:42 A.M. Shortly afterward, Martin was in the air, unconscious. Less than two hours later, his plane was on the ground.

"I woke up in a field in Kansas," he says. "They were announcing they were stuck in this part of the airport, but when I looked up it was just fields of grass everywhere. The pilot made an announcement: 'There's been a terrorist attack on New York. All planes are grounded.' We were like, 'Come on—there's no way.' We pulled in to the gate and saw all these planes. Every plane was grounded everywhere. It hit home at that time. It was insane."

Martin took out his recently purchased cell phone and tried to contact his friends. "The whole network was jammed. You couldn't get through to anybody. You didn't know if your friends were okay or not. We didn't know if it was the train stations, if it was the airports, if someone had bombed New York, if someone came in with a jet and started firing on the crowds."

Martin's plane neared the gate. The pilot got back on: "He told us, 'Two airplanes have crashed into the World Trade Center.' We were like, 'No way. How could that have happened?'" The Twin Towers' structural bearings were ruined; both buildings collapsed. Hijackers had rerouted another flight to Washington, D.C., and flew into the Pentagon, partially collapsing it. The fourth plane of the coordinated terrorist attack—diverted back to D.C. by a quartet of hijackers before passengers took action, crashing it into an empty field southeast of Pittsburgh—was United Airlines Flight 93: The one Martin switched out as a favor to a friend. No one on the planes had survived; altogether, the attacks claimed some three thousand lives.

Martin spent the next three days in a rural hotel room, trying to reach people. A month later, when Tommie Sunshine arrived in New York for Electroclash Festival 2001, the WTC site, now dubbed Ground Zero, was still on fire.

SUNSHINE ARRIVED in New York with David Alter and Ryan Paradise of St. Louis's Superstars of Love. Like a lot of people around the U.S., they had defected from the rave and club scene to the nervy new electro sound. In Chicago, Sunshine would start ElectroSweat, with

Detroit native Jordan Zawideh, at Red Dog, later moving it to Smart Bar and renaming it Degeneration. The Superstars had recently signed to International Deejay Gigolos alongside Fischerspooner and Crossover, who both played Exit during the festival.

All of them hewed to the new aesthetic promulgated by *Vice* magazine. Though it ran surprisingly deep reporting, its bread and butter was slickly produced cheap provocation, defined visually by Terry Richardson's starkly lit perv shots and Ryan McGinley's looking-for-America-with-my-rich-naked-junkie-friends scenarios, and by the infamous Dos and Don'ts—street-fashion photos with captions like coked-up verbal drive-bys, written by founding editor Gavin McInnes. Richardson, McGinley, and McInnes were all regulars at Luxx.

"Hedi Slimane from Dior and Dolce & Gabbana would come down," says Tee. "Kim Jones used to come from London, and now he's head of men's at Louis Vuitton. It was a real cultural moment of a new generation—a new aesthetic, the beginning of Hipsterville." *Vice* was Hipsterville's house organ; a cosign gave you instant cred. The final issue of 2001 paid tribute to the album that called its tune. On the cover, in construction-stencil lettering, was a lyric from *Kittenz and Thee Glitz*: "HAPPY HOUR SUNSHOWER 808S GIVE YOU POWER." Sunshine, the author, was thrilled.

If *Vice* was the scene's bible, its sacrament was cocaine, which had replaced MDMA as New York clubbers' drug of choice. In Williamsburg, people acquired it by going to the bar Kokie's, whose name was about as subtle as a leather jacket or a mullet or a porn-stache. "How the fuck do you keep open a business called Kokie's that sells coke?" says Sunshine, still amazed. "It stayed open until 2005." Ecstasy had encouraged PLUR-style egolessness; cocaine was egocentric, just the thing for a culture throwing off rave's now rote anonymity.

AT EXIT ON OCTOBER 10, the dressed-to-the-nines line went around the block for the guest list alone. Near the entrance was Sam

Valenti IV, a recent U-Michigan graduate, handing out promos of *Tangent 2002: Disco Nouveau*, a new electro compilation on his label Ghostly International. "There was a faint echo of really interesting, lost music that was coming back into view," he says. "Nowadays it seems kind of obvious, but at the time it was a breath of fresh air. Rock was happening, too—garage rock, the Strokes—[as well as] this international dance-music thing."

When Tommie Sunshine arrived, he went straight upstairs to see Linda Lamb, a Gigolo artist whose big record was "Hot Room," new wave redux so exact it could have come from Lene Lovich. Kicking off the main floor was the duo Crossover—Vanessa Tosti and Mark Ingram—who were subtle and had songwriting chops, two things most of the scene couldn't boast. "It's controversial—but I'm not Prince," Tosti sang over easy midtempo bloops on "Extensive Care" (2002).

Being Prince was Spencer Product's job. Upstairs he became Prance, performing flagrantly campy, robot-voiced rewrites of "Controversy" (as "Contra-Pussy") and "When Doves Cry" ("When Love Dies"): "The sweat of my body covers me / Candy Darling, can you picture this?" Yes, the audience of clubbers and ravers—ready to throw off nineties earnestness in favor of trashy post-Warholism much the way glam kids had left the Woodstock dream in their glittering dust—*could* picture it.

The flagrant sex appeal that rave had shunted aside for phat pants and PLUR was abundant at Exit. In the second room, Avenue D (Debbie Attias and Daphne Gomez-Mena) were still three years from their definitive recording, the self-explanatory "Do I Look Like a Slut?" (2004), but their scantily clad shtick was well in place. "The first time I ever went to Williamsburg, we went to Luxx," says Vivian Host. "The girls from Avenue D were bartending—or if it wasn't, it was somebody with duct tape over their nipples."

They looked like nuns compared to the night's first breakout star.

Born Merrill Nisker in Toronto, Peaches was a bisexual mid-thirties Jewish woman in hot-pink hot pants, tank top, and fishnet, wielding a persona not just horny but ravenous. Writhing around onstage to raw grooves she'd put together on the Roland MC-505 Groovebox (an all-in-one synthesizer, sampler, sequencer, and drum machine) and accompanied by keyboardist Chilly Gonzales (Jason Beck), Peaches had already appeared in New York three times over the previous year, the first time opening for Elastica. "She totally took over Bowery Ballroom," says Vincentelli. "Sweat was flying everywhere." At Exit, Peaches upped everybody's ante by appearing in a vinyl nurse's uniform and humping the stage while mewling "Fuck the Pain Away" and "Diddle My Skittle."

"Peaches blew our fucking brains out," says Sunshine. "If you were going to have a conversation while she was playing, good luck. No one had seen anybody put that much out there in so long—especially what we were used to. This was why Moby was so big—he was the only one that *kind of* got it right. If someone presented it the right way, it would've been so huge. But it wasn't about, 'How we can make this bigger?' It was, 'How can we make sure there's a next weekend?'"

LIKE THE ROCK STARS they archly pretended to be, Fischerspooner made the audience wait, coming on an hour late. Tee and others DJed between bands, but it was hard to miss the antici . . . *pation*. "It was going on and on: 'Are they going to fucking play or what?'" says Sunshine. "They took one step onstage, and we all went ballistic. It was everything you could have wanted—like the eighties on angel dust." Spooner, in greasepaint, enacted the role of a cyborg pop star, as is-he-serious? as Prance and confrontational as Peaches. "It was like you were at their rehearsal," says Sunshine. "When they would do a costume change, they would go two feet to the left and start changing onstage. You were in the show, catapulted into this world."

The audience reacted in kind, thrusting themselves toward the stage through machine fog as gold confetti flew and corn-syrup blood spurted. It was high drama with a raw edge, confrontational but interpersonal, connecting the dance floor's communal stardom to punk's audience baiting. "It was still very rough, but they had it so right already," says Sunshine. "If they're going to make this crash course in pop music, they're going to nail it to the wall."

Fischerspooner were in the midst of prepping the Exit show when the attacks happened. "We called off rehearsal that day," says Spooner. "I talked to Larry that day, and asked, 'Are you still going to do this?' He said yeah. It felt difficult at first. We had been making this celebratory, decadent thing about excess in the face of Y2K paranoia, and all of a sudden the world changed. 'Does this feel relevant? Does this feel disrespectful?' But, you know, when in doubt, go to work. It seemed the right thing to do, because it was a relief. All the paranoia about Y2K was transposed onto September 11—all this anxiety, all this fear [that had] built around the turn of the millennium."

Thomas Bullock, the Wicked DJ, had moved east in 1999; his black-leather-wearing and audience-baiting "science-fiction punk band" A.R.E. Weapons, unenviably, followed Fischerspooner. Their yammering electronic screech provided exit music for many. But Bullock largely avoided the hubbub, spending most of the night with two friends. "One was up to his fucking eyeballs in painkillers," he says. The other had "just escaped from a mental hospital, just to come to the show." He partied all night, still in his hospital gown. (Bullock had left A.R.E. by the time Vice Records issued the band's self-titled debut two years later.)

Sunshine left Exit that night riveted. "The rave scene had already run its course," he says. "All of a sudden, there was this whole world." Even *Vice*'s Gavin McInnes wrote a shockingly rhapsodic review of the show, lavishing praise on Fischerspooner: "A Vegas show with the honesty and unprofessionalism of a punk soundcheck," concluding: "Finally, something new." Others were more skeptical. "I was like, 'Are you fucking kidding me?'" says Ethan Brown. "Especially after going to see Fischerspooner play."

BY 2002, EVERY BAR IN NEW YORK had a pair of turntables. Younger indie kids didn't reject DJ culture—they resurrected it on their own terms, presaging the end of the 2000s, when the mass pop audience did the same thing. The catalyst for much of this was DFA Records, founded in 2001 by James Murphy and Tim Goldsworthy. Murphy, from New Jersey, had been an indie rock drummer, Englishman Goldsworthy the cofounder of Mo' Wax Records. "Tim was always at the computer, James was always at the mixing board," says Tim Sweeney, DFA's first intern, who started the WNYU mix show *Beats in Space* in 1999. The building was also the site of invite-only all-night DJ parties the two producers began to throw. "They were crazy, ecstasy-fueled parties," says Astralwerks founder Brian Long, who attended several. "There were people from a wide range of artistic disciplines." Murphy also began playing regularly at spots like Plant Bar and Passerby Bar.

DFA's planned first record set the tone: "House of Jealous Lovers" (2002), by the Rapture, a trio who'd formed in San Francisco and recently moved to New York. "Our goal before we met DFA was [to] tour with Fugazi," says singer-guitarist Luke Jenner. "James and Tim were like, 'You guys need to set your sights way higher.'" Recalls Sweeney: "They were thinking the Rapture was going to be the next Cure." Once, Murphy showed the band a piece in *i-D* magazine about England's then-emerging post-punk resurgence. "He was like, 'We're going to do this, I'm going to produce it, and it's going to take over the world,'" says Jenner. "I was like, 'Yeah, dude, sure.'"

"House of Jealous Lovers" seethed like a Gang of Four stripped of politics, its serrated edge rounded and floor-friendlier. Years of major-label Prodigy clones had made anyone with ears leery of "rocktronica," but here at last was an actual rock band, complete with Jenner's screamo-style vocals, making an actual dance record. The B-side featured a remix by Morgan Geist, half of New York duo Metro Area with Darshan Jesrani. Geist's remix of "Jealous Lovers" allowed DFA to sneak the twelve-inch into dance shops reluctant to stock a record by a rock band. DJs needed less convincing: Jenner was tending bar at Centro-Fly when Felix da Housecat played his record. "He came by the bar: 'You don't know it yet, but you're going to be really famous.' It was like, 'Yeah, yeah—it's after four in the morning.'"

"House of Jealous Lovers"—along with Murphy's bow as LCD Soundsystem, the wondrously tense and self-loathing "Losing My Edge" b/w "Beat Connection" (2002)—had an immediate, widespread effect. Like a canny remix of Brian Eno's famous formulation about only thirty thousand people buying the first Velvet Underground album, but all of them starting bands—and as if on cue from LCD's lyrics—seemingly all twenty thousand people who purchased "Jealous Lovers" either become DJs or bought drum machines. "And I'm sorry," says DFA label manager Jonathan Galkin with a laugh. "I'm sorry for what we were responsible for."

FISCHERSPOONER'S RECORDING CAREER was secondary to their gallery career; Deitch Projects put them on a monthly stipend. By the time they signed to a U.S. label, their signature song, "Emerge," had been issued three times already. Warren and Casey had been ready to sign to the newly opened U.S. branch of Ministry of Sound, the label offshoot of the British superclub. A&R men Andrew Goldstone and DJ DB, who'd just left F-111/Warner Bros., planned a straight reissue of their album, *#1*, with some extras. "Andrew and I were talking about a deal for seventy-five thousand dollars—considerable, but not crazy," says DB.

But after Electroclash Festival, Fischerspooner's gigs were crawling with major-label reps smelling money, and soon the offers became unignorable. Ministry's president, James Palumbo, says DB, "wanted to prove that he was going to be a serious record label and not just a compilations company." Adds Spooner: "It was a real marquee thing for Ministry. It turned ridiculous. All those stupid stories you hear about the music business doing to pursue someone? They're all true"—for example, Spooner flew the Concorde to England and back for a meeting.

Ministry's final offer gave them veto power over non-UK distributors, and the group didn't okay a U.S. partner for over a year. By the time Capitol issued #1 in America, it had been over a year since the UK release—and three since the DIY version went on consignment in New York. For this, they made a reported two million dollars. "I've had to live with everyone thinking I'm a millionaire, even though I'm not, and never was," says Spooner.

It was spectacularly bad timing. It sank Fischerspooner's Deitch deal, and came right as the big-label way of doing things was running off a cliff. The major-label dance departments were folding up tents—the beginning of mass belt-tightening to come. "Several overseas brands came over, opened up very flash offices during the dot-comedy era, and started handing out wheelbarrows full of money thinking that the party is on," says Errol Kolosine. "A lot of those people had to go back to the UK, or make their operations smaller." Ministry's American office was dismantled nearly as quickly as it had been established.

#1 made little money for Capitol, which had other things to worry about. On April 28, 2003, less than two months after its release, Apple announced the iTunes Music Store, selling MP3s for ninety-nine cents each, and with it a new world order.

The United States *lost something* with 9/11—the total expression of a generation, silenced off the airwaves, policed and beaten down, denied even the nostalgia granted to punk. Rave culture was not only underground; it has now been buried in the U.S., as if it never existed, as if the blurring of gender and color and dance never happened.

—TOBIAS C. VAN VEEN, REVIEW OF *SPEAKING IN CODE* (*DANCECULT* VOL. 2, NO. 1, 2011)

>16

COACHELLA

Indio, California
April 29–30, 2006

ON JUNE 18, 2002, Sen. Joseph Biden (D-Delaware) introduced to Congress the Reducing Americans' Vulnerability to Ecstasy —R.A.V.E.—Act. Yes, really. It basically extended the Crack House Law, levying fines up to $250,000 and prison time up to twenty years on promoters, venue, and owners alike for the use of MDMA on their watch or property. In short, the U.S. government was formalizing what it had been doing for years—and it seemed to work. In 2002, use of LSD in the nation's high schools had dropped to less than one-third of the previous year. "We have literally never seen anything like this," a drug policy expert said. "This isn't a trend. This is an event."

The R.A.V.E. Act lost two sponsors and left the table on June 27. The next day, Pasquale Rotella threw the sixth annual Electric Daisy Carnival in Long Beach. Typically, EDC was the smaller of Rotella's two pet events; inaugurated in 1997, it was two years younger than Nocturnal Wonderland. But in 2001, for the first time, Nocturnal lost money. "I couldn't get a venue. I'd also had a death at Nocturnal. It was really hard. But I still did Electric Daisy—I never missed a year." Still, the climate became brutal; EDC 2002 drew a meager six thousand. "It just dropped off a cliff," says Disco Donnie Estopinal, who briefly worked with Rotella. "When that happened everybody was shocked. It happened to me in lots of places I had shows set up. It had gone down to nearly nothing."

It wasn't just shows: After moving to Manhattan from Avenue U, Brooklyn, in the mid-nineties, Adam X, the manager of Groove Records, was forced to shut the business in October 2004, after profits plummeted to one-fifth of their peak. "It was all happening at once," says Adam. "You have 9/11, you have the advent of high-speed Internet, you have Final Scratch, you have the euro getting so much higher than the dollar, [all] within a two-year period."

In April of 2003, a year after the R.A.V.E. Act fell through, Congress passed a new Joe Biden–sponsored bill, the Illicit Drug Anti-Proliferation Act of 2003. A modification of the R.A.V.E. Act, the Anti-Proliferation Act was tacked onto the Amber Alert Bill, which dealt with child abduction.

Disco Donnie made do by tying together the various strands left over from the pre-crackdown years. He moved to Columbus in 2001, when his girlfriend (now wife) got an Ohio State residency. "I would do Cincinnati on Thursday, Cleveland on Friday, and Columbus on a Saturday. I started a hub system, like an airport. It wasn't an 'Aha!' moment. I knew a small percentage of the population still wanted to see DJs. If I was in Portland, I started calling about Seattle. Nobody wants to fly out to the Northwest without another flight." Estopinal also instituted cheaper prices: "I was doing five dollars for the first fifty tickets just to get the ball rolling."

ON AUGUST 29, 2002, Moby was in the audience at Radio City Music Hall for the MTV Video Music Awards; "We Are All Made of Stars" won for Best Cinematography. "Stars" was the lead single from

18, issued that May—an album that baldly retreads its predecessor. "Oh yeah, I wanted to repeat the success of *Play*," says Moby. "Everyone I worked with wanted to repeat the success of *Play*. I had been a marginal musician and I was suddenly getting all this attention. Part of me wanted even more attention. So I started thinking in terms of fame and public figure status. I wasn't trying to make more money—I wanted to keep being invited to parties."

Moby stopped being straight-edge after *Everything Is Wrong* came out, but September 11 spun his bad habits out hard. "I went from being a crazy drunk to being an even crazier drunk. I went from taking a lot of drugs to taking even more drugs. After 9/11, everybody I knew in lower Manhattan was doing everything they could to feel better in the next five minutes."

At Radio City, Moby was seated a few rows behind Eminem, who won four prizes that night. At the Grammys six months earlier, Moby had extensively criticized Eminem's misogyny and homophobia; Em responded by dissing Moby by name that spring on "Without Me," portraying him in the video: bald, reading a paperback while doing yoga and peeling a banana. "Moby" is body-slammed to the lines: "You thirty-six-year-old bald-headed fag, blow me / You're too old, let go / It's over, *nobody listens to techno*." America's long-simmering distrust of electronica had hit the pop airwaves. "You don't want to dis Eminem," Chris Rock said in 2003. "*Lots* of people listen to techno. But he said it so funny, and the timing was so perfect, I believed it."

"From about 2003 to about 2006, there was, especially in States, a massive backlash against me," says Moby. "Eminem both represented the backlash and perpetuated it. When he first started saying nasty things about me, I thought he was kidding. Then I found out he was quite serious. Every night on tour, someone dressed like me would walk out, and he would shoot that person with a shotgun."

At Radio City, Moby did a preplanned filmed bit with *Late Night with Conan O'Brien* hand puppet Triumph the Insult Comic Dog (head writer Robert Smigel). Unplanned, Triumph approached Eminem about quashing the beef. The surly rapper pushed the comedian's arm away. Smigel turned it into a sketch—a "press conference" that ended: "At the end of the day, he's just another white guy trying to make an honest living stealing black people's music." (For many, that applied equally to Moby sampling Lomax's recordings.) But Eminem wouldn't let go. Accepting an award, he startled the hall by sneering at "that Moby girl," adding: "I *will* hit a man with glasses." The audience booed. Moby later wrote that Eminem "called me a pussy (this was off camera) and then threatened to beat me up." They never met again, but no matter—the damage was done.

RICHIE HAWTIN WAS READY for bigger things. His longtime girlfriend lived in New York; so did his friends Magda and Troy Pierce, who copromoted Gel and Weave, a short-lived party at Openair (on St. Marks Place) with promoter-DJ Bryan Kasenic (Spinoza).

By 2002, Hawtin was living in Williamsburg, playing all over the city and throwing wild private loft jams. Magda and Pierce's roommate was Kevin McHugh, who put together electronic-music events for the public arts group Creative Time. "We were doing those DJ events to make enough money to pay for the art installations—one hand washing the other," says McHugh. Those events took place at the Anchorage, in a cavity of the Brooklyn Bridge. "We'd have nine hundred people who'd normally be at MoMA, going crazy under experimental electronic media installations."

McHugh fell in with Hawtin as a fellow conceptual art lover: "Richard Serra and classic sixties minimalism—I didn't know any DJ that could name-check that stuff." Not for long: The Anchorage shuttered for security reasons after 9/11, and both Magda and Pierce would abandon New York by 2002. Only a year after coming to New York, Richie followed them to Berlin.

• • • •

IN THE REUNIFIED NINETIES, the German government intended to vastly expand Berlin. "In 2003 it became the capital of Germany again, and leading up to that for ten years it was the biggest construction site in the world," says Mark Verbos, who moved there in 2000 and returned to New York around the time Hawtin left. But Berlin never turned into an economic powerhouse, so it remained not just affordable but cheap. Verbos knew only three Americans in Berlin when he arrived: "I would go to Tresor and never see any Americans except the ones who came to DJ."

Laptop glitch was big with Berlin techno hard-liners: "They were in love with American laptop guys because to them it was real," says Verbos. A number of producers there were using the same methods to make floor-ready tracks. At the same time, the locus of Berlin's dance scene shifted to the Friedrichshain/Kreuzberg area along the river Spree, where clubs like Berghain and Panorama Bar (in the same building), among others, sprung up. Thus the music shifted from Tresor-style bangers (and the tuneful trance that dominated the annual Love Parade) to the new strain of minimalism that, in *The Wire*'s July 2001 issue, San Francisco journalist-DJ Philip Sherburne dubbed "microhouse."

This stuff differed substantially from the artful whomp of minimal techno by Detroit producers like Robert Hood and Dan Bell, or dubby Berlin epigones like Basic Channel—a handful of elements occupying center frame. In Sherburne's formulation, microhouse "retained [house music's] essential features—especially its kick drum and off-beat hi-hat—[while] all the fat fell away from their hips and jutting collarbones . . . spawning a sound that wasn't so much emaciated as supple and lithe." He highlighted labels throughout Germany: Perlon and Force Inc. in Frankfurt, Kompakt in Cologne. But Berlin was the hub. "You could easily open a club there," says Kompakt cofounder Michael Mayer. "Just break into a building, open a club there for three weeks. It was like El Dorado."

In 2006, a Berlin apartment cost two hundred to four hundred euros (roughly \$275 to \$550) a month—less than a New York parking space. "People would rent a place for a year, and just live in it a couple months a year," says journalist Geeta Dayal, a Berlin resident for much of 2005. Equally key was the city's residence/artist visa, allowing one to live in Berlin as long as most of their living didn't come from Berlin firms. It helped that dance musicians frequently held tech-based day jobs (coding, programming) they could do remotely.

By 2006, it was a set pattern: If you were an underground U.S. dance producer or DJ beginning to attract serious attention, you either moved to Berlin or endured endless questions about when you were *going* to move to Berlin. "It was really depressing, to be honest," says Seattle DJ and promoter Sean Horton. "People began to have the perception that in order to become famous they needed to move to Berlin, and that's just bullshit." DJ Dave Turov, a software consultant born in Uzbekistan and brought up in Brooklyn, had been struggling to promote techno parties in early-2000s New York before going to Berlin in 2003. It wasn't just American DJs and producers defecting: "By 2007," says Turov, "we had all the Canadians, Chileans, Swiss, everybody."

IN 2003, HAWTIN ISSUED his first Plastikman album in five years, the woozy, introspective *Closer*, and he wanted to present it with a splash. The following year he made an early attempt at a full-on Plastikman live show at Montreal's MUTEK Festival, intending to one-up the festival's intensive digital audiovisual showcases. Hawtin brought McHugh, who'd done extensive multimedia work with Creative Time, and video artist Ali Demirel out to Berlin to work on it, telling them: "I want to control visuals, media, lights, and music."

"It took us six months to get ready for the MUTEK show," says McHugh. "We had a bunch of technical problems." During the performance, Hawtin's earphones fritzed out (they were fixed), and his visual controller was unreliable. It didn't crash and burn, but it wasn't remotely road-ready; moreover, it was a money drain. Finally, says McHugh, the team realized: "The technology just isn't there yet." (McHugh also used Hawtin's studio when Richie was out, eventually issuing music on M_nus as Ambivalent.) Hawtin would have to wait for the gear to catch up with his ideas.

He had also changed his look, growing out his blond hair and swapping his trademark black rectangular glasses for contacts. When he played the End in London, Magda recalled fans asking for Richie Hawtin when he was standing in front of them: "They never believed it. This really went on for a long time, maybe a year and a half, until people realized, 'Okay, he's got hair now.'"

Maybe he grew it out so he could symbolically let it down. In Berlin, where multiday partying was standard practice—individual events typically lasted twelve hours, most with after-hours attached—Hawtin became a fixture, getting visibly legless and spinning deep into morning alongside old friends like Sven Väth and new ones like the Chilean-born Ricardo Villalobos. The latter made long tracks full of minute but purposeful timbral shifts; more than anyone, Villalobos helped shift the city's club sound from bare-but-blooming micro-house to something tougher and itchier, typically dubbed just plain "minimal," or "mnml."

By mid-decade, Berlin's club scene was a tourist destination—what journalist Tobias Rapp dubbed the "Easyjet Set," flying in the continent's hardcore weekenders. Berlin's Schönefeld Airport, the hub for many bargain airlines, vaulted from 1.7 million passengers in 2003 to 6.3 million in 2007. For many, the undisputed destination was Berghain-Panorama Bar, in an abandoned fifties power station. "You won't find people there by mistake," says Israeli techno headliner Guy Gerber of Panorama Bar (heavier on house, while Berghain is heavier on techno). "They're really enthusiastic about the music. You can play for hours and hours." That is, if they can get in: Berghain's basement, the Laboratory, is a gay sex club, and the building's door policy is both strict and whimsical, giving it a basic snob appeal.

SEATTLE WAS A DIFFERENT KIND of techno city. There were big parties—local rave promoters USC could draw up to ten thousand—and candy raves at NAF Studio (also a rehearsal space for Queensrÿche and Soundgarden), which shut down in October 2002 after its final party, Organik. Far more upscale was Tasty Shows, the moniker of promoters Alex Calderwood and Jared Harler. In March 1998 they opened ARO.space on Capitol Hill—previously the rock dump Moe's.

"They started throwing parties and built up," says Matt Corwine. ARO.space was "this sleek, ultramodern, high-design club," with Spartan lighting and pale green walls—what Corwine calls "the sophisticated *Wallpaper* magazine grownup version" of the rave aesthetic. Calderwood applied the same ideas to other kinds of hospitality. In 1993 he and other partners opened Rudy's Barbershop, a vintage-style haircutters that grew to nineteen shops worldwide. In April 1998, a month after ARO.space opened, Calderwood helped launch the Ace Hotel near downtown. "It was like an ARO.Space you could sleep in," says Corwine.

Sean Horton shared Tasty's aesthetic. A Detroit native who'd spun at the popular dance-scene hangout Zoot's coffeehouse as a teenager, Horton had put on parties in Olympia while attending Evergreen State College in the late nineties, moving to Seattle in 2002. He was disdainful of USC's high prices ($75 a head), especially compared to his friends in the local dance scene's hippie contingent, with their ties to Burning Man and the tech biz. (Horton is a longtime Microsoft employee.) Additionally, he says, "I've always been a hardware guy: keyboards, drum machines, effects processors, outboard mixers. I saw more and more people producing music because it became less and less expensive."

In January 2002, Seattle promoter Fourthcity put on its first Laptop Battle: "People constructing loops and song structures in three minutes that people would vote on," says Horton, who participated in the first two. He also attended MUTEK 2002, in Montreal, where Villalobos participated in a festival-ending laptop jam that Sherburne feverishly called "something akin to the birth of house music or the very first scratch"—the moment when "microhouse" became "minimal." MUTEK was a revelation for Horton: "I came back to Seattle and said, 'You know what? We can do this." The city was full of young coders who doubled as digital musicians, but few played out much. The first Decibel Festival (September 23–26, 2004) gave them a showcase. Despite limited advertising and a mostly regional lineup, it drew twenty-five hundred people, highly respectable for a marginal style in a city where indie rock was still king.

Even indie rockers were starting to warm up. One was Ben Gibbard, the swoon-voiced singer for Seattle's Death Cab for Cutie, who'd contributed a vocal to L.A. IDM producer Dntel's (Jimmy Tamborello) third album, *Life Is Full of Possibilities*. On "(This Is) The Dream of Evan and Chan," Gibbard sang charming nonsense over skittering post-jungle beats, but the track reached clubs in the remix by Kompakt artist Superpitcher, who lovingly slowed Gibbard's vocal across foghorn synths and chugging bass, before an out-of-nowhere gurgle sparked a chain reaction—one bell dragging across a shipwreck floor, then a slew—a true what-was-*that*? moment. It paved the way for Tamborello and Gibbard's collaboration as the Postal Service. Their *Give Up* (2003) became Sub Pop Records' second-bestselling release, after Nirvana's *Bleach*.

WHEN BOOKING AGENT Tom Windish brought a rock friend to the first Coachella, they went to the Sahara Tent to see one of Windish's favorite Warp Records acts. "Oh my God, that's Autechre!" said Windish. "Where?" his friend asked. Windish pointed to the two men gazing into their laptops: "There! This is the show."

Long pause: "*Where*? They're onstage—but where *are* they? What are they doing?" It was a conversation Windish would repeat for years.

Despite those objections, Coachella was more attuned to electronic dance music than any other rock festival—especially then. In addition to many DJs and live dance acts, the festival hired Vello Virkhaus to run visuals in 2002 and 2003. "The Sahara Tent was a much smaller place then," says Virkhaus. "We brought all the projectors and screens. My favorite show was VJing Groove Armada."

The one dance act Coachella wanted but didn't get, year upon year, was Daft Punk. Not for lack of trying: Every year, Paul Tollette approached Gerry Gerrard, their booking agent, and every year Gerrard had to decline. "The whole country was asking for them," says Gerrard. "I remember I took Daft Punk over to Armand Van Helden's studio in 2005 and said, 'Do you know what my job is? It's to say no to people who want Daft Punk.'"

The demand wasn't because the duo had had huge American hits: "Around the World" had peaked at number sixty-one on the *Billboard* Hot 100; "Music Sounds Better with You," by Stardust—Thomas Bangalter and two collaborators—got to number sixty-nine. It was because, as Gerrard says, "They were selling three thousand records a week. It was just consistent, forever." He also noted that on their late-nineties tours, "Daft Punk were very proactive, like the Chemical Brothers: They spent money for extra lights and sound. They had the right idea." But the "French touch" sound they'd pioneered had burnt out: Philippe Zdar of Cassius recounted shopping for music in Paris, "listening to two hundred records, and all of them were shit."

No one in her right mind could dismiss Daft Punk's second album, *Discovery* (2001), as yet more filter-disco. Every shimmering surface conjured an aural utopia that offset and deepened the duo's knowingness, demanding you be swept away if you were a fan, in on the joke if you were a skeptic, and both if you were paying any attention at all. House music with the sweep of classic pop, it was bolstered by a pair of guests from New Jersey: Romanthony (Anthony Moore), who sang "One More Time" and "Too Long," was a singer-songwriter whose "The Wanderer (Journey Man Thump)" had been one of 1994's biggest house tracks; and Todd Edwards added his confettied samples to "Face to Face" as well as singing it.

Daft Punk could have swept up on tour, but stayed home, electing to dress as robots in their promo material. "They didn't do any DJ shows or anything," says their then-manager Pedro Winter—who, with less to do, founded Ed Banger Records in 2003, recording and DJing as Busy P. Ed Banger's second release featured the label's crucial track. Justice were Parisians Gaspard Augé and Xavier de Rosnay, in electroclash-uniform mustaches and black leather; Simian were British indie rockers who'd made a track called "Never Be Alone" that Justice had reworked into garish, fist-pumping electro-rock. Winter heard it and knew precisely which direction his label would take. Retitled "We Are Your Friends," and credited to Justice vs. Simian, the track kept Ed Banger in the spotlight for the next three years.

That amped, overdriven sound formed the bedrock of the third Daft Punk album, *Human After All* (2005). Rather than a return to *Discovery*'s Technicolor splendor or the swaggering grooves of *Homework*, *Human*, made in a mere six weeks, was the group's most determinedly robotic album. There were moments—"Robot Rock" punches up Breakwater's 1980 funk obscurity "Release the Beast" with sharp edits—but *Human* lacked ideas, sonics, grooves, and feeling. Daft Punk clearly didn't benefit from being hurried.

AFTER DETROIT'S MOTOR shut down in September 2002, Josh Glazer moved to L.A. to work for *Urb* magazine. "It was my favorite magazine," he says. "It was the only magazine seriously writing about the culture." He'd started freelancing there for fellow Detroiter Scott Sterling, who in the late nineties had run *Sweater*, a DJ-culture title sponsored by Camel Cigarettes. (Such direct corporate involvement was endemic in nightlife, particularly with Camel, which had several regional offices devoted to club outreach.)

Urb had first reached national newsstands in 1997, with a Chemical Brothers cover. By the time Glazer got there in late 2003, the scene in L.A. was "totally fucking dead": the clubs still played top-forty and hip-hop; bottle service was coming in. And aside from the hip-hop it had long covered, the magazine he'd stepped into didn't know its readership anymore: "It was, 'We've got to put a hot chick in a bikini with the 100 Greatest Electronic Albums of All Time.' This is when *Blender* had come out: 'This is what you need to do to survive as a magazine.'"

But much of the new blood coming into dance music came from places that were *not dance music*. Electroclash flouted the cult of the DJ, and a number of parties around the country followed suit. One, in New York, was MisShapes, started in 2002. "MisShapes was lawless," says Tommie Sunshine, a frequent guest. "There was security there, but for vanity purposes. It was a bar with lots of underage, coked-up kids having a really good time." They'd adopt pouts for the increasing number of digital paparazzi websites like Last Night's Party (launched October 2004), and its L.A. analogue, the Cobrasnake (launched January 2004), which further spread and codified the *Vice* "hipster" look.

MisShapes was responsible for the most insidious nightlife trend since bottle service: the celebrity DJ. Among MisShapes' guests were designer Hedi Slimane, actor-director John Cameron Mitchell (*Hedwig and the Angry Inch*), and Carlos D. (Dengler), the Eddie Munster look-alike who played bass for Joy Division sound-alikes Interpol. MisShapes further instituted a "no beat-matching and no electronic dance music" policy; DJs around New York even took to wearing T-shirts that said "NO BEATMATCHING." "It's more about having their presence than their music," co-organizer Greg Krelenstein said.

The height of this era came on October 22, 2005, when special guest Madonna "spun." "She grabbed the headphones a couple of times for some press shots, but she didn't fucking do anything," says Sunshine; the actual selections were handled by her producer, Stuart Price. "The place was out of control. The fact that she even did that became folklore. At the helm was Stuart Price, so you were getting real music. Just because you're famous doesn't mean you have to play bullshit." The *Village Voice*'s Tricia Romano was far more skeptical: "It's a downhill slide to Paris Hilton from here."

ANOTHER MISSHAPES REGULAR was an L.A. native who started out billing himself as Kid Millionaire. "He certainly didn't *look* like he had a million dollars," recalls Jason Bentley. "He drove around in an Isuzu Rodeo with a torn-up back: 'Kid Millionaire? Really?'"

Actually, yes: Steve Aoki was the son of Hiroaki "Rocky" Aoki, the Japanese-born restaurateur behind the Benihana steakhouse chain; his half sister, Devon, is a model. "He never invested in any of our businesses," says Aoki. "He never gave any handouts. That's a big part of the reason I've been able to take the tools in front of me and make something out of it." After spending his teens entrenched in DIY straight-edge punk ("I tour three hundred days a year; it doesn't faze me, because I was touring in a bus with four sweaty dudes, hauling gear, sleeping in a van every night"), Aoki founded Dim Mak Records in 1999. Five years later he struck gold with the Kills and Bloc Party, eventually linking with Vice's new Atlantic-distributed label.

At that point, Aoki and Franki Chan, a local talent buyer, began throwing parties under the Dim Mak banner at places like Cinespace, in Hollywood. "Instead of having DJs play, we'd have bands come and DJ: Carlos D., Yeah Yeah Yeahs' Nick Zinner. All of a sudden, we were the hipster kings of Hollywood—the L.A. contingent of what New York was doing. It was Justice and 2 Many DJ's leading the pack." Within a couple of years, says Jason Bentley, "Guys like DJ AM and Aoki decided to switch the format to dance music and electro. They were playing the trendy Hollywood Boulevard clubs. AM decided to apply his skill set to electronic records. He loved groups like Daft Punk, and everyone followed suit."

It was clear—*this* was what *Urb* needed to cover. "If these hipster kids going to see Carlos D. DJ were born ten years earlier, they would have been wearing baggy pants and going to see Bad Boy Bill," says Glazer. Founder-publisher Raymond Roker, who'd put "This is not the future of rock and roll" on *Urb*'s masthead a decade earlier, fumed: "You want to explain why you want to put a bass player from a rock band on the cover of my magazine?" That weekend, Glazer took Roker to a Dim Mak event; Carlos D. was the guest. "He showed up and loved it," says Glazer. "He only stayed for twenty minutes, but it sold him." Carlos D. appeared on *Urb*'s January/February 2005 cover. "It really did define the magazine for the next few years," says Glazer. "To the chagrin of Sandra Collins"—he laughs—"but I'm sorry."

BY THE FALL OF 2005, streaming video online had become faster than ever, and now there was a one-stop portal for it all: YouTube, which launched that Valentine's Day. One clip that surfaced early in the site's life originated on August 20, just south of Provo, Utah, at a party on a private ranch. The promoters had hired licensed security and EMTs and taken out a two-million-dollar policy. But they forgot to get the hundred-dollar "legal gathering license" thirty days in advance of any gathering larger than 250—making it an illegal assembly. Doors were at nine; police stood by as fifteen hundred people entered. At eleven thirty, someone began filming a drum and bass DJ from stage left. During a lull in the track, audible after about thirty-three seconds, a voice screams in the background: "SHUT IT DOWN NOW!"

Helicopter blades become audible. The people onstage look up, open-mouthed. Light is flooding their eyes. Somebody points off to the other side of the stage, past a fence, where police cars have pulled up. An officer is audible: "SHUT UP, KID!" Another, to the kids on-stage: "Get down now, or I'm taking your ass to jail." Men in riot gear replace the kids onstage. The camera swings in a slow circle; a few seconds later, a longer shot of the stage, and it now looks like a military invasion: kids held down by two to four officers at a time, police dogs barking, and, after two solid minutes, a beefy voice repeating menacingly, "Put your camera down." The video went viral instantly.

ONE OF THE TASKS of the *Urb* staff every year was to draw up a long list of Coachella suggestions. "Paul Tollett would come to our office one afternoon and we would go down the list," says Glazer. Not all their recommendations were dance-centric: Glazer recalls Tom Petty being mooted for 2006. So was Madonna: "She had just played MisShapes," he says. " 'Caught Up' was on every hipster-dance playlist." Glazer told Tollett: "Madonna was not cool last year. Madonna will not be cool next year. Right now, Madonna is cool. Also, Palm Springs is full of gay people, and you don't appeal at all to the gay community."

Tollett still had old-school reservations: "Paul comes from the eighties, where you like Black Flag and Madonna's the enemy." But this was 2005: The iPod had been on the market for four years, and the pop marketplace increasingly reflected that. "The tribes had been replaced by the shuffle," says Glazer.

Madonna agreed to headline the Sahara Tent on Saturday night. Putting a woman who'd sold three hundred million records in the dance tent meant enlarging it. "They bought a bigger tent that holds thirty thousand people instead of twenty thousand," says Glazer. "They'd installed extra speakers outside the tent, Jumbotrons, ready for this massive thing." Glazer was surprised to find out whom Tollett got to headline the Sahara on Saturday: No one at *Urb* had nominated Daft Punk. But, says David Prince, "Until then, Daft Punk was by far the most requested band Goldenvoice saw on their message boards."

In 2005, Daft Punk had turned down Tollett's quarter-million-dollar offer. They bit a year later, when he raised it to three hundred thousand dollars. Their acceptance was conditional—a typical deposit was 10 percent, and Daft Punk wanted 25. "It was constant, every week: 'We need more money,'" says Gerry Gerrard. According to Pedro Winter, Thomas and Guy-Man spent their entire fee producing their top-secret Coachella production—even he didn't know what it contained. Tollett told Gerrard: "I don't care if you and [Gerrard's number-two] Steve show up in fucking helmets, just so long as we can use the name Daft Punk."

TWO DAYS IN ADVANCE, Coachella added Kanye West to Saturday's main stage. In the blazing midafternoon sun, West peeled off a string of hits (introducing the previous summer's number one, "Gold Digger," he yelled: "White people! This is your only chance to say 'nigga'!"), brought out a string section, and danced awkwardly to a-ha's "Take On Me." "He was lean and skinny and constantly in motion," says David Prince, who watched the rapper from the side of the stage. "I was pretty blown away by the size of the crowd, and especially how many had come to see him."

Prince had gotten a production wristband from Tom Windish, on whose hotel floor he was sleeping ("His girlfriend was *not* happy about it"). Prince had just spent his third and last spring in Miami trying to turn his M3 Summit (Miami Music Multimedia) into a viable competitor to Winter Music Conference—"a Slamdance to their Sundance." High-minded and tech-focused, M3 was something Prince figured an ailing industry could use. "Things were falling apart and nobody knew what to do; I thought dance music would be the best place to capitalize on that. The tools used to make and play the music were the same tools people were going to use to sell and distribute."

WMC had other competition: the all-day, all-ages Ultra Music Festival. Founded in 1999 by Alex Omes and Russell Faibisch, the first Ultra brought ten thousand kids to a sandlot behind the Outback Steakhouse on Collins Avenue—not to mention the paramedics who hauled a kid on a stretcher past a city commissioner. But the event's numbers never went down; by 2006 it was drawing thirty thousand, expanding to two days in 2007. Ultra's crowd was neither WMC's old house crowd nor M3's tech-savvy hipsters, but local teenagers who'd grown up hearing plenty of dance music, yet still called everything "trance."

Three M3s had fried Prince's nerves. "Miami scared the shit out of me," he says. "When you get to that level you're dealing with the mob, with drug dealers—a layer of lawlessness that I was not prepared for. It was obvious from all that time in Miami that the music that was going to triumph was going to be the worst of the bunch—and that there was a lot of a snob in me." Coachella was more his speed. "I was there to recharge my enthusiasm for music. I was like, 'I cannot miss Daft Punk's return.'"

WHAT WAS DAFT PUNK going to *do*? Speculation ran rampant: "Is it going to be the robots with guitars and drums, like the 'Robot Rock' video?" guessed a friend of Glazer's. No one was allowed to find out early—around 10:30 P.M., in the middle of Londoners Audio Bullys' Sahara set, the backstage was cleared. "Only people who had special Daft Punk laminates could get back there," says Prince. "It was definitely headliner treatment." Taking one last look, he saw "Gerry Gerrard running around, working his ass off."

At 11 P.M., Depeche Mode finished playing on the main stage. "Everyone from the entire festival, basically, went to the dance tent," says Tom Windish. Prince took his place between the soundboard and right stage front. Closer to the center was local promoter-manager Danny Johnson; Vello Virkhaus watched from the wings. "It was insane," says Virkhaus. "People as far as you could tell, almost the next tent, and then the fence." Pasquale Rotella was on the left side, "probably five hundred to eight hundred people from the stage." In back, at tent's edge, nineteen-year-old Cinespace regular Dillon Francis made out with a girlfriend. Windish stood just outside: "It was so full I couldn't get any closer without fighting."

Glazer and his friends had been slamming Red Bull–vodkas in VIP before running to the tent. On the way, Glazer stopped at a plastic stall. "I was actually in the porta-potty, looking at the Jumbotron through the little vent screen, when I heard the *Close Encounters of the Third Kind* theme," he says. "Then the lights come up and there's the pyramid, and the robots are in the pyramid."

Daft Punk had been dressing as robots for years, so their outfits weren't exactly a surprise. But the suits lit up spectacularly; they made Rabbit in the Moon's glow-stick outfit look like cardboard. The stage setup was even mightier: a three-dimensional pyramid-cum-spaceship that both nodded to P-Funk's Mothership (and, by extension, the Electrifying Mojo) and served as a set of screens for vivid projection-mapped colors and patterns. "That was probably the first time I had seen 3D projection mapping done on that scale," says Prince. "There was a lot of wondering how it was being done." Gerrard was watching the show, he says, "with some of the most cutting-edge video people in the world, and they were like, 'How did they *do* that?'" Over a year later, after the show hit the road, *Spin* explained:

> Bangalter and Guy-Man . . . communicate with one another via mics and monitors built into the helmets, remixing on the fly from inside the pyramid. Wireless Ethernet links the Minimoogs and virtual synths at their metallic fingertips to offstage custom computers that have the processing power of nine tricked-out Mac G5s. While the musical and visual elements are scripted and pre-sequenced, both Daft Punk and their lighting director can improvise around set cues.

Whatever the specs, the effect was galvanic. "It was mayhem," says Prince. "It was group movement, but there's a lot of just jumping—especially down in front." Even the hard-to-impress Rotella was caught up: "I was extremely impressed. They were epic."

If you weren't there, your friends on-site were blowing you up. "The number of text messages and IMs I was getting from Coachella was amazing," says Bonnie Chuen, who went on Sunday: "'I can't even describe what's going on. This is the most amazing thing I've ever seen.'" It wasn't just the dance people. "It occurred to me when I was seeing them play how exciting this was to people, and how it was a revelation to a lot of them," says Vivian Host. "I had been doing this all along: 'Yeah, raves are awesome. We all love flashing lights and pounding dance music—duh. Obviously.'"

"All the tastemakers were at Coachella," says Estopinal. "They thought rave music was dirty and gross, and they were finally able to put dance music [together with] the visual aspect that was apparently so important. They were finally able to see what everybody else had been seeing the whole time. It made it cool." Prince calls the set "a moment of triumph. Think about the Stones, and the guitar riff of 'Satisfaction.' Daft Punk has twenty of those."

Steve Aoki was also in the tent: "One reason electronic music is such a successful big-group scenario is that you aren't watching a singer. You're just experiencing the feeling of the music around you, and being part of a larger experiential feeling. Watching Daft Punk, it's about absorbing the music: 'This is how you present it—with *production*.'" After Daft Punk at Coachella, says Tom Windish, "People realized what could be possible: 'Maybe if we spent more on our show, we could have *that*.'"

Walking back to their car, Glazer's friend smiled. "That's where that raver's been hiding."

"What raver?" Glazer asked.

"*You.*"

. . . .

BY COMPARISON, MADONNA was anticlimactic. Like Daft Punk, who went on a rock-star-like hour later than scheduled, she made the audience wait, albeit only an extra twenty minutes, for her six-song set. "I went early and forced myself to suffer through an entire Oakenfold set—he was at his cheesiest," says Prince, who was at the lip of the stage, "literally leaning on the railing." It was his first-ever Madonna performance. "It was cool, but there was definitely a feeling that it had peaked the night before." Host agrees: "Madonna was good, but she didn't *own*."

You'd never know it perusing the press coverage. Or rather, the print coverage: Online, Pitchfork devoted its final paragraph of its Coachella review to Saturday's finale ("Not to get hyperbolic, but people were crying at two French robots"), and the *Los Angeles Times*'s music blog ran a positive review (long since vanished). But *LAT*'s print review didn't mention Daft Punk at all. Neither did *Rolling Stone*. The *New York Times* and *Spin* both gave Daft Punk little more than a passing mention (the latter noted that they "performed in a makeshift spaceship"). For the American press, dance music was still marginal. The story was Kanye and Madonna, as symbols of the breakdown between divisions separating "pop" and "indie"—ignoring the band, and style, that would benefit most from this new openness.

FOR THE 2002 DEMF, Carol Marvin hired a committee of seven highly respected Detroit DJs, including Juan Atkins, Eddie Fowlkes, and Alan Oldham (in a reverse of his perceived first-year snub). Atkins was then living in L.A.: "I came into town, we made up our list of acts that we wanted, and it all went fine." It was the last DEMF proper; the name changed in 2003 to Movement. To keep it going, Derrick May stepped in—unwillingly, he says: "I was forced to do it. It was political. Had I canceled it for any reason my life would have been over in Detroit. I would've been blamed for fucking up the festival."

In both 2003 and 2004, May was promised money by Mayor Kwame

Kilpatrick's administration; both years, the mayor's office refused to deliver it. "I'm hearing the mayor's office thinks I'm rich and they're not going to give me shit. I had to take my Transmat staff and turn them into Movement staff." In 2003, May was given only four months to find sponsors; in 2004, after May lined up a deal with Saturn, a city official congratulated one of the auto company's execs, arousing the latter's suspicions: "They were like, 'Why the hell is somebody from the city's office calling us about a private festival? What business is it of the city of Detroit?' And they bailed, two months before."

May ended up sinking his personal savings into the festival—$450,000 per year; after the Saturn sponsorship fell through, he was forced to call a wealthy uncle twenty-four hours before opening day for an $86,000 loan. "He said, 'Man, if you need money don't wait until the last minute to call me.' Kwame Kilpatrick and that mayoral administration would have let me burn in hell. You wonder why Detroit is the way it is? It's because of people like him." (Forced from office in 2008, Kilpatrick was sentenced in 2013 to twenty-eight years in prison for a litany of charges, including bribery and fraud.)

Kevin Saunderson took over the festival in 2005. It was quickly apparent Movement couldn't continue as a free event, so they threw a fence around it and charged five bucks. (Many in Detroit were still under the impression the festival had drawn a million people the first year and would therefore clean up at five dollars a head.) Saunderson invited Paxahau—a promotion and digital-archiving company run by ex-Voom, -Motor, and -Hawtin hands Sam Fotias and Jason Huvaere—to run the Underground Stage. "No other promoter had curated an entire stage for an entire weekend at the event," says Fotias. "We wanted to make an impression."

Hawtin headlined the echoing concrete bunker. "Every day it was elbow to elbow," says Fotias. "We saw how everything worked and said, 'We could probably do this.'" They got their chance in 2006. Once again, the city dawdled: "We had eight weeks to execute the event," says Fotias, who nevertheless brought forth Hawtin, May, Nitzer Ebb, Robert Hood, and an all-star tribute to the recently deceased J Dilla. There were no hiccups. Paxahau has produced Movement ever since.

DOZENS OF FANS HAD uploaded their phone-shot footage of Daft Punk from the Sahara Tent onto YouTube; a user calling himself Freakboy put together a "supercut" of the entire show, synced to a leaked soundboard recording. "By the time Daft Punk got around to making a video for their live record, it was anticlimactic," says Prince. It was the best advertising three hundred thousand dollars could buy: A new stream of professional music blogs had come to the fore, all embedding YouTube videos—including the Daft Punk supercut. When Prince started his own music-news aggregation site, The Daily Swarm, in April 2007, he noticed immediately that Daft Punk were consistently "four or five of the top twenty posts. I made it Daft Punk news central. I felt that this was bigger than any record sales or ticket sales were letting on, that this had touched a nerve."

That summer, Daft Punk went on a short arena tour of the U.S.—the most anticipated concerts of the year. Gerry Gerrard didn't book it: In order to finance their art film *Electroma*, Bangalter and de Homem-Christo signed with Creative Artists Agency as filmmakers—which made CAA Daft Punk's live agents as well. "Coachella was the last show I ever booked for them," says Gerrard. "At least CAA let me keep my commission." At the Coney Island show, Host says, "Every single person I knew in New York was there—a good five hundred people. I thought, 'Okay, this is back.'" Eventually, Gerrard sold his booking agency.

In the tour's midst, on July 31, the night Daft Punk played Denver's Red Rocks, Kanye West released "Stronger," in which he boasts over a slowed-down chunk of "Harder, Better, Faster, Stronger." Pedro Winter's office got the sample request sometime after Coachella; it was immediately approved. On August 4, Kanye met Thomas and

Guy-Man in person for the first time, backstage in Chicago at Lollapalooza (now a destination festival à la Coachella, rather than a touring package). "There was an after-party at a place called Green Dolphin Street," recalls Prince. "Pedro Winter and DJ Falcon played; M.I.A. was dancing on stage. Thomas and Guy-Man played a couple of records, sans masks. It was a real Chicago rave-scene reunion. I literally bumped into Kanye on my way out—he was coming around a car and I walked right into him."

"Stronger" went to number one on September 29; *Graduation*, the album featuring it, was double platinum a month later. In his interviews, West put Daft Punk in the same category as Madonna, U2, and the Rolling Stones. The kids who'd grown up on them heard it exactly the same way. That summer, downloads of the original "Harder, Better, Faster, Stronger" leaped from a thousand a week to between five and seven thousand. "I don't think Daft Punk were more melodic than Derrick May," Pedro Winter said. "It was just a question of time."

WINTER MAKES A KEY distinction between "the children of Daft Punk" on his label, Ed Banger, and the robots themselves: "Daft Punk was influenced by Chicago and Detroit. For Justice, electronic music was Daft Punk." That went doubly so for the fans—especially in L.A., where the Coachella performance had spurred local teenagers to start hitting the hipster electro parties en masse.

"You saw the ripple effect almost right away," says Josh Glazer. "Everybody went from playing Snoop Dogg–Cure mash-ups to playing bonky electro. It got so big so quick. The Ed Banger DJs played the Detour Fest, a weeklong festival Goldenvoice did with *L.A. Weekly* in downtown L.A., and it was all fourteen-, fifteen-year-olds, just packed." Glazer recalls going to one club with Arthur Baker, the producer of Afrika Bambaataa's "Planet Rock," and "looking over the balcony at this seething mass of kids. None of them were old enough to drink. The bars were empty—no line whatsoever."

"The rooms themselves were still small," says Aoki. "But the energy level doubled. The feeling that what you're doing is significant is so much larger." Dillon Francis recalls Cinespace going from "a family-type thing—all the kids in L.A. knew each other who went there" to being packed out. "The minute Aoki fully embraced dance music, everybody else took his lead," says Tommie Sunshine. "Franki Chan started learning to mix and started playing Vitalic records instead of Britney Spears." Sunshine refers to Aoki as "Johnny Appleseed, laying the groundwork" for electronic DJing as a mainstream phenomenon.

In particular, Justice broke big, thanks to "D.A.N.C.E.," the single from their 2007 album *Cross*: a giddy Jackson 5 sample under noise-blare cuts and edits. Their mustaches and leather jackets made them look like a pair of seedier Strokes. When they played Coachella in 2007, Prince saw two anonymous Frenchmen watching from the audience, and said hello to Thomas and Guy-Man: "Not a single person knew who they were, of course."

#WMC – R.I.P. – It was a good run, we will miss ya! Now we can just start calling it what it really is: Spring Break. Guidos Unite!

—KASKADE, TWITTER, NOVEMBER 16, 2010

ELECTRIC DAISY CARNIVAL

Las Vegas, Nevada
June 24–26, 2011

GARY RICHARDS HADN'T THROWN a party in nearly fifteen years when he went to the L.A. Coliseum on June 30, 2007, for Electric Daisy Carnival—Insomniac's annual event, named after an old Richards party, now in its eleventh year. It had begun as Pasquale Rotella's secondary party; his "baby" was Nocturnal Wonderland, which by 2000 had taken over the Empire Polo Grounds, drawing forty thousand. Even in the post–Crack House Law era, L.A.'s numbers still dwarfed the rest of the country's.

In 2007, Rotella moved the EDC to the L.A. Coliseum. "That was his home run," says Richards. "It's a no-brainer—such a great location, all these cool rides, and the right talent." The production kept pace with the post–Daft Punk audiovisual deluge as well, hiring Bunny, from Rabbit in the Moon, as its creative director in 2008. "Electric Daisy Carnival has this sense of Cirque du Soleil performance," says Josh Glazer. "They hire hundreds of dancers—the girl wearing nothing but glitter, on stilts, doing backflips while the DJ plays, all that crazy shit." Rotella also got Vello Virkhaus, RITM's projection-mapping whiz, on board, giving him not just carte blanche to blow minds but also prominent flyer billing.

In 2009 EDC expanded from one night to two. By 2010, EDC was in Denver, San Juan, and Dallas as well as L.A. But the parties were well off the industry's radar. "Between 1997 and 2007, I don't think anyone was really paying attention," says Richards. "Pasquale had to slug it out." Richards was impressed by EDC's flair. But he vowed: "If he can do the Coliseum, I know I can get damn close."

He also knew he wanted different music—and found it at Steve Aoki and Franki Chan's Cinespace parties. "I would go on Tuesdays like, 'I want this energy.'" Hard on December 31, 2007, at Lot 613 in downtown L.A., was Richards' first event since Rave America. Aoki, Peaches, and Justice played, and it drew eight thousand. By 2010, says Richards, Insomniac "started coming after all my guys."

YOU DIDN'T HAVE TO GO to an event to hear electronic dance music, though—more and more, you could just turn on the radio. Daft Punk might not have hits, but Kanye West sampling them did—and was only part of a larger wave of R&B, hip-hop, and pop acts starting to pick up on dance-music tricks and grooves for source material. "You had the Lady Gagas of the world coming out," said Estopinal. "If you look into pop radio, you heard the beat changing behind most of the songs—a big dance influence going on." Look no further than Rihanna's singles catalog. "S.O.S." (2006) was an electro record (based on Soft Cell's "Tainted Love") that hit right as L.A. electro blew up, and she went to number one six years later with "We Found Love," a collaboration with the ascendant Calvin Harris.

"The commercial crossover that brought EDM to what it is was when Will.I.Am started working with David Guetta," says the Dutch producer Afrojack (Nick van de Waal). Guetta's production of the Black Eyed Peas' "I Gotta Feeling" became the biggest-selling song in iTunes history. "It was the first dance-crossover song where people were like, 'What is this music?'" says Afrojack, who was inspired by it. "I thought, 'I want to make a commercial radio dance song, just to try it.' Pitbull called me and said, 'Let's work together.'" The result, Pitbull featuring Ne-Yo, Afrojack, and Nayer's "Give Me Everything," went to number one in 2011.

By 2011, there was a wedge between the way the hardcore electronic-dance audience perceived dance music—contemplation-worthy, the locus of a cabal-like subculture—and how the pop audience thought of it—fun party music, the epitome of a mindless good time. Pop radio sounded more and more like a vintage anthems compilation with some reality-TV stars sprinkled on top. The epic-trance synths that dominated late-nineties superclubs were all over 2011's top *Billboard* hits: LMFAO's "Party Rock Anthem" and "Sexy and I Know It," the aforementioned "Give Me Everything," Britney Spears's "Till the World Ends," and Rihanna's "Only Girl (In the World)."

One of the few producers to successfully straddle commercial success and critical acclaim is Diplo (Thomas Wesley Pentz), a Florida native who made his name as half of the Philadelpia hip-hop party DJ duo Hollertronix, whose far-flung, self-issued-and-distributed mix CDs encompassed everything from *baile* funk from the Rio slums to moldy old psych-funk breaks. Diplo helped produce the brilliant first two albums by British-Tamil singer-songwriter M.I.A. (Maya Arulpragasam); "Paper Planes" went to number four in 2008. In '09, "Pon De Floor" by Major Lazer—Diplo with UK producer Switch (Dave Taylor)—became a club smash and the foundation of Beyoncé's "Run the World (Girls)," a top-thirty hit in 2010. Diplo's delectably spare track—coproduced by Afrojack and Free School—for "Look at Me Now," by Chris Brown with Lil Wayne and Busta Rhymes, hit number six in 2011.

A FORMER ROCK JOURNALIST, long-running BBC Radio 1 DJ Mary Anne Hobbs championed bass-driven music from a number of far-flung cities—L.A., Bristol, Glasgow, and especially London—for a global listenership estimated at six million, many of whom were hearing her online, either through the BBC Web site or mp3s of shows surfacing on blogs, message boards, comment boxes, and Twitter accounts. Her most legendary program aired on January 10, 2006—two hours given to a handful of producer-DJs from the South London neighborhood of Croydon. "The scent of revolution is high in the air tonight . . . now permeating every corner of the planet," Hobbs gushed. The episode's title: "Dubstep Warz."

Dubstep had emerged from UK garage. "Around 2000, there was MC-driven garage that was very dark," says Steve Goodman (Kode9), a Glasgow-born Londoner who runs the Hyperdub label and was featured on "Dubstep Warz." That turned into grime—inner-city London's idiosyncratic version of hip-hop, beats made on Playstations, biggest star Dizzee Rascal—but a gaggle of increasingly bass-driven instrumental tracks gained a following, particularly around Croydon's Big Apple record store, whose clerk Hatcha (Terry Leonard) had a Thursday residency at the Velvet Rooms called FWD>>. Upon hearing the *Tempa Allstars Volume 1* EP (2003), Untold (Jack Dunning), a Londoner who'd been producing jungle since 1993, had decided to switch allegiance to dubstep, a pattern that repeated throughout the world.

"Dubstep Warz" rippled far and deep—immediately. Dubstep Forum, the music's leading Web discussion board, promptly tripled its membership. As the scene crowded, the nights remained charged. Instead of growing stale, dubstep grew legs.

GOODMAN STARTED HYPERDUB as a Web zine in 2000. One of the first artists to send demos in for review was Burial (Will Bevan). "Around 2004 and 2005, I realized I was actually still listening to some of these CDs," says Goodman, who signed Burial to his label. "This stuff definitely had some kind of shelf life." At first, Burial chose not to reveal his identity—but his tracks, both haunting and urgent, appealed to people who couldn't have cared less which style of music they were hearing.

Burial's second album, *Untrue* (2007), made Pitchfork's top ten and was nominated for the Mercury Prize. London tabloid *The Sun* decided to unmask him. (Their nominee: Fatboy Slim.) Bevan sensibly stated his name for the public and asked to be left alone. "I am much too confrontational to be making these kinds of decisions," admits Goodman. "I drink way too much coffee to be reasonable."

But dubstep wasn't just popular with musos. "Dubstep managed to bridge the mainstream and underground," says Goodman—largely due to the way its consistent 140 BPM tempo could glue styles together in a set. "It sounds *ambiguous*," Untold said. "Depending on how you program the drums you can make a tune bump along like deep house, give it some garage swagger, even match the pace of drum and bass." Skream's "Midnight Request Line" (2005) got prominent play from Ricardo Villalobos, who in 2007 remixed dubstep producer Shackleton's "Blood on My Hands." That June, Skream played to a packed house of eight thousand at Barcelona's Sónar Festival.

IF BURIAL CROSSED OVER to artier indie rock listeners, dubstep's even more crucial breakthrough to the wider audience in the U.S. and UK alike came via Caspa (Gary McCann) and Rusko (Chris Mercer), who in 2006 started the label Dub Police. Goosing the slow-and-low menace of earlier dubstep, their tracks—e.g., Rusko's "Cockney Thug" (2007) and Caspa's "Floor Dem" (2008)—turned late drum and bass's po-faced metallic twist-and-morph into an absurdly lumbering cartoon, sub-bass frequencies tweaked till they made flesh the silly noises written out by *Mad* cartoonist Don Martin. Quickly, it got dubbed "wobble."

"People didn't like dubstep for a long time," says Vivian Host, who in 2006 started the Brooklyn label and party Trouble & Bass with Luca Venezia (Drop the Lime). "We would play it at our parties, and people would just be like, 'Huh?'—until Rusko started releasing tunes. He figured out the wobbly bass thing. College kids love songs about smoking weed. He gives you a vocal and more of a fun arrangement." In August 2009, Trouble & Bass threw its third birthday party with guests Benga and Skream. "There was a mosh pit," says Host. "It was crazy."

The response was even crazier in California. "When it became a little more loud and high energy, the West Coast kids really responded to that," says Danny Johnson. Most of the DJs had, like Untold, converted from drum and bass—such as John Dadzie, formerly Infiltrata, who listened to Hobbs online. Johnson, Dadzie's manager, encouraged him to make more dubstep; he then cross-promoted it to the Aoki crowd. "We started having dubstep guests in 2008," says Host, "and by the end of 2009, we could barely afford to book them anymore."

BURNING MAN BEGAN in 1986, when unemployed San Francisco landscaper Larry Harvey took over a friend's summer solstice party at Baker Beach. With then-partner Jerry James, Harvey added an attraction: a wooden effigy to be set aflame at party's end. By the third year, the Man was forty feet tall. Burning Man moved to Nevada's Black Rock Desert in 1990. "It's a culture in San Francisco, year-round," says Vivian Host. "Burning Man in its infancy was a lot more punk rock, a temporary autonomous zone in the way that early raves were." "The tech industry funded it: Google, Apple, Microsoft is why Burning Man has the amount of capital and the size and technical infrastructure it has," says Sean Horton.

Burning Man was hardly PLUR City. Says Brian Behlendorf, who first went in 1995: "There were drive-by shooting ranges. There was this sense of pushing against a frontier of some sort. The raver camp was jokingly referred to as the raver ghetto." In 1996, after the burn, someone drove through the rave camp—located two miles from the main camp—and killed a couple inside a tent, then crashed into another car and injured a third. Burning Man's rules tightened, but its crowds grew. The sound that typified its rave sector was John Kelley–style funky desert breaks—but the taste for breakbeats also included trip-hop/downtempo and scratch-driven turntablism.

That extended to "glitch-hop." Rather than a chin-scratching IDM derivation, this referred to laptop-centric hip-hop, in the style of Atlanta-bred Warp artist Prefuse 73 (Guillermo Scott Herren). The crunchy sound of his debut, *Vocal Studies + Uprock Narratives* (2001), resonated with equally tweaked Burners. "It was psychedelic," says Matt Tuttle, a longtime Burner. "They have sound systems out there that rival any nightclub. These bass frequencies are penetrating, and carry so far." It didn't take long for dubstep to seep into the mix.

San Francisco's Bassnectar (Lorin Ashton) was the pivotal figure—a death-metal guitarist turned electronic-music composition major at UC Santa Cruz, he started spinning trip-hop and psychedelic trance in 1996, gradually shifting into glitch-hop and dubstep. "Bassnectar started out making cool bleep-bloops to smoke weed to," says journalist and S.F. native Elissa Stolman. "Now it's face-melting midrange bass melodies and catastrophic builds and drops."

THE RABIDLY HYBRID NATURE of jam bands meant they'd inevitably adopt electronic-dance methodology. One of the first to do so was Philadelphia's Disco Biscuits, formed in 1995, whose guitarist, Jon Gutwillig, prefers to call his band's music "trance fusion," though it's better known by an uglier phrase, "jamtronica"; Sound Tribe Sector 9—STS9—came along in 1998. Gutwillig made a key distinction between his audience and that of older jam bands: Biscuits and STS9 fans were not just younger but coming in from outside the usual circuits. "I figured everybody's seen a lot of Phish shows. But not the kids! These kids, when Phish quit they were twelve! They were listening to G-rated Christina Aguilera!"

An exception was Ben Silver, who met the Biscuits when he booked them at UW-Madison in March 1999. "I saw Phish everywhere, I was really into electronic music, and the Disco Biscuits were kind of both," says Silver, now in Chicago DJ trio Orchard Lounge. "They were a lot darker—it wasn't really that happy-jammy feel." It was part and parcel of a scene-wide chemical intake notoriously excessive even by Grateful Dead standards. "Almost everybody was on ecstasy—and acid and mushrooms, too," says Silver. "The jam-band kids love ecstasy. People had that mentality where you can't have a bad time on it. You're probably not going to freak out, like on acid."

The Disco Biscuits decided to start their own festival, holding the first Camp Bisco near Philadelphia in the summer of 1999. "There were only five hundred people," says Silver, who's attended nearly every Bisco. "It was totally different back then. They had DJs at night, but there was barely anybody watching or dancing to them." Though Jerry Garcia's 1995 death meant a hippie influx into the rave scene, the two worlds had little overlap outside the West Coast. Bisco showed the way: The 2002 edition featured Alex Paterson of the Orb, DJ DB, and Scott Hardkiss. In 2003, Orchard Lounge made its Bisco debut—the first of eight consecutive appearances—to a crowd of five thousand. "That boosted our fan base exponentially," says Silver.

The more entrenched jam-festival scene was forced to adapt, booking an increasing number of glitch-hop-unto-dubstep acts nurtured by Burning Man—as well as a number of electronic-heavy gatherings aimed at the jam crowd. "After the summer festivals of '09, I started seeing weird ones pop up in Charlottesville, Virginia; Birmingham, Alabama; and Guelph, [Ontario]—all these small towns," says Dadzie. "The audience was more hippie influenced. It was less rager"—code for frat boy—"and more tie-dye and patchouli."

By 2011, Bisco drew close to twenty thousand; the following year it capped attendance at around thirteen thousand. According to Jonathan Fordin, owner of Bisco promoter MPC Presents, the cutbacks centered on "traffic issues and internal congestion and flow" surrounding Bisco's location, the Indian Lookout Country Club in Mariaville, New York, near Albany. Remedying the problems meant limiting the number of cars camping on-site, with many fans instead staying at the nearby Maple Ski Ridge and taking a twenty-four-hour shuttle. "There was an opportunity to sell more tickets, but we wanted the overall fan experience to be the best possible," says Fordin. By then, says Silver, "there were almost no bands. It was almost all electronic music." Camp Bisco went on hiatus in 2014.

MORE AND MORE, the kids in the Bisco scene were calling MDMA "molly"—a term floating around the Bay Area since the early nineties. "You started seeing [fewer] pressed pills and more little baggies in 2005, 2006," says Silver. "People would do finger dips—which is so gross, because it tastes bad and people's hands are dirty. As soon as you started to see that more, more people wanted that stuff. I don't do that stuff anymore at all, but when I did I thought, 'That stuff's not nearly as good as pressed pills.'"

Yet many kids were convinced of the opposite, even though powdered MDMA was easy to cut with any number of other substances. "In the last handful of years, I guarantee people who have pressed pills call it 'molly,'" says Silver. More alarming at a basic thinking-is-fundamental level are the number of young partiers in the 2010s absolutely convinced that "molly" (powder) and "ecstasy" (pills) are not different methods of delivering the same substance, but *different substances entirely.*

DECIBEL FESTIVAL'S CORE remains MUTEK-style producer-performers, but hippie/Burner favorites regularly salt the lineups. In 2007 Sean Horton booked Simian Mobile Disco—two members of Simian of "We Are Your Friends," now making techno—and Diplo; 2008 featured L.A.'s the Glitch Mob—whose twice-baked hip-hop cutups topped an outdoor showcase at Volunteer Park, the crowd full of kids and dogs on a perfect Saturday afternoon—and, headlining Neumos (capacity 650) on Friday night, Deadmau5.

The alias of Toronto producer-DJ Joel Zimmerman, Deadmau5 performed (still does) wearing a giant, instantly recognizable light-up LED mouse head—the Daft Punk robot suits boiled down to a witty piece of headgear. "Deadmau5 is a case study in really successful branding," says *Billboard* dance writer Kerri Mason. "[He] created a character and persona for himself, but at the same time is very connected to his fans. Instrumental electronic music that is not in a four-minute bite and has no vocal: no one has been able to popularize that [in America] before."

Decibel had caught him early: "We booked Deadmau5 before anyone had even heard of him, for probably about ten to fifteen percent of what he's getting now for shows," said Horton three years later. "It was an amazing show, probably one of the best I've seen with Decibel." Yet it didn't do amazingly: "It barely sold out," says Horton. "That tells you the level of exposure he had at that point. It was his first time performing in the Northwest." But the crowd was well up for it—Neumo's was likely the site of the weekend's heaviest imbibing, not to mention the most old-school *ravey*: "The kids in the crowd had made paper-plate mouse ears and were wearing Mickey Mouse rave gloves," recalls Rachel Shimp, who reviewed the show for website Resident Advisor.

Over the next two years, Deadmau5 would amass a veritable cult—able to sell out stadiums all by himself, no festival necessary. His persona—chip-on-shoulder hacker, fidgety around people he doesn't know, turns alpha dog when lost in music and/or costume—was offset by his willingness to play the game. In 2010, he performed for an Olympics party and as the house DJ at the MTV Video Music Awards. By 2011 he made $100,000 per show.

At that year's Ultra Music Festival, Tommy Lee showed up onstage with Deadmau5—they'd worked on tracks for Lee's band Methods of Mayhem. But the kids weren't there to see some old rock star—they were there to see the head. It was like 1992 in reverse—the year a Disney exec fumed that rave promoters using Mickey imagery "are, in fact, stealing from the Walt Disney Co. . . . Certainly we wouldn't want to associate that character with such activity." When Deadmau5 was invited to perform at House of Blues in Orlando's Disney World nearly two decades later, an executive told his manager, Dean Wilson, "We think this is the coolest thing that's happened to Mickey Mouse in the last forty years."

DECIBEL FESTIVAL 2009 (September 24–27) would have been the most internationally diverse edition yet even if Horton had limited his outreach to English dubstep producers. Playing that year, in alphabetical order: Benga, Boxcutter, Caspa, Mary Anne Hobbs, Mala, Martyn, N-Type, and Pinch—all champions of the music from early days. Horton also brought in Mad Professor, England's most storied dub reggae producer, for historical balance.

The track that walked away with Decibel 2009 was "Hyph Mngo," by Joy Orbison (Peter O'Grady), twenty-two, from South London, which at least three DJs (Hobbs, DJG, and Sub Swara) dropped that weekend. Its reappearances seemed to sum up the way dubstep had captured the dance-music mainstream, entering into conversation with house and techno without genuflecting to them. The track opens with a rumbling buildup to a synthesizer, big as a cruise ship and shiny as the ocean, plays a swooping riff that's soon joined by darting bass and a pair of women's voices, alternating the words "I do" and "Ooh!" The beat is slippery, eccentric, and funky, but it also comes down hard on the two and four. It reads rhythmically as dubstep but can be blended with anything.

Friday night at Motor, a psychobilly bar south of downtown, netting was up to keep drinks out of the hands of the eighteen-to-twenty-one-year-olds not allowed in the bar. It was a witty form-content match for the hardest-hitting dubstep lineup of the weekend. N-Type ripped through an obviously anthemic selection, dropping some old-school jungle to relieve things a bit, though when he downshifted back into slow and heavy new stuff, he did so without strain, and he closed, appropriately, with "Pon de Floor." Caspa followed with a similarly paced set, complete with his remix of Deadmau5 & Kaskade's "I Remember" and Chase & Status's grinding relick of Nneka's "Heartbeat," but while it was more explosive it was also more one-note: All that throttling low end began to seem kind of cheesy after a while. Still, the kids—hippies, Burners, jam fans, and students everywhere, along with Decibel's more archetypal rhythm-and-texture nerds—ate it up.

But the old guard was ready to move on. "By 2009, I was engineering a new place for myself," says Goodman. "I actually told my agent in the U.S.: 'I don't want to play on dubstep lineups anymore,' because I have nothing to do what they are doing at all." Booking agent Carter Adams remembers a similar conversation with Skream: "He wanted to play house and disco parties. It's splintered. One group has gone back to house and techno. And others have basically gone 'big room.'"

CRAIG KALLMAN WAS ONE of the few major-label record executives paying attention to electronic dance music's rising stock. In 1987, he'd founded New York house label Big Beat Records at age twenty-two; five years later Atlantic Records purchased it and brought Kallman onto the team. By the late 2000s, he "was really soaking up everything new on Beatport"—the online dance retailer, launched in January 2004, cofounded by Chicago's onetime mixtape king Bad Boy Bill, and overseen by Richie Hawtin and John Acquaviva's holding company. In early 2010, he reactivated Big Beat, throwing a launch party at Miami's Twelves Lounge, on March 25, during Winter Music Conference.

At the bottom of the bill was an artist so little known that the press release didn't even include a bio: Skrillex. Born Sonny Moore in

Los Angeles on January 15, 1988, Skrillex had discovered punk rock in tandem with Warp Records—then, at sixteen, found out he was adopted, a fact almost everyone else around him already knew. His version of therapy was to tour constantly with his screamo group, From First to Last. According to Danny Johnson, Moore blew out his voice. He'd already begun messing around with sample-filled, bass-heavy dance tracks on Ableton Live, so he shifted his attention to them.

Kallman first heard Skrillex's music when his A&R man Chris Morris handed him a demo. "I had Sonny meet me in the Peninsula Hotel in L.A. We were hanging out, and he started playing me everything on his laptop, till four in the morning. Basically, I signed him on the spot: It was all just wildly creative and innovative and different. It didn't sound like anything." The Big Beat party was his first-ever DJ gig. "He was on fire; he just tore it up," says Kallman. When Skrillex issued his first release, the EP *My Name Is Skrillex*, for free online in June 2010, Deadmau5 posted it to his Facebook page. Immediately, Moore became the face of American dubstep.

IN 2010, FOR THE SECOND YEAR in a row, Ultra Music Festival's attendance hit a hundred thousand. The same year, Winter Music Conference's registered attendance was 3,763. The sheer size of the millennial fan base flocking to Ultra swamped any previous dance-music generation—some seventy-seven million people, as large as the Baby Boom. For years, a WMC registration also got you into Ultra, but the difference between the two became vivid on November 16, 2010, when WMC announced its 2011 dates—two weeks earlier than usual. Within hours, Ultra announced it was staying put—and expanding from two days to three.

WMC's brass professed itself "blindsided" by this turn, but even Frankie Knuckles was criticizing them: "I think they went to sleep. . . . I've watched kids go up to the doors and their badges not be honored. And to me, that's so heartbreaking and disgusting. Because I know what it is to be those kids." Ultra 2011 drew 150,000 over its three days—nearly as many people as Coachella. In 2012, WMC expanded to nine days, March 16–25—the last three of which coincided with Ultra, which had sold out in January. The city papered over the cracks by calling the whole thing Miami Music Week. But nobody questioned who'd won.

IN THE EARLY NINETIES, says native Matt Tuttle (DJ Shoe), "Las Vegas was pretty much Everytown, USA, except there's slot machines in the grocery stores. Unless you're twenty-one, there's nothing to do." There were a few early-nineties "undergrounds" in the backs of bars, which were only moderately druggy, and a few parties along the lines of Candyland (1991): "On the flyers, you'd start seeing little X's that would indicate that there's going to be ecstasy here," says Tuttle. "The chief promoters had people running nitrous tanks near the front stage—definitely visible. You could hear them popping."

The early scene flared out the usual way—promoters calling the cops on one another. An attempt at a large-scale event, 1996's Desert Move, brought out only a few thousand. Even the scene's biggest names, Tuttle's college-radio colleagues Ken Jordan and Scott Kirkland, who became the Crystal Method—debut album: *Vegas*—didn't get anywhere until they moved to L.A.

Sin City probably still kicks itself for not thinking of bottle service before New York—but jumped on it immediately anyway. "Once they started seeing that revenue, that really revolutionized Vegas clubbing forever—not for the better," says Tuttle. "That spurred the VIP hostess. If you're coming to Vegas for a bachelor/bachelorette party, these VIP companies will set you with the limo, the club, take you to the strip club, get you extracurriculars to fill your party. The VIP industry has become part and parcel to the nightclub. These VIP hosts were able to facilitate transactions for their customers. That's still fairly common practice in the clubs today." Once upon a time in Vegas, says Tuttle, dealers threw illegal parties. "The dealers have just morphed into a different kind of entity."

But who is hosting may not be as important as where they do it. Vegas was always a magnet for brand names, and nightclubbing is no different. "You had New York brands like Tao come to Vegas," says Tuttle. "They also had Marquee at a hotel called Cosmopolitan. The Palms hotel was one of the first hotels to have an EDM headliner: Paul Oakenfold. That was a turning point for the mainstream acceptance of EDM. You still have the bottle-service contingent, but they also incorporated a lot of Cirque du Soleil performers in 2007–08."

"INSOMNIAC IS A HUGE institution," says Vivian Host, who as Star Eyes played the New York Electric Daisy Carnival in 2012. "In Orange County you get a captive audience of sixteen-and-overs with a lot of disposable income and nowhere to go. It's strip malls and churches and nothing. [They] mobilize all these kids with cars and money to spend. Trippy rave shit—they cornered that."

Yet only the kids seemed to know about it. "You can have a fifteen-thousand-person festival in San Bernardino that no one in Hollywood knows is happening, even though it's only forty-five minutes away," says Joshua Glazer. "It's such a big, big place." Charlie Amter recalls being caught in a traffic jam on the way to L.A. Coliseum in 2007: "Like the biggest football game you've ever been to. It was such a special vibe—like a tightly wound coil ready to explode." Amter joined the *Los Angeles Times* staff as a full-time reporter in 2009, and recalls: "I remember being blown away that this massive festival was not even a blip on the mainstream radar."

The incursion of Cinespace-style hard electro; the West Coast festival-sired rise of dubstep; increasingly electronic-heavy pop, hip-hop, R&B, and rock; the hard, clean-lined *whump* of a lot of younger new European producers; and the increasing self-marginalization of electronic dance music's artier wing meant the old guard was losing its footing to the kids. "I remember hanging out in Pasquale's private tent-booth with a bar that overlooks the whole football stadium with [UK house duo] Basement Jaxx," says Glazer of EDC 2010. "That afternoon they were frantically digging through their CDs trying to find something big enough, hard enough, epic enough for that crowd."

ONE THING PROMOTERS had learned to do was to avoid the word "rave." "When you see the word, the police are not having it, the city's not having it," says Richards. "No one wants to be involved in an event where underage kids do bad things." Adds Estopinal: "We knew what we were doing: We sold [them] as electronic music festivals or DJ concerts."

The term "EDM," as a shortening of "electronic dance music," originates in academia: Scholars began using it because it had no connotations to specific styles ("house," "techno") or sites ("rave," "club music"). "Electronica" evoked Warp-style listening music in England, the late-nineties major-label gold rush in America. So "EDM" was perfect—and then it started cropping up in online discussions of EDC 2010. "One of the basic reasons [it caught on] is because it fits in headlines, and lazy journalists want to hashtag stuff on Twitter," says Amter, who dislikes the term. Big surprise: Nearly everybody does—except scholars, who are probably more aggrieved by it now.

Besides, turn-of-the-2010s festivals have far more beefed up security than raves ever did. Also, "rave" connotes baggy pants and oversized T-shirts; "EDM festival" connotes hot pants and pasties. Those, combined with fairy wings (a perennial), came, says Rotella, "from people trying to replicate our flyers. My old flyers encouraged people to dress up. We wouldn't encourage them to dress naked." But many did. "Prostitots, we call them here—girls who dress up like prostitutes, who go to the events in just their bra and underwear," says Bonnie Chuen. The look took hold about the same time EDC went to L.A. Coliseum—as social media took over. "It's the Flickr effect," says

Glazer. "My theory is, it was four girls the first year; the next year, a hundred; then a hundred became a thousand."

THE COLISEUM'S DOORS admitted ages sixteen and up. But in 2010 a fifteen-year-old L.A. girl, Sasha Rodriguez, had snuck in. So had a lot of others—many kids jumping over an eight-foot fence. Rodriguez had taken an MDMA pill and then been separated from her friends. When they found her again, something was clearly wrong, and Sasha quickly collapsed. She'd been drained after dancing on E, gulped down cold water to counteract it, and started hallucinating. According to a doctor, her "sodium [and] electrolytes were so low that when she started replacing them so quickly, ecstasy [messed] up [her] body's ability to process that, so it threw her body out of whack." By the time she arrived at the ER, Rodriguez was comatose; she experienced multiple organ failure before dying at the hospital.

"When that girl died, different people were looking at it," says Rotella. "No one knew I was doing 180,000 people over two days in downtown L.A., just like they didn't know I was doing forty thousand people at the Empire Polo Fields. I was doing it under their noses, while people were sleeping. That situation [made people go]: 'This was doing 180,000 people? How did I not know about this?'" Says Amter, "That was when people started to pay attention: 'We'd better send a reporter.'"

SASHA RODRIGUEZ'S DEATH meant Los Angeles County was willing to turn away forty-two million dollars in profit generated by EDC. "I had other options," says Rotella. "I was looking in California, outside of L.A. city and county. I was going to do Electric Daisy Carnival no matter what. It was a little bit risky, keeping it in California. I felt like I was going back to the underground days."

Back in 2009, Rotella and Estopinal were talking with city officials in Las Vegas about doing a festival on the Speedway. "We were gun-shy," says Estopinal. But according to Rotella, Vegas initially gave him "a little resistance—they were worried about me coming there, actually, at first. I was coming off of this fiasco. I let them know about the political challenges, the deaths, everything I was dealing with, and they took me in and supported me." If anything, he worried about the fans' reaction: "Vegas was actually undesirable to people who loved dance music because it was fake. The clubs played hip-hop and it was cheesy. There was bottle service. They wouldn't let you in if you weren't good-looking enough or dressed well or wearing tennis shoes."

But by 2010, Afrojack had signed an exclusive contract with the Wynn, and soon Jason Strauss, who booked hip-hop for Tao, at the Venetian, was lining up EDM DJs for the Cosmopolitan, and a slew of other clubs followed suit. By the time EDC went to the Las Vegas Motor Speedway in June 2011, nine of America's ten highest-grossing clubs were in Vegas.

TICKET PRICES FOR EDC VEGAS ranged from one hundred to five hundred dollars, for which you could roam a thousand acres and dance to music from six stages. Some 230,000 fans came over three days; the event sold out some six weeks in advance. By contrast, Coachella had sold seventy-five thousand three-day passes, a decrease from 2010. Even before the first partier showed up, EDC had already outsold the most written-about rock festival in the country—and even Coachella saw a sharp increase of "prostitots" there to see Tiësto, Deadmau5, and Kaskade.

In sharp contrast to L.A., where Sasha Rodriguez's death had brought forth citizens' groups pressing to ban the parties outright, Las Vegas rolled the red carpet out. The spokeswoman for the local police told the *Journal-Review*, "We have big events here thirty to forty times throughout the year. We're not going to handle this any differently than we do any other big event. This is basically status quo." The gates were hectic on the first night, but everything ran precisely inside.

THE CRYSTAL METHOD played Friday night. They'd helped break "electronica" fourteen years earlier; Vegas was their hometown. They were veterans who'd lasted. And they got put on at 9 P.M. on the shaded Circuit Grounds stage, to a crowd that had barely arrived. Still, they sounded thrilled: "It's so good to be home!" Ken Jordan yelped. Their set was heavy on thick, fleet electro-house, but also on heavy-handed, super-obvious touchstones, remixed: Depeche Mode's "Strangelove," AC/DC's "Dirty Deeds Done Dirt Cheap," the Beatles' "Come Together," and Black Sabbath's "War Pigs."

EDC Vegas, like EDM as a whole, was both the inverse and the net result of electroclash's gleeful fuck-you to dance-music orthodoxy, and to the mash-up becoming the "secret weapon" of any DJ working the bar mitzvah salt mines. Like a drive-time radio host spinnin' the hits, the DJs at EDC Vegas returned, like clockwork, to the same handful of songs, typically the most popular hits of the moment, like top-forty DJs.

In a sense, many were: The weekend's most-played track was Adele's "Rolling in the Deep," then nearing the end of seven weeks at number one. (Also: "rolling"! Like you do on MDMA! LOL!) The next two number-ones also appeared: Pitbull, Ne-Yo, Afrojack, and Nayer's "Give Me Everything" (Afrojack spun it) and LMFAO's "Party Rock Anthem"—by four DJs, based on fewer than one-quarter of the weekend's set lists. Nearly as omnipresent were older songs like the Red Hot Chili Peppers' thirteen-week Modern Rock number-one "Otherside" (2000), the White Stripes' "Seven Nation Army" (2003), and Blur's "Song 2" (1997). This was the new "underground": an unblinking ritualistic celebration of music you'd been able to just turn on the radio and hear, every single day, for decades.

But this was something that had gone on for years, and only now was non-niche media paying attention. There hadn't been a party this big *ever*, in American history—and it dwarfed anything going on in Europe, where the market had dropped markedly. America was now leading the global market for electronic dance music.

ON FRIDAY THE TEMPERATURE in Vegas hit a high of ninety-five, but overnight it dropped to eighty-one, and the day's hard wind quieted. At 1 A.M., the Burner-sired fire-art troupe Flaming Lotus Girls accompanied Tiësto at the Kinetic Field to a heaving crowd of some forty thousand—not quite the 2004 Summer Olympics, whose opening he'd played, but not the Hard Rock Hotel, where he had a residency, either.

"People want more now," says Tiësto (Tijs Michiel Verwest). "They want the show to be amazing. Of course, the main part is mixing records, but the production value, if you bring it, will add thirty percent extra to the show." He also changed his sound—thanks in part to the instant feedback his podcast, begun in 2007, allows, he played darker, tougher house instead of the fluffier build-up-heavy trance of the mid-2000s. His set included Green Velvet's "Flash," recently remixed by Nicky Romano—the one older dance track to achieve the same kind of ubiquity of an "Otherside" that wasn't by Daft Punk, whose *Discovery* had become EDM's *Sgt. Pepper's Lonely Hearts Club Band*.

RICHIE HAWTIN PERFORMED twice at EDC: live as Plastikman at Cosmic Meadow Friday, and spinning at Circuit Grounds Saturday. By the time Hawtin got to Vegas he'd been on the road for a year and a half. The show that had stumbled at MUTEK in 2004 was a lubed piston. "The main idea of Plastikman live is to take control over the entire experience—controlling the lights, controlling the visuals, controlling the sound," said Hawtin. "We're talking high-end computers, networked together, talking together, to create that whole experience. It's really another, a totally different level."

The tour's spur was the 2010 reissue of the Plastikman catalog. The box set *Arkives* and a single-CD best-of fed into a general sense of dance-music nostalgia also pushed along by a number of reissue CDs and online mixes devoted to older dance music. "I felt I needed to at least describe the alphabet I've been working on and building to the new audience," Hawtin said. "I think it's important to let those new fans coming through the door to be able to find more information, and maybe feel more connected to what I've done in the past, and therefore to the whole story of electronic music."

The next several years of Hawtin's career have amounted to an extended PR campaign dedicated to reaching out to the younger, heedless, pop-leaning EDM crowd from the more entrenched underground. In the fall of 2012 he led the CNTRL: Beyond EDM tour, leading roundtables on dance-scene history, followed by DJ sessions, in college towns throughout the U.S.—right as Tiësto was out on a college tour of his own. ("If Hawtin's futurism could speed up the coat-check line, it would be a welcome advancement," Resident Advisor's Aaron Gonsher wrote.) In spring 2013, at South by Southwest, Hawtin played a back-to-back set with Deadmau5, and he issued a new Deadmau5 track as the first new Plus 8 Records release in over fifteen years.

Hawtin had other interests at heart besides the music. By 2008, Native Instruments had purchased Final Scratch, Beatport was up and running, and Hawtin was no longer using vinyl at all; he'd gone all digital. With Acquaviva, he'd become a wealthy businessman as well as a hardworking DJ; he knew what EDC's numbers could mean. And at EDC, embedded in a steel framework gradually exposed via dramatic lighting, Plastikman got the bros to pay attention.

FOR COACHELLA 2009, Steve Aoki had wanted to put on a damn *show*. He rounded up some wooden boxes, a life raft, and some Super Soakers. "You bring a whole bunch of ideas out and one will work. In

2011 I said, 'I need to introduce something different,' and that's when I introduced the cake." Meaning, when he started throwing cake at his audiences. He goes through some fifteen hundred sheet cakes a year. "You might be like, 'I don't want that shit on me,'" he reasons. "But you want to see *someone* get the cake. The people who want to be caked are the ones that are the most diehard—the most energetic, passionate, singing along with all the lyrics. They're getting their extra cherry on top. [Initially], people didn't understand the cakes were in the production part of the rider instead of the catering part. Now, they understand."

ROTELLA IS UNREPENTANT that at his events, spectacle swallows individual talent. "There are new guys no one has heard that are amazing," he says. "It's not just about the same ten guys over and over again. Even the ten guys know that." But musically, a blanded-out please-everyone aspect has risen to the fore, reminiscent, more than anything, of the soft rock of Peter Cetera, Air Supply, Journey, Michael Bolton, Richard Marx—eighties power ballads full of builds and drops.

No one exemplifies this trend more than Swedish House Mafia, who packed out Kinetic Field Saturday night; member Steve Angello played the same stage on Friday. The trio's fist-in-air anthems have all the gravitas of a Frank Stallone outtake; build-and-drop power ballads like "Save the World" (2011) could give Bryan Adams insulin shock. It too was inescapable that weekend. On stage left of Kinetic Field was a large VIP area. "We got inspired by Hollywood nightclubs," says Rotella. "I have so many old friends that do not want to be in the crowd, that love going to nightclubs—that I want to be there." Who needed clubs to have bottle service?

Not everyone at EDC Vegas was quite so quick to embrace the new EDM status quo. Porter Robinson, who appeared at the Neon Garden at 9 P.M. Saturday, was still a month shy of nineteen. "I feel like I've heard ten thousand DJs playing the exact same sets," he says. "I would rather play the worst DJ set with different music than play the same DJ set that's super-functional, and works every time and in every venue." His early-evening set got him the biggest response of his young career: "I remember getting a bunch of tweets like I'd never gotten before."

WHEN DAVID GUETTA invited some of his label execs to an L.A. edition of Electric Daisy Carnival, he says, they told him: "This is America. We don't really have a market for this kind of music." Guetta still sounds exasperated as he recalls it: "How can you say there's no market when a hundred thousand people are listening to DJs? It was becoming a real phenomenon, but people just refused to see it. No media, no radio playing this music, no journalists speaking about it. Record companies acted like it didn't exist."

For 2009's "Sexy Bitch," Guetta recruited R&B hitmaker Akon. "Everybody was telling me, 'This is great—but you couldn't make a record for America, because this is for Europe.' I said, 'What are you talking about? This can work in America.' 'Oh no, it won't work.' It was not seen as pop music at all."

The song's success necessitated a marketing shift. "We couldn't sell David Guetta albums, but we could sell David Guetta singles, so [it became], 'Let's stop trying to sell this thing called One Love and start selling this thing called "Sexy Bitch,"'" says Glenn Mendlinger, Astralwerks' general manager. That track would sell more than three million downloads; by contrast, it took nearly three years for One Love to go gold (five hundred thousand sales).

Guetta played Kinetic Field Saturday night to an audience that dwarfed even Tiësto's in size, so stuffed people spilled into the walkways. Guetta's hit-mongering set felt pallid, but up after him was Sidney Samson, from Holland, a pioneer of the "dirty Dutch" style—hard hitting, clean lined, flagrantly cartoony. His 2009 track "Riverside" blew up: "All the big DJs played it, from Guetta to Tiga." Soon he had a monthly residency at the Wynn. "I had a hardcore base in

Holland: thirty gigs per month, seven, eight a weekend. So I'm an experienced DJ. Performing is what I love to do."

That was clear from his EDC Vegas set—it slam-banged with far more finesse than his colleagues' turns. Letting a cappella vocals carry the rhythm instead of bludgeoning the crowd with an equally well-known beat, the set lended surprise to even "Riverside." He even made something as hoary as Bob Marley's "Three Little Birds" work *as DJing*.

"Las Vegas! Tonight we unite!" Samson told the audience. "For the love of house music, make some noise!" It's easy to imagine old-school Chicagoans bristling: *Y'all ain't house.* Indeed, house has evolved in so many ways that the connection of Samson's set to what Frankie Knuckles had done a generation earlier was, let's say, limited. Samson wasn't oppositional, a refusal; he was an affirmation of status quo. So was EDC Vegas, to a generation for whom house music has been lingua franca since birth.

SKRILLEX'S ANOINTMENT CAME at 3 A.M. on Saturday night in the Neon Garden. Earlier, around midnight, Skrillex paid an onstage visit to Dadzie, performing as 12th Planet, during his set at the Bass Pod— he knew Dadzie already from downtown L.A.—and got a huge round of applause. Onstage for his own show, Skrillex had a backdrop of some two hundred hangers-on. Playing "Scary Monsters," he leaped in the air, and the crowd went right with him.

Derisively, Skrillex's brand of music would become branded as "brostep." "It just skyrocketed across middle America so huge," says Johnson. "A lot of kids who were listening to metal appreciated it." The grotesquely warped bass lines were analogous to the bowel-scraping detuned guitars of Black Sabbath a generation earlier. He'd caught not the audience sired by the Bassnectar/Burning Man scene, but their younger siblings. "The Skrillex–12th Planet stuff was coming from the electro kids," says Glazer.

It wasn't just the partiers cottoning to dubstep. In 2009, rapper

Eve uploaded a track called "Me 'N My," for which producer Salaam Remi retooled Benga's "E Trips" (2008). "I had to get talked into doing it," admits Eve. Few people bit, but the August after EDC Vegas, New York's Hayden Planetarium held a listening party for Jay-Z and Kanye West's *Watch the Throne*. Under images of shifting constellations, the gathered press heard "Niggas in Paris" ("That shit cray")—not precisely dubstep, but clearly impacted by it, the way "B.O.B." had been by jungle. Another track, "Who Gon Stop Me," featured a hefty Flux Pavilion sample. Dubstep had arrived in hip-hop. A year later, Taylor Swift's "I Knew You Were Trouble" featured a bass wobble.

THE FINAL NUMBERS were a big turnaround from the previous year. There were sixty arrests total, and revelers all driving home at once clogged Monday-morning Interstate 15 traffic—but most important, nobody died. Vegas moved to turn EDC into a weeklong official event. "I almost felt like I could breathe," says Rotella. "I had been fighting this fight for twenty years. To get someone, a city government, to give us something like that was huge."

On July 27, the unpublicized premiere of Kevin Kerslake's *Electric Daisy Carnival Experience* documentary at Grauman's Chinese Theater in Hollywood was the site of a melee. One of the movie's performers, Kaskade, tweeted that he was going to DJ. Within an hour, the theater's small crowd of 250 ballooned closer to ten thousand. A riot squad was called in. "I parked—I couldn't believe I found a spot—and made it through the throngs and up to the theater," says Kerslake. "The number of people was alarming. Once the posture of the authorities became a little more aggressive, they started to get pushed back. Everybody misbehaved." More than five hundred screenings were canceled as a result.

DISCO DONNIE ESTOPINAL wouldn't be part of EDC Vegas going forward. "Pasquale told me in 2011 he did not think it was fair we were fifty-fifty partners on certain stuff," he says. "The relationship was going sideways." Estopinal formed Disco Donnie Presents and expanded beyond the middle of the country. "To see how many people traveled to [Vegas] was very eye opening. The writing was on the wall that we were all going to get eaten up. Promoters don't make any money."

Four months later, Estopinal sold the company to Robert Sillerman—who'd originally founded the company that became Live Nation, and had broken out on his own to revamp the earlier brand, SFX. Sillerman had announced plans to invest one billion dollars in EDM, to corner the parts of the market not already controlled by Insomniac or Live Nation—the latter of which purchased Hard from Gary Richards in late June 2012. Live music had become a bigger, more reliable profit center than the recording business.

Eventually Rotella threw in with Live Nation. "At one point I had eleven offers," he says. "Live Nation wasn't one of them." But once they got wind of the other talks, Live Nation got in the game. "I didn't go with the highest bidder," he says. "I went with the best partner."

"I do feel it's getting out of hand," says Richards. "Every time I turn around, someone's got an EDM-flavored gum and an EDM-flavored Popsicle they want to sell me on. I'm always wondering how far can it go. I thought this was going to happen twenty years ago. I put my whole life on it. And it just didn't do anything—'97, same thing. Now I'm just happy that everyone's into it."

No one man owns house.

—RHYTHM CONTROLL, "MY HOUSE (ACAPELLA)"
(CATCH A BEAT RECORDS, 1987)

>18

RANDOM ACCESS MEMORIES

Los Angeles, California
January 26, 2014

LOS ANGELES, February 12, 2012—**Skrillex** is accepting his first Grammy Award during the pre-broadcast ceremony, for Best Remixed Recording, Non-Classical, for his version of Benny Benassi's "Cinema." (There'll be two more: the *Scary Monsters and Nice Sprites* EP will win Best Dance Album, its title track Best Dance Recording.)

Accepting, Skrillex says: "I think Justice, *Cross*, should have won a Grammy; I think Daft Punk should have won Grammys. . . . There's labels out there that have been doing it for a long time, like Dub Police and Never Say Die, the list goes on—all the Croydon dub guys that started this all in 2003. It's crazy. I remember talking to Dieselboy one day and he said that all the boats rise in the water."

Daft Punk actually had two Grammys, for *Alive 2007* and its version of "Harder, Better, Faster, Stronger." Still, Skrillex's point stands: "Da Funk" lost to Donna Summer and Giorgio Moroder in 1998, "Around the World" to Madonna in 1999, "One More Time" to Janet Jackson in 2002. Also: Croydon? Dieselboy? In a *Grammy Awards speech*?

> 367 <

. . . .

Festival, the second (and last) annual traveling EDM showcase put together by the William Morris Agency, has no politics—only endless, nonstop logos and catchphrases, attached to various shades of neon. The actual term YOLO ("you only live once") is only on a handful of T-shirts, but it's the guiding principle. Everyone seems to be trying to outdo everyone else in the "I don't give a fuck" sweepstakes. Of course, this crowd is nearly all fourteen to eighteen years old, not so much advertising their own wantonness as advertising *that they're advertising* their own wantonness. It's still enough to make an adult queasy.

The operative word is "rage," which is better than the other words everywhere: "slut," "bitch," "whore." One girl in the roiling main-stage mosh pit who can't be more than fifteen has SLUT written on her neck, in hot-pink liquid gel. It's difficult not to feel sorry for them.

A brief, light downpour begins around 6 P.M. In a shaded corner is Morgan, twenty-three, a med student about to leave Long Island for Brooklyn. She began partying seven years ago, when a friend took her to see trance DJ Armin van Buuren at Pacha; the door price, she recalls fondly, was twenty-seven dollars. (She's also into Bassnectar.) Two years ago, that friend OD'd at a party. Today, she's chaperoning that friend's younger sister to *her* first party. Morgan left her charge in the pit after getting kicked in the back, and is keeping track via text message.

"There's a difference between people who just want to get fucked up and people who want to experience the music," she says. "If it isn't recognizable, they're like, 'Can we get some water?'" She adds: "I'm wearing two shirts—that's unheard of here. And *pants!* My friends tell me I look muted. I said, 'That's the point.'"

RANDALL'S ISLAND, NEW YORK, August 31–September 2, 2012—Electric Zoo, in its fourth year here, eschews both the Patrick Bateman 2.0 vibe of the midtown Manhattan club Lavo (see below) and

IDentity's twenty thousand fourteen-year-olds all on drugs for the first time. Produced by Made Events, it's state of the art, efficiently run, more collegiate than high school. Over three days, four stages, twelve hours of music per day, and well over a hundred DJs, the music is all over the place, both in quality and style.

What's immediately noticeable is the very different racial mix than in the nineties—the millennial generation is only 61 percent white, with 14 percent black and 19 percent Hispanic. At Electric Zoo, there's a heavy Asian and South Asian presence as well as a good-sized Hispanic one. Whites dominate and there are relatively few blacks—but those ratios are slipping too. Many younger listeners were drawn to dance music from hip-hop; calling it a "dance festival" and not a "rave" means it no longer auto-translates to "corny white people."

In one of the weekend's musical highlights, young Londoner Maya Jane Coles's percolating, effortless house grooves fill the tent dubbed Sunday School (a sop to the long-timers). The other highlight belongs to Skrillex, the last act on Sunday night's main stage. Coming out in a pod shaped like an insect villain from a Marvel CGI blockbuster—Friday evening, David Guetta came out in a spaceship—Skrillex has sharp instincts. He gets on the microphone too damn much; they all do. It's the EDM DJ's version of a sea of lifted camera phones. But the push-pull between him and the crowd is clear, their shared worldview suitably apocalyptic.

MIAMI, FLORIDA, March 15, 2013—The Bay Link Monorail between the Marriott and Ultra's location on South Beach goes past a billboard: two robot heads, silver and gold, fused down the middle, jumping out of a black background, with the Columbia Records logo in the right corner. No other words; none needed. Daft Punk is back.

The months-long run-up to the release of *Random Access Memories* is more memorable than almost all the album's songs. Its guest list filters out to the public before any music: Paul Williams, the elfin songwriter and seventies talk-show regular who'd composed the songs for *The Muppet Movie*; Chic guitarist-songwriter-producer Nile Rodgers; hip-hop and R&B superproducer Pharrell Williams; Panda Bear of Animal Collective; Julian Casablancas of the Strokes. Thomas and Guy-Man, as usual, say nothing.

On March 2, a fifteen-second segment of the album's first single, "Get Lucky," aired as a TV ad during *Saturday Night Live*; the Miami billboard (and one in Austin, Texas, for South by Southwest) followed. At Coachella a month later, a minute-long clip from the "Get Lucky" video appears: Thomas and Guy-Man in full robot gear, Pharrell on vocals, Rodgers on guitar—all wearing the glittering suit jacket Michael Jackson sported on the cover of *Thriller*, the title of the album in that one's font.

LONDON, ENGLAND, April 7, 2012—Glasgow producer-DJ Rustie (Russell Whyte) is spinning his edition of *Essential Mix*—a dizzying fifty-nine tracks in two hours, everything from Rick Ross and Nicki Minaj to Manix's UK hardcore anthem "Feel Real Good." The one that grabs everyone's attention is "Harlem Shake," by Brooklyn's Baauer (Harry Rodrigues)—a saxophone break treated to sound like a drunken kazoo, over distended low end and a sample of Philly rappers Plastic Little saying, "Do the Harlem Shake." It's the latest example of dance music's recent fascination with "trap"—the 808-led southern-rap style pioneered by Atlanta's T.I. (see 2004's *Trap Muzik*), fast becoming the DJ world's "new dubstep."

On February 2, 2013, a comic named Filthy Frank uploads a video—à la Psy's Korean rap novelty clip "Gangnam Style"—in which four people dressed like Power Rangers (or thereabouts) do a silly hip-thrusting dance for thirty seconds to Baauer's track. Within a few days, a slew of copycats join it on YouTube; within two weeks, they add up to more than 175 million views. All of them count toward the song's placement on the Hot 100, thanks to *Billboard*'s recent change in data gathering. The result: "Harlem Shake" spends all of March—five weeks—atop the pop charts.

Its ascendance makes a lot of people uneasy. The Harlem Shake is an actual hip-hop dance; the way Bauuer uses the vocal sample saying it on the track decenters it from any particular meaning—until the YouTube meme applied one, one that you couldn't have scripted to be more different than the original. And yet, says *Billboard* editorial director Bill Werde two weeks after the song hit number one, "There's no question that was the biggest hit in America that week. It's still the biggest hit in America. And I want the *Billboard* charts to reflect the biggest hit in America." Werde had worked for seven years to update the charts' data: "My fundamental belief was to reflect the entire music business—not just the major labels."

Tracking songs this way has its disadvantages, elevating many white performers without much black audience base to the top of the hip-hop and R&B charts. For many, this means Baauer, whose use of the phrase "Harlem Shake" comes under fire—a hip-hop dance's storied history suddenly brushed aside by white people acting silly. Many American pop fans are simply offended that a straight-up dance record is a number-one hit: *Where's the chorus?* Too late for them: "Dance music arrangements have broken through," says Beatport's Matt Adell. "This is fundamentally different than the sound of dance music breaking through. The arrangement style is now a badge of honor."

MIAMI, FLORIDA, March 16, 2013—At Bubba Gump's near the Ultra Music Festival grounds, a middle-aged black man is talking to the counterwoman about the previous year's event. "It was a life-changing experience," he says. "I'm used to a lot of aggression at concerts. I never knew people could be so friendly. It was like, 'I just stepped into Fantasyland.'" Is he going this year? "No. I can't afford it. It's too expensive for me this year."

That night, London duo Jack Beats is playing the jumpiest, friskiest, most irresistible music of the weekend on the OWSLA stage; near the front of the stage are a reporter in light gray jacket and straight black jeans, and publicist Lydia Fong, dressed similarly. A young woman in neon approaches, her eyeballs pinwheeling.

"You're not from around here, are you? I can tell."

"Really? How?"

"You're not *partying*." Meaning: *You're not on drugs. What are you DOING here? How DARE you?*

The live stage in the afternoon belongs to Disclosure—London siblings Guy and Howard Lawrence, twenty and eighteen years old, respectively, who make sharply updated UK garage. They come out to a small crowd—five hundred, maybe—which has grown to around twelve hundred by the time they leave. The brothers' youth and cheek—and cute looks—are a classically easy sell, and the kids, many wearing lensless glasses, aren't just out in force but dancing hard in their seats, as the Lawrences add live percussion to a new song called "White Noise." "That was only our second-ever trip to America," says Howard the following December. "A lot of the people at the Ultra Festival didn't really know who we were."

Disclosure's debut album, *Settle*, released in June 2013, turned into a long-lasting U.S. hit, launching the career of Grammy-winning vocalist Sam Smith on "Latch." The album also became an emblem of the EDM audience's maturing tastes. Maya Jane Coles's Electric Zoo triumph six months earlier was another sign—kids who'd come in as Afrojack fans were moving toward crisper styles. "That's exactly what happened to us in terms of popularity in the UK about two years ago," says Howard. "Dubstep, all that loud, aggressive-sounding dance music—people got bored of it in the UK a while ago, and they moved on to us. That seems to be happening in the U.S. now. That's very exciting for us—we're ready to tour the crap out of America. We love it there."

. . . .

DEREK VINCENT SMITH of Fort Collins, Colorado, swears he didn't choose his alias, Pretty Lights, based on his stage gear, but it's easy to think he did. Even among Ultra's endless eye-popping effects, Pretty Lights' visuals stand out. "The production element has become like a race to beat out the other artists in terms of cutting-edge technology onstage," says Smith, who performs inside a "disco ball" emitting colored light, synced in real time with help from his lighting director: "It reminds me of playing in a band. We get in sync with each other."

The music is less scintillating. Pretty Lights' easygoing stoner grooves replace dust-on-needle grit with EDM's rubbed-shiny quality. At one point Smith announces: "I'm gonna take you back to the old school. Y'all remember this one?" Out pours Etta James's "Something's Got a Hold on Me"—the source for his "Finally Moving" as well as Avicii's "Levels." Fans lie out in the grass to absorb it. A month later, a study will show more psychedelic drug use in the United States than ever, including the sixties.

JANUARY 21, 2012, midtown New York—Lavo is mobbed on a Saturday night for the young Swedish producer-DJ Avicii. It's the high-end superclub of nightmares—horrendous staff (journalist Puja Patel is refused an "I [HEART] AVICII" pin because, she says, "One of the bitches that work at Lavo said I was 'too ugly'"), offspring-of-Hooters visual presentation (the no-shorts policy does not extend to the dancers on raised platforms), and women who put their hands near your neck and say, "I work here. Do you want a shoulder massage?"

If this place is so upscale, why does the music sound so cheap? Avicii's set is utter undifferentiated slop; any pretense of building an arc is nonexistent. When he plays his Etta James–sampling hit "Levels," any built-in sense of tribute to James, who died the day before, seems like more coincidence.

The following year at Ultra, Avicii plays the Space Ibiza stage on

Sunday, on the first weekend, and commits the apostasy of bringing on a small band, including (gasp!) a banjoist, to perform some of his new material. "Wake Me Up," cowritten and sung by indie-label R&B throwback Aloe Blacc, has a Riverdance-ready violin sweep and galloping beat too close to "country" for this crowd, and the neon kids complain, loudly, online.

Not for long: "Wake Me Up" quickly becomes a global hit through the summer, and by the time Avicii plays Belgium's Tomorrowland festival's main stage the following July, a crowd of 180,000 from more than two hundred countries will be singing lustily along with it. With an appropriately overblown sense of drama, a thunderstorm begins right about when the chorus does. YouTube streams it to a global audience of more than sixteen million. "It's so big there that it changes everything," says Afrojack after playing his Tomorrowland set. "You're not just playing for the club—you're playing for the world."

SEPTEMBER 1, 2013, 11:24 A.M.—An e-mail arrives from Plexi PR, which handles press for Electric Zoo, about to begin its third and final day. It links to an official statement: Sunday is canceled due to a pair of deaths the night before—twenty-year-old Olivia Rotondo of Providence, Rhode Island, and twenty-three-year-old Jeffrey Russ of Rochester, New York, had ingested too much molly. There were five other deaths since the American dance-festival season began in March, some traced further to tainted or faked drugs—in some instances, bath salts sold as molly.

The first two days had felt sluggish, in large part due to a new setup—five stages instead of four, resulting in longer set times that reduced the sets' snap. The major exception was Baauer, headlining the Hilltop Arena tent—rapid fire but not ADD addled, draping clipped vocal samples over groaning low end. Remixes of Rihanna's "Diamonds" and Kanye West's "New Slaves" were both obvious crowd pleasers and, amid the largely tepid energy the rest of Friday evening, satisfyingly rude. He finished, naturally, with a truncated "Harlem Shake."

No one—no culture—rides a long serotonin high without crashing into the dirt. Though the press about EDM concerns itself primarily with Las Vegas, that isn't this scene's status quo. A festival like Electric Zoo is built for exertion, not creature comforts. Over Friday and Saturday evenings there's a visible loss of energy. There are a lot of festivals out there now; lots of fans hit as many as possible. By the time Labor Day comes around, everyone's tired—and along with the willful denial that "molly" is the same thing as "ecstasy," far too few are aware that MDMA depletes one's serotonin and leaves you bone tired if you use too much of it.

ROTELLA IS UNREPENTANT that at his events, spectacle swallows individual talent. "There are new guys no one has heard that are amazing," he says. "It's not just about the same ten guys over and over again. Even the ten guys know that." Familiarity sells, though—most of these festivals' lineups are more or less interchangeable.

Rotella thinks there are too many festivals: "And there's too many nightclubs and concerts that are dance music—there's too many events." It will likely shake out in the "next two years," he says. "There'll be casualties. People are going to cancel shows."

Interviewed weeks before the deaths at Electric Zoo, Estopinal's outlook is rosier. "At some point will there be some type of backlash, yes—but it will not go away. It will be a part of our lives and a part of our children's lives. The gross revenue for the last five to six years is growing thirty to forty percent per year—sometimes more. That's on average. If you see the attendance at the club shows and the festivals, the tickets are selling across the board. Every month this year is better from the month compared to last year."

Beyond the U.S., he says, is still untapped territory. "I've been in Mexico for almost ten months and it's been a learning curve for my local partner and myself. But it's a serious growth market. There are twenty-five million people in Mexico City. I can combine fifty of my markets and not hit that. The potential is exponential."

SKYPE, NOVEMBER 21, 2013—"You've seen how fast this market changes, right?" says Dutch producer Chuckie (Clyde Sergio Narain). "It doesn't even feel like [a big deal] if I put out an album now, because the kids are going to ask for a new album in about three months. The records have a shorter lifetime. They want new records every month. It makes more sense to feed them with singles or a small EP." This is part and parcel of DJ-music methodology, one the pop marketplace has adapted to: "It means that they're dancing to our tempo, our market, our scene. It makes the chance bigger for us to become successful on even the *Billboard* charts."

Chuckie's deal with Atlantic/Big Beat is a paradigmatic example of the new major-label EDM ecosystem. "They want me to do whatever I feel like as an artist," he says, and in trade he acts as a de facto in-house producer and A&R person, working with the company's roster (producing or remixing) to gain them toeholds in the dance market.

There's a gold-rush sensibility at work. "It's crazy," says Chuckie. "Major labels want a piece of this whole electronic-music pie. . . . But it's exactly where the market is. They know where they can sell the records."

SKYPE TO TELEPHONE, March 21, 2013—*What, if anything, have you had to adjust to the most in terms of doing your work over the last few years?*

Derrick May: "Time. You realize that the clock doesn't run forever. Listen, like Roy from *Blade Runner*, I've traveled the Orion system—sunbeams across oceans. I've seen the same things, and it's beautiful. But the reality is that one day, it has to stop. I'm really happy that I've had the chance to do that, and be happy."

You helped predict the future of music. Did you imagine what you were doing would have as much of an impact as it has?

"Yes, we did. We were scared, because we knew. And I knew that when we were doing it. I knew I was supposed to do something special. I didn't know what it was. I thought I was going to be an athlete. I scared myself—and I'm sure Kevin and Juan did, too—when I realized what it was. You know?"

BROOKLYN, NEW YORK, April 10, 2013—Boiler Room is basically a roving VIP room with a fixed webcam, streamed globally to over a million subscribers. Founded four years ago in London, it has outposts around the globe; its media kit lists nearly three dozen corporate partners, from Blackberry to W Hotels. Its lineups are increasingly eclectic—two weeks later, a rambunctious hip-hop session takes place at the midtown Manhattan W, complete with feather-flying pillow fight—but dance DJs are the bedrock.

Tonight's headliner is Frankie Knuckles. In 2000, he moved back to Chicago—which on August 25, 2004, renamed the corner of South Jefferson Street where the original Warehouse stood Frankie Knuckles Way, in a ceremony presided over by then–Illinois senator Barack Obama. But Knuckles had serious health issues—in winter 2000, he broke his foot in a snowboarding accident, leading to a bone disease exacerbated by late-onset diabetes. In July 2008, his right foot was amputated.

That year, Knuckles's profile received a significant bump when his remix of Hercules and Love Affair's "Blind" was issued—a deeply moving version that tops an already great original. "Blind" was the highlight of H&LA's self-titled album—the work of disco obsessive Andy Butler, released by DFA Records, then riding a citywide "disco revival." "They wanted 'that classic Frankie Knuckles/Def Mix' sound," Knuckles said. "I thought they must be kidding. No one was really playing anything remotely Def Mix sounding." But after his leg healed, he relented.

DFA was skeptical at first; Knuckles was "considered a huge risk" to work on the track, says label manager Jonathan Galkin: "Is he gonna get it? He's a main-room remixer a lot of times. . . . So going to that guy for our indie left-field disco record? He knocked it out of the park." Knuckles was "blown away" by the response, and began working on new tracks again with longtime confrere Eric Kupper, under the moniker Director's Cut, giving older material an updated sheen that's still true to Knuckles's classicist sensibility—high on drama, low on cheese.

Frankie is accompanied into the warehouse through a rear door and shown to a stool. The host gets on the mike, genuinely excited. "When he was defining house music, all of us were running around the Christmas tree with a fucking toy drum," goes the introduction. "So show some love, show some respect—*throw yourself in the dirt* for Frankie!" And from the opening kick drum it's clear: *This is Frankie Knuckles*. It's not the Power Plant or the Warehouse or Mendel High or the World or the Roxy or the Sound Factory Bar. It doesn't have to be; he can still deliver a present-tense moment on a dance floor like nobody else. The room's energy jumps; people get *down*. It's as joyous an hour as anyone in the room is likely to experience.

Almost a year later, on Saturday, March 30, 2014, Knuckles plays London's Ministry of Sound, then flies home the next morning. At five p.m., his manager Frederick Dunson finds him dead, age fifty-nine, by the side of his bed. Hundreds attend his memorial service at Chicago's Progressive Baptist Church, where a letter of tribute from President Barack Obama is read.

JANUARY 26, 2014, Los Angeles, California—It was obvious the minute the nominees were announced that Daft Punk was going to sweep the Grammy Awards. *Random Access Memories* is a comeback album (which the Grammys love) by a group that helped turn a corner on music-biz profitability (which the Grammys love) that, despite the group's claims on edginess, is a gigantic love letter to the past (which the Grammys love)—specifically, the big-budget blockbusters the Grammys festooned with awards in the seventies and eighties. It's the Christopher Cross Rule: Whoever hires the most session players wins.

Session players became much of *Random Access Memories*'s press hook. Daft Punk hired a series of legendary backroom pros; keyboardist Paul Jackson Jr., bassist Nathan East, and drummers John Robinson and Omar Hakim each worked with Michael Jackson. As Geeta Dayal wrote in *Slate:* "Here they've 'sampled' the vintage production of their favorite records, using the same analog equipment, techniques, and musicians." They also brought back Todd Edwards, who relocated to L.A. to work on the album; his patented sample confetti transformed the chorus of "Get Lucky" into yet another earworm in a song full of them.

Daft Punk had tuned the world to its wavelength. *Random Access Memories* was perfectly of its moment—despite the fact that nearly all the songs before "Get Lucky" are tediously bombastic and nearly all the songs after it are half-baked; first-week U.S. sales were 339,000. In a series of interviews, Bangalter and de Homem-Christo whined that younger producers had it too easy, and the music was suffering as a result, sounding for all the world like they'd walked six miles to school every day, barefoot, through a blizzard. Grammy bait, anyone?

Tonight, the album walks away with five awards: Album of the Year, Best Dance/Electronica Album, Best Engineered Album—Non-Classical, and, for "Get Lucky," Record of the Year and Best Pop Duo/Group Performance. (Kraftwerk is also given a Lifetime Achievement Grammy this evening.) Pharrell, in a Mountie hat, accepts multiple times "on behalf of the robots"—along with Nile Rodgers and a pair of soundless walking cyborgs in white.

During Daft Punk's performance, the robots appear onstage behind Pharrell, Rodgers, Hakim, East, Jackson, keyboardist Chris

Caswell, and—as if to bestow ultimate Grammy-osity—four-time Album of the Year winner Stevie Wonder. The stage set replicates—what else?—a recording studio. They start with "Get Lucky," bring in the "Harder, Better, Faster, Stronger" vocal hook as counterpoint, interpolate Chic's "Le Freak" and Wonder's "Another Star," and the groove builds. Crane shots show a studio on its feet, moving. Neon tubing reveals itself, changing colors, pulsing in time, like the Coachella spaceship.

Album of the Year is announced. The white-suited robots hold their hug in the audience for a full twelve seconds, a moment of triumph cut with whimsy—so very French, so very Daft Punk. Onstage, while Paul Williams does the thanks, Todd Edwards, to the right, is beaming. Now it's time to party.

JAKE SHEARS ARRIVES at the Park Plaza Hotel at ten sharp, the same time as Tommie Sunshine and his wife Daniela. (They married at EDC Vegas 2013.) "If I know something is going to be a big party with a lot of important people, I like to get in before the madness," says Shears. On the decks as they walk in is Chris Holmes, who'd recorded with Sunshine during the electroclash period, and before that played Furthur in 1994 with his band Sabalon Glitz. Now, Holmes is Paul McCartney's stadium-tour opening DJ.

The Daft Punk Grammy after-party, named for their winning album, takes place at one nominal birthplace of the L.A. (and U.S.) rave scene. Shears and Sunshine, of course, know one another from electroclash. The room has the ghosts of the entire U.S. scene, as well as its present: Skrillex, sitting on months'-old material for an album, *Recess*, that will land to critical shrugs in March; Zedd, who picked up Best Dance Recording for "Clarity"; and lo-fi synth-popper Neon Indian (Alan Palomo, plus live band), recently signed to Big Beat/Atlantic. Not to mention the stars: McCartney, Madonna (with her daughter Lourdes), Beyoncé, Jay-Z, Robyn, Queens of the Stone Age.

Nile Rodgers, who's maneuvered from "Get Lucky" to featured guest spots on a number of high-profile dance albums, like Avicii's and Tensnake's, is beaming. Sunshine hobnobs with Giorgio Moroder and Paul Williams, heroes since childhood, his head spinning. Shears already knew Williams; they'd collaborated on Scissor Sisters' second album, *Ta-Dah!* (2006). "It was really sweet," says Shears. "Paul looked at me and said, 'You guys were the first of the current generation of bands to pull me out.'"

This was a *party*. "No one had their guard up," says Shears. "The dance floor was crazy. Everyone was really letting loose." There's an opulent lighting rig—it's Daft Punk—and a DJ booth suspended three stories high. Shears jokes to Sunshine: "If you're having a bad set, you could always jump off." Equally impressive is the dance floor: "They put in this LED floor with disco squares all over it," says Shears. "Once the party got swinging, the whole thing starting doing this really trippy shit. Or maybe I was just drunk."

Holmes cedes the decks to DJ Falcon, a winner as one of the album's many coproducers; then DJ Premier. "In the middle of Premier's set, Disclosure jumped on for a hot minute," says Sunshine. "While they were playing 'White Noise,' Lars Ulrich from Metallica was dancing next to us. We were cracking up." Recalls Shears: "It was a lot of classics. It spanned about four decades of music— mostly dance music, stuff with disco and house roots, some awesome French house tunes I hadn't heard in a long time—nothing too obscure."

Daft Punk's first-choice DJ had been Questlove—but with the Roots playing on *The Tonight Show with Jimmy Fallon*, he had to nix the offer due to his NBC contract. "I am not supposed to be more than a thousand miles away from home on a Sunday night," he says. But when his 11 P.M. red-eye to New York is canceled, Quest has a free night in L.A. "Get here now!!!!!" his assistant texts; he's directed straight to the decks, and sprinkles the themes from *The Love Boat* and *Happy Days* alongside uptempo classics. He will board a 6 A.M. flight to New York: "I missed sound check, but I still rocked it that night on Fallon." He still hasn't met Daft Punk.

One party isn't the world—though some are so great they can make you believe it could be. But a party can be a beginning. The Grammys aren't so good at being the world, either—but their distance from the cutting edge signals when something is acceptable to the music business, whatever form it takes. Dancing till four in the morning on a psychedelic floor at a party for two men who'd heard the future in house and techno music played in warehouses, the dance-music underground and the big music biz, entities that had circled one another for a generation, finally embraced and said: *Welcome to the machine.*

ACKNOWLEDGMENTS

This book rests on more than three hundred interviews conducted between 2011 and 2014—not to mention the author's own presence at various events—and a plethora of archival material. I made extensive use of the extant archives for six of Hyperreal.org's regional mailing lists—MW-Raves, SF-Raves, PB-CLE-Raves, NE-Raves, NYC-Raves, and 313 (the Detroit list)—and several dozen old rave zines available as pdfs at RaveArchive.org, where I also downloaded hundreds of old DJ mixtapes. My first thanks go to Brian Behlendorf and Dan Labovitch, respectively, for maintaining these crucial resources, and for their insightful interviews.

A number of colleagues' work indelibly shaped this book: Charles Aaron, Jacob Arnold, Andy Battaglia, Andy Beta, Sean Bidder, Bill Brewster and Frank Broughton, Todd L. Burns, Geeta Dayal, Tom Ewing, Tim Finney, Will Hermes, Tim Lawrence, Lauren Lipsay, Dorian Lynskey, Kerri Mason, Joe Muggs, Piotr Orlov, Frank Owen, Puja Patel, Alexis Petridis, Tricia Romano, Mike Rubin, Andrew Ryce, Julianne Escobedo Shepherd, Mike Shallcross, Peter Shapiro, Philip Sherburne,

David Stubbs, Bruce Tantum, David Toop, Rob Young—and looming over us all, Simon Reynolds.

Many of these people are good friends; and several—Aaron, Battaglia, Dayal, Mason, Owen, Patel, Romano, and Sherburne—gave me interview time; my sincere thanks to all, especially Tricia and Geeta and Andy, who ran around with me in New York during the early 2000s—and Tricia and Geeta again for looking over early chapter drafts with a sharp eye. So did Andy Kellman, Kate Silver, and the incredible Mairead Case. Robert Ham, Elissa Stolman, Nathan S., and Camille Cushman kindly volunteered to help transcribe interviews. Thanks as well to Luke Bradley and Jess Harvell.

Major hat-tip to the colleagues who shared transcripts: Matt Diehl (Daft Punk), Miles Raymer (Derrick Carter), and Andy Kellman (Metro Area). Extra shout to Brad Owen for pdfs of his zine *Quadrasonic*, to Gerard Meraz for his thesis on East Los Angeles DJ culture, and most profusely to two fellow Midwesterners: David J. Prince, who gave me four sessions, countless follow-ups, and every back issue he had of *Reactor*; and Tommie Sunshine, who gave me four even longer sessions and loaned me a number of supplementary materials. For nineties issues of *The Wire*, I thank the New York Public Library for the Performing Arts.

From Red Bull Music Academy, I'd particularly like to thank Davide Bartot, and from Red Bull, Bonnie Chuen. Thanks to John Darnielle for dinner the night before I went to Palm Springs. My family—Lorie Town, Alexandria Matos, and especially Brittany Gomez-Matos, Miguel, Veronica, Olivia, and Mateo—is incredibly supportive. Paul Bresnick encouraged me to finish my proposal, then sold it fast and well. Mark Chait bought it and remained patient through several months of delays. Carrie Thornton picked it up from Mark and brought it home, nimbly aided by Sean Newcott. Greg Villepique copyedited out dozens of mistakes tiny and huge.

Thanks as well to Michael Daddino, Becky Ferreira, Angela

Ghesquiere, Nisha Gopalan, Rodney Greene, Angela Gunn, Kristal Hawkins, Nicole Kessler, Kate Koliha, Jessi Kramer and Eric Block, Jen Matson, Brian MacDonald, Kathryn McGrath, Nick Minichino, Chris Molanphy, Robert and Jaqui Myers, Jill Passmore, Nate Patrin, Lisa Jane Persky and Andy Zax, Ned Raggett, Kirk Semple, Joshua Sera, Alfred Soto, Anne Swan, Oliver, and Futurecat.

Special thanks to these editors, among others: Frannie Kelley, Sami Yenigun, and Jacob Ganz at NPR; Jon Dolan, Michael Tortorello, Keith Harris, Peter S. Scholtes, Melissa Maerz, Dylan Hicks, and Lindsey Thomas at City Pages; Kiki Yablon, Philip Montoro, and Mara Shalhoup at Chicago Reader; Greg Milner, Alex Pappademas, Caryn Ganz, Steve Kandell, Christopher R. Weingarten, David Marchese, and Jem Aswad at Spin; Chuck Eddy and Maura Johnston at The Village Voice; Nathan Brackett, Christian Hoard, Monica Damashek, Jonathan Ringen, Nick Murray, Simon Vozick-Levinson, and Jason Newman at Rolling Stone; Richard Martin, Mark Fefer, and Lynn Jacobson at Seattle Weekly; Zach Frechette at Good; Sasha Frere-Jones at The Daily; Jonathan Zwickel, Eric Grandy, and Grant Brissey at The Stranger; Ryan Keeling at Resident Advisor; Lisa Blanning at Red Bull Music Academy; J. Edward Keyes and Jayson Greene at Wondering Sound; Mary Huhn at the New York Post; J. Gabriel Boylan at Capital New York; Nick Catucci at Maxim; Mike Prevatt at Las Vegas CityLife; and Joe Levy and Louis Hau at Billboard.

Many people made time to answer my questions—sometimes just one or two via e-mail, sometimes for multiple sittings totaling several hours—either for this book or the pieces that fed into it. Not everyone I spoke to is quoted in the book, but their fingerprints are there whether it's obvious or not, and I thank them profusely. Besides many named above, they are, alphabetically:

Swedish Egil Aalvik, John Acquaviva, Carter Adams, Matthew Adell, David Alter, Charlie Amter, Nick Andreano [Nick Nice], Steve Aoki, Gregor Asch [DJ Olive], Nick Ashley-Cooper [Nick A.C.], Juan Atkins, Gamall Awad, Gavin Beiber [Gavin Hardkiss], Aldo Bender, Jason Bentley, Bethany Benzur, Jon Berry, Stefan Betke [Pole], Joel Bevacqua [Deadly Buda], Marke Bieschke, Matt Black [Coldcut], Matt Bonde [Matt Massive], Jen Boyles, Falko Brocksieper, Frank Broughton, Ethan Brown, Thomas Bullock, DB Burkeman [DJ DB], Screamin' Rachael Cain, Robbie Cameron [Robbie Hardkiss], Anthony Cammarata, Charles Chambers [DJ Funk], Dan Charnas, Oliver Chesler [the Horrorist], Spencer Chow, Joshua Kit Clayton, Eric Cloutier, Alexander Coe [Sasha], Kevin Cole, M. Tye Comer, Norman Cook [Fatboy Slim], Billy Corben, Justin Corbett, Matthew Corwine, Carl Cox, Carl Craig, John Dadzie [12th Planet], Vanessa Daou, Erik Davis, Adrienne Day, Mike Dearborn, Pietro DeMarco [DJ Repete], Marcel Dettmann, Seze Devres Kasenic, Leonardo Didesiderio [Lenny Dee], Kimberly Dietemann, John Digweed, Donato Dozzy, Jack Dunning [Untold], Abe Duque, Titonton Duvanté, Hobey Echlin, Kurt Eckes [Jethrox], Chuck Eddy, Jimmy Edgar, JD Emmanuel, Karl Erhard [DJ Movement], Disco Donnie Estopinal, Glenn Fajardo, Gene Farris, Ivy Feraco [Unjust], Brian Foote, Jonathan Fordin, Sam Fotias, Raymond Frances, Dillon Francis, Mark Gage [Vapourspace], Luis-Manuel García, Gerry Gerrard, J. R. Gibson [Julius Romero], Kenneth James Gibson [apendics.shuffle], Brian Gillespie, Robert Gilmore [Rob Gee], Frank Glazer, Joshua Glazer, Jonathan Golub, Rob Green, Darragh Guilfoyle [DJ Dara], Richard Hall [Moby], Wade Randolph Hampton, JD Harrington, Phil Hartnoll [Orbital], Matthew Hawtin, Richie Hawtin [Plastikman], James Healy, Thomas Heckmann [Kozmik Kommando], Will Hermes, Damian Higgins [Dieselboy], Robert Hood, Sean Horton, Vivian Host, Liam Howlett [the Prodigy], Lisa Hsu, Dave Huismans [2562/A Made Up Sound], Jason Huvaere, Karl Hyde [Underworld], Brandon Ivers, Alex Jarvis, Boyd Jarvis, Eve Jeffers, Marshall Jefferson, Darshan Jesrani, Danny Johnson, James Johnson (Dayton), Curtis A. Jones, Nathaniel Pierre Jones [DJ Pierre], Dory Kahalé [DJ Apollo], Bryan Kasenic [Spinoza], John Kelley, David Kennedy [Pearson Sound], Shawn Kent, Kevin Kerslake, Zak Khutoretsky [DVS1], Shel

Kimen [Klevervice], Leyland James Kirby, Errol Kolosine, Karl Kowalski [Jetstream], Nicola Kuperus [ADULT.], Eric Kupper, Dan Labovitch, Laura La Gassa, John Larner [Cyberjive], Howard Lawrence [Disclosure], Vince Lawrence, Tom Lea, Jane Lerner, Kate Lesta, Steve Levy, Charles Little II, Andrew Lochhead, Brian Long, Justin Long, Joseph Longo, Luciana Lopez, René Löwe [Vainqueur], James Lumb [Electric Skychurch], Ed Luna, Drew Lustman [FaltyDL], Dean Major, Dan Martin [Dan Doormouse], the Martinez Brothers—Chris and Steve, Davey Mason [Davey Dave], Kerri Mason, Manoj Mathew, Derrick May, Michael Mayer, Woody McBride [DJ ESP], Steve McClure [DJ Monk], Kevin McHugh [Ambivalent], Keith McIvor [JD Twitch—Optimo], Chris McNaughton, Michael Meacham, Hector Merida [Huggie], Imri Jonas Merritt, Berkeley Meyer, Daven Michaels [Daven the Mad Hatter], Adam Lee Miller [ADULT.], Christopher Milo [Three], Dave Minner [AK1200], Adam Mitchell [Adam X], Frank Mitchell [Frankie Bones], Sheneza Mohammed, Kevin Moo [Daddy Kev], David Morales, Terry Mullan, June Nho-Ivers, Pavel Niakhayeu [Pavel Ambiont], Cosmin Nicolae [Cosmin TRG], Charles Noel [Archetyp], Alan Oldham [DJ T-1000], Melvin Oliphant III [Traxx], Neil Ollivierra, Todd Osborn, Scott Osman [Scotto], Brad Owen, Frank Owen, Jon Ozias, Fred P, Tamara Palmer, Puja Patel, Phil Pelipada [Phil FreeArt], Thao Phan, Sam Pitmon, Derek Plaslaiko, Stacey Pullen, Dave Quintiliani [Dave Q], Riley Reinhold [Triple R], Gary Richards [Destructo], Porter Robinson, Riz Rollins, Tricia Romano, Maria Rotella [Maria 909], Pasquale Rotella, Neil Rushton, Patrick Russell, Graham Ryan, Jana Sackmeister, Santiago Salazar, Andy Salzer, Sidney Samson, Jeff Samuel, Kiran Sande, Chris Sattinger, Kevin Saunderson, Rita Sayegh, Laura Schebler Rammelsberg, Dave Segal, Jason Sellards [Jake Shears], John Selway, Anthony "Shake" Shakir, Praveen Sharma [Sepalcure], Jonah Sharp [Spacetime Continuum], Erika Sherman, Rob Sherwood, Rachel Shimp, Chris Shively [Chrissy Murderbot], Adam Shore, Jacek Sienkiewicz, Ben Silver, Kate Simko, Mike Simonetti, Todd Sines, Aram Sinnreich, Vicki Siolos, Andrew Smith, Derek Vincent Smith [Pretty Lights], Marian Smith, Rod Smith, Alex Smoke, Sean Smuda, Freddy Snakeskin, Martin Solveig, Tiga James Sontag, Carlos Sosa [DJ Sneak], Alan Sparhawk [Low], Patrick Spencer [Jedidiah the Messiah], Casey Spooner, Charm Stadtler [Gabber Girl], Noel Steen, Ariel Meadow Stallings, Tim Sweeney, Gabrial Szakal, John Tasch [JT], Danny Tenaglia, Todd Terry, Rob Theakston, Lawrence Thom [Larry Tee], Ahmir Thompson [Questlove], Criterion Thornton, Mystic Bill Torres, Seth Troxler, Barbara Tucker, Dave Turov, Matt Tuttle [DJ Shoe], Nikki Usher, Sam Valenti IV, Michael Vance, Nick van de Wall [Afrojack], Paul van Dyk, Armand Van Helden, Peter van Hoesen, Little Louie Vega, Mark Verbos, Tijs Michiel Verwest [Tiësto], Elisabeth Vincentelli, Vello Virkhaus, Wolfgang Voigt, Clark Warner, Tamara Warren, Lisa Weatherston, Marci Weber, Tamara Weikel, Michael Weiss, Bill Werde, Christina Wheeler, Daniel Lee Wherrett [DJ Dan], Jenny Reynolds Willis, Debby Wilmsen, Tom Windish, Josh Wink, Pedro Winter [Busy P], Peter Wohelski, Mike Wolf, Garth Wynne-Jones, Sioux Zimmerman.

My thanks to the publicists and other folks who helped facilitate many of those interviews, in particular: Kim Booth, John Bourke, Leeor Brown, Brian Coleman, Inge Colsen, Jerome Derradji, Dean Driscoll, Alastair Duncan, Marybeth Feeney, Lydia Fong, Sarah Foote, Jordan Frazes, LJ Gacho, Alexandra Greenberg, Shannon Herber, Bruce Jones, Betty Kang, Justin Kleinfeld, Zane Landreth, Matt Learmouth, Fallon MacWilliams, John Ochoa, Ellie Shaw, Mark Stewart, Andrea Sutherland, Melissa Taylor, Elizabeth Ward, and Sean West.

R.I.P.: Scott Hardkiss, Frankie Knuckles, Dean Major, DJ Rashad, Romanthony, Dan Sicko, Thomas Spiegel, Donna Summer.

My apologies to anyone I've forgotten. You know how parties get.

Finally, thanks and love to Rahawa Haile, who read and polished and enabled and encouraged. Go get 'em, tiger.

MIXOGRAPHY

MIXOGRAPHY

Note: Rather than compile a thorough discography, I'm listing ten chronologically ordered DJ sets per chapter—recorded and live, some legitimate releases and many not—that capture some of the flavor of each period and/or region. (DJ sets, not live PAs—hence, neither Daft Punk's Even Furthur '96 nor Coachella performances are here.) Official CD releases are italicized; radio program titles, mixtapes, live sets, and podcasts are not. This listing is in no way definitive or complete. Happy hunting.

CHAPTER ONE: The Power Plant (Chicago, Illinois—Early 1983)

- Tom Moulton: The Sandpiper, Fire Island, New York (1974)
- Larry Levan: *Live at the Paradise Garage* (Strut 2CD; rec. 1979; rel. April 17, 2000)
- Frankie Knuckles: Live at the Warehouse (August 28, 1981)
- Ron Hardy: The Muzic Box (June 19, 1984)
- Farley Keith: WBMX-FM, Chicago (August 31, 1985)
- Julian "Jumpin'" Perez & Farley "Jackmaster" Funk: WBMX

102.7 FM, Chicago (mid-eighties)
- Frankie Knuckles: WBMX-FM (1986)—*often tagged as 1979*
- Frankie Knuckles: Friday Night Jams, WBMX-FM, 107.2 FM, Chicago (October 31, 1986)
- I-f: *Mixed Up in the Hague Vol. 1* (Panama CD; mixed November 1999)
- Greg Wilson: Big Chill (August 8, 2010)

CHAPTER TWO: The Music Institute (Detroit, Michigan—November 24, 1989)
- Ron Hardy: Live at Club C.O.D., Chicago (1987)
- Ron Hardy: RA.415 (rec. 1987; uploaded May 12, 2014)
- Armando: WBMX 102.7 FM, Chicago (1988)
- Derrick May: The Music Institute (1988)
- Derrick May: WJLB-FM, Detroit (1988)
- Graeme Park: Live at the Garage Club, Nottingham (1988)
- Mike Pickering: Live at Nude, Haçienda, Manchester (October 1988)
- Tony Humphries: Live at Zanzibar, New Jersey (March 5, 1988)
- Derrick May: Live at the Barn, Essex (August 24, 1989)
- Richie Hawtin: Power 96, Detroit (November 24, 1989)

CHAPTER THREE: Stranger than Fiction (Los Angeles, California—September 9, 1990)
- Frankie Bones: Bones Breaks Production (Studio Mix) (1989)
- Tony Humphries: Mastermix Dance Party, KISS-FM, New York (December 29, 1989)
- Frankie Bones & Lenny Dee: Live at the Barn, Essex (1990)
- Nightmares on Wax (DJ E.A.S.E. & the Boy Wonder): Studio Mix (1990)

- 808 State DJs: Sunset FM, Manchester (April 3, 1990)
- Frankie Bones: Amnesia House, Sky Blue Connexion (August 23, 1990)
- Alan Oldham: Fast-Forward, Public Radio Channel X, Vol. 2 (October 11, 1990)
- Andrew Weatherall: Live at Kaos, Leeds (1991)
- Jon Williams: 1991
- Larry Levan: Live at the Sound Factory, New York (March 22, 1991)

CHAPTER FOUR: The Finale of the Gathering + UFOs Are Real (San Francisco, California—April 11, 1992)

- Barry Weaver: Untitled 91 (1991)
- Mark Farina: Live at Shelter, Chicago (November 1991)
- Jenö: Live at Toon Town (December 31, 1991)
- Scott Hardkiss: Circa 92, Los Angeles (April 14, 1992)
- Mercury: Live at Come Unity, San Francisco (June 2, 1992)
- Robbie Hardkiss: Om Labs (July 19, 1992)
- Garth: The Gathering, San Francisco (October 1992)—*marred audio*
- Josh: The Gathering, San Francisco (October 1992)—*marred audio*
- Tony: The Gathering, San Francisco (October 1992)—*marred audio*
- Garth: Live at Basics, San Francisco (November 28, 1992)

CHAPTER FIVE: Grave (Milwaukee, Wisconsin—October 28, 1992)

- Bad Boy Bill: B96 Dance Party, Chicago (1990)
- Jeff Mills: KDGE-FM, Dallas (December 21, 1991)
- Derrick Carter: Genre (1992)
- Hyperactive & Terry Mullan: DJs Unite Volume 1 (1992)
- Miles Maeda: Bliss (1992)

- Spiral Tribe: Live at Castlemorton Common (May 1992)
- Alan Oldham: Fast-Forward, Vol. 5 (July 31, 1992)
- Nick Nice & Roz B. Liquid: Alice in Raveeland, Madison, Wisconsin (August 28, 1992)
- Nick Nice: French Invasion 1 (1993)
- ESP Woody McBride: Mind Safari (1993)

CHAPTER SIX: Storm Rave (Staten Island, New York—December 12, 1992)

- Grooverider: The Shark Bar, Brighton (1991)
- DJ Rap: Live at Eclipse, Coventry (1991)
- Frankie Knuckles: Live at the Sound Factory, New York (April 8, 1991)
- Deadly Buda: Intro (1992)
- DJ Pierre: Kiss FM (1992)
- Joey Beltram: The Orbit, Leeds (August 22, 1992)
- Lil Louis: Live at the Haçienda, Manchester (September 25, 1992)
- Goldie, Rufige Kru, DJ Phantasy, MC Reality, NRG, James St. Bass, and more: Harddrive, 89.5 FM, Toronto (November 1992)
- Lenny Dee: Live at Universe Big Love (August 13, 1993)
- Josh Wink: Live at Liquid Sunshine, Toronto (August 14, 1993)

CHAPTER SEVEN: Rave America (Los Angeles, California—December 31, 1992)

- Liam Howlett: Rave Party, East London (1991)
- Doc Martin: Live at Gilligan's Island (September 1, 1991)
- Steve LeClair: Live from the 808 State Rave (September 14, 1991)
- Ron D. Core & DJ Dan: DX2 Volume 3: Live at the Funny Farm (1992)

- DJ Dan: Wicked Burning Frenzy (1992)
- Doc Martin: Live at Citrusonic (May 27, 1992)
- Jason Bentley: October 1992
- Jon Williams, Tony B, Bad Boy Bill, Eli Star, and DJ Juanito: PowerTools Mix Show (October 24, 1992)
- Megabass, SL2, Two Little Boys, Unity, Carl Cox, and Krome & Time: *Hit the Decks Vol. 1* (Moonshine CD, rel. May 21, 1993)
- DJ Trance: Live at Bassrush 3, Los Angeles (September 1, 2002)

CHAPTER EIGHT: See the Light Tour (Thirteen North American cities—October and November 1993)

- Richie Hawtin: For Those Who Like to Groove, Dutch radio, Holland (April 4, 1992)
- Adam X: Live at NASA (1993)
- Ellis Dee and Easygroove: X-Static (1993)
- DJ Pierre: American Classics (1993)
- Sven Väth & Moby: *Mixmag Live! Vol. 2* (DMC CD; rec. 1993, rel. April 23, 1996)
- Jeno: Full Moon, Palo Alto, California (May 5, 1993)
- Joey Beltram: Rezerection (May 29, 1993)
- Doc Scott: Testin Nu Tunes Studio Mix (November 1993)
- John Acquaviva: Empire (January 22, 1994)
- DJ DB: *History of Our World Part 1—Breakbeat & Jungle Ultramix* (Profile CD; rel. June 28, 1994)

CHAPTER NINE: Spastik (Detroit, Michigan—August 8, 1994)

- Scott Grooves: RA.225 (rec. 1993; uploaded September 20, 2010)
- Robert Hood: Deep Space London, Mastermix, Kiss 100 FM (April 20, 1994)

- Kevin Saunderson: Live at Harmony (April 30, 1994)
- Richie Hawtin: Flavor, Denver, CO, USA (November 19, 1994)
- Jeff Mills: *Live at the Liquid Room, Tokyo* (React CD; rec. October 28, 1995; rel. March 21, 1996)
- Kenny Dixon Jr., a.k.a. Moodymann: Live on Radio Nova, Paris (December 1995)
- Claude Young: Dexit Mix Tape (1996)
- Carl Craig: *DJ-Kicks* (K7 CD; rel. March 26, 1996)
- Derrick May: HR3 Clubnight—Harmony House Tour (March 30, 1996)
- Matthew Hawtin: *Once Again, Again* (M_nus CD; rel. April 13, 2010)

CHAPTER TEN: Even Furthur '96 (Eagle Cave, Wisconsin—May 24–27, 1996)
- DJ Tron: 27 Hits of Acid (1994)
- Adam X: Live at Descension, Milwaukee (March 19, 1994)
- Aphex Twin: Live at Furthur (May 1, 1994)
- Terry Mullan: New School Fusion Vol. 2 (May 1995)
- Woody McBride: Live at Beyond, Chicago (May 13, 1995)
- Spencer Kincy: Experiments (c. 1996)
- Hyperactive: 04 of 12 (April 1996)
- Scott Hardkiss: Live at Even Furthur '96 (May 26, 1996)
- DJ Funk: Bootyology (1999)
- Thomas Bangalter: Live at We, Dolton Expo Center, Chicago (October 9, 1999)

CHAPTER ELEVEN: Organic '96 (San Bernardino, California—June 22, 1996)
- Massive Attack: Essential Mix (December 11, 1994)
- DJ Trance: Too Much Going On Upstairs (March 1995)
- Bob: Demo III (Live at the Double Door, Chicago) (August 27, 1995)

- Scott Henry & Charles Feelgood: Fever—Time to Get Ill, Volume 5 (1996)
- Darren Emerson & Underworld: Essential Mix (February 4, 1996)
- Sasha & John Digweed: Live at Simon's, Gemini Party, Gainesville, Florida (May 27, 1996)
- The Chemical Brothers: *Live at the Social* (Heavenly Social CD; rel. July 18, 1996)
- John Kelley: *FunkyDesertBreaks* (Moonshine CD; rel. August 6, 1996)
- Doc Martin: Unlock the House (August 9, 1996)
- DJ Icey: *The Funky Breaks* (Fontana CD; rel. August 5, 1997)

CHAPTER TWELVE: Woodstock '99 (Rome, New York—July 22–25, 1999)

- Armand Van Helden: Essential Mix (January 21, 1996)
- Kruder & Dorfmeister: *DJ-Kicks* (K7 CD; rel. August 19, 1996)
- Daft Punk: Skyrock (1997)
- The Freestylers, *FSUK2* (Ministry of Sound 2CD; rel. May 25, 1998)
- Fatboy Slim: *On the Floor at the Boutique* (Skint CD; rel. August 25, 1998)
- The Chemical Brothers: *Brothers Gonna Work It Out* (Astralwerks CD; rel. September 21, 1998)
- Danny Tenaglia: *Global Underground 010: Athens* (Boxed 2CD; rel. February 15, 1999)
- The Prodigy: *The Dirtchamber Sessions* (XL CD; rel. February 22, 1999)
- Josh Wink: Essential Mix (September 10, 2000)
- Timo Maas: Essential Mix (August 18, 2002)

CHAPTER THIRTEEN: Detroit Electronic Music Festival (Detroit, Michigan—May 26–29, 2000)

- DJ Assault: *Straight Up Detroit Shit Vol. 5* (Electrofunk CD; rel. 1998)
- Richie Hawtin: *Decks, EFX & 909* (Novamute CD; rel. November 2, 1999)
- Daniel Bell: *Globus Mix Vol. 4: The Button Down Mind of Daniel Bell* (Tresor CD; rel. June 22, 2000)
- Matthew Herbert: *Globus Mix Vol. 5: Let's All Make Mistakes* (Tresor CD; rel. November 3, 2000)
- Claude Young: Live at Fuse (November 4, 2000)
- Magda vs. Mike Servito: M&M Mix (2001)
- Derrick L. Carter: *Six Eleven Mix Series Vol. 3: About Now . . .* (611 CD; rel. October 23, 2001)
- DJ Rolando: Live at Groove Club, Detroit (November 24, 2001)
- Scion: *Arrange & Process Basic Channel Tracks* (Tresor CD; rel. August 13, 2002)
- Metro Area: Live at Weekendance (December 28, 2002)

CHAPTER FOURTEEN: Phuture Phat Hong Kong Phooey (New Orleans, Louisiana—August 26, 2000)

- Sasha: Vol. 7 (1993)
- Rabbit in the Moon: DJ Promo (1994)
- Micro: Caffeine Long Island—In-Ter-Dance (mid-nineties)
- Shy FX & DJ Ash, One in the Jungle (August 17, 1995)
- A Guy Called Gerald: Essential Mix (October 7, 1995)
- Sasha & John Digweed: *Northern Exposure* (Ministry of Sound 2CD; rel. September 27, 1996)
- Bad Company: Live at Renegades Sessions (1999)
- DJ DB: *Shades of Technology* (F-111/Warner Bros. CD; rel. March 30, 1999)

- Frankie Bones: *You Know My Name* (Moonshine CD; rel. November 14, 2000)
- John Digweed: Kiss 100 (at Fabric, parts 1 and 2 of 3) (December 23, 2000)

CHAPTER FIFTEEN: Electroclash Festival 2001 (New York City—October 10, 2001)

- Tiga: *Montreal Mix Sessions Vol. 5: Mixed Emotions* (Turbo 2CD; rel. February 6, 2001)
- Doc Martin: Essential Mix (February 11, 2001)
- Richie Hawtin: *DE9: Closer to the Edit* (M_nus/Novamute CD; rel. September 18, 2001)
- Playgroup: *Party-Mix* (promo CD, late 2001)
- James Murphy: Beats in Space Radio Show #111, part 2 (WNYU-FM, New York; May 9, 2002)
- 2 Many DJ's: *As Heard on Radio Soulwax Pt. 2* (PIAS CD; rel. June 18, 2002)
- Felix Da Housecat: Live at the Love Parade, Berlin (July 13, 2002)
- DJ Hell, *Electronicbody-Housemusic* (React 2CD; rel. November 26, 2002)
- Tim Sweeney: Beats in Space Radio Show #150 (February 20, 2003) [part 1 a.k.a. *Dance to the Underground*—DFA Records' cover-mount CD for *Muzik*, April 2003]
- The Rapture: Essential Mix (October 26, 2003) [bootlegged as *You Are There*]

CHAPTER SIXTEEN: Coachella (Indio, California—April 29–30, 2006)

- Panytec, Live at Beta Lounge, Hamburg (May 22, 2000)
- Andrew Weatherall, *Hypercity* (Force Inc. CD; rel. May 1, 2001)
- Ellen Allien: *Weiss.Mix* (Bpitch Control CD; rel. July 8, 2002)

- Triple R: *Friends* (Kompakt CD; rel. October 22, 2002)
- Ricardo Villalobos: HR3 Clubnight (September 6, 2003)
- Michael Mayer: *Fabric 13* (Fabric CD; rel. November 3, 2003)
- Daniel Bell & Dave Turov: Club WMF, Berlin (June 10, 2004)
- Black Strobe: Essential Mix (November 28, 2004)
- JDH & Dave P: *Go Commando* (Defend CD; rel. March 20, 2007)
- Justice: Rejected Fabric Mix (December 2007) [a.k.a. *Xmas Mix*]

CHAPTER SEVENTEEN: Electric Daisy Carnival (Las Vegas, Nevada—June 24–26, 2011)

- Kode9: Groovetech Radio (November 6, 2002)
- Switch: Essential Mix (January 11, 2004)
- Armin van Buuren and Tall Paul: Essential Mix (April 25, 2004)
- Eric Prydz: Essential Mix (March 13, 2005)
- Tiësto, Essential Mix: Live from Disneyland, Paris (April 24, 2005)
- Mary Anne Hobbs, Mala, Skream, Kode9 & the SpaceApe, Vex'd, Hatcha, Loefah & Sgt. Pokes, and Distance: Breezeblock—Dubstep Warz (January 10, 2006)
- Rusko: Cockney Knees Up Mix for Mary Anne Hobbs (May 4, 2008)
- A-Trak: *FabricLive 45* (Fabric CD; rel. April 4, 2009)
- Untold: FACT Mix 58 (June 18, 2009)
- Sidney Samson: Electric Daisy Carnival, Las Vegas (June 25, 2011)

CHAPTER EIGHTEEN: Random Access Memories (Los Angeles, California—January 26, 2014)

- Rustie: Essential Mix (April 7, 2012)
- Maya Jane Coles: *DJ-Kicks* (K7 CD; rel. April 17, 2012)
- Disclosure: FACT Mix 327 (April 30, 2012)
- Hercules and Love Affair: *DJ-Kicks* (K7 CD; rel. November 13, 2012)
- Jack Beats: Live at Ultra Music Festival, Miami (March 16, 2013)
- Frankie Knuckles: Boiler Room New York 007 (April 10, 2013)
- Eric Prydz: Live at Coachella (April 14, 2013)
- Skrillex: Essential Mix (June 15, 2013)
- Mat Zo: Live at Electric Daisy Carnival, Las Vegas (June 22, 2013)
- DJ EZ: *FabricLive 75* (Fabric CD; rel. September 16, 2013)

BIBLIOGRAPHY

Note: Detailed notes are available online at tuimfootnotes.tumblr.com. Below are some titles of published sources that were particularly helpful.

BOOKS

Sean Bidder, *House: The Rough Guide* (Rough Guides, 1999)

———, *Pump Up the Volume* (Channel 4 Books, 2001)

Bill Brewster and Frank Broughton, *The Record Players: DJ Revolutionaries* (Black Cat, 2011)

Jeff Chang, *Can't Stop Won't Stop* (St. Martin's Press, 2005)

A. James Fisher, *SWAT Madness and the Militarization of the American Police: A National Dilemma* (Praeger, 2010)

Jonathan Fleming, *What Kind of House Party Is This?* (MIY Publishing, 1995)

Walter Huegli, ed., with Arsene Saheurs, photos, *Raw Music Material* (Scalo, 2002)

Peter Kirn, ed., *Keyboard Presents the Evolution of Electronic Dance Music* (Backbeat Books/Hal Leonard, 2011)

David Lubich, ed., *Catch the Beat: The Best of Soul Underground 1987–91* (DJ History, 2010)

Tara McCall, *This Is Not a Rave: In the Shadow of a Subculture* (Thunder's Mouth, 2001)

Frank Owen, *Clubland* (Broadway Books, 2003)

Tobias Rapp, *Lost & Sound: Berlin, Techno, and the Easyjet Set* (Innervisions, 2010)

Luc Sante, *Kill All Your Darlings: Pieces 1990–2005* (Yeti Books, 2007)

Philip Sherburne, liner notes to Plastikman's *Arkives* (M_nus box set, 2011)

Dan Sicko, *Techno Rebels: The Renegades of Electronic Funk (Second Edition)* (Painted Turtle, 2010; first edition 1999)

Mireille Silcott [Silcoff], *Rave America: New School Dancescapes* (ECW, 1999)

WEB SITES:

- Dancecult (https://dj.dancecult.net/index.php/dancecult)
- 5 Magazine (http://5chicago.com/)
- Gridface (http://www.gridface.com)
- In the Mix (http://www.inthemix.com)
- Little White Earbuds (http://www.littlewhiteearbuds.com/)
- MTV News (http://www.mtv.com/news/)
- NPR Music (http://www.npr.org/music/)
- Pitchfork (http://pitchfork.com)
- Red Bull Music Academy (http://splash.redbullmusicacademy.com/)
- Resident Advisor (http://www.residentadvisor.net/default.aspx)
- Slate (http://www.slate.com/)

ARCHIVAL MATERIAL

- RaveArchive.org [enormous collection of Midwest-focused rave zines and mixtapes]
- Hyperreal.org/raves/ [the source of archives for MW-Raves (February 1993 to June 2001), NE-Raves (June 1992 to December 1999), NYC-Raves (December 1995 to December 1999), PB-

CLE-Raves (October 1995 to December 1999), and SF-Raves
(March 1992 to December 1999)]
- Music.hyperreal.org/lists/313/archives/ [the source of the 313
list archives, September 1994 to July 2001]

PERIODICALS [sometimes via digital, sometimes not]
- *Billboard*
- *Chicago Tribune*
- *City Pages* [Minneapolis-St. Paul]
- *CMJ New Music Monthly*
- *Details*
- *DJ Times*
- *Entertainment Weekly*
- *The Guardian*
- *The Independent* [UK]
- *Las Vegas Review-Journal*
- *Las Vegas Weekly*
- *Los Angeles Times*
- *Massive* [Milawukee zine]
- *Metro Times* [Detroit]
- *Miami New Times*
- *Mixmag*
- *New York*
- *New York Daily News*
- *New York Times*
- *Orlando Weekly*
- *Philadelphia Inquirer*
- *Quadrasonic* [Milwaukee zine]
- *Reactor* [Chicago zine]
- *Rolling Stone*
- *San Francisco Bay Guardian*
- *San Francisco Examiner*

- *SF Weekly*
- *Spin*
- *Under One Sky* [NYC zine]
- *Vice*
- *Village Voice*
- *Wall Street Journal*
- *Washington Post*
- *Wax Poetics*
- *The Wire* [UK]
- *Wired*
- XLR8R

INDEX

ABOUT THE AUTHOR

MICHAELANGELO MATOS is the author of *Sign O' the Times* (Continuum, 2004) and contributes to several magazines, newspapers, and websites. He lives in Brooklyn, New York.